Hollywood Enigma

HOLLYWOOD LEGENDS SERIES
CARL ROLLYSON, GENERAL EDITOR

Hollywood Enigma
DANA ANDREWS

CARL ROLLYSON

University Press of Mississippi • *Jackson*

www.upress.state.ms.us

The University Press of Mississippi is a member of
the Association of American University Presses.

Photo on page ii courtesy Dana Andrews Collection.

Copyright © 2012 by University Press of Mississippi
All rights reserved

First printing 2012

∞

Library of Congress Cataloging-in-Publication Data

Rollyson, Carl E. (Carl Edmund)
Hollywood enigma : Dana Andrews / Carl Rollyson.
   p. cm. — (Hollywood legends series)
Includes filmography.
Includes bibliographical references and index.
ISBN 978-1-60473-567-3 (cloth : alk. paper) —
ISBN 978-1-4968-4955-7 (paperback)
ISBN 978-1-61703-648-4 (ebook) 1. Andrews, Dana, 1909–1992.
2. Motion picture actors and actresses—United States—Biography. I. Title.
PN2287.A615R86 2012
791.4302'8092—dc23
   [B]   2011052332

British Library Cataloging-in-Publication Data available

CONTENTS

            Acknowledgments *VII*
            Introduction *3*
CHAPTER 1. Don't Miss *6*
CHAPTER 2. The Patriarch (1881–1924) *17*
CHAPTER 3. "Go Hollywood, Young Man!" (1924–29) *36*
CHAPTER 4. To Be an Actor (1929–32) *43*
CHAPTER 5. "Mediocrity Is Not My Lot" (1932–35) *58*
CHAPTER 6. Holding On (1935–36) *73*
CHAPTER 7. Pasadena (1936–38) *77*
CHAPTER 8. Goldwyn (1938–41) *99*
CHAPTER 9. Fox (1941–44) *117*
CHAPTER 10. *Laura* (1944) *150*
CHAPTER 11. Stardom (1944–45) *165*
CHAPTER 12. *The Best Years of Our Lives* (1946) *191*
CHAPTER 13. The Name above the Title (1947) *199*
CHAPTER 14. "What Is This Thing I Do to Women?" (1947–50) *203*
CHAPTER 15. Hollywood Fights Back (1947–57) *215*
CHAPTER 16. Period of Adjustment (1950–53) *226*
CHAPTER 17. Home and Abroad
            Dr. Jekyll and Mr. Hyde (1953–57) *238*
CHAPTER 18. Sobriety (1958–64) *256*
CHAPTER 19. Ruin and Recovery (1964–72) *270*
CHAPTER 20. Curtain Call (1972–92) *279*
            Sources *287*
            Filmography *295*
            Bibliography *297*
            Index *302*

ACKNOWLEDGMENTS

I DECIDED TO write this biography after I had a long telephone conversation with Susan Andrews about her father. At the time I knew relatively little about Dana Andrews, although I had watched *Laura* three or four times, entranced with the actor playing Mark McPherson. He reminded me of my father, a plain-clothes detective in 1940s Detroit. Like Mark, my father was a romantic who kept his emotions hidden behind a male mask. If I were to recreate my father's biography, it would be as a film noir.

Susan described the substantial archive her father had amassed: a diary, letters, photographs, and other documents. I could already see that I would be able deal not only with a career I admired, but also with the whole man. And I would have the enthusiastic cooperation of his family—not just Susan and her sister, Katharine, and Katharine's husband, Tim Smith, and Dana's son Stephen, but also Dana's grandchildren: Abigail, Ilena, and Matthew. I explained that I would need complete freedom to research and write the book, but that I would value their contributions and wanted them to review what I wrote before it was published. In the end, however, it was to be my book and subject to no one's censorship. Susan readily agreed, and so did her siblings. So I began. My biographer's blood was up.

To say that the members of the Andrews family have been helpful is an inadequate acknowledgment of what they have contributed to this book. In the course of many interviews and hundreds of email exchanges, they provided candid and openhearted memories, often writing passages that have been integrated into the narrative of this biography. They also sent me DVD copies of the 16-millimeter film that Dana shot or had taken of him, his family, friends, and those he encountered on trips abroad.

That generosity is a tribute to Dana Andrews, who was about as open about himself as a human being can be—while remaining, in certain fundamental respects, enigmatic. Of course he told the truth in his own way. We all do. And like so many self-invented figures, he constructed a life narrative that looked somewhat different from the way I have fashioned it. That is the difference, of course, between autobiography and biography. I have tried to let him have his say, even as I choose other angles from which to take his measure.

I have had the great good fortune to speak with Jeanne Andrews, the wife of Charles Andrews, Dana's younger brother. She was able to take me back to the time when Dana first hit Hollywood. She also knew Dana's father and the rest of the large Andrews family, and could share with me her memories of Texas in the 1930s and 1940s, when she and her husband returned to stay for twelve years before going back to California. Her son, Dana, named after his uncle, spoke with me about sailing and drinking with his father's favorite brother, and in addition provided the precious resource that is Charles's unfinished novel about Charles Forrest Andrews, the father who made such a deep impression on his progeny. A conversation with Dana and his sister Jeanne Marie also added considerably to my understanding of their Uncle Dana and his family.

Angela Fabry, the daughter of Dana's brother David, devoted herself to answering my innumerable questions about what Dana and his brothers were like. She knew them all and has taken a special interest in the family's genealogy. Angela put me in touch with Aimee Abben, the daughter of Dana's sister Mary. Aimee sent me photographs and other memorabilia full of invaluable details that helped to paint a picture of what it was like to grow up in Texas during Dana's lifetime. My narrative would be much poorer if I had not had access to reminiscences contained in the material Aimee sent to me.

At a crucial moment, Sheila Simpson came through with valuable information about Janet Murray, Dana's first wife, and about Janet's family. Sheila also made many helpful suggestions, and I benefited from the dozen or more email exchanges I had with her.

Through David Andrews, a sixth cousin of Dana Andrews who had warm memories of meeting Dana at the Coconut Grove Playhouse in Miami, Florida, I received DVDs of Dana's movies and help with genealogy and the history of Holmes County, where Charles Forrest Andrews was born. David is an important contributor to the "Descendants of Thomas Andrews 1795" website at myfamily.com. There I made contact with Shawn Pearson and Rhett Farrior, who helped me understand the cultural and religious background of Charles Forrest Andrews.

I also have to thank Clyde Williams, who began work on a biography of Dana Andrews in the 1970s. He deposited his interviews in a Dana Andrews collection at Mississippi State University. Without Williams's work, I would not have had direct access to the reminiscences of Dana Andrews, Dana's wife Mary, and his brothers David and John. Williams also did interviews with Susan and Stephen Andrews, who kindly supplied me with transcripts Williams made of their conversations.

Other librarians and archivists who have been especially helpful include the resourceful Ned Comstock at the Cinema Arts Library of the University of Southern California. At the University of California, Los Angeles, I received invaluable assistance from the indefatigable Julie Graham, Performing Arts, Special Collections; Mark Quigley, Manager, Research & Study Center, UCLA Film & Television Archive; and Jonathon Auxier, Curator, Warner Bros. Archive. I was also aided by Erin Chase, Curatorial Assistant, The Huntington Library; Mattie Abraham, Manuscripts Coordinator, Special Collections Department of Mississippi State University Libraries; Ashley Adair at the Dolph Briscoe Center for American History; and Mark Ekman of the Paley Center for Media in New York City. The staff at the Academy of Motion Pictures Arts and Sciences provided me with many important production and clipping files. And in so many ways my work would have been more difficult if I had not been able to rely on Valerie Yaros, historian of the Screen Actors Guild.

Thank you to Howard Prouty (hprouty@labridge.com) who at the last minute found for me that interview Dana did with Allan Eyles. Robert Lightermoet at Roberts Hard to Find Videos did indeed find the videos of Dana Andrews's movies I was seeking. Another helpful supplier was lovingtheclassics.com. Similarly, Jerry Haendiges (jerry@otrsite.com) was able to send me on CD those two "Hollywood Fights Back" broadcasts. Old Time Radio (otracat.com) sent me a marvelous CD that included the complete run of *I Was a Communist for the FBI* and many of Dana Andrews's other radio performances.

In Collins, Mississippi, not only did Marie Shoemaker at the chamber of commerce arrange for me to meet with several Speeds (Dana's mother's side of the family), she also organized a well-attended talk I gave at the Blackwell Library.

In Uvalde, Texas, Virginia Davis of the El Progresso Archives supplied a clipping file and a transcript of the day Susan Andrews, Steve Forrest (William Andrews), and others came for a Dana Andrews celebration.

In Rockdale, Texas, Denice Doss of the chamber of commerce organized a talk for me in the local library, where I was also able to glean much important material from the *Rockdale Reporter*. I am also very grateful to Jeanne Williams of the *Temple Daily Telegram* for sharing with me her research on the period during which the Andrews family lived in Rockdale.

On my trips to Huntsville, Texas, I had the opportunity to meet with several people who knew the Andrews family, some of whom came to a talk I gave at the Wynne Home Arts Center, organized by Mike Yawn, a professor in the political science department of Sam Houston State University. He was ably assisted by the Political Science Junior Fellows, which helped arrange funding for my visit. Mike was a wonderful host who introduced me to many important sources, including Professor Ralph Pease, who hosted one of Dana's visits to the university in 1986, and to Mac and Leeann Woodward, who were able to help me get in touch with Mary Sue Coffman, one the daughters of Norma Felder, who became engaged to Dana when they were still in high school. For his willingness to answer my questions about local history I am thankful to James Patton, who knows more about the subject than anyone else. Just as crucial was Barbara Kievit-Mason in Special Collection at Sam Houston State. Not only did she keep the doors open after closing time to accommodate me, she went out of her way to supply me with items I would otherwise have missed. I know all this sounds too good to be true, but it is true. I met more helpful and hospitable people than I could keep track of while in Huntsville, and to all of those whose names do not appear here, I extend an apology. I should have kept better records.

My debt to Norman Lloyd is substantial, not only for his memories of Dana Andrews, but also for his comprehensive knowledge of Hollywood history. And I really appreciate the conversations I had with others who appeared in pictures with Dana Andrews, including the late Anne Francis and John Kerr. And a special thanks to Eric James for his vivid memories of *Bright Promise*. Alas, many of those I wanted to interview have died—some, like Karl Malden and Farley Granger, just as I was getting started. Fortunately, I was able to speak with Peggy Cummins, who confirmed much of what Norman Lloyd said about Dana's strengths as a man and as an actor. Some actors who appeared in pictures with Dana did not answer my letters or declined to be interviewed. Especially regrettable is the silence of Harry Morgan, who appeared in several pictures with Dana. The two men were quite close during the early years of their respective careers. Elizabeth Taylor's assistant wrote to say she had made it a policy not to be interviewed about her fellow actors. I am grateful to late Ken Orsatti, who shared his memories of working with Dana at the Screen Actors Guild. Katharine Weber put me in touch with Linda Viertell, whose mother met Dana Andrews in the John Douglas French Center during the last years of his life.

I have had wonderful support from fellow biographers, including David Stenn, Jeffrey Meyers, and Bernard F. Dick, who promptly answered my queries, and Donald Spoto, who once met Dana Andrews and was a good friend of Dana's co-star in *The Best Years of Our Lives*, Teresa Wright. While in San Francisco reading Dana's papers at Susan's home, I had an opportunity to meet and discuss my biography with Eddie Muller, the Czar of Noir. Check out his comments (and Susan's) on the Fox DVD of *Fallen Angel*. To Carol Easton, a special thank you for putting up with me and putting me up during my stay in Los Angeles. My fellow biographers know how depressing it can be away from home after an exhausting day of reading papers or running around doing interviews. "You feel like going to your hotel room and slitting your throat," one colleague said to me. Well, Carol's friendship and advice made my trip happy and fruitful. Similarly Felicia Campbell, an old friend, providing an encouraging forum for my talk on Dana Andrews during a Far West Popular Culture Association meeting.

Leila Salisbury, head of the University Press of Mississippi, championed my biography right from the beginning and provided wonderful support all along. She has a mighty fine staff that is a pleasure to work with.

Lisa Paddock, my wife, and sometime co-author, knows that every line of this biography is better because she has edited it.

It seems to be an unwritten rule in biographers' acknowledgments not to say a bad word about their sources. Who knows when you might need them again? And, at any rate, it would seem ungracious to criticize those who have hindered as well as helped you. So I feel it necessary to reiterate how extraordinarily welcoming the Andrews family has been to every query I have made. Too many biographers heap praise in their acknowledgments and then tell you (off stage, so to speak) what a pain it was deal with family members. Not me. What I have written is the same as what I would tell you if we ever met.

Hollywood Enigma

INTRODUCTION

HE WORKED WITH distinguished directors such as John Ford, Lewis Milestone, Otto Preminger, Fritz Lang, William Wyler, William A. Wellman, Mervyn Le Roy, Jean Renoir, and Elia Kazan. He played romantic leads alongside the great beauties of the modern screen, including Joan Crawford, Elizabeth Taylor, Greer Garson, Merle Oberon, Linda Darnell, Susan Hayward, Maureen O'Hara, and most of important of all, Gene Tierney, with whom he did five films. Retrospectives of his films often elicit high praise for an underrated actor, a master of the minimalist style. His image personified the "male mask" of the 1940s in classic films such as *Laura*, *Fallen Angel*, and *Where the Sidewalk Ends*, in which he played the "masculine ideal of steely impassivity." No comprehensive discussion of film noir can neglect his performances. He was an "actor's actor."

Directors like Otto Preminger and Lewis Milestone thought of Andrews as a director's actor because he delivered lines flawlessly and never, *never* hogged the camera or made a fuss. In contrast to stars like Joan Crawford, he never "indicated," playing up emotion and milking a scene. He imprinted his image not only on the minds of millions of moviegoers, but also on the imagination of novelists. "It is possible to stand at the window, loosen my collar and rub the back of my neck like Dana Andrews," wrote Walker Percy in *The Moviegoer*.

That neck rub indicates a character and an actor under considerable strain. Anxiety ate away at Andrews even during his prime in the 1940s. The narrator in Susan Isaac's novel, *After All These Years*, describes the "unrelieved sadness at the human condition" in the characters Dana Andrews played. In "The Spanish Lady," Alice Munro refers to Andrews's "willed and conscious, yet easily defeated, charm." Susan Andrews wrote to me: "Lately, I've been watching the new hit TV series *Madmen*. The lead character reminds me in some ways of my father. He's got this secret past and all the trappings of success: the wife, the children, the home in the burbs, and yet he's strangely dislocated. Reviewers have called him an existential hero."

One critic attributed Andrews's alcoholism (not full blown until the late 1940s) to a style so tightly wound that the actor sought relief in drinking. His daughter Susan confided to me that she thought her father found the pressures of filmmaking and celebrity difficult and craved an outlet. Sailing proved a godsend to him. He could chart his own course and be his own man, hanging off the bowsprit. But as a contract player beholden to Samuel Goldwyn, Darryl Zanuck, and other producers, he succumbed to drink as a way to bolster himself. Susan thought that this country boy from Mississippi and Texas was never quite comfortable among Hollywood's formidable moguls. These explanations only go so far, however, in explaining this troubled actor's behavior. He was part of a generation of men who felt inhibited and introverted. "It's not difficult for me to hide emotion, since I've always hidden it in my personal life," Andrews admitted to interviewer Lillian Ross. He equated openness with vulnerability. Yet this is the very thing drinking signified: an attempt to open up—or at least loosen the actor's mask.

This self-defeating behavior damaged his reputation, which he began to repair in the 1970s. He candidly discussed his alcoholism at a time when most public figures and actors like William Holden hid the malady. In public service announcements for the National Council on Alcoholism, he announced, "I'm Dana Andrews and I'm an alcoholic. I don't drink anymore, but I used to—all the time."

Proud of his profession, Andrews worked hard as vice-president (1957–63) and then as president (1963–65) of the Screen Actors Guild, taking a tough line against the exploitation of women in gratuitous nude scenes. He promoted the idea of pay-tv (a forerunner of pay-per-view), so that actors could be properly compensated for their work. He also believed that television had degraded public taste and demoralized actors. In 1964, he rejected six television jobs (they would have netted him at least $30,000) and also rejected the offer of a three-year, $300,000 contract to promote a brand of cigarettes.

During the last twenty-five years of his career, Dana Andrews turned increasingly to the theater, scoring significant successes in *Two for the Seesaw* and *The Glass Menagerie*. He would also have good moments on screen—some of them in television—but he never again captured the allure, the complexity, and the mystery of the screen persona he perfected in the 1940s in *Laura*, *Fallen Angel*, and *Where the Sidewalk Ends*. These three films, products of a remarkable collaboration with Otto Preminger, and his inimitable performance in *The Best Years of Our Lives*, constitute the core of Andrews's contribution to Hollywood film history.

Since the arc of Dana Andrews's career peaked in the 1940s, that period—and what it took to get there—inevitably become the focus of this artist's story, with later chapters simply detailing the denouement of the whole man. For some of his friends and family he would always remain Carver, the name he was given at birth. The first part of this biography will use both names—sometimes even in the same paragraph—to capture the bifurcation of a character who never really made Hollywood his home, even though, like Thomas Wolfe, a fellow Southerner, he could never go home again.

Dana's daughter Susan understood the dynamic of his life:

> Dad's story is a classic. I've always believed so. The striving to be somebody and then when he gets there it doesn't fill the empty place he so dreamed it would. I've always connected with the theme of the big guys toying with the talent and then moving on; the "talent" having to cope with the reality of being a star, of handling the sex, drugs and rock n' roll of celebrity, good looks, and the talent that comes from somewhere and eating at the insides while the money guys rake in the dough. The not really being prepared for the big time somewhere in the small town soul, yet never able to go small town again. What saves a guy? What happens to him? What nourishes him when the passion of the climb is gone? I feel like "they" took something from my father (the fans, the producers) and left him to figure out what to do with what remained. He forged ahead and he maintained his dignity. He always had tremendous dignity.

A certain sadness may creep into the later stages of this book—a kind of mourning for the waning of Dana's talent—but it is alleviated by the way he soldiered on, confronting his alcoholism and keeping his family together and thriving. His nobility is striking, quite unlike what you would expect of a Hollywood star. Many actors are, as human beings, actually smaller than their roles. Dana Andrews, although an admirable artist, was greater than even his best work.

CHAPTER 1

Don't Miss

I WAS BORN on January 1, 1909, in the village of Don't, which is now part of the town of Collins, Mississippi. I was the third of thirteen children, five of whom are dead. My father was a Baptist minister, and I was named after Dr. Dana, who taught at the seminary my father went to, in Louisville, Kentucky. My first name is Carver, after another of the teachers, but I dropped it in college.

So says Dana Andrews, movie star, in Lillian Ross's collection of interviews, *The Player: A Profile of an Art*, published in 1962. Dana gives us the bare bones of his beginnings. Now that I've made it my business to tell the story of his life, I wonder what he was thinking when he said these words.

Ross, a celebrated *New Yorker* writer who had re-created Hemingway's talk in a pitch-perfect magazine profile, had a knack for turning her reporting into her subject's self-revelation. How much Dana knew about her I don't know, but he was well read in the sense that he kept abreast of contemporary culture. He liked to stay at the Algonquin Hotel, the famous hangout of *New Yorker* writers like Dorothy Parker and Robert Benchley. Dana admired writers, and while still in his twenties he kept a journal and dreamed of becoming a writer. He would have been eager to speak with Lillian Ross. I'm sure.

Dana was almost always an amiable, receptive person. He seemed quite open about himself and others. And yet, I don't think he told Ross, or anyone else, the whole story. You can be the friendliest person in the world, but that does not mean you want to tell the truth about yourself, or about aspects of your background that you wish to remain buried. I'm reminded of the leading man role Dana played in the musical *State Fair* (1945). To Jeanne Crain, playing the girl he is courting, he confesses: "Everybody has trouble explaining me." Dana delivers the line with his usual offhand grace. He wraps the enigma in an envelope of geniality.

So what was it like for Dana growing up in a Mississippi hamlet? You'll be disappointed to learn that he does not say. He was only five when his family moved to San Antonio. But something occurred in Don't, whether he remembered it or not. "I recently went back to Collins, for the first time since 1913 and visited relatives, mostly on my mother's side, and mostly named Speed," he told Lillian Ross. He then added, "There are hundreds of Speeds in the area—a prolific family consisting of good, solid country folk." In fact, Dana had himself filmed walking the land near Collins where he was born, going into old abandoned homes (where he almost fell through rotten wooden planking), and pointing to the rusted tin roofs he lived under as a boy. He filmed his father's Leaf River Baptist Church, looking not much larger than a one-room schoolhouse. Dana wanted to remember and record where he came from.

Dana's daughter Susan noticed that in the brief shot with his Speed relatives her father demonstrated the way he helped people who might have been a little uncomfortable in front of the camera—as well as uneasy around a confident movie star:

> He becomes sort of uber-friendly and supportive in his demeanor, kind of buoying them with his own comfort level, good humor and kindness, that was maybe only very partially feigned. He did this a lot with us kids, and I never thought about it til now really. It was like he was going to be jolly and comfortable for the whole crew!

Carver was quite close to his mother. "I remember the many things my mother told me about Collins," he told an audience gathered for "Dana Andrews Days," a two-day affair in Collins (November 16–17, 1978). He would always think of himself as a country boy who made it in the big city. Unlike some country boys, he never lost sight of where he came from and what it taught him. In 1943, just after he had co-starred with Tyrone Power in a war film, *Crash Dive*, and was on the cusp of stardom, Dana wrote to his younger brother Charles, expressing disgust over the Hollywood that had lured him West. As he struggled to retain his dignity, Dana did not see much integrity in the studio system. And war made him dwell on his down home years, a period that made the present seem

> too cold, too calculating; too much head, too little heart. Actually I can't tell, so I must ask you: has the mood and temper of people changed so much, or is it just because I am living in Hollywood?

—or that I am older and have lost my boyish ideas? Sometimes I get so sick of this nasty place I could throw the whole thing up and move back to Texas where people are not any dumber and a lot more honest. Guess it's just because I'm from the country and don't like "city ways."

So why did Carver Dana Andrews stay in Hollywood? I think he realized the country ways he remembered so fondly were just that—memories. He continued: "I suppose with radio and such things, the good old country people are just as glamour conscious as the rest." The world was changing, his letter acknowledged, and the place he had come from no longer existed.

To look at him, Dana Andrews did seem in a class all his own. In 1933, a good ten years before he wrote that Hollywood Babylon letter to his brother, Dana—still only a Hollywood hopeful and a good five years away from securing his first movie contract—was already aware that he had re-invented himself. Educated as an accountant, Carver Dana Andrews wrote a sort of cost-benefit analysis of his move away from Texas in his journal:

If a man has that staunchness of character that stays the same in any environment, is it a virtue or a fault? Since coming to California after many years in the South, I don't talk, think, or act like a southerner. Many people I see everyday have the stamp of some locality on their personalities, their speech, their actions. Chameleon-like I have changed almost without being aware of it. Now I wonder if that shows a weakness of character, an inability to hold one's own against environment, or is it evidence of that type of imitativeness which I covet and admire in actors and such like—that sensitiveness to personality and environment that might mean a great elasticity, indicating that a more beautiful model could be molded from such plastic material.

Carver believed in "good, solid country folk" because he wanted to say it straight. When I spoke with Norman Lloyd, who appeared in two films with Dana, he called his fellow actor "one of nature's noblemen." Norman admired Dana's no nonsense acting style. Norman was not flattering Dana, nor was he flattering me for my choice of subject. Norman Lloyd *loved* Dana Andrews. I could tell not just by the glint in his eye, but by the way his wife stood in the doorway, watching us talk and smiling as her husband poured out his heart. "I knew Dana Andrews," she proudly affirmed, as though some kind of blessing had been conferred upon her.

So Carver Dana Andrews had to return to Collins even if Don't no longer existed, even if the village itself could not have been more than a dim memory to him. He needed contact with his mother's kin, and I think it anchored him to believe in those hundreds of Speeds who were like her. He was used to mingling with lots of family. He had seven brothers—Wilton, Harlan, Ralph, David, John, Charles, and William (who became the actor Steve Forrest)—and only one sister, Mary (four others died before the age of two). Wilton drove everyone crazy talking in tangents. The studious Harlan liked to ask you questions about yourself. John, a little high strung, later became the most religious brother. Dana always seemed to deviate in some way from the family line. He was hard to control but always a charmer. He made all the women in his family feel like beauties. David most resembled Dana and later was often asked for his autograph. Ralph was self-described as the ugly duckling. He was shorter than his brothers and did not look like any of them. But like the rest of them, he had a great sense of humor. Charles, who later aspired to be a novelist, adored Carver, the only brother not to earn a college degree. His siblings took jobs as educators, businessmen, engineers, and executives.

Their charismatic father, Charles Forrest Andrews (CF), is described in family lore as a kind of Elmer Gantry figure, high on the Lord but also a hugger of the flesh. As Shawn Pearson, an Andrews relative, observes, CF (1881–1940) "grew up and lived during the lives of some of what could be considered the founders of fundamentalism": Charles Spurgeon (1834–92), Dwight Moody, (1837–99), and Billy Sunday (1862–1935). These powerful preachers fumigated towns all across America known for their drinking, gambling, and other vices.

CF had a hold on his people because he could preach The Word. He had reserves of energy and erudition that tantalized his flock. Shortly after he died, Edwin C. Boyton wrote about his pastor in the *Huntsville Item* (March 7, 1940), describing his "oratorical force": "His face alight with the message of the moment, he always left the impression of being one who could say much more than he had ever said upon the theme in hand." Preachers have a tendency to overstate, but CF apparently understood—as did Dana—the power of understatement and suggestion. As his son Charles wrote, CF had a "flair for the dramatic action which he exercised with fervor and sincerity."

About the last thing in the world Charles Forrest Andrews wanted his son to be was a movie star—or any kind of actor, for that matter. On September 12, 1917, when Carver was eight years old, the First Baptist Church of Rockdale "met in regular conference," with Pastor Charles Forrest Andrews acting as moderator. The following resolution was read:

> Whereas our covenant contains at present the promise that we will refrain from such of the world's games & amusement as having a tendency for evil, or are immoral in their nature, therefore be it resolved by this church that it considers, the dance included, together with 42 games for prizes, the moving picture as at present operated, and playing pool and participation in or attendance upon any of these, shall hereafter be considered as a breach of its covenant.

The church minutes reported that "an overwhelming majority" adopted this resolution.

There's not much leeway here for an aspiring Hollywood actor—although any boy with Carver's pluck would seize on that slight waffle, "the moving picture as at present operated." He was ambitious, but not rebellious by nature. He had a father who believed in higher callings. Dana would have to find a wedge to pry himself out of strict conformity to the covenant, but such would not occur to him until he was well into his teens.

Carver Dana Andrews was still in grammar school when the family moved to Uvalde, Texas, a town that, he told Lillian Ross, "left the strongest imprint on me of all the places we lived in as I was growing up." He kept pigeons that always seemed to migrate to the attic of Uvalde's most famous resident, John Nance Garner, who would later become one of FDR's vice-presidents. Dana reveled in his years in Uvalde, a "wild, colorful part of the state." As he recalled: "A friend of my father's joined him in trying to clean up the town, and was shot to death in the street by a crony of the sheriff's, because the sheriff was in charge of an operation to sell bootleg tequila brought in from Mexico."

He said no more about Uvalde in the Ross interview, leaving many questions unanswered. What about that Uvalde imprint? Carver would certainly have seen in his father a principled, educated man dealing with a frontier mentality. CF set high standards and persevered even at some risk to himself. Carver never outgrew the protestant notion that an individual must account for himself. Well into his twenties, Dana wrote letters to the father justifying himself and his choice of profession.

But how in the world did a Texas boy ever suppose he could become a movie star? The notion took root in Huntsville, Texas, Dana told Lillian Ross. In Huntsville, he attended high school while his two older brothers enrolled at Sam Houston State Teachers College. In high school, he got his first taste of acting, appearing in both modern plays and Shakespearean drama. But acting, per se, had not yet proven its allure. Carver needed to see the performing arts on a larger scale and on a broader platform. The full impact of what he might accomplish was not apparent to him.

During his first year in college, Carver got a job taking tickets and ushering at two local side-by-side movie theaters owned by Sam Parish, one of Huntsville's entertainment entrepreneurs. By Carver's third year in college, Parish made him manager of both theaters. But it was not the business side of the work that intrigued Carver: "I used to watch those damn movies over and over, and after a while I began to take some notice of the way the actors went about their work. It didn't look so difficult to me," he told Ross.

That last sentence is key to understanding the young Carver Dana Andrews. He had the insouciance of youth. How hard could breaking into the movies be? In college he had the encouragement of a mentor, his drama coach Charles O. Stewart. Stewart is a notable figure in the Lillian Ross interview, one who, Dana said "encouraged me to make theatre my goal." Indeed, on the very day Stewart singled out Carver, the young man made a commitment:

"That night in bed, I realized that the only thing I had ever done that made me feel good was acting in those plays. The other students had told me how good I was, and some of them had really appeared to mean it. I had watched all those pictures, and being in movies seemed to be as far away from business as I could get, so now I began to think seriously about movie acting."

The decision is striking and entirely convincing. It is like the moment when Marilyn Monroe, working in a World War II airplane factory, attracted the attention of a professional photographer who told her she was a "natural" and should think about modeling and movie acting. For a certain kind of person, it takes only one authority to sanction an ambition.

Carver appeared in several plays at Sam Houston, including the 1928 production of Oscar Wilde's *Lady Windermere's Fan*. In 1925, just as Carver was beginning his movie theater job, the play received sumptuous silent movie treatment. This version starred the incomparable Ronald

Colman, a master of the subtle gesture that Dana Andrews would perfect. Watch a movie once for the story; watch a movie a second time and you begin to notice how it is put together. Carver was a young man creating his own film school, closely following the work of actors like Gary Cooper, Richard Arlen, and Douglas Fairbanks, Sr.

What happened next is, I imagine, a unique occurrence, one you won't find in biographies of other movie stars: This college boy became part of the movie production process. Nearly thirty-five years later he would explain to Lillian Ross how constructing movies became an integral part of his psyche: "This was before we had talkies, but some movie companies were experimenting with adding music and sound effects on synchronized phonograph records, which they sent around with the films. I decided to get together a collection of records and use them to provide scores of my own. I even recorded some of my own sound effects." Lillian Ross heard a lot more about how Carver fashioned sacred music recordings into a score for Cecil B. DeMille's celebrated *King of Kings* (1927), and adapted George Gershwin's "Rhapsody in Blue" (1924) for the Douglas Fairbanks epic, *The Thief of Baghdad* (1924). If some of the results were—by Carver's own estimation—"corny," he also realized they were impressive, especially in an era just beginning to explore the possibilities of sound. Carver Dana Andrews would remain fascinated with sound and sight technology all his life, buying the most up-to-date recording equipment and shooting his own film and photographs. Indeed, he had a kind of mania for recording his own life—even asking family members to repeat their entrances for the camera.

In the 1920s, momentous changes were occurring in an industry that would be able to magnify and amplify the human figure and voice in magical ways. Motion pictures defined the modern—as documentary filmmaker Robert Flaherty illustrated by staging a scene *Nanook of the North* (1922) where his Inuit hero marvels at a phonograph and its hard metal disk that could reproduce the human voice.

Ross recorded the first stirrings of that quest for stardom as told to her by a movie star, one who kept returning to the moment of inception: "One night, after I'd gone to bed, I began to think about what I wanted to do with the rest of my life. I didn't *like* business. I didn't like keeping accounts, which was what I was learning to do in college. I didn't want to be ordinary." Carver had experienced an epiphany that nearly annihilated whatever else his family, culture, church—you name it— told him. I say "nearly" because it is a long way from Huntsville, Texas, to Hollywood, California. And New York City, where filmmaking had begun and was still active in the Astoria studios in Queens, was even further out of reach—especially for a country boy without funds facing a father who opposed his son's proposed line of work. What sort of character was he presenting to CF?

In 1929, after three years of studying business administration at Sam Houston State Teacher's College and earning passable grades (plus a slew of incompletes), Carver was far from the Coast of Dreams, as California historian Kevin Starr calls it. He had tried to seize the day during a two-week trip to New York City, but no one in the theater had a job for an untested twenty year old. Carver came home broke, having spent the two hundred or so dollars he had saved up for his show business debut. He was obliged to take a job in Austin working as an accountant for a large stationery store.

But he was restless, and his father had moved the family to Van Nuys, California, to begin a pastorate at the First Baptist Church. So Carver quit his job, threw a big party for his friends, and—now penniless—hitch-hiked to California. He stayed with his family for three months while he made the rounds of movie studios. Quickly he realized, as he later told Lillian Ross, that he was just a "punk kid with a little amateur experience." He made a living driving the Van Nuys High school bus while he attended night school drama class.

Now here is where the Lillian Ross version of Dana's story veers from veracity—at least in so far as it is an account of what happened next. Texas drops out of the story as Dana (he has stopped calling himself Carver) becomes involved with the "socially prominent towns people" that patronize the local little theatre. In his own words, "a great time was had by all," even though he is the "only one in the group burning with serious ambition." Soon he is offered a lead role in a community theater production. Cast with him was Janet Murray, "a wonderfully vivacious local girl," Dana told Ross. Murray had just earned a masters degree in journalism from Northwestern University. On December 31, 1932, they were married.

Dana covered this early period of his life in California in about one hundred words. Was he really that concise, or did Ross judiciously edit a longer version, distilling his reminiscence? Perhaps it does not matter since the result is the same denouement: Texas no longer had a hold on him. Janet now provided the support he could no longer count on back home:

> She was an inspiration to me in the days that followed; unlike everybody in my family, who refused to recognize acting as a legitimate occupation, she consistently encouraged me. She liked my baritone voice and urged me to become a singing actor, like Lawrence Tibbett. I began to study singing seriously, taking lessons with a local teacher who had sung in the original company of "The Desert Song." Janet and I were very happy. In 1933, our son, David, was born, and when he was two, Janet contracted pneumonia and died.

True enough, Dana had broken free from Texas, but at great cost to himself. Before meeting Janet, he had been engaged to Norma Felder, a Huntsville girl. I would later learn from her letters that he had met Norma when he was fourteen and that by the following year, they considered themselves engaged. I also learned from Jeanne, the wife of Dana's brother Charles, that the marriage to Janet was not, in fact, such a happy one.

Ignoring Norma would negate an important part of Dana's life, a part that he often thought about and that shaped his attitudes toward Hollywood and stardom. Dana wanted to move his story along for Lillian Ross, I suppose, but revisiting what happened in Huntsville and those first two years in California are crucial to his biography. When I first began work on this book, Dana's younger daughter, Susan, told me the story of Norma—but without much detail. Susan only knew what her mother told her, since Dana never talked about Norma. The Felders were a prominent Huntsville family who deemed Dana, the son of a poor preacher, not good enough for their daughter. At one point, her family sent her abroad to separate the couple. In the end, Norma simply could not buck her family's opposition.

My first inkling that this story could not be accurate occurred in the spring of 2009, when I visited Huntsville and spoke with local historian James Patten. In a matter-of-fact manner, he told me that Charles Forrest Andrews would have been a respected member of the town, somewhere on the level of a community leader or college professor. Dana's family was poor, to be sure, but the picture I had formed of a shabbily dressed Dana being shown the door by his sweetheart's family now seemed more fable than fact. On that same Huntsville visit, I reviewed the First Baptist Church minutes: In 1924, C. F. Andrews had been offered a salary of $2,500 a year, not an inconsiderable sum and on a par with what college professors made. Of course, he had a very large family and wanted all of his children to do well. He held out for $3,000 and got it.

CF Andrews presided over a considerable establishment with a distinguished history. The First Baptist Church was founded with eight members in 1844 in the Republic of Texas, erecting its first building in 1851. Its original evangelical theology and preaching style had not changed much when CF arrived in 1924. His mission would have been the same as that described in this October 19, 1848, report of a Huntsville revival meeting:

> The meeting here is exciting a tremendous influence on this community. General Davis has been converted; Doctor Mosely, Colonel Watkins and many prominent citizens are rejoicing in Christ as their Savior. General Sam Houston is at the anxious seat crying for mercy, with many others of the best citizens of Huntsville. God is working. None can hinder. Thirteen have joined the church; six or seven will join tonight; sixteen have professed who have not joined.

On July 2, 1925, the *Huntsville Item* reported that the First Baptist Church of Huntsville, Texas, had 450 members and was preparing for the opening of a new structure built at a cost of $100,000. The building had four entrances and six marble columns, an auditorium that seated 464, and a balcony that seated 300, with additional space for Sunday school rooms at the back of the auditorium. Ivory colored plaster and woodwork with an oak finish graced the interior. A modern furnace heated and cooled the building. The choir had robing rooms, and the pastor had a room across from the pulpit that served as his study. In this grand edifice Carver once climbed four stories and—to the alarm of his mother—swung from the rafters.

A year after my first trip to Huntsville, when Susan and I began to go through her father's correspondence, the Norma story came into focus. Norma never gave up on Dana; he had left her behind. The myth of the rejected Dana, Susan supposed, arose from her father's guilt or conflicted feelings about what he had done. Evidently he never gave a full account of his involvement with Norma even to his second wife, Mary Todd. And God knows what he told Janet Murray. I cannot help thinking that for him it was important to see the move to California not as a choice, but a necessity, because no one at home believed in him. Perhaps it was just too painful to relive the elation and desolation of those years between 1925 and 1929, when Dana conceived his dream of becoming a movie star. And yet the full story remained important to him. He did not try to obliterate the record—indeed, he assembled all the materials vital to this biography. He was not by nature a deceptive man, and he was far more open about his failings than other movie stars of his generation.

In Huntsville in the spring of 2009, I began to piece together Norma's story. I wanted to speak with her daughter, Moselle, but she rebuffed me. Later, she wrote movingly in a letter to me about her sad childhood memories and her mother's multiple sclerosis. I would need to get to Dallas, where Mary Sue, Moselle's younger sister lived, to get more of the family history.

In the meanwhile, I had to puzzle out what Huntsville and the Felder family thought of Carver. What kind of a person was Norma? How had Janet Murray and then Mary Todd replaced Norma Felder in his affections? And why did he remain in contact with Norma until her death in 1970?

The Felders had lived in Texas since the 1860s, settling in Huntsville in the 1880s and opening photographic and real estate businesses. In 1908, Victor Felder married Sue Parish, a local girl, and a year later she gave birth to Norma, their only child. This was also the year that Robert Phillips opened the first picture show (as movie theaters were called then) in Huntsville. "It was more of a novelty than art or entertainment and would have been abandoned if a young musical couple, Sam and Maud Parish, had not taken over the business," I read in a history of Huntsville. The very Sam Parish who would hire Carver Dana Andrews was Norma Felder's uncle.

How I would like to know more about Sam Parish, who had trained as a singer and who relished the improving technology of the cinema that Carver loved to manipulate. As the Huntsville history book puts it, Sam had "held the fort," awaiting the advent of bigger screens and other refinements that would allow him, in 1913, to open up the two theaters—the Dorothy and the Avon—where Carver worked a little over a decade later. By 1923, "fabulous Hollywood controlled the world of make-believe," in Huntsville, Texas. And Sam Parish cared about the quality of his product: "He has always been known to show only the finest productions, including the first showing of academy award winner pictures," reported the *Huntsville Item* (March 6, 1941).

The tantalizing details gathered during my spring 2009 trip to Huntsville left me with a familiar problem: There was more to tell about the origins of Dana Andrews's ambition. Where and when did he really set out on his life's course?

CHAPTER 2

The Patriarch
1881–1924

CHARLES FORREST ANDREWS liked to regale his family and congregation about his boyhood on the farm in western Florida. His forebears settled in Holmes County sometime in the 1840s and stuck to the soil. These first years working the land, CF's fourth son, Charles, speculated, "must have had something to do with the steely courage he was later to stand in great need of . . . ." At just over six feet tall, this lean and lithe man—with his brisk walk, penetrating grey eyes, and angular face softened slightly by wavy brown hair—seemed ready for any contest. CF was "a man fit to live," as Charles put it.

Yet CF was not robust as a boy. "As for a healthy body, I did not have one to start with," he told Dana. "In my early childhood I came near dying with bronchitis and asthma." He lacked "bodily vigor," if not the powers of concentration and determination. But he liked to hunt and fish and became good at both, always outperforming those who hunted with him in his later years. Sandy Creek, clear and cold, was nearby. At night, he could hear the coon- and fox-hunting hounds. When meat was scarce, dogs were used to tree squirrels. Turkey, and sometimes even deer, was fair game. Foot races, baseball games, and of course church socials provided entertainment. CF probably enjoyed "dinner on the ground," a custom whereby families brought food to share, "laying it on elevated wooden tables."

Home was rudimentary, with a stick-and-clay chimney and a cast iron Dutch oven in the hearth. You washed yourself by pouring water from a wooden bucket into a washbasin, wetting and smoothing your hair with your fingers, and cleaning up with strong lye soap if necessary. Breakfast might consist of dried, cured meat from the smokehouse.

Good times and bad were seasonal. The end of winter meant corn and hay were short, and you made do with dried cowpeas. A good supper consisted of poke-greens with bits of white bacon buried in them, together with "sand-buggers made of potato and onion" and orange biscuits. In this hardscrabble place, salvation appeared in the form of a preacher who might very well look like the God of the Old Testament. He would also likely be the man with the most education in an otherwise sparsely schooled community. Early on, CF decided he wanted a life that did not involve plowing. He had a powerful voice and wanted to find a use for it. He was equipped with only a rudimentary grammar school education, but CF, a "voracious reader," scored high on the scholarship exam for Florida State Normal College at De Funiak Springs, from which he graduated, intent on a teaching career.

Just north of Holmes County, De Funiak Springs, situated on the foothills of the Appalachians, appeared as "beautiful little table land, in the center of which its great Springs boil up in a perfect circle of one mile in circumference, around which that town is artistically laid off and built," records John McKinnon's History of Walton County (1903). The town ascended to its "great Spring," seated atop "quite a hill." Judging by McKinnon's prose, written even as CF neared graduation, De Funiak inspired him. Or, as McKinnon summed up the site: "All is upward."

Well, not quite all. Why CF left Florida became the stuff of legend, a species of Southern gothic worthy of a William Faulkner novel. One account has him, the baby of the family, going to live with his sister and her husband and impregnating their black maid. CF may have been alluding to this incident when he later vowed to Wilton that he had never "crossed the race line." Another version has CF murdering a man in a barroom brawl. One of CF's brothers rushed him out of the state, which is how he landed in Don't, Mississippi, in 1904. Whatever happened in Florida, Charles Forrest Andrews seemed determined to become someone else. Never again would anyone call him "Charlie," as he was identified in the 1900 Census.

Apparently CF's brother, successful in the lumber and turpentine business, had a contract on some land near Don't and sent his wayward brother there to work it. Soon, however, CF began life anew, working as a teacher at the Leaf River School, where he promptly fell in love with one of his teenage pupils, sixteen-year-old Annis Speed. Annis was by all accounts a fast-maturing girl, and she had received her first marriage proposal at the age of eleven. Her wary father, James Monroe Speed, a prosperous farmer, withdrew his daughter from Leaf River School. "My grandfather Speed didn't think much of my father at that time," recalled

David, CF's fifth son. "He thought my dad was one of a bunch of roughnecks. He probably was, at that time." CF and Annis continued to see one another in secret. To Annis and other girls her age, the young dynamic schoolteacher was quite a catch.

William, CF's seventh son, remembered his mother telling him that CF would leave love notes for her in an oak tree near the cotton fields she worked with her black neighbors. Not a man to avoid confrontation, CF called on Annis at home. "She's going with me," he said, walking past James Monroe Speed, who was standing behind the screen door of his house. CF took Annis's hand, and the couple eloped.

CF, having accepted Christ as his personal savior in a ceremony apparently conducted by a traveling Baptist evangelist, later reconciled with Annis's father, who gave CF a thirty-seven-acre farm to manage. In 1905, when her husband took her home to his Florida family for a visit, Annis was only seventeen. There she learned, the story goes, the shocking events (including the existence of a love child) that led to her husband's hasty departure for Mississippi. Annis also witnessed the crude conditions of her husband's upbringing. When she saw the house he had grown up in and the holes and cracks in its floor, she exclaimed: "[C]olored people [back home], they're living in better houses than that."

Annis, "patient to the point of saintliness" and a "foil to the firebrand," had a forgiving nature and a reverence for her husband's words that steadied her in the years to come, as she bore him thirteen children and put up with his wayward behavior. Whatever CF did, good or bad, Annis took it to the Lord in prayer. "Mama talked very personal about God as though he were in the next room," Charles recalled. "The fact that Papa was this lord of life and mother his obedient and tender footstool was the most real and important thing in the entire scale of things."

Life for a schoolteacher in Don't was "rugged and the pay was calculated to maintain those conditions. To the hard-bitten natives of the region, education was something you got on the fly when you could not hoe corn or pick cotton. Three months a year and five grades vertical was the menu." Just making a living proved daunting, and CF and Annis had a burgeoning family. "Four sons in four years. They were blessed by the first, disturbed by the second, scared by the third [Carver] and blitzed by the fourth [Charles]. And of course this was only the fifth year of marriage," marveled Charles.

CF recalled that Carver, born in Annis's father's home, seemed eager to discover his new world and was a "very husky chap with a tremendous voice almost in the bass range and determined to use it." The boy "walked rather early," although he was heavy on his feet and so "bow-legged that you could not have hemmed a hog in a ditch," CF later wrote to his son. Dana could not remember much from his four years in Don't except the smell of the woods. Nothing in Texas would ever smell like the Mississippi woods, with their great old oaks dripping with Spanish moss. Don't, Mississippi, no longer exists. A cyclone destroyed nearly everything in 1912.

On winter evenings CF played the piano and the family sang by the hour. CF would sing what his father taught him. Only CF sang those songs, which gave Carver an "eerie feeling." In the summer evenings, Annis regaled the family with tales about her father's cotton plantation. Sometimes, as Charles intimated in his novel, the boys became too much for her, and she would dump it all in the Lord's lap: "He sent them to me, so He must have known what He was doing. I've tried everything, now it's up to Him."

Carver joined Wilton (born 1905) and Harlan (born 1907) and soon had a baby brother, Charles, born on September 16, 1910. Wilton served as the family caretaker during periods when CF ran away from his responsibilities, and Charles became the novelist manqué who memorialized the patriarch's powerful impact, calling CF Andrew Sampson in one of his unfinished stories, which had the tentative title "Papa Wasn't God." Charles described his father's futile return to farming when part-time preaching assignments yielded poor pay: "With Old Bess patiently dozing in the harness Andrew read his books in the shade of a black gum. After an hour's earnest scanning he would drop the book, grab the plow handle, and chase the startled beast up and down the rows like the devil was after them both." This "read awhile and plow awhile" system resulted in catastrophe when "Andrew" miscalculated the mule's "capacity for speed, sending plow and plowman nose first in the furrow. Patting the heaving animal to a sitting posture, he walked out of her life and away from the plow for good."

In 1910, the family joined CF in Louisville, cramming into a small flat where the boys all slept together in one bed in the kitchen. Wilton remembered his mother making their clothes. He often had to do the shopping, taking along his infant brother Carver, who one day toddled out into traffic and was almost run over by one of those electric cars that traveled about ten or fifteen miles per hour. At the age of seventy-two, Wilton still remembered the awful screech of automobile breaks and the policeman who came running to escort the boys across the street.

In 1912, CF accepted his first pastorate in Braxton, Mississippi, a village of 286 souls. Two-year-old Carver was already performing, as CF later recalled in a letter to his son:

> You always liked to show off and let no opportunity pass to demonstrate some feat or talent when visitors dropped in. Mother says the most embarrassing moment of her life was on one occasion when she was entertaining a man and his wife, sort of "ritzy" folk, and had neglected to pin a diaper on you. They were all sitting out in the hall talking, and you toddled in from the yard and concluded it was a capital time to get attention. Down on all-fours you dropped, your little dress very short, and shouting: "Watch me gallop!" went cantering away with all your scenery in full view.

Wilton remembered Carver's first public recital:

> When I grow up to be a man
> I will not drink or smoke or chew
> And do what other bad boys do.

During this performance Dana flubbed one of his lines and insisted on performing it all again—to everyone's considerable amusement.

The next year, the family moved to Waelder, Texas, arriving in a horse drawn wagon that almost pitched the family, furniture and all, into the creek. The boys now had a little sister, Hazel, born in early January 1912. She died nine months later when a doctor used an adult's stomach pump on the little girl, who had swallowed some pills she had found under her mother's pillow. It was the first of several devastating deaths.

The hard times continued. As the oldest, Wilton often functioned as a surrogate father and made do with the family's poor accommodations—bathing his brother Harlan in the well, for example. Wilton also had to cope with yet another brother, Ralph, born on January 11, 1914. Like Carver, Ralph was rather precocious, walking at eight months and talking shortly thereafter, although a speech defect exposed him to his brothers' teasing. The long-suffering Wilton always looked after his brothers. "You were my Daddy," David (born on April 4, 1919) later told him.

CF "never did devote much time like fathers do now . . . seeing that their kids play little league ball, that sort of thing," David remembered. "Mother . . . was really the stronger person of the two, her will of iron, you know, very dogged type of personality, she'd keep after, keep on keeping after...." In a movie magazine profile, Dana mentioned childhood whippings. This claim was apparently no exaggeration. According to David, "I knew that if I got out of line, I was going to have to pay the price. Well, he really didn't deal out that much, but when he did it it was pretty severe. And, I guess under today's standards it was considered brutalizing, but he never injured me." CF used a little peach tree switch or a belt. "It was always eight licks when he spanked you," David said.

In 1915, CF took his family to the Prospect Hill section of San Antonio, where he worked as state evangelist, acquiring a formidable reputation as a fundraiser. He liked to set wealthy church members against one another, competing to show their piety with their pocketbooks. Annis quailed, though, when CF began the giving with a fifty-dollar donation they could not afford. CF traveled a good deal, and one time after he returned home, a grass widow from Waelder showed up, "making a play" for the preacher, not an uncommon occurrence. Preachers were susceptible to that kind of pursuit, Wilton told his brother David. But apparently CF did not respond in this instance.

The Andrews family did not have much. The boys relied on the local barber college for free haircuts, losing the long curls they all had as young children. With one pair of roller skates between them, they joined in a nation-wide craze that resulted in lots of tears in their knee britches and ribbed black stockings. Wilton often did the family shopping—even picking out a Christmas tree and ordering presents from the Sears & Roebuck catalogue on the advice of his mother. He got the fireplace going in the morning and learned to use the wood stove when his mother taught him how to make biscuits for breakfast (a job Carver would take over when he got a little older).

Wilton remembered a San Antonio hailstorm that undid Carver. Hailstones rained down a foot deep and made a terrifying sound on their tin-roofed house. The world was surely coming to an end. Years later, CF recalled that during the storm six-year-old Carver "rushed to the center table . . . seized a Bible and frantically thrust it into your mother's lap, crying: 'Read the Bible, Mother, read the Bible!'" Wilton never forgot the sight of Carver tugging on his mother's skirt, as she frantically told her boy she had to shut the swinging shutters. CF's dry humor is apparent in his postscript to the story: "If your gesture of religious devotion fooled the Lord, I have not to this day been informed." The family had a good laugh over Carver's panic, but the incident also reflects the terrifying impact fundamentalist Baptists could have on children, who heard a good deal about the Lord's punishment and very little about His forgiveness.

CF remembered it otherwise when he wrote Dana (still calling him Carver) on February 19, 1939:

> As to your having the idea in your younger days that God was "an old meanie" (your words)—it is either a reflection on your powers of comprehension or the influence of your home life. I never preached that way, never taught you that way. Hundreds of others were convinced by my preaching that "God is Love, that thru this love He sent His Son, Jesus Christ, into the world to redeem it by his blood: and that eternal salvation might be had through finding Him . . . I neither preached nor practiced long-faced religion, and I despise it as heartily as you ever could do. . . . Since you mentioned "hell" and your early fear of it, I'll venture to say that the bible seems to teach that the essence of hell will be that same cheated self, with its realization of the tragedy of its mis-spent days and years.

Take CF at his word, and you have to believe that what he preached is not what his son heard—except for his father's words about the "cheated self." The plight of a person who does not do for others and claims none of their love certainly drove Dana Andrews to create an examined life, one in which his responsibilities to family and community remained paramount.

The birth of a daughter, Margaret Alton, just as the family prepared to move from Waelder to Rockdale, thrilled not only Annis, but also her boys, especially Wilton and Charles. To Wilton, it all seemed miraculous, since he had watched his mother, eight months pregnant and suffering from double pneumonia, declared beyond saving by the family doctor. Yet she recovered. "Mother was made of iron," Wilton told his brother David. It had been quite a year. Ralph, barely more than a year old, also had been infected with pneumonia and nearly died.

Charles's fiction evokes the family dynamics at this time. Already Carver (renamed Dan in Charles's story) had become a hero, the leader in their fishing and rabbit-hunting trips. Unlike Charles, who treated Margaret like a princess, Dan was "too old and too wise to be encumbered with a little red headed girl all the time. And too, he was reserved about things." Dan had bigger boys to play with, but he always made time for Tim (the name Charles assigns to himself). Early on, Carver—who would remain close to his brothers all his life—was a standout, a soul who did not quite reveal himself even to his younger, adoring brother. CF used mock biblical language to describe this period, deeming the next two years a time when the "child grew and waxed strong, and was filled with a hankering for 'sweetmeats' from his mother's womb! How you did love candy!"

In February 1916, the year Wilton learned to use one of those increasingly popular electric irons, the family moved to Rockdale. To a man settling down with a growing family, this town of about two thousand inhabitants could not have been a more pleasant residence. "Wide tree-lined streets and weathered buildings" seemed its main features, along with an "air of indolent contentment." But perhaps that very air of contentment is what stirred up CF, who did not believe complacency led to salvation.

At first, all seemed to go well. CF auditioned for his part, so to speak, giving his first sermon in Rockdale on January 20, 1916. By February 10, he had received the "call," and he used his second sermon to announce his acceptance. The *Rockdale Reporter* touted his reputation as an orator and had announced the repair and renovation of the three-bedroom parsonage to coincide with his arrival. It would have seemed a cozy cottage for a small family, but eight children plus their parents would have to jam themselves into close quarters, with the boys sleeping on a closed-in porch at the back, all four lying sideways on the same bed.

With such a large family, the boys had to help out with chores like making beds and scrubbing floors. They fought about whose turn it was to do what, but they performed their domestic chores, as well as delivered newspapers, hoed weeds for fifty cents a day, and made their own Christmas presents—such as wagons, breadboards, and tie racks—when they could not afford to buy them. Somehow the resourceful Annis always managed to provide a birthday cake. A good seamstress, she always dressed well herself. She wanted her family to look good, no matter how modest their means, a trait her son Carver emulated for the rest of his life.

Meanwhile, the family kept growing with the arrival of another little girl, Evelyn, born at 3:00 a.m. on July 17, 1917. It was a night Wilton remembered, because Annis had shouted out to her eleven-year-old boy to run for Dr. Wilson, the family physician. Wilton never seemed to question why his mother charged him with the mission, even though CF was home, if sound asleep. Later CF was rather put out with his son for not waking him up. But even if Annis never admitted as much, and Wilton never acknowledged it, he was always the one who could be depended upon.

An article in the June 15, 1916, issue of the *Rockdale Reporter* noted that "Pastor C. F. Andrews is doing some strong preaching," signaling trouble: "Some people are getting uneasy, but loyal Christians see the guidance of the Holy Spirit in the fearless attacks made upon popular worldliness which has been 'at home' in this church. It is encouraging to see that many are swinging back to the high standard that Jesus Christ set for his followers." But many were not. A resolution had been adopted the previous day putting the congregation on notice by forbidding "profanity and obscenity on the streets, in our homes, and elsewhere," and proscribing "use of intoxicating liquors as a beverage, the frequenting of saloons and pool halls." Dancing, no matter where, was condemned, as was card playing. It was a losing battle, especially when it came to the local movie theater, another target of Baptist disapproval. "Motion pictures are of great educational value," announced R. L. Long, manager of the Dixie Theater, in the July 20, 1916, issue of the *Rockdale Reporter*. "They have come to be recognized as being in a class with newspapers and good books. People demand them and they have come to stay." And, of course, the "theater is cool and pleasant," Long observed, "as we have installed a big windmill fan which gives splendid circulation and keeps the house well ventilated at all times, day and night. We also have plenty of overhead and wall fans." Business was increasing week-by-week, Long told the *Reporter* two months later. Feature length pictures like *Gloria's Romance*, and serials like *The Goddess* and *Stingaree*, were drawing record-breaking crowds. Charlie Chaplin, of course, was a sell-out. And all for ten cents—even the eight reel epic production of *Romeo and Juliet* starring Francis X. Bushman and Beverly Bayne. By the end of the year, Long was upping the ante against the Baptist church by exhibiting *The Rosary*, "a play that bears the highest endorsement of every religious body, carrying with it, as it does, a moral lesson that is appreciated by all faiths. It is a good sermon."

The counterattack began on January 18, 1917, at the mid-winter revival meeting. "Large numbers have been saved" and the churches "made strong and aggressive," the *Rockdale Reporter* announced. CF did his part by issuing a call: "The pastor wants you to come and let's have a great choir. We are going to have great preaching. Let's do our part toward having great soul-stirring song." Charles would later note that Andrew Sampson, the preacher he based on CF, liked to announce hymn numbers "in the deep cheery voice he used for song services." CF realized that his habit of sermonizing had put off some of the faithful. Again, Charles identified the problem: "He always prayed in a kind of scared groan and for twenty minutes sometimes. Other times he was a nice friendly man, but praying seemed to give him the blues something awful. Somewhere along in evening prayer he always said, 'Oh Lord! We are going down the road to wreck and ruin as fast as the wheels of time will carry us on. Have mercy on us Lord!'"

The enterprising Dixie Theater manager forged ahead, in January 1917 compensating for the town's lack of streetlights by offering a free $1.25 electric flashlight with every sale of a $2.00 book of tickets. This offer met with a response from CF on February 22, 1917, when the pastor described the "feast of good things" to be had at the "largest congregations we have had in several months." At the same time, church minutes show that CF was hard at work organizing members to help pay down the church's debt.

The nation's declaration of war on April 6, 1917, seemed, Wilton thought, to set off a kind of spree in Rockdale. People went wild, getting drunk and on Saturday night even swapping wives—at least that was the rumor. The Andrews boys dug trenches in the back yard, staged mock wars, and even excavated a tunnel under the garage, engaging in their own chemical warfare by setting on fire a pound of sulfur to smoke out the neighborhood kids who had infiltrated the underground passage. Dana later told a movie magazine that the best days of his childhood were spent in Rockdale. Perhaps so, since he began to attend school there, and he liked to recite stories in class and cause a stir.

CF's Rockdale trouble began when forty or so congregants left the church, complaining about a pastor who seemed to pay more attention to the poor than to the town's prominent citizens. Church minutes also reveal expulsions of members for "gross immorality" and "ungodly living." A more supple or conniving preacher—a true Elmer Gantry—might well have smoothed over the church's internal struggle, which was taking place amidst a rapidly changing culture. The advent of this modern world meant that parents worried about the role mass entertainment played in their children's lives, usurping the power of example and precept that preachers like CF depended on for their authority. Although Lewis's novel was not published until 1927, it accurately reflected an early twentieth-century world in flux—one that CF had not begun to make his peace with, and one that would motivate his third son to seek a world elsewhere. CF was an absolutist, no doubt believing in what Lewis's novel characterized as "the historic position of the Baptists as the one true Scriptural Church."

On Thursday, January 10, 1918, under the headline "Why the Pastor Has Not Resigned," the *Rockdale Reporter* reproduced the complete text of the sermon CF had given four days earlier, titled "We Ought to Obey

God Rather Than Men." CF admitted, "[T]here have been hours when my very soul cried out to God for relief from the burden of it all." But he would not bow before those powers intent "upon the task of crushing a man who had only tried to do his duty; and doing it because he would not compromise with sin and worldliness." Arrayed against him were not only those with hard feelings, but also those "in the wrong place, under wrong leadership." In effect, he admitted to a lack of diplomacy that his opponents used against him: "I have not softened down the hard sayings and rebukes of the Savior nor sheathed the sword of the Spirit, the word of God, in the velvet scabbard." Comparing himself to the besieged David, CF developed a truly grandiose conception of himself, one fraught with biblical phrases about the "wrath of both Jews and Gentile, bond and free" that made him a martyr to the truth.

What had really riled the well-heeled was CF's practice of seeing to it that the "common people have a voice in church affairs." A radical democrat in this respect, CF may also have been acknowledging what Wilton later noted: It was the poor who often came to the pastor's house with gifts of food and affection. CF said as much, expressing gratitude for the "food and clothing for my wife and little children." CF may not have been a good politician, but he understood the politics of the attacks on him: "Many have stood against me when their hearts are with me, and some of them have said to me that the stand I have taken is right." Indeed, according to Wilton when the family later moved to Uvalde CF received letters saying as much.

CF's adversaries had not followed Baptist usage or even common courtesy, he felt. To those who said his very presence was dividing the church, causing some to leave because they could not sever life-long friendships with others who were also leaving, he replied: "I happen to know that some of them did not run over anybody getting in to church before I came." Zeroing in on his target, he admonished his congregation: "You cannot have a Baptist church where the will of favored classes counts for more than the will of the great rank and file of the membership." He was fighting for the "principles of Democracy." He freely admitted his mistakes, but he was staying "not because of stubbornness but because of conviction." Wilton estimated that something like three hundred church members supported CF, while forty wanted to be done with him. The church minutes for January 16, 1918, disclose that a motion was offered and passed to organize a counsel of three pastors who would attempt to reconcile the opposing factions. By July 6, it was apparent that the conflict could not be resolved. CF offered his resignation, to take effect immediately, and the conference, meeting in regular session, accepted.

In the late summer of 1917, CF moved his family to Uvalde, a little over 220 miles from Rockdale, and settled into a home on the edge of town. Uvalde was twice the size of Rockdale, with an appealing "broad plaza divided into four landscaped parks, in each of which is a public building. Hundreds of native pecan trees shade the streets." Without a church of his own, CF accepted a position as "general missionary" of the Del Rio Baptist Uvalde Baptist Association. Then, on March 17, 1918, the First Baptist Church of Uvalde unanimously elected Charles Forrest Andrews as their pastor. Wilton remembered the family then moved to the center of town, into a home (a parsonage) with trumpet vines that attracted hummingbirds. Next door was the church, a wooden structure built in 1893. As he had done in Rockdale, CF immediately began raising funds for the construction of a large brick church.

The boys took on all sorts of odd jobs as their contribution to the family income. Wilton remembered their work with bees: "Dana and I . . . worked all day [on a centrifugal extractor] separating honey and capping it off, used the old honey to sell around town." Their employer had a contract to supply the Waldorf Astoria with pure honey. They worked on sixteen hives using masks and a smoke pot. But Dana also enjoyed riding horses on W. D. Bunting's ranch on the Nueces River, where he also could swim and fish. Bunting, who remained a friend of CF's for life, would later invite him back to Uvalde to preach.

In the early spring of 1918, everyone got measles. Little Evelyn developed dysentery and was treated with laudanum, an opium mixture commonly used as a home remedy. Many years later Wilton's voice broke when he described her "wonderful sweet personality." On April 22, she died in his arms. On May 1, Margaret, now two years old, also died. Wilton remembered the funeral ceremony and the ritual of throwing dirt on her grave. "It breaks your heart," is all he managed to say. Carver's reaction seems to have been similar, judging by Charles's fictionalized version of events. Margaret, renamed Julie in his story, was Charles's heart's joy. When she died, he looked to Carver (Dan in the story) for some sign of how to go on. Tim (Charles) watches Dan, as he flips a knife over and over:

> "Damn." He had gotten to where he said that word when he was mad or displeased. Tim had been sent to bed for saying it at the supper table and didn't think Dan should say it like that when

everybody was so sad, and told him so. Dan just said it again and kept flipping the knife. . . . Brushing a tear away Dan said "Damn." Then he softened a little, "Timmy, crying don't do no good. There won't nothin do no good." He squared his jaw picked up the knife and got up brushing the seat of his pants and said, "Let's go to the house."

He put his arm around Tim awkwardly then took it away. They both walked stiffly toward the house not saying anything. But Tim kept thinking about faith moving mountains and things like that.

It is apparent from Charles's story that neither he nor his older brother could ever reconcile these two deaths with what their father had taught them. In fact, the deaths of these two girls seemed to confirm the doubts that Carver and Charles—alone among all their brothers—would have about their father's religion.

In Charles's story, Tim reflects on his earliest understanding of the world:

If anything really went wrong there was Dan or mama or papa to fix it, or to say it couldn't be fixed. Either way, it was understandable. If the problem was too big for even papa it was shunted off on God and everybody seemed satisfied. And though Tim sometimes wondered why God didn't take a more active part in things he let the matter rest like the others did.

From what they said in Sunday school he [God] must have gone a long way off, and when Papa said in the pulpit that no one would know the day or the hour when he returned Tim thought God must be a cagy and distrustful sort of person to want to sneak up on people like that without giving them a chance to get the chickens cooked or even to dress up a little. Still Tim believed in the best way he could and looked solemn in church the way everyone else did.

CF was soon to learn that, in Carver's case, he was already losing the hold that faith can enforce. Both of these boys already had an inkling that their father's beliefs were inadequate for the immense world they were beginning to encounter. Charles could no longer live "in any fashion that separated him from the flow of things."

Annis seemed to feel terribly alone after the girls' deaths. David, born on April 4, 1919, believed he was spoiled because his parents were still grieving over the loss of their two daughters. "I got by with a lot that I'm sure they [his brothers] didn't. At least I've heard that from my brothers," David recollected. Annis also had the consolation of giving birth to another daughter, Mary, born in Uvalde on October 14, 1922.

Then CF put his heart into supporting the Ku Klux Klan, extending its popularity in the South, parts of the Midwest, and as far north as New Jersey. Uvalde's most famous native son, Congressman John Nance Garner, denounced the Klan as an "organization which had no place in American life," even though some members of Congress from Texas had joined the KKK. Klansman, "hooded and gowned," burned a fiery cross in front of Garner's home and conducted a campaign against him. He lost Uvalde County but still managed to get re-elected. To some citizens, the Klan seemed admirable because of its opposition to alcohol consumption, one of the evils CF constantly campaigned against. Wilton remembered Garner saying to his father, "Brother Andrews, I didn't believe in Prohibition. But I will enforce the law until we get it off the books. You know I got a cellar full to last the rest of my life."

On June 1, 1923, the *Uvalde News Leader* reported: "All doubts as to the Ku Klux Klan having an organization at Uvalde were dispelled last Sunday night when 13 hooded Knights marched down the aisle of the first Baptist Church of Uvalde." In a written statement, the Knights proclaimed:

> We have watched the unselfish efforts and works of Rev. C. F. Andrews, pastor of the Uvalde Baptist Church, towards making Uvalde a better place spiritually to live in, towards winning souls for Christ and in teaching men the fellowship of Christian religion, and we believe him consecrated and dedicated to his work in body, in mind, in spirit and in life, and we are in sympathy with him and give him our most hearty commendation, and it being one of his desires to erect an edifice in Uvalde for the worship of God and the advancement of God's cause, we UVALDE KLAN, in recognition of his services for the cause and in furtherance of the cause, and in the name of our blessed Savior who died on Calvary that we might have ever lasting life, hereby donate the sum of $100.00 toward assisting in building a Baptist Church in Uvalde.

At a crowded public meeting on June 18, CF introduced Rev. Lloyd P. Bloodworth of San Antonio, who spoke on behalf of the Klan. The *Uvalde News-Leader* reported that CF "spoke of the good work he considered the Klan doing in bringing men to a better understanding of the gospel of

Christ," noting that "82 per cent of the Protestant ministers were members of the Klan and 95 per cent were in sympathy with it. . . . It was a great brotherhood and stood for the church to the last ditch and for Americanism to the last ditch." Later, on April 25, 1924, CF addressed a Klan Hall meeting of "several hundred members and invited guests," endorsing the views of a guest speaker who expatiated on the "great menace to our American institutions by the great hordes of foreign speaking population especially in the large cities where they were not assimilated and where their ideas and inclinations were absolutely foreign to American ideals."

This kind of zealotry appalled CF's third son, even if, like the rest of the family, he still attended church. "I think from my early memories of Carver, he was always sort of skeptical," David said. Carver was a good student—he made seventh grade honor roll—but he was already sneaking out to the local movie theater, the Strand, where the owners, amused at the antics of the preacher's son, let him in for free. Wilton remembered his younger brother hopping their home's back fence and slipping down an alley to enter the theater's rear doors. Even when his father caught him and punished him by refusing to take him swimming, Carver continued his movie going.

Charles set one of his novel's scenes in the Strand, where his protagonist, Jeff Harvey, watches the "amorous manipulations of Greta Garbo and John Gilbert" thinking, "[h]ow delicious and secret it was. What strange things people did out in the world." The movies sure beat the watering and weeding Charles and his brothers did around the house. Attending movies put him and Carver among the souls "past the redemption point." But the thought of the picture he had just seen gave Jeff a thrill: "Well it was a pretty nice way to be lost at least for awhile."

Already attracted to the stage, Carver sang "Your Star on the Flag" at a school assembly on February 25, 1921, and appeared in a school play, *At the Photographers*, on March 9, 1923. He was popular with girls, who did not want to have parties without him. "Is Carver coming?" they would ask Wilton, who acknowledged his brother's good looks. Carver always picked the prettiest girl to go out with, and he was—as Wilton put it—devoted to his choice, while Harlan seemed always to have several girls on hand.

Dana remembered Uvalde fondly. He loved hunting and fishing. Wilton took his brothers camping for three or four days at a time. The hill country was their playground, where they were unhampered by adults. "Wilton's old enough to take care of himself," Annis said serenely, "and smart enough to look after the younger ones." Carver loved riding horses. His daughter Susan remembered: "[W]hen I was about 3 he put me on the horse with him, in the front of the saddle with his arms around me. Now THAT was a formative experience."

Unlike his brothers, Carver resented the constraints put upon a preacher's boy. He was always a bit wild, "a rebel," Wilton said and David later confirmed. Dana, a generous spirit, liked to treat his friends at the local drugstore, until his father put a stop to this largess by informing the store's owner that he could not afford his son's expensive habits. Whenever Dana came home late, he would say he had been playing the church organ, which he did—but this was also a stock answer used to cover up other activities his father frowned upon.

David could not have been more than five at the time, but he remembered that his teenage brother once took off during a Wednesday night prayer meeting. "What a catastrophe it caused around the house," David said. Wilton, as usual, knew more of the details. Carver went missing that night and with a friend hopped a train to San Antonio the next day. "They were about to freeze," Wilton recalled. They had two pasteboard suitcases (one for food, the other for clothes), which they tried to use as a "windbreak." Dana later recalled "the fog in San Antonio and those deep voiced pre-dawn factory whistles announcing the dismal hour of 6 A. M. And that walk along the highway and the nap in an empty fruit car."

Nearing San Antonio, Carver noticed that the train was curving in the wrong direction and called to his friend to jump off, but another train got between them, separating the boys and their suitcases. Out of money and food (he had the suitcase with the clothes), Carver wandered around for a day or so until he had enough. Then the homesick boy looked up one of his father's friends. "Dad had called and told Dr. Gates the boys had run away," David said. When Carver showed up at Dr. Gates's house, the doctor said, "Son I've been expecting you." Dr. Gates called CF and said, "Guess who I've got here." CF replied that he would pay for his son's trip home. "I remember when Carver came back from San Antonio, Dad picked him up on the train . . . in his Model T Ford," Wilton said. CF just said, "Well, son, I was expecting you." CF talked to Carver, going over the whole episode. Carver said he had run away because he was tired of being poor. He had set out to get rich so that his mother could have a servant and not work so hard. But now he realized how hard it was out there in the world and how wonderful home now seemed.

CF announced to his sons that he didn't want anybody else to say anything about the incident. According to Wilton, CF told Carver: "Any other time you think you want to go, tell me. I don't want you to go. But if you want to go, you don't have to run away."

About a year before he died, CF wrote a letter responding to Dana's request that his father write about his son's early years. CF wrote about Carver's escape from Uvalde, "where you decided to throw off the yoke of parental authority, turn your back on the cramped surroundings of a preachers home and go out into the big world on your own, packing up and charging a lot of canned goods to dad." That his son ran away "while the rest were at church . . . gave me the hardest jolt I had ever had up to that time, it was so unexpected. For the next two days I hardly slept or ate." The rest of the story is as Wilton, David, and John recalled it.

If CF saw any greater import in his son's departure, he did not let on, except to say the episode cured Dana of his "wanderlust." CF remembered, instead, another incident that demonstrated his son's "dramatic tendencies at Uvalde":

> [Carver] rushed out into the street in front of the home of the old, flat-footed Catholic priest, waving an old red jacket at a savage and dangerous Jersey bull which had torn out of his stall and was on a rampage thru town. You had read of matadors or bull fighters, waving red flags at bulls; so you decided to be a toreador yourself . . . The old priest did not love me any too well; but he came rushing out on his porch, shouting at you—"Go back you little fool—don't you know that bull will kill you?!" But it was a chance to "act" before your public, and you forgot the danger. I'm still grateful to old Father Simone! But for him your one-act play might have ended disastrously.

As a Klansman, of course, CF was fervently anti-Catholic, David recalled. Charles described a character based on his father as "a good man, but a fire eater if you ever saw one. He had been brought up among the pine thickets of the deep south, by folks devoutly protestant who used the words Catholic and devil with the same tone of fear and hate." Annis shared these sentiments, fearing that an apple Father Simone gave Wilton might be poisoned.

Near the end of his life, CF summed up his view of the Uvalde years in a letter to Dana:

> [W]onderful days—days of hard work, heavy responsibility, but interesting and full of joy: with a lot of sturdy boys growing up

around me in the home, each one as distinctly different as if they had been no kin. I know now that you must have often felt the limitations imposed on a preacher's boy somewhat galling; but the quality of the men they have become lends strength to my life-long conviction that boys who are held under sensible restraints make MEN; those who do as they please make—*trouble.*

CF mentions at the end of this letter that he is "very tired." He could no longer work, and he had time to reflect on the man he had been: the one who often had no time for his boys and counted on Wilton to father them; the one who apparently never saw the incredible selfishness of many of his actions; but also the one who represented a lofty standard, even if he did not always live up to it himself.

None of the Andrews brothers would follow their father into the ministry, although Ralph considered it, and John (born in Uvalde on August 8, 1920) remained in his father's faith. John's wife, Anne, remembered waking up at three in the morning during one of Dana's visits and hearing him say, "John, you're stirrin' the hell out of me." As usual, the brothers were arguing about religion. John also knew the story of his brother running away from home and had his own interpretation, saying Dana "got crisscrossed." "Dad represented God," John told biographer Clyde Williams,

and Dad . . . had some real problems, and Dana saw a lot more of that than I did . . . Dana was very perceptive, very . . . He's got a mind like a steel trap in a lot of ways . . . But, he didn't, I don't think ever discern that Dad was a fallible human being, and although he had a connection with God he still was largely motivated by fleshly things, and this—I don't think he ever, ever put—uh, I'm trying to find the words for that . . .

CLYDE. Reconciled

JOHN. Reconciled, so therefore . . . I think he found it immoral. . . . he saw the inconsistency in Dad's life . . . and he [Dana] just never recovered.

From conversations with Dana Andrews, Clyde Williams gathered that Dana had "heard too much hell, fire and brimstone in his early life and saw people terrified by that." "He said in effect that a God that can strike that kind of terror in the people made him wonder about the nature of the deity," Clyde told John. Dana sang the hymns "Almost Persuaded" and "Just As I Am" on the phone to Clyde and remembered those relentless revival meetings working people up to be saved. "One way to do it was to exhaust everyone so they would have to come forward or they wouldn't get out of church. We had a good laugh about that," Clyde told John.

CHAPTER 3

"Go Hollywood, Young Man!"
1924–29

IN MARCH 1924, CF was offered the pastorate of the First Baptist Church in Huntsville, the home of Sam Houston State Teacher's College. He wanted his sons to be well educated, and settling in Huntsville, where he had friends, seemed the most congenial and affordable way to achieve this goal—especially after the birth of his eighth son, William (Billy), on September 29, 1925.

Unlike CF's troubled departure from Rockdale, his farewell to Uvalde seems to have been a pleasant, sociable occasion. On May 2, 1924, the local newspaper described a reception for the pastor and his wife, as well as tributes to the pastor given by several prominent citizens and clergy. Presented with the gift of a three-piece silver service, CF thanked everyone for the loyalty and love shown him not only by his congregation, but by so many others in Uvalde.

Carver joined the high school debate team and did well. In his senior year, he won the leading role in *The Lovebug*. He also met and fell in love with Norma Felder. By the time Carver was fifteen, the couple considered themselves engaged. Pledging himself to Norma Katherine, as her friends called her, meant Carver would have no time for other girls. But like everyone else in the family, Carver worked—in his case, earning $30 a month making deliveries for the local butcher. A few years later, when the family moved to Madisonville (about thirty miles from Huntsville), he remained behind to attend college, working for a farmer in exchange for room and board. He also worked part-time at the local bank.

Huntsville, the home of Sam Houston, its founding father and the patron saint of Texas, had a population in the vicinity of five thousand. The state college, founded in 1879, had a year-round enrollment of approximately a thousand students. At first, Carver thought he might enjoy a career in teaching or business, but he soon grew interested in drama.

Like Charles, Carver may have noticed that teaching was not really a career for truly successful men. "For from the time of its establishment to the present that profession has ever been the hope for the aspiring poor, the ambitious mediocre," Charles wrote in his novel, describing a college in which "all the good ones, all the sleek ones, all the well fed, all the brilliant ones were aiming at engineering, medicine, law, and business. . . . Teaching was for dolts." Charles's protagonist, Jeff Harvey, "could remember no occasion when . . . the super teacher was ever asked to air his views, his methods and techniques before the associated student body. . . . By and large the people of the town and the school population looked down upon teachers."

Twice the size of their home in Uvalde, their new house in Huntsville had three bedrooms and a parlor. Across from the college and atop a hill, the "grim gray towers of the Texas State Penitentiary," overshadowed what the WPA Guide called "this dignified old town." Executions by electric chair began in Huntsville in 1923. The prison, a considerable enterprise, housed a machine shop and facilities for shoe making and printing, and for the manufacture of candy, mattresses, and license plates. The prison could be seen from Old Main, the building that dominated the college campus. "When we lived in the parsonage," Wilton said, "every once and a while a convict would escape. They brought bloodhounds up to our front door. The escaped convict came right through our house. Another time a convict went right over the front porch." College girls sometimes fell in love with prison trustees, who were allowed to go into town. Most of these men were not violent and were in prison because of liquor violations. College students were not allowed to visit the penitentiary, Wilton noted, but the boys often found rubbers on the church floor.

Huntsville had a social hierarchy, its own "400," as Wilton put it. Although Harlan dated Julia Smither, daughter of a prominent local family, a poor minister's children generally did not socialize with the well to do. This prohibition became a sore point when Carver began to go out with Norma Felder. She had an active social life, often hosting parties for girlfriends to celebrate their engagements. The *Huntsville Item* printed lavish descriptions of weddings, just the sort of ostentatious events that neither Carver nor his family would be invited to attend. But high school and then college provided a natural meeting place for a couple that shared many interests. At Sam Houston State, Norma and Carver were members of the Spanish and drama clubs. Carver got good reviews for his performances in school plays, especially for the role of Cecil Graham in *Lady*

Windermere's Fan. Norma was president of the Eclectic Society, dedicated to developing the "social and literary qualities of young womanhood," and to supporting "college activities, such as athletics, literary and musical organizations." She was assistant editor of the college yearbook and was nominated as one of the twenty-four "beauties" featured in the college annual. At a "women's forum," she gave a talk on proper etiquette. "As a result," the *Huntsville Item* reported, "they now know how to acknowledge an introduction, what to do when the name is not distinctly heard, and most important of all, they know how to avoid the awkward pause that often follows an introduction."

In fall of 1928, Norma departed from New York City on a world cruise as part of the "floating university," an impressive yearlong trip that included 450 students and forty faculty members. By many accounts, this voyage had a profound impact on students and faculty alike, many of whom described the life-changing experience in memoirs and on resumes. Norma joined students from the best schools, studying world geography, history, and literature. She took extensive notes, and, like other students, wrote that the highlight of the trip was a visit to India and the Taj Mahal. She also mentioned a meeting that was to become a treasured memory for many of the students: "Cannot touch India without feeling the spirit of unrest. The young people in India do not hesitate to tell you that at 1st opportunity they will throw off this yoke of England. We were privileged in seeing Ghandi [*sic*] the famous leader of the revolt for a few minutes."

Carver's brother David believed Norma's family had spirited their daughter off to separate her from Carver. Mrs. Felder wanted her daughter to marry a Smither or a Gibbs, a member of one of the two prominent families in town, David said. Although he was studying to be an accountant, Carver's prospects were uncertain. But Mrs. Felder's granddaughter said her grandmother was just wild about Carver, who joined Mrs. Felder when she came to New York to welcome her daughter back from her trip. David, however, believed that Carver had insisted on driving Mrs. Felder to the rendezvous. It seems likely that Norma's attachment to Carver caused some anxiety in the Felder family, even though they did not forbid her seeing him. Annis later wrote to her son that Norma's mother was "crazy about you," but disapproved of Carver's plans to head for California. Mrs. Felder could not bear the idea of having a daughter live so far away. In the end, though, Annis thought her son lucky not to have married Norma: "You and Mrs. Felder couldn't have gotten along. At that time any way."

In her floating university notebook, Norma listed Carver's address as: c/o Dorothy Theatre, Huntsville. Her letters to him have not survived, but on two pages of class notes she carefully practiced her monogram, NFA. Whatever her family's concerns, it appears that she intended to return to Carver and to an engagement that she never considered repudiating.

For Carver, working at both of Sam Parish's movie theaters, the continuous showing of *Wings* for three days, beginning on December 12, 1928, presented him with exactly the kind of future he wanted. Although not a talkie, *Wings* marked a new epoch, "with complete sound effects . . . the first sound picture ever to be shown in Huntsville," the *Item* reported. Carver did publicity for the film, stenciling wings on sidewalks and talking to various organizations about the exciting new film, which featured amplified with sound effects during the aerial combat scenes.

Directed by William Wellman, whose aerial exploits during World War I provided him with material for this "epic of the air," *Wings* depicts the competition of two young men for the love of the same woman. The plot mattered less to Carver than the nuanced performance of Richard Arlen. Compared to the callow and impulsive Jack Powell, played with adolescent vigor by Buddy Rogers, the cautious, self-doubting David Armstrong is the type of gentleman hero that Dana Andrews would perfect. Wellman called his pilots "knights of the air" in this chivalrous story: When David's machine gun jams, a German ace declines to shoot him down. This aerial jousting must be on equal terms. Although David realizes he has won the love of Sylvia Lewis (Jobyna Ralston), he cannot bear to break Jack's heart by telling him. The rivals have become best friends during their combat missions against the Germans. And it is only after David's tragic death that Jack realizes how his noble friend has sought to protect him: Jack shot down a German plane, not realizing that David was piloting it after having escaped a German prisoner of war camp.

Dana mentioned to Lillian Ross that he watched films like *Wings* over and over again. In Arlen, he would have detected an actor who knew how to hold his emotion for the camera—as he does during his farewell scene with his mother. He is perfectly poised to develop the poignancy of the moment: his desire to go to war struggles against his yearning to remain home. Later, critics would single out Dana Andrews's ability to convey just such conflicted emotions. "I felt I might even be able to do better than Richard Arlen," Dana told Lillian Ross. To Hedda Hopper, he confided: "Just to entertain myself, I'd reconstruct how they played the parts and imagine how I'd do it."

Silent film acting often depended on broad gestures to convey what words would otherwise explain. Arlen, like Dana's other hero, Ronald Colman, understood how silent film training pertained to talkies, which required actors to concentrate emotion much more subtly in their faces, postures, and gestures while delivering dialogue. Body language alone could sometimes sum up a character—as Arlen does twice when he forms a circle in the air with his finger: first when he is shot down and is watching the planes above him, and then again when he is dying. The circling motion of his finger imitates revolving propeller blades, and also the cycle of life and death that the war encapsulates.

Arlen's frown, his deep-set eyes, suggest hidden depths and reserves. Dour and taciturn, withdrawn and hesitant, he remains a fascinating psychological study. You can't quite read his emotions. He holds back and draws you in with his innate dignity. Arlen's introspective melancholy contrasts with Rogers's extroverted behavior and even with the latter's facial contours. Rogers's eyes seem closer to the surface of his face, as befits a character who does not know his own mind. He thinks he is in love with Sylvia, but in fact he ought to be romancing Mary Preston (Clara Bow), whose personality and affinity for him makes her far more suitable for him. Arlen performs his part as a divided personality—exactly what Dana Andrews, the actor and the man, would experience when he left home for Hollywood, a place that excited him but could never truly be his home.

Quite aside from the love story and the stunning aerial action scenes, *Wings* is a film that spoke to Carver Dana Andrews because it is concerned with what it means for a man to leave home and abandon the woman he loves. He was not yet prepared, however, to believe he had forsaken Norma. Like David Armstrong, he would wrestle to find the noble course of action. And like David Armstrong, Carver Dana Andrews would continue to question himself. Although Carver had rejected his father's religion, he could not renounce the need for self-examination that CF always returned to in his sermons. "The first requisite of a man is honesty with himself and with God," CF preached. "To each soul is open a highway and a low, / And each soul must determine on which highway he will go."

After serving less than two years as pastor of the First Baptist Church of Huntsville, Charles Forrest Andrews resigned and moved his family twenty-eight miles to Madisonville, where he sold insurance, thinking himself unworthy to be a preacher. As Wilton later told his brother David, "It all started in 1926. I talked to him [CF] at the time, and I didn't like what he was doing. He lied to me. That's when I blew my top. Little Ralph was up in Dad's study, and Dad tore up a letter, and Ralph pieced it together, and he showed it to mother. That's the way she found out about it. I was keeping it to myself." David knew about "it" too: His father was having an affair. The situation seemed so serious that Wilton thought the family might have to break up. CF spent part of the time in Houston seeing this other woman, and at one point, Wilton remembered, he and Dana went to Houston to confront her. Wilton did not think the woman physically attractive, but she was a marvelous musician and poet. She had all the talents that his father admired but none of the character his wife had. Wilton thought his father prone to a certain immaturity that he never quite outgrew.

By 1927, the affair was over, but the damage was done, not just to Annis—who decided to keep the affair under wraps so as not to harm her husband's reputation—but also to Dana. He never spoke against his father except about the way CF had treated Annis. Wilton made excuses, saying CF's poor health and a weakened constitution that made him susceptible to the other woman. How CF extricated himself from his affair is not clear, but by 1927 he had returned to Madisonville. There he resumed his ministry in a town of about a thousand people that featured a castle-like courthouse where Sam Houston "made one of the most impassioned speeches against Texas secession."

CF seemed to do well by Madisonville, which greeted his resignation on May 29, 1929, with considerable disappointment. The *Madisonville Meteor* reported:

> The membership of the Madisonville Baptist church were greatly grieved when the announcement was made that Rev C. F. Andrews had received a call to one of the leading churches in Los Angeles, California and would tender his resignation at the services Sunday morning to accept the work in that field of labor. Rev. Mr. Andrews has been here only a short time and his work was just getting under headway it seemed and for him to be called away so soon was indeed a very great shock to his membership. He is one of the outstanding preachers of the Baptist denomination and not only that but a real man with it. Not afraid at any time to preach the truth of the Holy Bible and to fight sin from every angle, he has not only been a great help to the Madisonville Baptist church during his short stay here, but he has been a real asset to the town in advocating law enforcement from the pulpit and as a citizen as well. His

last act for the Baptist church here was to baptize three converts and to receive two others into the church Sunday night.

The church feels very keenly the loss of Rev. Andrews at this time and many regrets from other citizens of the community have been expressed.

Carver had another year of college to complete and did not join his family in Van Nuys, where his father became pastor of the First Baptist Church.

For some time Carver's teacher and drama coach, Charles Stewart, had been telling him, "Go Hollywood, young man. Get out of Texas. Become an actor. You have the brains. The looks. Acting ability. Go." Carver took no more classes after the spring semester of 1929, but he delayed heading to Hollywood. In one movie magazine account he alludes to a quarrel with Norma—some kind of crisis that led to his leaving Huntsville, but not Texas. Norma would later mention their "misunderstanding" in a letter to Carver, adding, "neither of us could adequately explain." Nonetheless, she conceded, it was a misunderstanding that led to his decision to leave for California as soon as he could afford the trip.

Carver found work for a few months as an accountant for Gulf Oil in Houston. Later in the year, he moved on to Jack Tobin's stationery store in Austin, where he earned $295 a month keeping accounts. In Austin, as he later confessed to Norma, he was unfaithful to her. Wilton, who remembered visiting Dana at this time, seemed both impressed and a little appalled by how many women Dana had around him. Perhaps Dana's betrayal—a kind of bridge burning—is what finally provoked his decision to depart for California. After announcing to Jack Tobin that he was quitting to become a movie star and turning down his boss's offer of a raise to $350 a month, Carver splurged on a farewell party for himself, exhausting the thousand dollars he had saved. Squandering this much money sounds like an exaggeration—but perhaps it isn't, given the number of dunning letters that would dog him all the way to California. He hitchhiked the 1500 miles to Van Nuys in three days.

CHAPTER 4

To Be an Actor
1929–32

CARVER WROTE NORMA sometime after he arrived and received this response on December 30, 1929:

> I don't know why I'm writing to you immediately after getting your letter. I should wait a month or so and torture you as you have tortured me the past few weeks. But I don't believe I could hurt you—not like you have crushed me. You promised to write me a letter before you left Texas—and then you promised to wire me as soon as you arrived in California. I don't hear from you for over four weeks. What was I to think?—that you had quietly walked out of my life for all time. Just when I was beginning to see light again after months of darkness—just as I was about to regain that self-respect that I'd completely lost—and you plunge me right back into darkness and self-disgust. That was cruel, Carver.

Norma wanted him to know about her horrible holiday season. She described the dire impact of the October 1929 stock market crash on her relatives, "all in a terrible state financially unless the stocks rally soon. And Daddy continues to try to drown his worries in liquor, and is just about to drown Mother and me in sorrow." The dry good store was doing very little business. She told Carver about someone they knew who had been caught embezzling $3,000 from the local bank, which had to close when too many depositors tried to withdraw their savings. Without access to her account, Norma was stuck at home—although she made a little money substitute teaching and had gone to the Palace Theater to moon over an actor who resembled Carver.

By January 8, she had received three letters from Carver. Apparently he had done much to repair their rupture, although she recalled how he laughed at her when she recited Elizabeth Barrett Browning to him. She quoted, "But love me for love's sake, that evermore, / Thou mayst love on—through love's eternity." Did she also put herself in the poet's place, wondering whether Carver would play the part of Robert Browning and come to her rescue? No longer angry, Norma now worried that she would lose her man: "Sweetheart, ever since you told me of being unfaithful to me before you left Austin, it has grieved me." She did not blame him, though, her "mind was in such a turmoil then that I wasn't really responsible." What she said had driven him away. Now she wanted him to know that she loved him "heart, soul, and body" and hoped he would stay true to her. She quoted Shelley's "Love's Philosophy":

> Nothing in this world is single;
> All things by a law divine
> In one spirit mist and mingle.
> Why not I with thine?

"It seems it might have been written for us," her letter ended. She wanted him to write her every day. "That was one of our old conditions, wasn't it?" she reminded him in letters that she sent every two or three days. He did not write that often but made up for lapses with long letters.

When Carver arrived in Van Nuys, he found his mother presiding over the nicest house she had ever occupied, the first one with indoor plumbing and situated on an attractive corner lot. CF had rented the home for fifty-nine dollars a month. His ministry had begun well. He had the powerful support of a patron who had heard him preach and had persuaded the congregation to issue the "call" to CF. At the same time, CF's former mistress followed him out to California. Wilton watched his sly mother go to work. Annis invited the woman to visit the Andrews home in Van Nuys, where the woman would have to see the family she had almost broken up. The kindly Annis then invited the woman to stay the night, insisting they sleep in the same bed. The woman left the next day and never returned. Wilton chuckled in admiration at his mother's maneuvers.

The cultural shock of the move West never wore off. Wilton described the family's trek across the continent in a British-made Star motorcar as similar to what the Okies would experience a few years later escaping from their Dust Bowl misery. Wilton marveled at the lush surroundings, the pepper trees that seemed to him like mesquite on a grander scale, and orchards that would gradually disappear as the property values rose and speculation in real estate escalated. But only Dana and Charles could conceive of a permanent life for themselves in California.

After Carver's arrival, Annis asked him, "Vacation?" "Nope," he answered. "I'm going to Hollywood. To be an actor." The confident aspirant then did the rounds of the studios and soon learned they had no work for him. He stayed with his family for three months and ended up driving a Van Nuys school bus for ten dollars a week, the first of many poorly paying Depression-era jobs.

Norma had heard that Carver's family was planning to return to Madisonville. Was it true, and would he join them? She hoped not, since she loved the idea of living in California. She wanted to know all about his new life and projected herself into it: "Wouldn't it be just a picnic for us seeing every thing together." She assured him, "Sweetheart, I want you to know that I have all the confidence in the world in you. I *know* you will make good. I think the whole trouble so far has been that you have never found what you really want to make your life profession." She would wait for him. "It all depends on you now." Norma's relationship with Carver had evidently become a touchy subject at home, since she advised him in mid-January 1930 that she had to destroy his "nice long letter" after having read it a "dozen or so times." She added, "Please be extremely careful about how you write to me, dear. You know how things are here."

Norma confessed that she was disappointed to learn that he did not get a $200 a month job he had been counting on: "But, Darling, if you want to go into the movies, *by all means* do it. You'll never be happy unless you like the work you're doing, and I've always secretly thought that you were cut out for the stage or the screen." She even fantasized about being the wife of a John Barrymore, jealously fighting off her female rivals and then kissing and making up with the man she was so proud of. Norma's faith in Carver, however, would gradually have the paradoxical effect of driving him away. She constantly reminded him of the risks: "It's such a long, hard pull—and so uncertain. Of course you'll have to begin as an extra—and that means that some days you'll have work and that most days you won't. And *that* means longer for *us* to wait. But you know, honey, I'll wait for you forever."

Norma had another worry. Carver's brother Charles had recently married, even though she doubted he was in a position to support himself. If the Andrews family did return to Madisonville, and Carver and Charles stayed behind, Norma suspected that Carver would feel obligated to help Charles and his new wife. That obligation would mean putting off marriage to Norma. "*Don't* agree to it, Dear. *Please* don't put him before me." Apparently they had quarreled about Charles before, and Carver had told her off. "I hope you won't *ever* write another letter like that," she signed off, "I'm relying on you."

It would take Carver nearly two years to work out why Norma—who had known him since he was fourteen and had seemed inseparable from the life he wanted to make for himself—should not become his wife. Did her plaintive letters wear him out? She told him that she was sitting by the radio listening to a man singing "All Alone," and that she could not bear to stay in Huntsville "another week," in spite of going to social events like dances and earning at least a little income teaching. Of course, she had to tell him how she felt, but how was he, so far away, to deal with what was a joy but also a burden for both of them? How to explain it all to himself—let alone to anyone else? He proposed that she come to California that summer. Norma replied that she did not have the money. "I'm not just *talking* hard times. Daddy's feeling them terribly," she told him.

Every letter from Norma included the hope he had landed a job. She mused that the movie people would change his name—"Don't be 'Dan' again, please" (the name he used in Austin)—and require him to remain single to please his fans. She offered job advice: Maybe he could sing on the radio. And her letters always had the same bifurcated message: She would wait forever but please hurry.

He kept her letters as a treasure of her love, but read in chronological order they reveal the excruciating nature of his attachment. At the end of February, after seeing Harlan happy with his new wife, Norma wrote, "I could almost beg you to come back to Texas and take just any little job, future or no future, to have that contentment. You don't know how lonely and desperate I am, darling." She complained that he had not written for two weeks. Nearly a year after Carver had come to California, Norma wrote him: "Did it ever occur to you with how little you and I could be perfectly happy?" She recalled a poem he had recited to her:

> There isn't much to life but this—
> A husband's smile, a baby's kiss,
> A home, a book, a fire, a friend,
> And just a little cash to spend.

But Carver had no cash and still owed plenty of people money. His father was so worried that he wrote to Norma on January 13, 1931. No doubt Norma would be surprised to hear from him, CF began, but they both cared deeply about Carver, and CF needed her help. His son had not been able to find a position other than the make-do, temporary, and usually part-time jobs available during the Depression. "He is living a fine clean life as anyone could wish," CF emphasized. "It is not his morals that disturb me. But he does not seem to realize the value of a dollar, and should he get a position, I am afraid he will still spend all he makes as he has been doing the past few years." CF thought that because Carver loved Norma, she better than anyone else could influence him to be "more responsible in a business way."

CF was also writing to learn whether Norma still loved Carver. "I had hoped when I left Texas that you and Carver would marry," CF told her. "If you do love him, I believe you could make a real man of him. He has not even noticed any other girl out here and has no bad habits of any sort, except spending all his money when I wanted him to pay his debts. He has been just as fine and noble as I could wish him to be, and you know how old fashioned I am. He says he has learned his lessons and means to settle down and save when he gets a position." But CF was worried: He would probably return to Texas soon and leave Carver and Charles behind. "I know you are good and sweet and would be a blessing to him." He hoped they would marry soon and not wait to "make a fortune" before they marry. "It is not so bad to start poor," he suggested. CF asked her forgiveness for any presumption on his part, but he assured her he was only interested in her happiness and Carver's. "He does not know I am writing you."

How did this moving letter from a father who could be very hard on his son come to be in Dana Andrews's papers? Presumably Norma gave it to him at some point, perhaps when Carver decided he could not marry her. As agreed, she apparently destroyed his letters, but he kept hers—a characteristic gesture by a man who never wanted to erase where he had come from, even if he could not bear to reveal what it had cost him to become Dana Andrews. CF's letter, which goes a long way toward explaining why his family never forsook him, also raises questions about both Norma and Carver. That they loved one another cannot be doubted. But the reasons why they kept postponing their marriage are open to question. It was certainly prudent not to marry in the midst of the Depression. On the other hand, as CF himself had proven, marriage could be hard but not impossible without much money—especially where there was love and devotion. Charles was only nineteen when he married. The truth seems to be that both Norma and Carver wanted something more out of life than a man of CF's generation and convictions expected. Both Norma and Carver wanted to live on their own terms and tried to persuade one another that they shared the same aspirations. Indeed, the very notion of aspiration united them. Perhaps if Carver, like Robert Browning, had come home to Huntsville and swept his beloved off her feet, their story would have had a different ending. But Carver could not and—probably like the young Thomas Wolfe—would not return. Not yet, not when he still owed people not just money but an explanation.

A letter from R. W. Miller, Vice-President and General Manager of Huntsville Oil Mill Company is typical of several others that CF alluded to:

April 25, 1931
Dear Carver

Mr. Parish has been talking to me repeatedly about your past due note here and says that although he has written you a number of times, you have failed or refused to answer his letters, and he knows that you got them or else they would have been returned. I am hoping that you will handle this matter in such a way that Mr. Parish will not demand payment of me at this time which he has been threatening to do.

I am ashamed that you stayed in our office as long as you did and not getting it ground into you most thoroughly that you must attend to your obligations promptly even if you cannot pay them.

Such letters made it impossible for Carver to make an appearance in Huntsville—not only because he would have to confront men to whom he owed money, but because he would have to confront himself at a time when his own sense of self-worth was open to challenge.

As for Norma, how could she leave a family fallen on hard times and scrape together the cash for a trip to California? Money aside, what would it say about her if she pursued Carver, especially at a time when he could not support her. What kind of a drag would she be on him in an environment alien to her, expressing a love that had flourished in such a different culture? She would be coming to a man who was still a boy living with his family, a point CF evidently did not consider when he wrote to Norma. Although CF's letter is full of love for his son, it also presents the picture of a young man everyone is *hoping* will turn out all right. Right then, was Carver any more than a good Southern boy who "meant well"?

Helen Wood, a Huntsville friend, had written to Carver playfully, warning him not to be seduced by Hollywood, city slickers, and blondes. But Carver's nobility of purpose was never in doubt—at least not to himself or to those closest to him. His father's letter might give the impression that Carver was oblivious to his plight, or at least that he failed to see the implications of his behavior. In fact, Carver had set out to study himself and to examine his motives in a journal he began just about the time that CF wrote to Norma. It is striking how self-consciously and deliberately he set out to write the book of his life:

> The following pages, be they few or many, shall, by the regularity of their consummation tell the tale of another good intuition of one, Carver Dana Andrews (Born Jan 1, 1909 near Collins, Miss.), which intention, it is the endeavor and hope of the writer, shall not grease the already paved road to Hell but shall on the contrary aid in a complete reconstruction of the path in the opposite direction. The following is intended to be more than a diary—less than an autobiography, in fact, far from anything to be made public in any other manner than to my own needs and in a manner suitable to my own psychological processes in order that they might be readily retained not herein alone but in my mind and be a part of my daily life and thought. I shall call it my "scrap book" and transcribe therein only those things which I conceive to be uplifting, instructive, balancing, or any of those qualities which make for a fuller understanding of life, its problems, and immortality—the greatest thing about any man.

For the next ten years, he would keep a record—sometimes detailed and sometimes sparse—in an accounting ledger of his thoughts and actions. It was not a scrapbook, really, but a journal, an accounting to himself, of what he hoped to accomplish, and an examination of his character. He may have rejected his father's church, but the urge to examine his soul remained strong.

By March 1931, Carver's family (except for Carver and Charles) had returned to Madisonville. CF decided to leave Van Nuys because he could not accustom himself to the ways of the Northern Baptist Convention. The organization seemed too worldly. Although CF remained a popular preacher, certain members of his congregation never did get used to his Bible-based strictness with church members who had not fully accepted Christ as their savior.

Carver's journal entry for March 14, 1931, read: "Can imagine that Norma thinks I have forgotten her, light of my life—this is getting terrible. I *will* write tomorrow." What could he say? He had no job. He was doing housework and reading Woodrow Wilson's book, *On Being Human* (1916), copying out passages that spoke to a certain regret over his new urban existence: "We shall find men sane and human about a country fireside, upon the streets of quiet villages, where all are neighbors, where groups of friends gather easily and a constant sympathy makes the very air seem native." Isn't this why CF had returned to Madisonville? Carver had forsaken this kind of community, and Wilson's essentially regionalist temperament spoke to Carver's troubled mind: "Men have indeed written like human beings in the midst of great cities, but not often when they have shared the city's characteristic life, its struggle for place and for gain. There are not many places that belong to a city's life to which you can 'invite your soul.'"

In letters home to friends Carver wrote eloquently, even telling Helen Wood that his letters to her were his way of practicing his style. Like Benjamin Franklin copying out passages from *The Spectator*, Carver not only memorialized his reading, he started keeping lists of words and their definitions: pellucid, penchant, and objurgation were the words for March 14. Charles and his new wife Jeanne seem to have been Carver's only companions. He noted their trip to the beach on Sunday, March 15, adding that he would begin driving a bus on Monday "until something better shows up." He played with the neighborhood children and finally wrote to Norma, "not such a good letter—not half what I wanted to say but then: there was *no insincerity* as has been my custom; quite ponderous." He was lonely and not much entertained by Emil Ludwig's biography of Goethe—although his reason for reading such a book is apparent in this reflective journal passage: "I look at people of littleness and narrowness and find it difficult to kindly make concessions for their lack of the knowledge of what the composite parts of life are." His urge to making "cutting remarks" was "not right!" he admonished himself.

Carver seemed to have ambition but no purpose: "If it is ever realized," he wrote on March 16, "I will very much pleased—but I can be happy without it—; but I cannot be happy without trying to do something about it. That would not be fair to myself." Music on the radio inspired him. Listening to a program about Victor Herbert, he exclaimed, "How I would like to sing a love-song of my own composition (to Norma)." Sometimes these early journal entries bemoaned his lack of accomplishment and will power. He felt sorry watching a middle-aged man gardening for thirty-five cents an hour, and then thought, "Maybe he was as big a fool as I have been (when money was mine)." Eventless days made him remark: "Too much involved with little things to be concerned with much that is worthwhile."

Carver's mood brightened on March 19 when he received a letter from CF, now happily ensconced in Madisonville, and the "best Dad in the world." But soon Carver became despondent, noting: "I go to bed, cast myself upon it, draw up the covers with the firm conviction that tomorrow I will be a different man." In the morning his dreams seemed unsound, "colorful effusions of youthful fancy—the dream palace *only* of night's romantic touch." He feared he was a "little man . . . consumed with little things." Like a preacher's son, he decried his "evil thoughts," although what those might be he did not say. After this month of intense self-examination, he did not record another word in his journal until August 1931.

Norma still expected Carver to return to Huntsville to "claim my hand in the true conventional manner." She said that she would like to follow the "dictates of my heart" and leave for California, and that she did not "give a hang" for what the gossips would say. But she did care, noting how much public opinion meant to her mother. Carver had apparently called Norma's bluff, inviting her to bring her mother with her. Norma stayed put, although she wanted to know if Carver really meant what he said about bringing her mother. "I know it wouldn't be the Heaven we've planned, but I simply couldn't leave her alone." If Norma ran off, her mother would lapse into hysteria. Norma mused about getting her parents to drive out to California, but her father did not like car trips. Clearly, she wanted Carver to come for her. It seems that for this couple, it was not just love, but a certain conception of love that both united them and broke them apart. She signed herself, "Your wife, Norma."

By the end of April Norma was "peeved" after Carver sent her a "curt and reprimanding letter." They were bickering, she admitted: "Do you realize that it's been seven long years ago tonight since I was first introduced to you—and about six years since we've been engaged!" And now he was telling her it would probably be another two years before he could come for her. She was embarrassed because she had led her parents to believe it would be sooner. Norma complained that Carver's letters got shorter and farther apart: "Do you realize how little I know about your life in California?—I who ought to be sharing it!" And now she had just had a big fight with her parents. She would come to him, as long as she could bring her mother, even though they would have to put up with Mrs. Felder's "smothering interest." Carver did not answer.

During this period Norma would occasionally visit with CF and Annis. It is unlikely that she confided in them, but CF, attuned to his son's moods, seems to have wondered if the long separation from Norma might be leading his son into temptation. On May 31, he wrote to Carver about how it "steadies a fellow and puts a bit of brightness into his gloom to know that somebody thinks about him, loves him, and is hoping he'll 'make the grade.'" Such thoughts had helped CF himself "struggle toward high ground" after being stuck in mud. "I remember once when I was planning something that was below my standards, I received thru the mails a bottle of perfume and a note, on my birthday, from one who loved me. It left my heart stricken, and made me hate my unworthy plans." He knew his son was lonely, but it could be much worse, he assured Carver.

When Norma stopped writing in what she called a "siege of punishment," Carver resumed regular correspondence. "At least you know now what agony I've endured dozens of times when you've been negligent," she wrote on June 4. She was happy at the prospect of his employment on a ranch outside Fresno, where, she supposed, they might settle for a while. But the job never materialized, and Norma's letters that month began to fret about what was happening to Carver. She detested hearing that his friends in California called him "Dan," but was heartened to hear that he was now thinking of becoming a writer. "I honestly think, aside from being prejudiced, that you have talent," she wrote on June 16. She cautioned him against using so many poly-syllabled words in his short stories. "About your poetry—I can't save your letters for reasons which you know," Norma told Carver. "But I've cut out every scrap of poetry you've ever written to me and carefully cherished it." She thought some of his work sublime, but overall he had to work on structure. (None of his verse seems to have survived). Then, to her chagrin, he stopped sending letters. But all was right again when he sent her a birthday letter and poem.

Norma kept Carver up-to-date about doings in Huntsville and the activities of their friends, even as she hoped he would secure a good job—this time employment at Bullock's, a Los Angeles department store. She was also worrying again that he might, as she put it in a July 21 letter, let "grosser attractions intrude." His silences worried her, and she wearied of waiting for him. A letter would come, talk of a promising job, and then—nothing. "Writing to you lately seems like talking yourself hoarse to a blank wall—absolutely no response. It's terribly discouraging." Someone was always asking about him, and it was "humiliating besides heartbreaking not to know anything." And yet she would love him until the end of time.

Carver could not write to Norma because he was having a perfectly dreadful time, as he admitted to his "sort of diary" on August 27. The job at Bullock's had lasted three days. Carver was no good at sales. "Despondency grows on me as money, clothes, and friends dwindle away which is no more than natural, I believe." He was reading a good deal: Bulwer-Lytton's *Last Days of Pompeii* and *The Cream of the Jest* by James Branch Cabell. The latter intrigued Carver with its portrait of the "dream-woman of all poets and, for that matter, every man—which dream-woman vanishes immediately upon being touched." He admired Sinclair Lewis's *Babbitt* but was bothered because the author is "foolishly radical in his desire for reality. He takes too large a discount off of man's higher emotions." This said after a day of picking figs for twenty-five cents an hour.

What had happened to Carver's ambition to be an actor? An essay in his journal, "Why I Want to Write," provides some explanation. Writing appealed to him because of his "natural interest in people" and his pleasure in studying them and figuring out their psychology. "To work upon the emotions of people seems to be the one great enjoyment to be derived from the writing of stories and it seems to me that the basic reason for the existence of narrative in this world of drab routine is to furnish an outlet for the many emotional energies that lie dormant ordinarily." Of course, this explanation applies just as well to acting. But writing needs no equipment, no vehicle, no platform other than the writer's own imagination and discipline, and that simplicity appealed to Carver, as it did to Charles, at a time when neither man had steady employment. CF was trying to find a school for Charles—presumably one where he could teach in or work as an administrator—but Carver had long ago abandoned any interest in either business or education.

Carver's authorial ambition also seemed an expression of his desire to distinguish himself as the noble aspirant CF had described in his epistolary exhortation to Norma. No wonder, then, that Carver's first autobiographical story (included in his journal) should have her in mind as the narrator's "one girl that was to receive my devotion so long as life should last." But the story lacks drama and a plot, and it ends in wish fulfillment, reuniting the couple after a misunderstanding. Like Charles, Carver lacked the talent to develop his fiction. But also like Charles,

Carver yearned for a means of self-expression that would project him onto a public stage.

After an August flurry of writing in his journal, Carver fell silent again. On September 20, 1931, Norma wrote, "Your letter . . . came nearer breaking my heart than anything I've ever experienced." He was approaching his nadir. And Norma, too, seemed at a loss. Her father had just overdrawn his bank account. He could not pay for the stocks he had bought on margin, and his daughter watched him walking the floor after his broker called to demand $1,400.

Carver did not respond to Norma for quite some time, but she kept sending letters, trying to bolster his confidence, telling him much older men than he were in dire circumstances but hanging on. She was working in an office of the Retail Merchants Association to supplement her family's income. She had withdrawn everything from her meager savings account and given it to her father to pay his debts. Like Carver, she had turned to writing (travel articles), confessing it was a way to occupy her time and lift her spirits.

When Carver finally wrote to Norma in early October, he seemed to be considering a return to Texas, where a friend might find a job for him. But a paragraph in her letter of October 10 unwittingly revealed why he could not return:

> There's only one reason that I hate to see you leave California—that's because I always will believe that you could have made good in the movies and you never will have another chance. But you might stay out there five years and never get a break—and if you didn't come back to Texas within five years I'm sure you'd find only my corpse.

Since it might well take five years—or more—to get his break, did it make sense to keep her waiting? Not to Norma. But to Carver? What was becoming intolerable was not merely their separation, but Carver's confrontation with himself. At what cost to himself and Norma was he willing to pursue a dream that might never come true? How could he be fair to her and to himself? She identified with his dream, but she also had invested *everything* in her vision of their love, which always came first and which meant other compromises might have to be made so that they could be together. By the end of her letter she had only one message for him: "Please write to me, and please hurry, hurry, hurry back home." Carver's ensuing silence signaled trouble.

Was 1931 the longest year of Carver Dana Andrews's life? Reading his journal, his correspondence, and contemplating the long days he put in with little result makes it seem so. Norma—and everyone else—counted on him, and he worried that he could not count on himself. His December 8 journal entry recalls that a year earlier he was "in route via highway to California":

> The year has been wasted. I have not accomplished anything. My life is one year shorter and my capacities have not been trained accordingly.
> I was to have had a job and married by this time.
> Well, I still have many things to look forward to; if I had attained them, I would be denied this pleasure. That is something for which to be grateful.

But how long could he hold out on his great expectations? His letters near the end of the year to Norma—judging by her dismay—were angry, the product of much frustration. He looked too thin in a recent photograph, and she worried that he had been ill. A letter from CF said he had no money to pay his son's way home, and the prospects for employment there were dismal. Both Wilton and Ralph were out of work. Even worse, CF said:

> But the truth—just plain unvarnished fact is, you have been utterly wasting a very unusual and gifted life . . . prodigally, as if it would last forever; thoughtlessly, as if there would never be an accounting. Your present unhappy limitations are due to the invention of a God who would intervene, to make you think. You have "denied" Christ; and you have been denied.

If Carver prayed, God would speak to him:

> He helps people who trust in Him. . . . PRAY. You don't feel like it? You doubt the value of it? Maybe. But do it anyhow—tell God you doubt—that you don't feel like praying; but you need Him, and want to get right with Him. Boy, He'll do more for you than you can imagine. TRY IT!

Although Carver never again attended church after leaving his father's home, he apparently did take his father advice—or so his mother believed. "Carver you can't ever know how glad it made my heart to know you are praying and depending on God to help you," Annis wrote on April 1, 1932.

Carver had still not paid his debts, including a note for $127.40 that his father wrote him about on January 14, 1932. It was becoming embarrassing. "Lots of people can't pay their debts now," CF wrote, "but anybody can show a debtor the courtesy of explaining why they can't, and that helps a great deal to keep the respect of those who have favored us. You and Charles have both made inexcusable mistakes along that line." By now, it was clear that CF, and probably the whole family, thought he should return home. CF said a friend of Carver's might have a position for him at Gulf Oil, the company that had employed Carver briefly before he departed for Austin in the summer of 1929. CF advised: "I wish you would get work here, and come right back where you made your mistakes and live them down. Don't you think that would be a fine thing to do? A man can 'come out of the worst sort o' kinks—I *know*, because *I've done it.*"

At the same time, Norma's letters were getting more importunate. She needed Carver home. The new year had begun with a devastating fire at the Dorothy Theatre, and a friend of theirs had died in the projection booth that Carver had once commanded. Then Norma's Uncle Eddie Parish died, leaving a large family fatherless. "I need you dreadfully," Norma said, and then with typical remorse added, "But I don't mean to keep dragging it before your eyes." Carver considered returning to Texas if the Gulf Oil job materialized. She wrote him on January 28: "I can't marry you until those horrid debts are all paid." She now knew not only about his Huntsville debts, but also about a considerable bill he had racked up in Austin, as he had just confessed to having misled her about how much debt he owed. She blamed herself: "The mistake came when I went on the cruise. If I had stayed with you, you would have finished school that year and started into some job and stuck to it. I have spent the past three years regretting taking the trip." She was now considering leaving home to take a teaching job, so sick she had become of her family telling her she was a burden. And yet she hated teaching "with a *passion.*" Her writing seemed to take on a new tone of lament: "Oh my God, for the dreams and ambitions we had six years ago!! Air castles—fading back into the air."

But Carver was taking voice lessons, and his teacher thought highly of his prospects. Norma noticed a buoyancy and cheerfulness in his latest letter that had been absent in most of what he had written her in the past year. "I've always known your voice was magnificent. Haven't I told you time and again!" The same was true of his acting. Suddenly the Gulf Oil job vanished as a subject of discussion, and Norma was exulting again in the prospect of joining Carver in California. But he was terribly vague on exactly what his prospects might be. What did his talk of a "rising sun" actually mean? Norma wanted to know. Still, she felt "somewhat like I did just before our boat docked in New York." She could relinquish the thought of his returning to Texas in the spring, she wrote in February, if they were that much nearer to "permanent bliss."

Carver's "anticipatorial" letters continued to excite Norma. But the emotional toll of their separation also enervated her. She had sobbing fits and could not concentrate, could not divert herself with reading or playing bridge. A great reader of literature (Aldous Huxley and Willa Cather were among her favorite authors) she had been railing against fate much as Thomas Hardy does in his novels. She was feeling better by the time she wrote Carver on February 16, 1932, but it is chilling to read her description of the "false spring" that had just come to Huntsville. She did not know that the temperature of her life was about to change unalterably.

CHAPTER 5

"Mediocrity Is Not My Lot"
1932–35

CARVER HAD BECOME INVOLVED in the Van Nuys High School evening theater program and had a part in a play. Norma wanted to know all about it, but he provided few details, and she was beginning to feel resentful. Realizing how unappealing this mood made her, she switched to reminding him of all the pleasures they shared. She wanted him to tell her what he liked to listen to on the radio. He was finding his voice lessons rather tiresome—all that singing of scales—but such drills were absolutely necessary, she insisted. She always seemed to feel better when she could take an encouraging tone and believe she was helping to shape his future. "Have you heard 'Everything Must Have an Ending But My Love for You?'? I just heard it over the radio," she wrote on February 28. She could hear him singing it. She was willing to accept the mystery of what he was actually doing in "this venture of yours of which I know nothing." So special did he make her feel that after reading his letters over and over she burned them. "I don't want anyone reading them—regardless of their content!"

However hopeful Norma tried to sound, she acknowledged that she had "bombarded" Carver with "blue letters." She urged him not to pay attention. Perhaps she realized that her very neediness might drive him away. The nagging mother, the drunken father, the infuriating substitute teaching jobs—this refrain of frustration was not, she realized, very appealing. "Pay it no attention," she urged him on March 6. She wanted him to remember, instead, summer evenings on the porch and winters by the fire and their hours of "make believe." She lived on memories of their "supreme happiness" in their "struggle with Fate." For the first time, though, she wrote, "[E]ven though He should see fit to never bring us together again, Dear, I think that we have been fortunate in knowing true love—love at its most beautiful—love in its purest and highest state."

How much Carver's life had changed by March 24, 1932, is apparent from an item in the *Van Nuys News* identifying him as one of the leading players in the cast of *The Thirteenth Chair*, a murder mystery performed by the Valley Playmakers and sponsored by the Van Nuys Woman's Club. The cast met in the homes of prominent citizens and cast members for meals after rehearsals. On the "women's page" for April 14, the day of the play's performance in the Van Nuys High School auditorium, Carver appears in the second row of a cast picture, which includes Janet Murray.

On March 24 he wrote to Norma:

Darling Girl

I have something to write to you, something that will astound you at first but you will understand I hope after you have thought it over for a while. I have given it more thought than anything I have ever given anything in my life. I have held an unforgivable silence in the hope that things would change, that I would be my normal self after a while. The thing has haunted me for days now seriously interfering with my work, play, and sleep. And the more I think of it the more firmly I am convinced that the thing I should do is the thing I am doing in this message.

I don't know how to say it so you would best understand. I'd like to be able to be with you to tell you, but since I can't I shall do my best to get the idea roughly across this way. About the best way to start, I guess, is to make a flat statement of the whole thing then explain it best I can. Here it is:

You must give up the idea of ever expecting to marry me, my dear. For I have given up hope of enjoying a life of companionship with you. "Things" have changed a lot since I saw you last. I have changed a lot. In fact, I'm too changeable, and I haven't been fair to you in my correspondence recently. This has been on my mind for a long time, but I haven't been able to write you about it. I've concluded that it is bad enough to have to be so undependable without adding to the fault by keeping you in the dark about it. It would be easier for you to understand, I think, if there were someone else—a girl in this case. But there is not. So it is all very difficult for me to understand try though I might since I have not lost my affection for you at all. I have never thought seriously of anyone but you and still think of you very tenderly. But I must be frank to confess that I've discarded the thought of matrimony and resigned myself to the loneliness of "single blessedness." You must not think that I am

unselfishly or magnanimously granting you your freedom because of my futile efforts to gain an income, name or fame in the world. It is not that. Quite contrarily, I am asking you for my own freedom for the most selfish reasons imaginable. There's really nothing more I can say. Feeling this way after weeks and weeks of careful consideration I feel duty bound to tell you about it and ask you to forgive me and forget me. No, I don't want you to forget me, ever. You must remember that you are the only one I have ever loved or will ever love in the highest sense of the word. I shall await your answer with misgivings.
Carver

He did not get around to sending this letter—or some version of it—to Norma until May 1. Since she seems to have destroyed his letters, it is impossible to say whether he altered this draft, but it obviously reveals the reasons for the silences that troubled Norma, and for the letters in which he repeatedly left her thinking he was not telling her the whole story. This draft is as definitive as possible about how he had cut himself off from the kind of life Norma represented. Realizing that his ambition had put him in a class of his own, Carver could no longer bear the burden of carrying Norma along with him.

On April 18, the *Van Nuys News* reviewed *The Thirteenth Chair*, briefly complimenting Janet Murray's performance. But the review devoted a paragraph to "Carver Dana Andrews, who should continue to cultivate his dramatic art. In the role of Roscoe Crosby, he did splendidly. Although it is the colorful, romantic, and dashing part, which Andrews should take, he is adaptable to any characterization."

On May 6, Norma replied to Carver's May 1 letter, admitting that it was a "staggering surprise," since she always thought they had a telepathic understanding. She had expected him to return on May 1, and when she did not hear from him assumed he was coming and wanted to surprise her. Norma's reaction to this terrible blow reveals just why Carver had loved her. She appreciated his frankness and courage. He had been faithful to their vow to set the other free if asked. She wished him health and happiness. Although she had many questions she'd like to ask him, the pressing one had to do with her worry that he regarded her as an impediment to his career. She still did not understand exactly what he intended to do with his life. She wanted him to destroy her letters and to send her pictures back to her. And she would return his. She ended by saying she would never stand in his way. Carver did not return Norma's letters to her, and Norma, who had said earlier that she burned his letters after receiving them, does not seem to have returned what remained of his, for it is difficult to believe he would have destroyed his letters and kept only hers.

Three weeks later, Norma wrote to say that she would like to continue their correspondence. She missed his letters and hoped he would continue to send them if they did not have a negative impact on him. She did not attempt to resume their intimacy. Instead she wrote him about the books she was reading and the movies she enjoyed, and she wanted to know what he was reading. She signed her letter "Sincerely, Norma."

Carver's reply is no longer extant, but her letter of July 27 reveals that he regretted breaking off their engagement:

Oh, Darling, Darling, Darling,
Don't you know that if I had had the price of a ticket to California I would have been out there long ago? In fact I would have been out there just as soon after May 1st as possible. You wrote to me on May 1st saying it was the end. Down in my heart I knew that you still loved me—knew that you were making a mistake—knew too that if I could only see you I could convince you that it was a mistake. And I tried every way under Heaven to get ahold of some money to get out there—but to no avail.

She now explained that before he left Texas, when he was making $135 a week, she expected him to marry her. Although marriage on those terms would have been a struggle, she believed they would have been happy. "But you didn't ask me to marry you then. You'll never know how that hurt me. It was largely responsible for the break that occurred soon after." She knew why he had not asked her:

You were having a good time in Austin. You were running with a jolly crowd—but a wealthy one. It took money for you to keep up with them. The money that you might have spent coming to me over the weekends went to bootleggers and what not. I'm not blaming you. You thought that you were entitled to a good time for once in your life and you thought you could play around a few months and that I'd still be waiting.

And he was right, Norma admitted. She had heard stories about his wild parties but preferred not to say anything about them because she loved him. She knew, as Dana once said, that his strict Baptist upbringing did not "leave a guy much time to be bad." She kept on loving him because in California he seemed to have sobered up. And then he had just cut her off without consulting her feelings about the matter. And now he wanted her again and was asking her to come to him, "now or never." Could she make him happy without even knowing what his circumstances were? "Wouldn't there be times when you'd get so discouraged you'd wish me back in Texas? Wouldn't there be times when you'd yearn so for this career that you have a chance at that you'd almost hate me for depriving you of it?" Carver had always praised Norma for her common sense, and now she said she was using it. On what terms, exactly, was he offering to share his life with her? "God only knows how much I love you," her letter concludes.

Norma's note the next day suggests that sometime in the spring of 1932, Carver had begun seeing Janet Murray. Norma wrote that she could not put what she had to say in a wire—as he had done in a telegram to her. Although she had always insisted she did not feel bitter, this time her anger erupted:

> There seems to be a veiled threat in your letters and in the telegram. When you didn't answer my letters did I wire you, "Win me back or this will be the end"? You can't do me that way.
>   If you mean that you are going to marry this other girl if I don't wire you—then God forgive you. You will be ruining three lives.

Norma assured him of her love and that he could make her or break her, but she was not prepared to beg him.

By July 4, Carver had begun socializing with the Murray family. A July 4 item in the *Van Nuys News* announced "Murray Home Scene of Smart Series of Fetes." Indeed, Independence Day marked a month of entertaining to celebrate the new Murray home on Van Nuys Boulevard. An outdoor barbecue party featured a fireworks display on the lawn. "Miss Murray and Carver Dana Andrews" rounded up a paragraph describing the guest list.

Norma kept writing to Carver: "Oh, the pity of it! To think of all our brave young dreams gone blah!" By November 8, Carver was engaged to Janet Murray. Just the thought of Janet had "poisoned" Norma's mind. Was it Carver, or just her dreams of him, that she still loved, she wondered? A letter sent at the end of November revealed that she was dating other men, including "Doc" Smither, an eligible male from a prominent Huntsville family. She wanted to know all about the plays Carver was appearing in.

Norma did not inquire about Janet Murray. Janet was born September 1, 1908 in Eldora, Iowa. Her father, William Murray, was a banker active in organizations such as the Masons and the Shriners. Like Carver, Janet appeared on stage early, on April 5, 1917, singing "The Cheerful Robin," one of the few solo performances at the Methodist church morning program, as reported in the *Eldora Herald*. But Janet never thought of acting as a career. Although performing in public continued to amuse her, she seemed early on to be attracted to journalism. In 1921, Janet's family moved to California. Her father became director of the California Trust Company and also a vice-president of California Bank at the Van Nuys branch. Her mother was president of the Van Nuys Woman's Club and active in community affairs. In 1926, Janet graduated from the Cumnock School for Girls in Los Angeles. She lived in a world where the *Van Nuys News* reported her visits in 1927 and 1928 to relatives in San Diego and the East, as well as a weekend spent entertaining school friends. By the following year she was giving dramatic readings at meetings of the Van Nuys Woman's Club, and participating in evening programs, including a "gypsy scene," appearing in "Romany" costume. In 1930, Janet earned her BA in English from the University of Southern California and an MA in journalism from Northwestern University in 1931. In June 1932, she began writing a column about local history and community life for the *Van Nuys News*.

On December 29, 1932, the *Van Nuys News* announced that at 8:30 p.m. on December 31, 1932, Janet Murray would marry Carver Dana Andrews in her parents' home in a "quiet" ceremony officiated by David Farquarhson of the First Presbyterian Church. "Relatives and a coterie of intimate friends" would witness the marriage. Janet's picture appeared on the woman's page of the *Van Nuys News* (January 2, 1933) with the heading, "Charming New Year's Eve Bride" and a caption, "Mrs. Carver D. Andrews." Describing "one of the season's most exclusive weddings," the newspaper account resembled just the kind of notice that would have appeared in the *Huntsville Item*. The newspaper devoted a long paragraph to the accomplishments of this "talented and popular member of the younger set." She was now teaching a class in short story writing at the Van Nuys night school and was a *Van Nuys News* columnist. Her father was identified only as a prominent citizen, and the newspaper summed up Carver Dana Andrews in one sentence: "The groom is a member of the office staff at Wardlaw's Motor Inn, has a wide circle of friends and is the son of the former pastor of the First Baptist church of Van Nuys."

Dana was still determined to make his own way, but he also enjoyed the thought of having married well. Many years later, Wilton remembered the time a socially prominent and pretty girl said to Carver, a popular, good-looking boy, "Why should I dance with a poor preacher's son?" Later he ignored her and turned away when she tried to greet him in Austin, and still later did not answer her letter asking him if he would meet her children when them came to Los Angeles. His reaction reminded Dana's daughter Susan of his response to Chaplin's *City Lights*. The fancy people love the Chaplin character when they think he is wealthy, but they don't recognize him when he is poor. "Dad experienced it at both ends," Susan said, calling this rags-to-riches-to rags story a "formative" experience. Dana once told a reporter, "I worked at 21 jobs before the movies paid me regularly," including ditch digging and driving heavy trucks for four dollars a day. "That's supposed to be heroic. Algeresque. Baloney. I'd just as soon have been born rich!" Never one to romanticize poverty, Carver Dana Andrews had married a woman whose "Post Nuptial Fete" was celebrated on the February 2, 1933, woman's page of the *Van Nuys News*: "Inspired by society's newest fad, the hostess presented her guests with tallier—each divided into two parts, which were matched to find partners for jig-saw puzzles. The first couple completing their picture had their choice of gifts, although there was a 'prize' for everyone."

Charles wrote from Madisonville on his brother's wedding day: "It will be funny to think of big handsome Carver getting married," although Charles had expected this event for some time. The marriage came as a surprise to CF and Annis, who still expected their son to wed Norma. In fact, in early December CF had seen Norma, he reported to his son, and she looked as "sweet and 'cute' as ever." CF thought it odd that Charles had not called on Norma, but at this point Charles, who had returned to Texas and was corresponding with Carver, knew about Janet Murray and probably wanted to avoid a painful meeting. Something in Carver's letters during the fall of 1932 provoked CF to write on November 9: "Our hearts are a bit sore, mothers [sic] and mine, because you seem to have forgotten the old love and the old days when we were all you had, and our love was the only support of your helplessness."

But right from the start, Janet charmed CF. "It's no surprise to me that Rev. Andrews found Janet charming. Charm runs in this family—meet any of Janet's collateral descendants and you would most likely agree," declared Sheila Simpson, who is married to Janet's great nephew. A former professor of Janet's at Northwestern University recalled what a "good looking girl" she was. Janet came from a family that remained close, and her involvement in civic affairs as well as amateur theater suggests an outgoing and gregarious nature that appealed to Dana. He may have told his family as much, although his perplexed mother had a more pressing question: "We all were surprised to hear you were going to marry any lady besides Norma Kathryn.... Is your wife a Christian?"

Annis nonetheless quickly took to her new daughter-in-law and delighted in her son Ralph's account of his California visit. Janet had sent clothes as a gift to the family's only daughter, Mary. "Janet you are indeed a sweet daughter-in-law," Annis wrote. "I sincerely appreciate them every one. I can make every one of them to fit her as she needs them." Annis enclosed a recipe for cooking sweet potatoes that Janet had requested after hearing about it from Ralph.

Dana, always interested in the newest recording equipment, had begun sending records to his father, including one of himself singing his version of "Danny Boy." Janet, impressed with Dana's voice, encouraged him to continue his voice lessons. "Charles and I sing rather well together," CF wrote his son. "The Church people like to hear us. We sang 'Christ Returneth', at church last night. Had a house full of folks, and you could have heard a pin drop." When Dana wrote his father about the "god" he had fashioned for himself, CF replied that as a young man he had indulged in similar "vaporings." His son would find his way back to the true church as he grew older and realized that man could not create a god who was merely the result of man's self-absorption. This was a sore subject between father and son, but as CF said, Carver himself had brought it up.

On May 23, 1933, CF wrote his son to tell him of Norma's plans to marry Wilbur "Doc" Smither. Not a word from Norma herself. The *Huntsville Item* (June 1, 1933) announced the wedding, which took place at the home of Norma's aunt, Mrs. C. B. Henderson. As was customary then, the newspaper described the setting. Almost a full column was devoted to detailing the wedding ornaments and table, the food and those present. This was not the life Norma had projected for herself. It would take a year for her to absorb the experience before she dared write to Carver, who commented in his journal: "I can only say here that, in my opinion, her life promises to be a very sad and barren one. May God bless her and give her happiness is my sincere prayer. She deserves more than she will likely ever enjoy."

On June 6, 1933, Carver summed up in his journal: "Just to remind myself that I am still alive, have been married and am well on the road to having a family since the above was jotted down, I will write in few words, a thought or two to show what I am thinking about at this stage in life." He had been reading Napoleon Hill's eight volumes on *The Law of Success*, a popular self-help series, which Carver recommended to family members. He had decided on a career as a "singer or actor or both—my preference undoubtedly being in favor of the latter but the opportunities of the moment seem to point to the former." At any rate, he saw both as "closely related." He was studying with John Pratt, "a former baritone of some negligible Broadway fame, who seems to think there are possibilities in my voice, and as well as I am able to judge, his statements are not ungrounded."

Carver Dana Andrews's first performance occurred on an arts program for Eastern Star on September 7, 1933, performing "Goin' Home," "Danny Boy," and "Brahms' Lullaby." He sang with "splendid artistry," according to the *Van Nuys News*, "Smilin' Through, Drink To Me Only with Thine Eyes" for the Van Nuys Woman's Club on October 23. It was a start—although not one he wrote about in his journal.

On November 30, 1933, Janet gave birth to David Murray Andrews. Carver's journal records almost nothing about Janet. Carver's brother David said Carver respected Janet, but David doubted that Carver ever loved her or quite got over Norma. After discovering another life partner who believed unquestionably in him, he seems to have retreated into a solitary communion with his hopes and dreams—at least in the journal. Dana, as he was beginning to call himself, was candid with his brother Charles and Charles's wife, Jeanne. "He was not happy," Jeanne recalled. "He would tell us that he was not in love with Janet, and she would keep telling him, 'But you will find you *do* love me because we get along so well together.' Which they did," Jeanne affirmed. Dana had married Janet thinking perhaps she was right, but the birth of their son David made matters worse—especially when he learned she was pregnant again. "I can't live like this," Dana told Charles. And yet Dana did. He understood that his ambition could isolate him, and that may be one reason he could not break with Janet. She was so "personable," Jeanne emphasized. "You could not help but like her. And she doted on Dana."

"I must not become too selfish, self-centered—and egotistical," Dana wrote in his journal on June 8. Indeed, the very next day he wrote that remarkable passage about how much he had changed since leaving Texas. No longer a Southerner, he wondered how much he had lost as well as gained by becoming a new man. Acting presented him with an infinitely elastic sense of self. It was a source of strength but also of insecurity. If he could become someone else, someone not from Texas, then who—at his core—was he? This question bedevils many actors, who turn to performing to find themselves in defining roles. Perhaps for those growing up during the Depression, the very idea of starting over again had a particular poignancy. It meant so much to succeed in the 1930s. Charles had just secured a good job in Texas, Dana noted, "at a salary of $135.00 month—pretty good for him—or anybody in these times."

The Dana of the journal never fooled himself about the immense effort it took to overcome his own doubts and the scorn of others: "There are too many people who want to discourage those who, unlike themselves, have determined to move up ahead; they appear to envy yet try to destroy all creative genius." The corollary to his self-doubt, however, was his sense of mission and accomplishment: "After running over a few songs with 'the maestro' today—I was pleasantly aware of a new richness in my voice." Now he needed to work on making it stronger, more colorful, and more expressive through "painstaking practice." He read "only good literature" and told himself, "Life is simply a matter of concentration; the things we read today are the things we become tomorrow." What Dana could not do, as he admitted, was record his everyday life, which seemed devoid of inspiration. Too often he did his duty, but opportunities to do more eluded him. Conversations with Janet, he admitted, led nowhere. "Energy! Will Power! Enthusiasm!" he wrote, urging himself on. "I must realize my ambition or die a miserable man. Mediocrity is not my lot." The summer months went by as Dana made fitful progress with his singing lessons.

Dana and Janet moved into a larger, better-furnished house, and he concluded he had to work even harder, disciplining himself with a "set time each day to practice. I must let nothing interfere with that schedule." He spent three hours a day working on his voice and learning how to perform "without self-consciousness or nervousness—with utter relaxation—relaxation—relaxation. To sing—that is the thing!" He would not write another word in this journal for another four years.

Dana's doings for the next two years are documented mainly in letters to his father, other family members, and friends. On August 16, 1933, CF wrote to express his relief that Dana was finally paying his debts. How Dana was able to do so is not clear, although it is likely he had help from Janet and her family in meeting his responsibilities, especially after

David's birth. Dana sent CF a photograph of father and son. CF replied that a friend had seen the picture and remarked, "[Y]ou looked as if you though you had done something great—with that baby in your arms."

Janet's faith in Dana, apparently as strong as Norma's in Carver, and her family's solid and secure standing in the Van Nuys Community meant a good deal to Dana—as he made clear when he boasted of his marriage to an angry Austin businessman who was still attempting to collect on Dana's debts. Dana was ready to pay up, adding:

> I suppose I should relegate myself humbly to that vast lot of poor souls who just do not seem to get along. However, such a life has its compensations and I just won't feel sorry for myself. Self-pity is such a vicious thing. In this regard I might say I am very well satisfied to be the husband of a beautiful and charming wife who is the daughter of the state inspector of banks, the father of a handsome one-year-old boy, the humble beneficiary of that fickle dame called fortune, and the proud possessor of a circle of friends who have proven themselves to be both good friends and valuable acquaintances.

As Dana's daughter Kathy said, her father never forgot the hand-me-downs he had had to wear, and marrying Janet meant "something above."

Still, relying on Janet and her family posed a problem. On June 19, 1934, CF wrote: "As to your problem which you discussed at length in your letter . . . I believe in every tub standing on its own bottom, even though it has a weak bottom." It gratified CF to think his son felt the same way: "It is mark of manhood and self-respect." But he added, "Certainly I think that you and Janet should be fully agreed on whatever course you take." Janet, CF acknowledged, was not used to living on a "modest income." Still, their "mutual cares and sorrows" would bind them together better than luxuries. CF sensed, however, that his son was holding back: "Why will you not tell me what you are endeavoring to fit yourself for? Are you ashamed of it? If you are ashamed of it you ought to let it alone." More likely, as the eloquent silence of the journal implied, Dana was not sure that he was getting anywhere. When Dana did finally tell his father about his plans for a singing and acting career, CF's response, predictably, included a sermon on the immorality rampant in Hollywood and the "few successes in that line."

Norma had given birth to a 9 ½-pound daughter, Mary Sue, as announced in the *Huntsville Item* on March 3, 1934. On April 1, Norma's mother replied to a letter Dana had sent to Norma a few weeks earlier. Norma thought it best that she not write, Mrs. Felder explained, "best for you, Carver, and best for her." Instead, Norma had asked her mother to send him news of the "blessed event." Doc was all Mrs. Felder had ever hoped to find in a son-in-law:

> They both seem to be so supremely happy, Carver, that it must go on, if possible. Doc has a marvelous disposition, but you mustn't take advantage of it. I understand, of course, dear boy, that you are interested in her future and any time you feel you would like to hear of her I'll be so glad to write you. Doc had nothing to say of your letter, but maybe next time he wouldn't be so nice. Then unpleasantness may start between them, and I know you wouldn't want that to happen.

Norma remained interested in Dana's future and would like to hear from him, "but it seems best if she doesn't," Mrs. Felder advised. "It would be much better if you could just forget each other." Nevertheless, she was always available to tell him about her daughter's life: "Norma suggests that I do this. She knows she mustn't write to you." Mrs. Felder closed the letter with kind words about his family, her interest in his brothers—especially Charles, who was making a success as a school principal, and she then related news about Carver's Huntsville friends. She promised to give him the "lowdown" on others. "I'd love to see your boy. I know he is lovely," she added in the only reference to his own new life.

Norma had resumed her role in a proper Texas family. To go outside of it had always been a risk. The pressure on Norma to stay put was perhaps the reason—more than lack of money or any other factor—she expected her beloved to return home and claim her. Dana came from an "outsider" family. CF had a position but was never a power player. If his son had been content to take a position in a local bank or other establishment, Mrs. Felder, who was very fond of Carver, might have been content, if still disappointed in her daughter's prospects. Carver was intense and charismatic, but not reliable. Red Allen, Carver's Huntsville friend, wrote to him about Norma on September 23, 1933: "I wouldn't think too much about the old girlfriend. The Smithers, Gibbs, and Felders seem to be a closed organization."

In light of what Mrs. Felder had written, it is surprising to learn that Norma resumed writing to Dana just two months later. But then, as Norma's letters reveal, she never thought her mother really understood her that well or realized that Norma did not share all of her family's values. On May 5, 1933, Norma acknowledged his good wishes and said it was "so nice" to hear from him. She detailed the exciting and busy events of the past few months, even telling him her six-week-old was twenty-one inches long at birth. She filled him in on local news, including his brother Charles's marvelous appearance in *Smiling Through*, a Huntsville Little Theatre production: "Your entire family has the talent for stage careers. It's a shame that some of you didn't follow it as a profession." She hoped he had not given up the idea of a movie career. She wanted to know about his son and if he was still taking voice lessons. Norma seemed, judging by her letter, to want a connection to Carver—as she still called him—and wanted to establish a new, friendly, but socially correct, relationship with him. On May 27, Norma found her May 5 letter in a stationery box, saying she had been so busy she had forgotten about it. She added another sociable note, concluding: "In Huntsville life goes on very much as it did when you lived here. But it's a serene and comfortable spot, if none too exciting."

Carver replied to Norma, telling her about his son David and the generous Murray family, which prompted Norma to caution him not to "let them spoil David. . . . They're so much better off, not only as children but in later life too, when they learn that they can not always have their own way." After all, success depended on getting along with other people, she noted. Norma, an acute observer, sensed what Dana would later admit: The Murrays, especially his mother-in-law, tended to indulge his son.

Together with Janet, Dana was involved in a re-organization of the little theatre movement in Van Nuys. The term "little theatre" came into use just as the movies were becoming a popular form of mass entertainment. The Little Theatre in Chicago and the Toy Theatre in Boston—both established in 1912, the same year *Poetry* magazine began publishing—were reflections of an arts movement organized around local communities. The movement was spearheaded by groups of amateurs and professionals who wanted to create and perform work that entertained but also edified, dealing with serious issues in a more realistic style than that of the melodramas of the nineteenth century and the current fantastical stories of Hollywood and popular periodicals.

In the East, the little theatre movement culminated in the dramas of the Provincetown Players in Provincetown, Massachusetts, and the

Theatre Guild in New York City, featuring new dramatists like Eugene O'Neill and Elmer Rice and the controversial realism of Ibsen and Strindberg. In the West, the idea of a community mounting ambitious productions of significant contemporary plays as well as the classics took hold with the Pasadena Playhouse. By 1925, a complex of six stages accommodated experimental, popular, and classic works produced with high professional standards that attracted the attention of Hollywood studios looking for new talent. With its own theatre school, the Pasadena Playhouse offered actors both training and employment.

Under the sponsorship of the board of education, forty people met at Van Nuys High School on September 3, 1934, to establish a fund-raising plan for a self-sustaining community theater similar to the Pasadena Playhouse. "Dana Andrews Has Title Role in First Play," read the September 13 headline on the woman's page of the *Van Nuys News*, announcing his role as Dr. Peter Pepper in *Pepper's Prescription*. Although still an amateur company, the Van Nuys group was beginning to draw the attention of theater and film professionals, the paper reported. Just as importantly for Dana, little theatre provided him with a following. He now had a constantly attentive audience that helped create for him a community of interest that had been lacking during his earliest, futile attempts to establish an acting career. In Van Nuys, he finally began the process of seasoning himself.

On October 25, 1934, Gilmor Brown, founder of the Pasadena Playhouse, addressed a luncheon at the Van Nuys Woman's Club. "No greater changes are going on in the world today than in the theatre," Brown declared, extolling it as an institution where young people "find themselves and stand on their own feet." Janet's mother spoke after Brown's lecture, and if Dana was not present, he would have been inspired to hear Mrs. Murray relate Brown's inspiring vision of the theater's importance.

In November, Dana had the role of Uncle Rod in a Zona Gale play, *Uncle Jimmie*, set in a country village. The *Van Nuys News* critic called the part "a very difficult characterization that a player less capable would probably have been reluctant to undertake." The critic went on to say, however, that "Andrews accompanied his work with a certain dash and gusto that fitted nicely into the setting." In the cast, as well, was Janet's sister, Marjorie Laub (Margo to her friends). She became close to Dana and seems to have had considerable talent as a "finished and comprehensive performer." On December 2, Dana sang "At Dawning," the musical prelude to the wedding of Pauline Hall and William Frederick French. On December 13 and 14, he played Captain Sharpe in *Yip'ee*, a

Christmas play and charity show sponsored by the Elks. At the December 23 Candlelight Service of the First Methodist Church, he sang a solo, "O Come to My Heart, Lord Jesus." In May 1935, Dana headed a cast of twenty-five in a Little Theatre production of *Uncle Tom's Cabin*. Described as the "singing star" of the play, he gave an impromptu performance at a meeting of the Little Theater on early August, and on September 20 he sang at another wedding. October 17 found him singing at another Woman's Club event.

Then on October 28, the *Van Nuys News* reported on its front page that Janet was "critically ill." Three days earlier she had caught a cold that rapidly developed into pneumonia. During the last week of October, she had given birth to a second child that did not survive. On Tuesday afternoon, October 30, she died. She was only twenty-seven, and "one of the community's most popular matrons," her obituary in the *Van Nuys News* reported on October 31, 1935. Dana sent a telegram and then a special delivery letter, which his father received on the day the obituary appeared. Norma learned of Janet's death the same day and sent a consoling letter to the grieving husband, who would now, more than ever, depend on Janet's family to help care for David as Dana continued to pursue his dream of an acting career. A friend of Janet's wrote to Dana, "I'm sure you realize how she never changed in her devotion to you—almost idolatry!"

CHAPTER 6

Holding On
1935–36

AS DANA TOLD LILLIAN ROSS, he dealt with Janet's death by training his voice and working like a "maniac." He ran two miles a day to build up his diaphragm and learned operatic roles in French, German, and Italian. He found no consolation in religion, and when his father wrote a pious letter asking his son to trust in God, Carver (as CF still called him) replied that God "had nothing whatever to do with it."

CF's unsparing theology now showed itself in stark relief, explaining much about his son's journey away from home:

> All your life you have wanted to have our own way; you have thought much of self-gratification; you have left Christ out of your life's program by your own admission. What would be your hope if it had been you instead of Janet? The Father loved the Prodigal son, but he let him go away, and there was no rejoicing for the Prodigal till he came back—he only lost what he had in the far country. When he came to the end of his resources, "no relief anywhere", he came back to the father's house. That was the only hope for the Prodigal,—and the only way out for you. God knows all your sorrow and He cares; but He cannot help if you shut him out. We are praying for you everyday.

After Janet's death, the bills came due. Dr. Edward Kellog, writing on February 20, 1936, wrote to express his sympathy for Dana's loss: "I can well understand the difficulties that you are having at this time. However, it is unfortunate that you did not advise me of them sooner inasmuch as no reply was received to several bills sent you the account was placed in the hands of a collector." What money Dana had went to paying for voice lessons, as the receipts he kept shows.

As Dana later told Ida Zeitlin, a writer for *Modern Screen*, Janet's mother (called Aggie) believed she could still do something for her lost daughter by taking Dana and his two-year-old son into her home. "In a way it was a family tradition when the Andrews moved in since Aggie and her husband had resided with her parents in their home in Eldora," noted Aggie's great-niece, Sheila Simpson. While Dana seemed in perpetual motion pursuing his career, Aggie watched over David. Returning at night he would find her sleeping on a couch near his son's room. Only then did she retire to her own bed.

Janet's father had been a well-known singer and had studied music briefly in Boston, but had become a banker after dropping out of college in his third year to support himself. His thwarted ambition may well have contributed to his identification with his son-in-law's aspirations. Dana could not afford to visit home, and his parents did not have the money to travel to California, but Aggie, apparently wanting to maintain family connections, sent a fur coat Janet had worn to Dana's sister Mary.

And Dana received still more help from outside the family. Stanley Twomey, a partner with John Wardlaw in the Wardlaw Motor Inn, told Dana he was wearing himself out working at the gas station and going to singing lessons. "I want to put you on salary," Twomey said, "Your job'll be to go on with your singing lessons and spend the rest of the day figuring out how to get into motion pictures." When Twomey asked how long Dana thought it would take for him to get a movie contract, Dana said, "six months at the outside." It would take much longer, but Twomey and Wardlaw backed him all the way, and Dana promised to provide them with a substantial return as soon as he secured a contract.

The extraordinary story of how two businessmen invested in an amateur singer and actor would become sensationalized in movie magazine profiles, which reduced the facts to a fable in which Dana was heard singing while pumping gas, attracting the attention of his employers, who promptly funded his studies. But Dana had been working at the Wardlaw Motor Inn for more than two years when Janet died, and he had become well known in the Van Nuys arts community as its most promising Hollywood hopeful. Stanley Twomey's wife, nearly as prominent in civic and social affairs as Aggie, was one of Aggie's bridge partners, and the two women lived on the same street. Mrs. Twomey had seen Dana perform, and—as Dana told his erstwhile biographer, Clyde Williams—she "discovered" him. "Such a nice-looking boy," she told her husband. "Ambitious too. He came from Texas to get into pictures." Everyone could see that Dana would exhaust himself before he obtained his dream—unless a way could be found to rescue this driven young man. In retrospect, he noted that even with his frenetic ambition, "I almost did give up."

In public, Dana never expressed anything but gratitude toward Wardlaw, Toomey, and Aggie, but a letter written on February 24, 1937, by one of his mentors, the German actor Rudolph Amendt ("Rudi"), reveals that Dana had an ambivalent attitude towards his benefactors. It seemed strange to Rudi that the apparently "self-sufficient" Dana sometimes felt the need to assert himself "too vigorously" because he resented being "hemmed in" by his patrons. He should not feel beholden to them, but to his talent that had brought him to the attention of his backers. He was intelligent and had "marvelous assets." His troubles, slight as they were, Rudi believed, came from the stubbornness of people like Aggie and Twomey. But Dana's "enormous power of true conviction" sometimes made him resist the suggestions of those who saw other ways that might lead him to his goal. He was like a horse who would not walk between trees, preferring to "take a detour of an hour than cut off a corner of a wood."

Although Dana work diligently on his voice lessons for the six months following Janet's death, he seemed to make little progress obtaining professional roles. He wanted to sing opera and perform the classical repertoire, he told his father. CF replied on February 17, 1936: "I am really pleased that you are not satisfied with mere mediocrity—to be a cheap crooner of cheap jazz and nonsense. The man who inscribes 'Excelsior' on his banner may expect to be lonely; for there are so few that can share such a vision with him."

Twomey took Dana to audition with John Columbo, an agent and brother of singer Russ Columbo, according to Zeitlin's account in *Modern Screen*. As Dana told Lillian Ross, the agent said, "I had a fair voice but couldn't make any money as a singer. Second-rate actors, he said, could earn more than first-rate singers." By April 1936, Dana was having his teeth straightened and would soon try for work at the Pasadena Playhouse.

Letters home to CF seemed to steady Dana, even though he could not have appreciated his father's view that besides straightening his teeth he should straighten his heart. It had been nearly five years since father and son had seen one another, and both seemed to crave a meeting. In their letters, they exchanged memories about fishing together. Did Carver remember when he had saved Charles from drowning? CF asked. Charles had stepped off into deep water: "You were holding him up on your neck, with your own face under water, as you stood tip toe on a rock, when I reached you in a boat," CF wrote. "You were the one who was about to drown—but you held on." CF admitted he did not appreciate what he had then: "I didn't realize how happy were those days which you recalled in your letter—not while they were passing. We know this, yet we go on singing, like one of Tennyson's characters: 'Ah! Death in life—the days that are no more!'"

CHAPTER 7

Pasadena
1936–38

IN JUNE 1936, Dana went to a Sunday night open reading at the Pasadena Playhouse. Maudie Prickett, a character actress at the Playhouse, described this great democratic proving ground for actors. Callbacks came on Tuesdays and Thursdays for actors who were up for roles, and by the next weekend the play would be cast, then it was rehearsed for a month. Dana was cast as "a French gentleman" in *Cymbeline* and as Menecrates in *Antony and Cleopatra*—roles that gave him seven and two lines respectively. He carried a spear in *Julius Caesar*.

On July 19, the *Van Nuys News* reported that Dana had a singing role in *Cymbeline* during the Pasadena Playhouse's Shakespearean Festival. The previous night Janet's mother and sister were in the audience. Oliver Prickett, a Playhouse veteran, remembered that a "chap like Dana Andrews would come in just to be a singer. He wanted to amplify his light-opera career. . . . A beautiful voice." But he wanted to do more than that, submitting to the theater's demanding regimen. As Dana wrote his parents: "From early morn til late at night I run from one appointment to another—dramatics, voice, orthodontist, dance (for free body movement) speech, fencing, and beside all this I have to study for parts and go to rehearsals every day." This was the Pasadena Playhouse program that also included classes in makeup, costume design, manners and customs, various kinds of vocal training, and the history of literature.

According to a story Dana told *Modern Screen* reporter Ida Zeitlin his career at the Playhouse began unfortunately when he showed up late for his scene in *Antony and Cleopatra*. While he was nervously fingering his false mustache, it fell off, and by dashing off for more spirit gum he missed his cue. Embarrassed actors struggled to improvise lines to cover his missed entrance, and afterwards Dana had to placate an irate director.

Making no excuses for himself, Dana pleaded for a second chance—and got one.

Dana did not record what it was like for him to enter the Playhouse as a performer. It has rightly been called a temple of the arts, a cathedral built in mission style with a baroque fountain in a courtyard of Florentine proportions. Anyone steeped in the theatre, watching young apprentices gaze at the warm pastel facade, senses their profound pleasure upon arriving at the site of their aspirations. Walking up the steps into the foyer marks the ascent to a magnificent 820-seat auditorium built like an opera house, with a balcony that hangs like a heaven over the rear of the theater. The main stage is huge and able to accommodate the largest casts of Shakespeare plays (all of which had been performed at the Playhouse by the year Dana appeared there). The green room, the haunt of actors awaiting their time on the stage, is located below ground adjacent to and accessible from the orchestra pit. This abode of actors is a tunnel-like enclosure, twenty-two by forty-four feet, and has the feel of an elongated living room. Buttressed with massive beams and festooned with shields and crests, its paneled doors lead into ten three-person dressing rooms. A locker room, a kitchen, and bath and shower rooms complete a design that makes the theater a self-contained world. Here a society of actors in various states of dress and undress and sharing the dream of performance congregated, creating the world that Dana Andrews had sought for so long.

Maudie Pricket, Oliver's sister, explained how Dana was able to master a repertoire of roles quickly and discover his strengths: "You had a chance to be in all kinds of plays, and no favoritism was ever shown because somebody could play this part or that part better than others. And of course . . . lots of times you were given the thing that you were least suited for, but it was a great challenge for you to try to play that part. After all, you were in the process of learning and trying to find out what is the thing you can play best." By the end of the year, after playing a few other roles in plays performed on smaller stages, Dana was a rousing success in Irving Cobb's play, *Paths of Glory*. His triumph meant something special to the Van Nuys community, which had watched him in performances for the past four years. An excerpt that the *Van Nuys News*, reprinted from Richard Sheridan Ames's review in *Script*, singled out Dana's performance as one of three innocent soldiers court-martialed and executed. The critic noted it was difficult to "restrain my praise": "In that terrible and shocking guardhouse scene, wherein the doomed men mock the priest, Mr. Andrews not only contributes his share of savage indignation but portrays as well the helplessness, the manly terror, even the physical revulsion felt by an intelligent youth who must walk unflinchingly to a senseless death."

Dana told Lillian Ross that "it was a demanding role, and I worked on it with a private coach to get every shading just right." That coach was Rudolph Amendt, who "pleading, pounding, cajoling, calling him hard names and soft" pushed Dana to the "brink of nervous exhaustion"—all to get the perfect performance. Dana could feel the audience's excitement building when, as Langlois, he handed his coat to the sergeant charged with taking him to his execution, and dropped his eyes on his uniform's medals. Stan Twomey ran backstage to tell Dana that it was "just a matter of time now." Dana told Ross that "reviews of that show are still among my most treasured ones." The role anticipates the lynched man he would play in *The Ox-Bow Incident* (1943), giving a stunning performance that moved him closer to stardom.

Dana sent the *Script* review to his elated father and told him about the offer of a movie contract he had rejected. CF wanted him to accept it so that Carver could visit home. CF, referring to his failing health, was already dreaming of a movie contract that might make it possible for his son to buy him and Annis a retirement home. "How would you like to do that?" CF asked Carver. On January 19, Annis wrote to her son, thanking him for the delicious Christmas present of fruit. She hoped he would make good in his profession: "I know the picture show could be one of the finest influences for good that we have to day. If they were conducted in the right way." She trusted in God to make him a "pure and good" movie actor. He seemed to question her support, for she wrote on February 20, 1937: "You ask if I wanted you to succeed. I can only pray you succeed as I wrote Janet, if it be God's will. I know to be a great singer of great songs is great. I had hoped and prayed God would give me one great Gospel singer. Are you going to be the one?" Annis was pious, and she was also perceptive: "I hope the Murrays are still kind to you. I imagine you will have a time ever getting David away from them. I'm sure we couldn't blame them."

Sometime in February 1937, Dana attracted the attention of Oliver Hinsdale, "quite famous as the man who had trained Robert Taylor," as Dana later recalled. Hinsdale arranged for Dana to meet an MGM casting director. Exactly what transpired is not clear from the story Dana later gave in an interview, although another story had it that his braces got locked during an embrace with the actress doing a scene with him. A letter from Rudi Amendt in mid-February noted: "Your test at MGM cannot possibly be bad if you felt about it the way you describe. There is enough in it of you to show you in a just way." But the MGM casting director told Dana to return to his work as an accountant. He did not think Dana was leading man material: "You'll work now and then, but you won't really make a living." Dana, used to conflicting opinions, did not then give up hope of an acting career.

But appointments at Warner's and RKO yielded discouraging results. The studios did not want to test him and thought, at best, he was fit for small character parts. These seemingly obtuse responses may not have been entirely off the mark. Dana told Ida Zeitlin that Gilmor Brown had tried him in a "young man-about-town" role, and having "no polish" he flopped. Irving Cumin, the talent scout at Warner's, told him to keep on working: "I don't think you're ripe yet." Cumin thought Dana need at least another six months of work before he screen tested again.

Dana finally made it home in early 1937. Jeanne, Charles's wife, remembered CF's response to Dana's return. "Aren't you excited," Jeanne said to CF, who replied, "He's not coming home to see *us*. He's coming home so that we can see *him*." But after his son's visit, CF wrote to him: "To have you home was a great joy to all of us. . . . I can't express the joy it was to me to have you come into my room and sit down and talk with me . . . down deep you cherish the same ideals that we always sought to develop in all the boys." Dana's youngest brother, Billy, was thrilled to have his brother home. Dana took him to the movies and told him tales of Hollywood. Equally impressive, Dana sang Figaro from *The Barber of Seville* for Billy. CF believed his son when he said he wanted to "bring the family riches." Dana did not believe his father understood him, but Billy thought otherwise.

"Well, I've read story after story when the old sweetheart appears when the girl looks her worst and now I know it actually happens!" Norma wrote to Dana on March 5. She had just undergone an appendix operation and suffering from diphtheria while caring for a new baby (Moselle). Norma had not seen enough of him during his visit home and wanted to know all about his role in a new play, and all about David. Dana's visit to Huntsville was brief, but he also may not have wanted to intrude on Norma's married life, even if in her letter she seemed quite eager to show him her home. She wanted him to come back soon and would have invited him to dinner but did not want to encroach on the time he was spending with his family. Any lingering bitterness about their breakup, or yearning for what might have been, seem absent from her open-hearted letter: "Carver, I can't begin to tell you how proud I am and how happy I am that you are on the verge of realizing your lifelong ambition. I suppose I'm particularly proud because I think that at one time I made a sacrifice for that career." Seeing him succeed seemed some kind of recompense for her devotion to someone confronting daunting odds. She wanted him to write her whenever he could make time and tell her if he was appearing in anything she might be able to hear or to watch.

But Dana's reappearance disturbed Norma more than she let on. One of her cousins, Dorothy Parish Farr, wrote him:

Dear Carver,
I received a letter from Norma just after you left. One of about four I've ever received including the one from abroad. Something *must* happen to cause her to write, and when she does I always feel that it's a vent to those emotions she's afraid to let show down there. I suppose you're better acquainted with her emotions than I am but I always felt that if I closed myself up tight like that I'd surely pop.

Although Norma's mother had thought it best that her daughter and Dana forget one another, they never did. Norma and Huntsville exerted a pull even in Hollywood: "Whatever made you decide on using Dana?" Dorothy asked. "It used to be your pet aversion—I always did like it in spite of your protestations and rather approve of the change but you'll forgive me if I stick to the former. I think you'll always be just Carver to me."

Just after his visit home, Dana's brother John wrote him, "I had thought you would be so different from what you really were, but you turned out to be just as formerly, with numerous added assets to the better. I hope you stay like that as long as possible." His sister Mary wrote: "We got those pictures of yours today . . . You look like a regular movie star now." She thanked him for all the wonderful clothes (some of them Janet's) he sent to her, and said his visit home had heartened their father: "Dad said if personality ever got any one where they wanted to go that you would be at the top in no time. . . . Here in Texas (rather this part of it) where everyone is like everyone else, with the exception of some few, you can tell when someone with a personality comes around." Wilton wrote encouraging letters saying he was sure his brother would "make good." Like Mary and his father, Wilton assured Dana that he had the "personality to succeed." Wilton nevertheless understood his brother's anxiety. For a man with ambition there was "no letup." Although Dana had "considerable encouragement from the studios," he told a friend, to his parents he confessed: "I'm working hard and getting nowhere yet."

On May 19, 1937, Dana returned to writing in his journal, continuing what he had written nearly four years earlier on August 20, 1933: "To sing—that is the thing!" He now added: "—and sing he does. At least he still tries. . . . I'm some older in experience: some rather tragic things have transpired *but* I imagine I'm still the same foolish boy that penned those silly lines above." He was preparing for a June 6 recital. He had a new music teacher, Florence Russell, his third, he noted. She observed what is also apparent in Dana's diary: his indefatigable, perfectionist drive that resulted in impeccable performances. One time, when he came to one of her parties with champagne that did not have the appropriate amount of bubbles, he drove ninety minutes across town and returned with two effervescent bottles.

A Pomona College graduate, Russell had been teaching music since 1917 and began specializing in voice lessons in 1925. Although trained in classical opera, she was soon teaching stage, nightclub, and radio performers. She employed over fifty exercises for developing vocal technique, showing her pupils drawings of the anatomical parts used in singing and providing explanations of their functions. She also schooled her pupils in the history of great singers. Like her other protégés, Dana presumably appeared at her studio to observe her teaching while filling out an application. At the same time, she sized up the applicant, looking for a resourceful, hopeful aspirant, not prone to sudden slumps or ecstasies, but endowed with "a sense of humor related to themselves."

Singing seemed to be in the Andrews blood. Through the years Dana would get letters from his brothers and his sister Mary that mused about a singing career or mentioned the singing each still did in church. Singing had been CF's way of lightening the load of his fearsome sermons. For Dana, singing was throughout his life a discipline and a means of expression that he could not do without. And then Phil, a fellow Playhouse actor who had spent "thirty years on the boards," told Dana "what a terrific gamble is this thing called 'show business'" and that "pictures were on the way out . . . you had better stick to your singing." In an undated letter sent to Dana just as he was on the verge of success, Phil noted:

> I have always judged people by their voices. To me the voice was the man and yours was such a delightful thing to hear as I remembered it from the dressing room at Pasadena Community. I just could not bear to see it thrown away when it could bring so much

pleasure to all of God's children. Voice has been the passion of my life and I am thankful that yours is coming into its own even tho it is not in the way I had thought it should—(I still think you'll be an opera star—the career of all careers).

At the Pasadena Playhouse, Dana socialized with fellow actors, including Victor Jory, Preston Meservy (Robert Preston), and Dorothy Adams. As for his professional work, Dana commented: "I don't seem to have the lightness that I need—both for my singing and dramatic work. Rudolph [Amendt] seems to have given me a complex about that—but today I feel much better about it." Often he spent a day taking classes with both Amendt and Russell, while still seeing an orthodontist. He was a few years away from his signature style, a relaxed but concentrated manner that hardly seemed like acting at all, but that allowed the role to take possession of him.

Dana was also dating again, recording this cryptic note on May 21: "Have a strong sense of having accomplished something last night"—a tryst by a lake in the foothills with someone identified only as H. J. "This sexual problem has been worrying me some of late; possibly this is the solution. I have no regrets today at all—so I guess I'm a hardened sinner." Occasionally he brought girls home to meet Aggie, who had said to him that of course one day he would marry again. It relieved him to hear so, although she would often say, "She's not the one, is she?" He could feel Aggie relax when he answered, "No, she's not the one," to which Aggie would say, "I didn't think she was."

Dana worried about spending enough time with his son. "He is growing into quite a young man and is developing some tendencies that alarm me, nothing bad but just no concentration. So much has been done for him that he has learned to do nothing for himself," he wrote his parents. Dana talked it over with Aggie, noting she did not agree with his "theories but I don't suppose anyone even a wife would." Dana's daughter Kathy later observed that he thought the Dr. Spock school of children rearing too indulgent. Dana thought his son was a "pretty good boy and I hope I can instill in him the same principles that were so thoroughly drilled into me."

Dana would spend part of a day with Aggie and David, taking scenic drives up San Gabriel Canyon. He wrote his father about his days with Davey, and predictably CF worried that his grandson would not get to know Christ: "You can't begin too early with a child, especially in such atmosphere as Los Angeles, where to be a movie star, or able to put on a little more empty show than some one else is the summum bonum of existence." Dana did not Christianize David, but CF's scorn for Hollywood would carry considerable weight with his son, who shared a good deal of his father's belief that the movies existed "in a circle of unreality and false show, hurtful both to those who produce them and those who pay to see them. It will demand much manhood to resist the atrophy of those finer things that make life healthful, helpful and wholesome, and to forestall the growth of an abnormal ego which smothers the soul in the smoke of its own selfish combustion. Maybe you can make the grade—I hope so, without paying too much for what you get! Money NEVER made any one happy. Fame has the same weakness."

But at night Dana went alone to the Van Nuys Theater to watch Fredric March and Janet Gaynor in the "excellent" *A Star Is Born*. Aggie was a problem, especially after Dana's midnight return from a date with H. J. Aggie said "she was through trying to be of assistance to me since it seemed I was only interested in Pasadena *cheapness*." Aggie had discovered on his desk a "little tin box partly empty." He does not say what was in it, but he noted that he "admired her very much for not having been more incensed." Unquestionably she had found a tin of prophylactics. "Since she showed more 'guts' than diplomacy—I showed more of the latter and declined to discuss it with her," Dana noted in his journal: "It seems to me this problem I must work out for myself so long as I can do it without injuring other people." A few days later Aggie apologized for her "shameful conduct." She hoped Dana did not think she was snooping. "You have the right to work out your own salvation," she told him. Dana remained grateful for her "great help" to him and hoped she would not be too hard on him. He did not seem, at this point, to feel any resentment toward her, probably because, as he said, "God knows she has had enough trouble of her own."

Dana's journal entry for May 29 marks the first time he mentions his drinking. He had not returned home until 4:00 a.m. At this stage, he still had the stamina the next day to accompany David and the Amendts to the zoo. "Had a grand time in spite of the fact that I was dead on my feet," he noted. Aggie was upset with him again about his late nights, but he would not give way: "I *need* friends for my own happiness and contentment—and if I'm not rationalizing, I think I need to associate with all sorts of people in my work. I have observed that it helps me to gain poise, and ease." This explanation was not mere rationalization—a certain stiffness and earnestness remained in this Texas boy, and it took years to obliterate that quality in the man and in the actor. The very next sentence, though, expresses a sorrow that shows why he could not break the tie to Aggie: "Today is Memorial Day. God bless and keep my Janet. No one will ever take her place and I think she understands now that our little difficulties were not a result of lack of affection."

The self-improvement program continued, with Dana learning new words ("salient" on May 31) designed to make him a confident and polished performer. His recital on June 6 went well, but still not well enough to satisfy him. But it was dramatic training he needed now, even though he was also spending part of his time driving a truck. He quoted a June 7 article in the *Van Nuys News*: "'a brilliant future is predicted for the promising young baritone'—Quien Sabe!" He needed the good notice, writing to his father about the daily "grind" of his work. Relieved that the performance was over, he noted: "I think I showed less 'stage-fright' than ever before. That is very encouraging."

Dana had the Twomeys drive Aggie home after his recital so that he could celebrate with his friends. Getting home at 1:30, he noted in his journal the continuing drama with Aggie:

After numerous scotches—none of which took effect—I found a note on my pillow which began, "How *could* you be so forgetful of dear Janet tonight?" and proceeded to picture her as being neglected on this *night of nights* (because I didn't come home and talk about it) and it ended, "well I had a good cry and it's over. Such an aftermath to this long anticipated occasion."

Dana's character comes through in his reaction:

I hardly know what to think. It isn't like Aggie to be cheap, but that is just what that note was to me. I have a life to live and I honestly try to live the way Janet would want me to live. Last night I did precisely what Janet and I would have done on this occasion. I went out and had a jolly good time within the bounds of decency and liberal propriety. So I have no guilty conscience but I do wish Aggie would be less insistent on my living the tragic life of a widowed young husband.

As if to counter the claims Aggie was making on him—and the constant demands of a father and family that would have been perfectly happy if he had dragged himself back to Texas—Dana wrote out this passage from Elbert Hubbard, as quoted in Dale Carnegie's *How to Win Friends and Influence People*:

> Try to fix firmly in your mind what you would like to do; and then without veering off direction, you will move straight to the goal. Keep your mind on the great and splendid things you would like to do, and then, as the days go gliding by, you will find yourself unconsciously seizing upon the opportunities that are required for the fulfillment of your desire, just as the coral insect takes from the running tide the element it needs. Picture in your mind the able, earnest, useful person you desire to be, and the thought you hold is hourly transforming you into that particular individual. Thought is supreme. Preserve a right mental attitude—the attitude of courage, frankness and good cheer. To think rightly is to create. All things come through desire and every sincere prayer is answered. *We become like that on which our hearts are fixed.* Carry your chin in and the crown of your head high. We are gods in the chrysalis.

Dana wrote Norma about his June recital, and she replied in late August, expressing her vicarious thrill at the "scope and magnitude" of his program. They shared news about mutual friends and about their children. Carver's expressed concern that David did well with adults but had no children to play with. Why not put David in a nursery school as she had done with Mary Sue for six weeks that summer? "Directed play helped her marvelously," Norma said, although she would understand if her suggestion received the "snub" it probably deserved. But this idea was what Dana wanted to hear. David had to learn to paddle his own canoe. As CF wrote to his son, "It is a serious blunder to rear a child like royalty in the midst of a Democracy."

In late September, Dana added exhibition ballroom dancing to his repertoire. He was immediately taken up by a nineteen-year-old dancing partner, whose father used to work for Cecil B. DeMille. She invited him to the Beverly Hills Tennis Club, where he mingled with Groucho Marx and other celebrities, including tennis greats Don Budge and Fred Perry. Dana spent his evenings savoring grand motion picture performances—like Paul Muni's in *Emile Zola* and Ronald Colman's in *Lost Horizon*—performances that capture the sort of nobleness of spirit Dana wanted to embody on and off screen. As his journal demonstrates, he tied conviction as an actor to conviction as an individual: "developing a definiteness in my characterizations." He had his weak moments, writing on September 28 (his last entry for 1937): *"I'm pretty well worked up tonite.* Over my apparent inability to do the very thing that I most want to do. If I can't develop my imagination, I will never be able to get anywhere in the art business. I'll try a few things and see how I come out." He wrote to his father about his doubts, and CF answered: "You come by your lying awake nights quite honestly—burning up inside, 'wish-thinking,' dissatisfied with your attainments, disappointed with your level, trying to stretch your wings." CF thought marriage would soothe his son but despaired of Dana finding the right woman among the "romance hunters" of Hollywood. Charles and Jeanne seemed to embody the type of happy married life suitable for Dana as well. Everyone loved Jeanne. She fit in so well that the brothers thought of her as a sister.

By late January 1938, Dana had found a new confidant, Mary Olive Todd. He had first appeared with her in the January 1937 production of *Money* at the Playbox Theatre, one of the smaller stages at the Pasadena Playhouse. "You would say that it is a 'mother play.' All the doings of her trashy family and her snooty in-laws falls at last upon her shoulders. Mother has to do this, has to stand that. . . . Mary Todd, Dana Andrews . . . bring the young characters to life," a reviewer wrote in the *Pasadena Star News* (January 13, 1937). Mary had been at the Playhouse since 1935. But she had always loved the stage and knew much more about it than Dana did. She cared about actors and their roles. "It was 'John Barrymore in . . . ,'" her daughter Kathy remembered. In the Todd house attic in Santa Monica, Mary tacked up pictures of her favorites, making the space into a kind of museum, full of costumes, hats and helmets, fencing gear, and souvenirs from her trips abroad with her parents. As a teenager, she adored Ruth Chatterton (1892–1961), a magnificent stage actress who successfully made the transition from the silents to the talkies, starring in *Dodsworth* the year Mary and Dana met. Chatterton came for dinner years later in Weston, Connecticut, when Dana was performing in *Two for the Seesaw.*

Mary began her freshman year at UCLA, but convinced her parents of her commitment to acting. Before meeting Dana, Mary had performed in Pasadena Playhouse productions as Helen in *The Trojan Women* and as Emma Woodhouse in *Emma*. In the latter role, she had received wonderful reviews in a production that moved from the Playbox Theatre to the main stage in February 1937. She was, everyone noticed, a gifted comedienne. And she also performed well in serious drama. "Mary Todd is lovely as Hermione [in *The Winter's Tale*]; in the early scenes she reads her lines with clarity and feeling; in the final tableau she shines with a still inner radiance that takes the place of all forgiving words," wrote the *Pasadena Star News* critic on November 23, 1937.

Mary and Dana appeared together in *First Lady*, in which a president's granddaughter schemes to put her husband, the secretary of state, into the White House. A collaboration between George S. Kaufman and Washington columnist Katharine Dayton, the play opened on the Pasadena Playhouse main stage on January 18, 1938. Emmy (Mary) is "a soft and fluffy young woman, very young, naive," visiting Washington, D.C., for the first time and finding it "awful confusin'" because no one means what they say or even knows what they are saying. Keane (Dana) is a "boy Senator . . . good looking, Western, and doesn't know a thing," which makes him a good presidential prospect in this farcical play about national politics. He eventually becomes engaged to Emmy.

After rehearsals Dana and Mary joined the cast at Sheetz's drugstore for sodas, or at the Waldorf for coffee and sandwiches. According to an account Dana gave Ida Zeitlin, Mary began to blot out his interest in other women—but there was a problem. She had gained weight since her performance in *Emma*:

> Back in the safety of his own room, he'd talk to himself. "Andrews, this can't be happening to you. You're crazy if you think you can fall in love with a fat girl."
> "Who says I'm in love with her."
> "Then quit hanging around. There's no law that says you have to go to the Waldorf."
> "I'll never step foot in the joint again."
> Not till the next night he wouldn't.

In fact, Dana had felt the same way about Janet's weight gain. "All his life Dana abhorred fat girls," Zeitlin explained, while reporting (without explanation) that Mary soon slimmed down to 108 pounds.

Mary had first become aware of Dana after his performance in *Paths of Glory*, but as she herself said they were A and Z people. He did not seem to be her type. Compared to her self-dramatizing, Stanislavsky-studying contemporaries, he seemed rather ordinary—in a breezy sort of way. He was not an Orson Welles's stentorian THEATRE MAN. She did not really begin to take Dana seriously until she returned from doing summer stock in Martha's Vineyard, when he seemed prepared to listen to her impressive store of theater lore. If the difference between them "was part of the attraction for both of us," as Mary later said, it took more than a year for them to realize as much. Dana did not mention Mary in his journal until 1937, and he apparently made no reference to her in his correspondence until 1938. Then on February 18, 1938, writing in his journal after "a few months of neglect," he announced that on the closing night of *First Lady*:

> I discovered with a shock that I was in love—seriously with the girl playing opposite me in this opus. I have known her since my first play in Pasadena but never had the opportunity to really get acquainted. She has an unusual charm that fascinates me. She is very intelligent or so I believe, though a bit critical, and exceedingly clever. She possesses a good sense of comedy on stage and this carries over into her private life. I believe she is good for me and I'm entirely going into this with my eyes open not to mention wholeheartedly.

At a Waldorf Astoria opening night party for *First Lady*, Dana bumped into Mary emerging from a phone booth, grabbed her, and after a kiss said, "I've been wanting to do this for four weeks." She then followed him back to his table without saying a word until she accepted his invitation to see her home. It was a long drive to Santa Monica. Ida Zeitlin's dialogue wraps up the romance too neatly, like a movie:

> "I'm in love with you. What're you going to do about it?"
> "What would you like me to do about it?"
> So he told her, and they sat holding hands and talking till daylight.
> Aggie met her when Dana took them both out to a show. Afterwards, he dropped Aggie at the house before driving Mary home. But she waited up for him.
> "That's the one," she said. It was a statement, not a question.
> "Oh, Dana, I'm glad. She's wonderful."

It was not so easy as all that with Aggie or with Mary, as Dana would later acknowledge in his journal.

Mary recalled that on that first evening together, "[W]e talked of our future plans for ourselves; we were both looking for more exciting and meaningful lives than we had led in our hometown. We wanted to become fine artists." Mary was an only child from a prominent Santa

Monica family, and her early years had been comfortable. Dana fascinated her with stories about the "real world" life he had led before entering the Playhouse. She learned about the "dynamic, complicated" CF, and how Dana had run away from home and returned to a surprisingly receptive father, whose mercurial temperament was balanced by the attentions of a warm, strong, and devoted mother. She enjoyed Dana's depiction of himself hitchhiking his way to California in a "'classy' black overcoat, Homburg hat, and white scarf."

Mary's critical intelligence would become essential to the success of Dana Andrews, providing him with a perspective that neither Norma Felder nor Janet Murray could ever have matched. Mary had character and finesse, developed perhaps during her own upbringing by a rather Victorian mother and a more arty and unusual dad, who was nevertheless an upright businessman. Mary had to stand up to her mother, who liked to run the show. "She didn't tell her mother nuthin' that she couldn't get out of. She really didn't," said Minnie Carter, who later became a part of the Andrews household and took care of the children.

Dana needed more than worship, and he realized Mary was a woman he could not sideline. Moreover, this new partner had wit and could hold a room—not to mention an audience—with her stories. She had, he realized in wonder, opened his eyes and had already taken him away from the purely romanticized version of himself and his relationships that he had indulged in more than he realized. So certain was he that he wrote home to his father, who cautioned him about marrying a woman, especially an actress, in a climate where the "matrimonial harness fits too loosely." What kind of family did she come from, and what kind of life had she led before meeting him? "Too large a proportion of actresses are handled goods; they have known too many men," he warned in a letter sent on February 24. Dana's response to his father's admonition has not survived, but he was, in fact, careful, confiding to his journal on March 6 that he had not pressed Mary to be more intimate with him: "I am not now so sure that we are as compatible as it first appeared. Our interests are at considerable variance, which in itself is not as serious as the difference in our attitude toward things in general." He was determined not to make a "hasty or foolish decision."

Spending enough time with David remained a problem, and some of their outings now seemed less successful. "David has been a little captious today," Dana wrote in his journal, trying out one of the new words he had committed to memory that day, along with "arbitrary" and "puissant." Dana sought to reassure himself that "withal," his son was a "most charming and delightful lad." Even the wording of this last personal remark has the patina he was attempting to apply to his manner of expression, which remained a little stilted. When Mary first met him he seemed a bit of a rube, and perhaps that is why he initially felt somewhat out of his element with her.

Besides Dana's uncertainty about Mary, he was struggling with his role in *Knights of Song*, a play about Gilbert and Sullivan, which had opened on March 1. Dana did not think much of the play or of his part, as he confided to both his journal and his father. After opening night, Florence Russell, still his vocal coach, told him the character he had developed was "too weak," and so he "stepped it up a bit" the following night. He admitted he still had some "bad spots to iron out." Once again, his problem seemed to be how to bear down without becoming overbearing: "I have a tendency to be easy-going about everything. I'm going to try to change that without becoming either hard or ruthless," he vowed. How to combine "natural kindness and congeniality" with "a strong determination and dominant quality to be impressive and satisfying"? There had to be a middle way, he reasoned. He talked it over with Toddy, as he called Mary: "She told me which spots in the show she thought were bad. I appreciate this sort of criticism and hope to be able to profit by it."

This would be the hallmark of Dana Andrews during his greatest period as an actor: to admit his shortcomings and absorb shrewd criticisms of his performances and his style. At the same time, all wasn't easy. He was still getting used to Mary: "My love affair is very unsatisfactory at the moment," he wrote in his journal on March 8, promising he would explain "when more time is available." Days were taken up with learning new words, taking music lessons—including sessions of singing *Pagliacci*—and nights performing at the Playhouse. Two days later an evening out with Toddy resulted in a "bacchantic, bibulous, crapulent orgy, a collocation ensued until daylight." He was still not certain they were compatible, but he was happier because "we have at least hauled the bones out of the closet so we can see how to pick them."

Reading the record of dozens of performances at the Playhouse, it might seem like Dana went from success to success, but it did not seem so to him. He recorded his devastating disappointment when he did not get an important role in *Merrily, We Roll Along*, a Kaufman and Hart play. "Am having a hard time keeping up my morale as I seem to be getting nowhere," he confided to his journal. Continuing work on *Pagliacci* perhaps kept him tuned and in touch with mentors like Russell. But Dana's darkening mood—"pretty hard days," he wrote on April 10—persisted:

"I've (or had) developed a most convincing complex of inferiority that I found it hard to live with myself—am better now but still need a good round of encouragement from some source." He does not explore the source of that sense of inferiority. He was never one to psychologize himself, but it seems that what he calls inferiority had to do with feeling out of place. Dana doubted himself because he could not seem to fit in or feel comfortable in the green room of an actor's life, in a setting where everyone was in costume and acting a part—even though that bond with his fellow actors is precisely what he needed.

Mary Todd provided that bond. She had fallen in love with him while remaining her own person. She was an actress, but she did not pretend with him. He had to adjust to her as much as she adjusted to him. He needed the give-and-take of equals. He had to believe that with Mary he could find a world elsewhere, outside the boundaries of the very circumstances that now defined him as another one of those struggling actors. "I'm terrifically in love and being able to do nothing about it has probably brought on the above mourned feelings," he wrote in his journal. Toddy had spent the last two weeks living with her parents, and visiting her in Santa Monica had palliated his plight, giving him a respite from the "foul atmosphere of Pasadena." To sing or perform was the thing, but only on *the stage*. To be other than himself outside the confines of a theater seemed inauthentic.

He wanted to keep his distance from the pretensions of performers. He did not, ordinarily, take his fellow professionals into his confidence. Nowhere in Dana's journal does he appear to revel in his fellow actors or in the adulation that so many stars thrive on. Dana was a loner, and that solitariness explains why Mary had become so precious to him. To see her other life outside of Pasadena consoled him. He did not think her a great beauty, but he still thought "hers the loveliest countenance my dull orbs have looked on for many a turn of the season. Love does things to your senses and (may I tritely add) How!"

On May 1, Dana re-read everything he had written in his journal since resuming it in 1937, and then commented: "I have had some terrific feelings of inferiority of late but at this writing I attribute them largely to fatigue and the resulting over-anxiety for my career." He was obviously pleased to report the review in *Script* of his performance in *Criminal at Large*: "Dana Andrews, cast in a minor role, shows assurance and polish. The Pasadena Playhouse should keep him in mind for an important romantic lead." "[N]ot bad for a notice on a stooge part," Dana remarked.

Stanley Twomey encouraged Dana to quit the Playhouse. Dana should work up a scene to impress the studios and see if he could secure a contract. Twomey was still paying Dana $50 a week and waiting for the day when Dana would make good on his commitment to pay Twomey and Wardlaw together 25 percent of his movie contract salary for five years. Dana did not quit the Playhouse, but he did turn down a Pasadena Laboratory stage production: "To hell with this playing around: I'm going to do something to justify my passing as an actor." His choice "passing" is revealing, suggesting fakery or impersonation, even as he declared his increasing fondness for "La Belle Todd." Dana then copied out the lines from sonnet XXXI of Edna St. Vincent Millay's famous collection, *Fatal Interview*, the last five lines of which seem especially apposite to the way Dana's love for Mary and devotion to his career were converging:

> When we lie speechless in the muffling mould,
> Tease not our ghosts with slander, pause not there
> To say that love is false and soon grows cold.
> But pass in silence the mute grave of two
> Who lived and died believing love was true.

Dana thought about Mary but stayed away from the Playhouse. "Maybe wise—maybe no," he concluded after calling up Paramount and learning that no new talent need apply. Business had been terrible: "[A]nother depression or the continuance of the old one," Dana wrote on May 9.

The next day he was with Toddy seaside in Santa Monica. She looked "very sweet in a new beach suit which looked like what we used to call rompers." They talked about the theatre as usual. Then Dana returned home and washed dishes for Aggie, who was preparing for a woman's club outing. Dana had kept up his connections with the Van Nuys community, dining with Janet's sister Margo, and taking David to a music school run by Portia Young, who had appeared in several amateur productions with Dana. This period, for all its momentary gratifications, seemed, in Dana's words, an "eternal waiting for something to show up." Would he look back on this time as having been wasted for "not having the habit of industry"? As his days were crowded with self-improving activities, he seems to have been unduly hard on himself. "I'm trying to utilize every minute by having it previously planned—either for work or pleasure," he wrote. And he sketched out this schedule for himself: "An hour for reading, two hours for study, two for music, two for work on dramatics etc." He allowed for "upsets and recreation" between his perusals of Bertrand Russell and Marcus Aurelius, not to mention self-help books like *Learning How to Learn*. In a journal passage about concentration and remembering what he read, he sounds remarkably like a latter-day Benjamin Franklin, the self-advancing genius of the autobiography. It would not be out of place for the Dana of the diary to enumerate his errata. Later, to erstwhile biographer Clyde Williams, Dana would present himself as a Horatio Alger hero.

In the spring of 1938, however, it had been discouraging to hear from an agent who told Dana he "photographed *heavy*" and could expect to play only "character leads." This comment, coupled with Dana's earlier concerns about developing a more relaxed style, may have prompted this sudden analysis:

> At this point it occurs to me that I would likely be much happier and less introverted if I would think of other people a little more and myself a little less. I'm not nearly so important as I try to make myself believe and even if the worst should happen—what would it matter. If I can impress this thought with force upon my consciousness it might possibly decrease my self-consciousness.

Dana would always have a temperament more suited to drama than comedy, which is perhaps why he sought Mary's countervailing comedic sensibility. He confessed that he got "a wee bit on the silly side when I'm in her company. She is very charming and loads of fun." Just the antidote for an actor who knew he took himself too seriously and yet could not do anything about it on his own. After a day on the beach with Mary at the end of May, Dana exulted in a successful voice lesson, exclaiming, "me—me—me." He had returned to the Playhouse to read for a part in *Major Barbara*. He was also getting more rest, retiring to bed by ten, and doing some running. And capitalizing on his new determination to pay more attention to others, he appeared open to this contribution from a short, squat passer-by on a Van Nuys street: "If I wuz as big as you are I wouldn't give a fuck for anybody in Los Angeles." Laughing all the way home, Dana was greeted with four-year-old David's claim that he could lay an egg: "Hearing the call I detoured via the refrig.," Dana reported to his journal, "and got a real egg. Feeling around in the shredded paper of the large Bullock's box, I produced this egg to the surprise and amazement of all present. Dave, imaginative as he is, believed he had laid it and I didn't disillusion him."

On June 8, Dana confessed to himself:

This can't go on for long as I should soon lose my mind. What the hell has happened to my old cockiness? I haven't always been like this. Fear of impotence, fear of failures—fear-fear-fear. I'm all tied up—so completely afraid that my nerves are all tensed all the time.

He was going to see a psychoanalyst:

My God! It would be better to die trying to do something than to go on like this, never getting any peace from myself. I'm not inferior; I have many qualities that are outstanding and I should be able to develop these and not blame myself for not having everything. I have a good voice, I'm manly looking. I'm sincere in almost everything I do, I have a fairly good brain, I've had some valuable experience. I've demonstrated to myself that I can act well enough to get started and it can be improved from there. With all these assets my liabilities consist chiefly of: a lack of energy (not a great lack at that), possibly not the most artistic temperament in the world, a gross lack of confidence in my ability to do anything well—this last being fatal to a frame of mind that might aid in the improvement of the others. But be it resolved that from here on out, I shall rid myself of this and develop even an overbearing confidence in myself or die in the attempt—just how this last will be accomplished (the dying, I mean) I don't quite know. To say the least, I'm thoroughly disgusted with myself tonite!

Yet six weeks later, the world had turned again: "The part in *Major Barbara* which opened July 4th was good experience and turned out rather well." It is easy to see Dana playing the part of the Cockney Bill Walker with conviction, fiercely repudiating the Salvation Army's religiosity: "Rot! there ain't no sach thing as a soul. How kin you tell wether I've a soul or not. You never seen it. . . . It's this Christian game o yours that I won't have played agen me: this bloomin forgivin and noggin and jawrin that makes a man that sore that iz lawf's a burdn to im."

"Outlook—better," Dana reported tersely in his journal on July 18, while rehearsing another Shaw play, *Back to Methuselah*, and feeling healthy after consulting with Dr. William S. Casselberry on "a method of problem solving and life planning . . . If it does nothing else it keeps me in a better frame of mind than I have been for quite some time." Dana kept a June 10, 1938, receipt for $10 for a "psychological exam."

In early August, while playing Barnabas and Martellus, respectively, in *Back to Methuselah*, Parts II and III, something happened to Dana Andrews that he had been anxiously awaiting for years. He put it in a sentence quoted later in a Twentieth Century-Fox press release: "I learned to stop stewing, relax, and get into the spirit of the play." Some final element of reserve had dissolved in Dana's performances. There is no telling exactly why, but it is likely that Mary Todd had made the difference. As Dana explained to a reporter, "Mary was light-hearted in many ways and by being with her I found my own attitudes becoming less oppressive. Not that she was flighty. But she helped to show me that I couldn't look upon everything as being world-shaking. That there had to be some laughs scattered here and there." Toddy was that lover/critic that broke through his inhibitions—that stiff earnestness that he could never quite relinquish until he embraced both her authority and devotion to him. "She knew more about acting than I did," Dana admitted many years later, but even more importantly, Mary was committed not to the dream of what he would become but to the man that was about to fulfill his dream.

Dana's moment came nearer on the opening night (October 11, 1938) of *O Evening Star* on the main stage of the Pasadena Playhouse. Ivan Kahn, who reported to Lew Schreiber, the casting director, at Twentieth Century-Fox, was in the audience. Dana replied to Kahn's admiring note, thanking him for his encouragement, and agreeing that he was suitable for playing "character leads." On November 9, Stuart Heisler wrote to Dana: "Just to let you know that I saw the show last night and enjoyed it a great deal. I thought your performance very smooth and delivered without a great deal of effort—which to me is good acting." Heisler had been in Samuel Goldwyn's employ for more than a decade, earning his gratitude for rescuing a slow-moving *Stella Dallas* (1925) with a superb editing job that resulted in one of the studio's greatest box office and critical triumphs. Shortly after hearing from Heisler, Dana wrote his father that a movie contract was in the offing, and CF responded warmly, noting that perhaps Dana's acting ability had, to some extent, been influenced by his preaching—although CF never consciously tried for a performance but simply spoke naturally and with conviction. But perhaps that was the best kind of acting, he mused.

On January 1, 1939, his thirtieth birthday, Dana Andrews did a "summing up" of the last three months in his journal. Dr. Casselberry, who

Dana depended on for an "objective point of view," assured him that his roles in *Back to Methuselah* had been "impressively interpreted." An agent, Lew Golder, had taken an interest in Dana's work, first spotting him when Dana did some work at Neely Dickson's summer theater: "You may not know it, but you're the best man to hit this town since Spencer Tracy in *The Last Mile*. I've already talked to a big producer about you." This sounded like agent's talk, but Golder had lined up Reeves Espy, vice-president at the Goldwyn studio. The agent had also told Gregg Toland, Goldwyn's best cinematographer (later to gain fame for his work on *Citizen Kane*), all about Dana. After Dana had Golder meet with Stan Twomey, the latter said to Dana: "If the kike isn't lying, he's got something on the ball." Dana concluded: "Since Golder seemed thoroughly sold on me, I decided to sign up with him." Golder then persuaded Espy to watch a performance of *O Evening Star*.

On October 29, 1938, Dana took his screen test on stage 4, "without make-up and in a gray wales stripe suit and a pale blue shirt (which I purchased for the occasion from Bullocks for $7.50) and dark blue tie with small red figures." He did a scene with Sigrid Gurie, a Norwegian actress just beginning her career in Hollywood, having first appeared in *Algiers* (1938). Goldwyn was engaging in yet another futile effort to build up his version of Greta Garbo. The test took all day. During a lunch break, Dana forgot to remove a temporary porcelain cap. Resuming shooting the cameraman told Dana he noticed "a little space between two of your teeth." Then Dana realized he had swallowed the tooth along with his oyster stew.

The following morning an anxious Dana asked Mary to accompany him to a viewing of the screen test in Goldwyn's projection room. As they entered Espy's office, Espy gave Dana a serious look and said, "Well, it looks like you're a success." Dana's response is exactly what you might have imagined: "Sweeter words were never spoke nor more gratefully received." Then they went to see the test. "It was quite a strange experience to see myself moving and talking but I thought the test fairly good," he wrote in his journal. When Mary laughed at the awkward "stool gag," Espy said, "You're getting a razzing, young man." Dana had told Mary beforehand that the test was "no good so she was surprised to learn I was just ribbing her." Espy told him not to say anything about the forthcoming contract until the publicity department put out the story.

Dana sent roses to Sigrid Gurie and telegrams to Espy and Stuart Heisler—and kept his good fortune to himself, "which was, *oh so hard*." In fact, he did tell a few people he trusted, and celebrated the new year, his birthday, and his contract at the Graystone Manor garage, "all the rooms being taken by Rose parade spectators. Never spent a happier or more satisfying night." He returned home to Van Nuys, David, and dinner the next day.

CHAPTER 8

Goldwyn
1938–41

DANA'S EARLIEST MEMORY of Samuel Goldwyn seems to be a scene in which the producer screened footage of Gary Cooper playing Abraham Lincoln. Goldwyn wanted Dana's opinion. "I later learned from many years of experience with Mr. Goldwyn that this is one of his practices," Dana told an interviewer:

> He asks everybody, from the hairdresser on the set to the head of the business department, what they think about little things like hairdos, or whether a man's clothes fit properly, or questions about his personality. A lot of people say, "Goldwyn asks everybody what they think and then does what he thinks." But I think what he thinks is made up to some extent (or influenced, certainly) by what he hears from various people.

Goldwyn often did the same thing with stories he proposed to film. First he had several writers retell the story, until Goldwyn believed he had identified the key elements that would work in a picture. Only then did he authorize the writing of the screenplay. Dana's story also reveals how accessible Goldwyn was—in part because he was an independent producer with a relatively small studio. He could be quite annoying and intrusive for actors and directors alike, but his presence was also a godsend when crucial decisions had to be made quickly.

The Goldwyn contract, dated November 28, 1938, was the standard seven-year agreement with six-month options: Employment commenced on January 19, 1939, with the first six month option paying Dana $150 a week; the second $200 a week; the third $300 a week, escalating to $2,000 a week by the end of the contract. He was guaranteed forty weeks of employment. The agreement contained the usual morals clause that obligated the "artist to conduct himself with due regard to public conventions and morals." Any action the studio deemed degrading, or which incited "public hatred, contempt, scorn or ridicule" or shocked community values and was detrimental to the entertainment industry, could be grounds for dismissal. Changes in the actor's voice, appearance, or mental capacity could trigger suspension. As a salaried employee under contract, Dana had no control over the roles offered to him. Refusing to perform an assigned part could lead to a suspension lengthening the seven-year contract: "[T]he producer shall exercise the right to extend this agreement for a period equivalent to all or any part of the period of such suspension."

Nothing about Dana's situation changed during the first three months of 1939. This was the first of several delays that resulted from several factors. As a small independent producer, Goldwyn made only one or two pictures a year and had trouble placing actors under contract in appropriate roles. He often quarreled with his distributors, United Artists, because he did not get the favorable terms he believed he deserved as their main producer; consequently, he would suspend production rather than capitulate to their conditions. Goldwyn solved part of his problem by loaning actors out to other studios and pocketing payments that far exceeded the actors' salaries. But Dana was not yet an established star who could be employed in this way.

With Goldwyn's permission, Dana continued to perform in a variety of roles at the Playhouse. This was a downtime (six weeks) as specified in his contract, which meant he drew no salary until March—although the studio used him once to screen test a Broadway actress. Stan Twomey agreed to keep him on the payroll (Dana took inventory at one of Stan's gas stations) until he got his first check from Goldwyn.

Dana read David stories at night, drove him to grammar school, went to music lessons, met with Dr. Casselberry, played tennis with Mary, saw a lot of movies, visited with old friends in Van Nuys, did his work at the Playhouse, and socialized with a few actors like Robert Preston, Dorothy Adams, and occasionally Victor Mature. Dana believed he had gained considerably in confidence and poise as an actor, but still chided himself for laziness and for not doing "wonders." It suited both the Goldwyn Studio and the Playhouse to have Dana on stage so long as he was not on call for a picture—the word Dana would also use, pronouncing it quite distinctly and respectfully as "pik'cher." So he continued to accept parts, most notably the role of George Washington in Maxwell Anderson's *Valley Forge*. Dana did considerable reading about Washington, resulting in a performance that may have been the best Dana ever created on the stage. He was especially impressed with his character's self-control.

Dana attended a PTA meeting, afterwards going home to tell Aggie all about it. The school principal told him David was "one of the most extraordinary children she had ever seen but we must be extraordinarily careful not to spoil him. We *must* teach not to be always the center of attention—this for his own good." Other teachers confirmed the principal's words. "Seems he's quite the boy around the kindergarden. How Janet would enjoy hearing what I heard tonite," he wrote on January 24.

Dana took David and sometimes Aggie on drives into the foothills. He loved to watch his precocious son play and would occasionally record David's observations, including a report on his day at a Christian Science Sunday school. David raised his arms and brought them down sharply, imitating his teacher's way of saying: "There is no Life, Truth, intelligence nor substance in matter." Then there was the time David got into a "terrific argument with Aggie." He wanted to play with his train in the shade, while Aggie insisted he take advantage of the winter sun. When Aggie "put her foot down," a petulant David said, "Aggie, don't you think you ought to *apologize* to me?" When Dana asked his son what they should get Aggie for Mother's Day, David suggested: "Let's get her a clock that stops once in a while so she can get caught up."

Dana did odd errands and chores for Aggie that included washing dishes and taking her to a Republican woman's meeting on January 23. A lifelong Democrat, he was surrounded by Republicans at home, including not only Aggie's husband William, but also Janet's sister Margo and her husband Hal. Even Janet had been a Republican. If he ever argued politics with them, however, neither his journal nor surviving letters show it. What is certain is that he never forgot his debt to the Murrays, writing on a photograph: "To Aggie, who has been advisor, Mother and inspiration to me through many struggling years. Dana."

He wrote a "long, chatty letter to Mother & Dad," which CF responded to on February 19, noting that "you let yourself loose and wrote more than a mere note." The letter "seems more like you," CF told his son. "What you said about being home-sick was rather pathetic." CF, looking at a picture of Dana and Janet taken shortly after David was born, could not help but think of Frost's poem about the road not taken, which Dana had sent him. Dana's sister Mary wrote her brother telling him what CF himself could not say: "I thought dad would not be glad about your contract since he has preached against the movies all his life, but you would be surprised at his 'pride' when he tells someone about his son being in the movies." Dana's mother pretended to be less thrilled, Mary noted, "but in reality she is just as proud as we are." Mary seemed disgusted with people in Huntsville bragging about how they knew Dana "'when' . . . I get quite a bit more attention since it has been found out that I have a brother under 'movie contract.'" Charles chimed in, telling Dana how Hollywood crazy his students were, and now so impressed that he had a brother under movie contract. Shortly after getting his first paycheck, Dana apparently sent money home, because his father sent a note in early April, admitting that he had "always protested against much found in the movie pictures and now I'm receiving money from that industry ha!"

Sometimes in the middle of the day Dana would steal an hour to sit on the beach, thinking often about Mary, "so sweet and charming and attractive, interesting, thrilling. At times it seems too good to be true," he confided to his journal. Sometimes Mary would join him for some "plain and fancy caressing." They spent a lot of time together at her family's home in Santa Monica. Then he would drive home and play cribbage with Gramp (William Murray).

In one of his rare journal comments on world affairs, Dana wrote: "Hitler's speech from Germany today was rather epoch-making in its length and nonsense—the kind of stuff with which the German minds are poisoned but nothing was said that made much difference except that he (Hitler) publicly pledged aid to Mussolini in any further territorial ambitions he might have. He commended Japan on her 'fine work' in China—this being about the bitterest pill for U. S. listeners to swallow." Fascinated, Dana even set his alarm for 3:00 a.m. to hear another one of Hitler's speeches in late April.

By the spring of 1939, Dana was ready to marry, but he reported in his journal that Reeves Espy said the studio would not like him to wed—presumably because it was worth more to them to promote a new, good-looking, and seeming unattached actor. Dana and Mary decided to "humor the studio." It was late April when Dana was first called for costume fittings and rehearsals for a film tentatively titled "Sailor Beware." On April 17, Dana reported in his journal that he had received six checks: "$150.00 ea. 94.50 per wk is mine." The Murrays, he wrote, "are in pretty bad shape financially so I'm paying all the bills except the utilities, which the Laubs [Margo and Hal] pay." He was sending $10 a month to Texas, and of course he was starting to repay Twomey and Wardlaw for their years of support.

On April 25, Dana reread some of Norma's old letters. "I can understand a lot now that slipped by before," was his only comment. He wrote more about his petunias—which were "coming along nicely"—than about his feelings. Indeed, like his mother he loved to garden and mentions gardening often in his journal. A May 2 bill from the Sherman Oaks nursery lists his order: one Camellia, four gardenias, one flat of zinnias, one flat of verbena, five delphiniums, one sack of leaf mold, and one bale of peat moss, for a total of $12.41, including tax. He had loads of topsoil and fertilizer trucked in. "We ought to have a fairly good garden one day," he wrote on May 1. He took pleasure in building a sandbox for David and assisted the family cat when she gave birth to four kittens. David, who stroked them all day, wanted an explanation of their arrival—"which I answered as plainly as I could," Dana reported.

Mary spent early May preoccupied with a new production at the Playhouse, leaving Dana feeling lonely: "Wonder if she knows how completely dependent I am on her." Then after seeing her again, he sensed some kind of "under-current." A few days later he seemed perplexed because she seemed a "little strange," sitting at a bar in the Waldorf drinking beer when he was making a tremendous effort to refrain. After another outing, he was even more certain that something was wrong. In fact, the couple had become so worked up that "we each thought the other was acting a little strangely and being proud, neither of us would unbend." Of course both did unbend after several days, when they confessed their misgivings to one another. Dana became jealous when Mary went off horseback riding with another man. He decided to break it off with her. But the moment they met again, he got over his outburst and they were, in his words, "like two doves." Their quarrels now just seemed silly to him. The only discordant note seemed to be his drinking, although it is hard to judge from his journal just how severe a problem it had become.

An agent's offer in the middle of May to set up a screen test for Mary at MGM troubled Dana. "Looks like she had forgotten that I don't want an actress—even to be in love with. Have always been afraid that something like this would come up," he vouchsafed to his journal. He would not ask her to refuse the offer—not if that is what she wanted—but he did not see how he could go on with her. "Something is happening to our little dream," which did not include a wife and husband both "in the public eye." It would be useless to pretend that he was other than "old-fashioned." He just hoped that somehow "time and further developments" would make it possible for him to fulfill his "idyllic plans." The waiting was agonizing, especially when Mary said she was "just curious" about the offer. "I'm so damn much in love it just about kills me to think of anything coming between us," he admitted. He was "eating his heart out like a damn fool over a situation I have created in my own mind." Mary had given him every reason to be happy, although he felt especially low after accompanying Mary to *Dark Victory* with Bette Davis, George Brent, Humphrey Bogart, and Geraldine Fitzgerald—a "four handkerchief" tearjerker.

Dana did not say exactly when Mary dispelled the suspense, but two months later he was writing the next entry (dated July 18) in his journal, announcing that she had convinced him "she could be happy without a career and that I could be happy with having asked her to give it up for the sake of our usual contentment." She had shown no signs of regretting her decision. Who knows? Perhaps his elation contributed to the glowing reviews of *Valley Forge*, especially this one in the *Pasadena News*:

> Dana Andrews' Washington is a splendid figure, a truly amazing tour de force for a young actor only just launching himself on a professional career. If this be genius—let Samuel Goldwyn studios make the most of it. . . . He renders his character with superb control and mature understanding. Now aloof, now passionate in vituperative anger. Now depressed and lonely—the full gamut of dramatic emotion, courage, honesty, nobility of purpose, rings true.

A sense of nobility and restraint—that was Dana Andrews at his best. Yet all he said in his journal is: "I didn't get what I wanted out of my characterization. Notices were good." The preacher's son did not care for self-congratulation. He tried hard not to act the part of the star (Stan Twomey had warned him about this) and friends were beginning to ask if he was still going to be the same old Dana. Sounding a little irritated, he wrote that he thought he had gone out of his way to be "cordial to every one."

But Dana had missed sending Norma her usual birthday letter, and on July 14, she wrote him a plaintive note—unusual for her—to say she realized he had to change. He was no longer the nineteen-year-old boy whose photograph she treasured, even though she still preferred to think of him that way. Her letter evidently disturbed him, because she wrote again to say that she had "come up against the obdurate wall of conflicting loyalties. So I make one of the necessary compromises you mention." From now on she would not let her "reminiscing get out from under control." If she kept a "tight rein" on her emotions, could they still be friends? "It was my own thoughtless rambling that led us to this cul de sac," she concluded. His reply is not extant, but he never broke the connection she wanted to preserve.

Around the same time, he and Mary decided to get married. It was not solely their decision alone, though. "Look, you haven't worked in pictures yet," said Reeves Espy, "and we need a little publicity. What about squiring some girls around town to the nightclubs, so we can get a little publicity for you which will help you along? I would suggest you wait a while." Mary was not happy about it, but the couple waited several months before Dana sounded out Espy again. He told Dana: "Well, you're no good with the Hollywood nightlife. But why don't you talk to Sam? He'd like to feel that you thought enough of your responsibility to him to ask him."

In late July, during a special effects fire, and amid the raucous sounds of sirens and bells, Dana noticed Goldwyn, who signaled that he wanted to talk to Dana. "You want to talk to me?" Goldwyn said. "I certainly thought I'd had a speech all prepared," Dana recalled,

> about my wanting to get married and so on, how long I'd been going with this girl—I had it really worked out to a very fine point, with the clincher at the end and all that. I certainly didn't think this was the place to do it. I said, "Well, Mr. Goldwyn, if you don't mind, I'd rather wait and beard the lion in his den." He sort of smiled and took me by the arm and led me over two paces, which helped not at all, but away from the crowd just a little bit, and said, "Beard me now." So I blurted out that I wanted to get married and wanted to know what he thought about it. He smiled very benignly and said, "I'll think it over and let you know."

Dana liked to tell this story, sometimes imitating Goldwyn's accent as he shouted over the clamor of the fire: "I UNDERSTAND YOU VANT TO TALK TO ME. VAT DO YOU VANT TO TALK TO ME ABOUT?" The mercurial studio mogul could be cordial one day, cantankerous the next. As imperious as his competitors (Adolph Zukor, L. B. Mayer, Jack Warner, Harry Cohn, and Darryl Zanuck), Goldwyn sought to control virtually every aspect of an actor's life. In the silent era, Goldwyn had expected Ronald Colman and Vilma Banky to marry because they were his two biggest stars, and he was put out when Banky chose, instead,

Rod LaRoque. Goldwyn eventually got over his pique, but the Banky-LaRoque marriage had to become a Goldwyn production, carefully managed by his publicity department.

Determined to marry, in early August Dana "broached the subject to Aggie," who tried to discourage him. Tensions developed as Aggie made cutting remarks that hurt Mary, who was getting "touchy." Dana could not blame her. He was now determined to go ahead, whatever the risk. Mary was the "most genuine person I have ever known and my devotion to her is neither wasted nor misplaced," he declared in his August 13 journal entry. Finally on August 23, after another meeting with Goldwyn, Dana secured his employer's consent to marry. "He was very pleasant and assured me he had me in mind for a picture at the first possible moment," Dana wrote. At the end of August, Lew Schreiber, the A-list casting director at Twentieth Century-Fox, sent for Dana's screen test. Jim Ryan, the B-list man, took a look. Schreiber and Ryan conferred, and both talked to Dana.

As the world situation worsened, Dana, like millions of other Americans, hoped "we can keep out of this mess," even as he was planning an October wedding. Dana admitted in his journal that he had little time to think about his feelings. It was just so satisfying "when you can do the thing you have chosen to be"—as well as "being terrifically in love." The prospect of war seemed distant as he prepared to "peacefully retire" to his bed.

"It is now 12:10 on the fateful morning of Sept 1st—Janet's birthday—a day that will go down in History as the beginning of the worst war the world had yet seen," Dana noted. He wanted America to stay neutral: "I believe that I would go to jail before going to war. I don't believe that they really settle anything and the thought of the millions of young lives they cost is appalling." Before Pearl Harbor, this was a widespread sentiment among members of a generation that grew up in the aftermath of World War I. As for the aggressor, it was the "same old gag": "It appears that Herr Hitler expects the world to believe that he is only protecting German nationals against 'Polish terrorism.'" Dana spent all night listening to the radio and Hitler's rants against the Versailles Treaty, claiming his efforts to promote peace had failed.

By late September, a dismayed Dana wrote that the Germans had overrun Poland. Roosevelt already seemed to be moving the country closer toward war with his "cash and carry plan" (which became known as lend-lease, the arms and equipment program that kept Britain resupplied during the early stages of the war). Reeves Espy phoned Dana to say he was slated for two pictures. Dana had quit smoking (temporarily), but he continued to drink so heavily that Mary could not keep up with him. They were performing together in *Dear Octopus*, a Playhouse production, and he admired her "superb performance."

David was upset, adamantly saying "he just wouldn't have it" when his dad told him he was going to marry Mary. David had said something similar on a visit to the Playhouse, and a hurt Mary overheard him. David liked Mary but told Dana he did not see why his father could not just continue to see her. "He was so serious and so touching," Dana wrote. Dana had David spend time with Mary, and slowly David adjusted so that Dana began to take pleasure in seeing his son playing quite happily with his wife to be.

Still without a part, Dana wandered about the Goldwyn lot, wearing a costume for the leading role in *Raffles* (1939). Neither Dana nor the film's star, David Niven, understood why Dana had been assigned to follow Niven around. But this was a typical Goldwyn ploy. "I was afraid stardom had come so suddenly and so easily that he [Niven] might take it a little too lightly," Goldwyn later explained. "Everywhere David went, there was another actor, ready and made up to take his part if he fell down. When the picture began, David put his heart into it, and did a wonderful job."

Near the end of October, Dana finally was up for a very small role (a couple lines in two scenes) in *Vinegaroon*, later retitled *The Westerner* (released September 20, 1940), starring Gary Cooper and with Walter Brennan in a strong supporting role. Cooper made one of his first screen appearances in *Wings* (1927) when Dana was still a picture projectionist in Huntsville. Cooper's two-minute role as a doomed aviator in *Wings* was a standout. Now, twelve years later, Dana felt the pressure of making his own screen presence palpable. He had tea with director William Wyler's wife, Talli (Margaret Tallichet), while also doing a test scene with her. Brennan, a superb character actor and Academy Award winner, welcomed Dana with sound, comforting advice. Dana, who was having trouble adjusting to this formidable cast of veterans, greatly appreciated Brennan's concern. He watched the wonderfully droll scenes between Cooper (Cole Harden) and Brennan, who plays the legendary saloon keeper and hanging judge, Roy Bean (c. 1825–1903). Dana had admired Wyler's work on *Wuthering Heights* (1939), just one of several achievements that included *Dead End* (1937), with Humphrey Bogart and Joel McCrea, and *Jezebel* (1938), starring Bette Davis. Of his own work on *The Westerner*, Dana wrote in his journal, "Wyler didn't seem to particularly like the scene and I can't say that I blame him. I couldn't seem to do what I knew he wanted but trying didn't seem to help." Wyler's habitual treatment of actors may have unnerved the neophyte, since the director rarely said what he wanted. Instead, he would shoot take after take until he was satisfied. This grueling process would demoralize all but the most confident actors. Even Bette Davis sometimes threw fits over Wyler's dogged direction of her.

Without a challenging role, a frustrated Dana took in college football games with Janet's father, played tennis with Mary, and looked for apartments the couple might move into after they were married. He dined with the Todds, played with David, played with Michael, the family dog, watched lots of movies, continued his singing lessons, read scripts, and waited for his chance. He even suggested to Reeves Espy that Goldwyn film *Valley Forge*, giving Dana the opportunity to play George Washington, a very unlikely role for a movie actor just turned thirty in a town that expected someone like Paul Muni or Raymond Massey to perform such parts.

Mary was overdue, and Dana worried they might have to move up the wedding date. He was ready for this new life with her, but he would have preferred not to have a child right away. On November 12, the couple obtained drugs from a drugstore "intended to precipitate her overdue menses. . . . One of the most harrowing experiences of my life was seeing Mary desperately ill after dinner," he recorded in his journal. Yet they went out to see *Mikado in Swing*, a live show at the Paramount Theatre. Mary immediately went to the ladies room and emerged feeling a little better, but looking wan. "Shall never forget the black, glistening black dancer going through whole convolutions while I was wondering how Mary was," he wrote. The next day Mary called to say, "All was well and we need not start our family right away."

Then Dana learned he would have to leave town for Tucson to shoot *The Westerner*. He immediately took David out horseback riding, something Dana had not done for years that resulted in "two raw places on my rump." The other raw spot was Aggie: "Really 'mixed it up' with Aggie today over her attitude toward my marrying Mary. We ended up crying on each others shoulder and I think going from now on will be smoother," he reported in his journal. He soothed himself by taking Mary with him to view their new apartment at 92 Doheny Drive in West Hollywood, where they put dishes on the shelves, "fixing planning, and dreaming." An ecstatic Dana declared, "I'll make a much better husband now than before." He was whirling with excitement: "Such packed days!" he exclaimed on November 14. And Aggie had apparently settled down: "I showed her the apt. She liked it," Dana noted. With little to do at the studio, Dana and Mary worked on wedding arrangements and picked out a ring.

On November 20, Dana recorded his reactions to the wedding that had taken place three days earlier. He named the guests, friends and members of the Todd family. David "strewed the floor with orange blossoms, and after the ceremony said to the minister, 'Thank you for what you did.'" Dana thought his son enjoyed the wedding more than anyone else. Wedding pictures in the papers showed an unshaven Dana (part of his preparation for *The Westerner*) with an explanation that he was an actor.

With David in tow, Dana carried Mary over the threshold of their new apartment. Then Dana returned his son to the Murrays. David still spent nights with his grandmother, but that too changed as he became absorbed into the Andrews household. Instead of a honeymoon, Dana was off to location shooting in Tucson, after farewell dinners at the Todds and the Murrays. Mary was in tears, but Dana was "happy as hell." Arriving on the set, Wyler looked at Dana and told him to shave. There were too many beards in the picture.

Norma was annoyed to learn about Dana's wedding from his mother and wrote to tell him so—although she wanted to know all about Mary and his movie contract, and expressed her hope that he would be bringing his new bride home to Huntsville. "Give us a chance to really know her," Norma wrote: "Please don't ever travel quite so far that you lose all interest in our small town doings. If you should I will miss your occasional letters greatly." CF wrote to his son expressing his pleasure with the wedding pictures Dana sent. CF liked that twinkle in Mary's eye. He then included this characteristic reminiscence and injunction: "Remember how you used to use 'Stay-Comb' to slick back your hair and keep it in place? Well, Hollywood needs to smear a lot of 'Stay-Put' on their marriage licenses, and I am pleased that you and Mary agree with my ideas in that."

Bad weather in Tucson gave Dana time to socialize with cast—mainly with supporting players like Forrest Tucker and Chill Wills—with trips to the movies at night. Shooting started in earnest shortly after Thanksgiving. Mary had written to him that the "curtains are up the dishes are washed the check has come, in fact God is in his heaven all's right with the world except that you aren't with me and that's very wrong indeed." The whole business was over in a few days, and he returned home to Mary.

Dana's scenes in *The Westerner* involve conflicts between ranchers and the homesteaders. As Hod Johnson, a homesteader, he appears for less than a minute—not enough time to make an impression, but long enough to almost cost him his life. A right angle turn in a speeding wagon dislodged the fence posts on top of the wagon bed, and for a moment Dana thought he would be killed. Wyler cut the unusable scene, saying not "What happened to the actors?" but "What the hell happened to the fence posts?" As Dana told interviewer Allen Eyles, "the importance of my part in the picture was less than the fence posts!" Filming on location meant that Dana had missed David's birthday. On November 30, Aggie wrote to him about his son's birthday party. "Mary was over for part of the time" to watch David's delighted reactions to the tools and gadgets he received as gifts. He seemed a "contented and happy boy," although characteristically Aggie added that the last thing he said before going to sleep was how he wished his dad could have been there. David enjoyed Dana's letters, Aggie reported: "I have to read and reread them."

Near the end of the year Dana's salary had risen to $200 a week for a forty-week contract, now split between Goldwyn and Twentieth Century-Fox in a "pooling agreement" dated December 14, 1939. Although Dana always said he abandoned his singing career as soon as he signed his movie contract, in fact he talked over his music lessons with Reeves Espy, who suggested that Dana make a recording for Goldwyn. Apparently nothing resulted from this conversation. Dana celebrated Christmas by buying new recording equipment and testing it out on Mary and himself as well as her parents.

These were happy holidays spent with the Murrays, the Todds, and Playhouse friends like Jorys. All the celebrating had added a roll to Dana's midsection that meant he would soon be "starting on a regime to take it off," since he would be beginning work on a Fox picture on January 18, playing Scrappy Wilson in *Sailor's Lady* (shot between January 18 and February 12 and released July 5, 1940), a ship and shore romance. Just how new Dana was to motion picture work is evident in his journal entry for February 1:

Strangely—I can't seem to recall anything important except that I've been working on the picture pretty regularly and getting up awfully early. My God—this movie business is a business of waiting. You wait around for hours waiting for something to happen—act a few minutes and the stand-ins do the work. Was a little worried about my part but since no great criticism has been offered, I may at least say it will pass. However I don't think much of the story or the director It's not the sort of thing you could get very worked up about.

Dana's comment on Allan Dwan (1885–1981) is understandable, even though Dwan had been involved in making motion pictures since 1911, directing Douglas Fairbanks in the acclaimed *Robin Hood* (1922), Gloria Swanson in *Stage Struck* (1925), and the incomparable Shirley Temple in *Heidi* (1937). Dwan had been among the first directors to use dolly and crane shots, and *Sailor's Lady* is an example of fluid, if uninspired cinematography, including relatively mobile shots of sailors lining up on deck and reporting for duty. Some of the best scenes are set below decks. Dwan, often praised for his "effective use of visual space" has the sailors, including Dana, hit their heads on a beam as they walk back and forth trying to soothe a baby. But as Dwan admitted, his best work had been in the silent era.

Sailor's Lady stars Jon Hall as the sailor (Danny Malone) who is supposed to get married when he returns to shore. But life gets complicated when his girlfriend, Sally Gilroy (Nancy Kelly), becomes a foster mother who leaves her baby aboard his battleship during a visitors' tour in a desperate effort to reconcile with him. As Scrappy Wilson, Danny Malone's shipmate, Dana does a creditable job playing a soured divorced sailor. Scrappy's girlfriend says that all he really wants is the navy and its guns and boats. Scrappy thinks he is doing his friend Malone a favor by concocting a plot to separate Danny from his intended. But the adorable baby softens even the cynical Scrappy, so that Dana gets an opportunity to croon and get down on all fours to play with the child. The part demanded very little from him, even though it provided significant screen time to play a rough-and-ready type. "When this comes out, you'll be in," Allan Dwan said, using a typical example of Hollywood hyperbole—although he apparently meant it, because he advised Fox studio head Darryl Zanuck that the studio had signed "a terrific new personality."

By mid-February, Dana had completed his work on the picture and almost immediately started on another month-long assignment, *Lucky Cisco Kid*, reporting to the set on February 27. During the shooting in March,

CF had a stroke. Less than a week later he died, at 8:15 p.m. on March 3. "Mother came on the line and in a broken voice wished I could be there and blessed me," Dana recorded in his journal:

> It was hard to believe even though it was not unexpected. For days there was a dull stubborn resistance to the fact. Being compelled to work steadily every day promoted this attitude of non-acceptance but when a let-up came there was a terrific feeling of loss—of something being gone that was there to depend on. Always having held him in great respect for his vitality and leadership, I now found that there was a great affection for this man who was my father.

CF had been ailing for years with a weak heart and spent his last few years at home virtually unable to work, although he tried to sell insurance and keep up appearances. His letters never lost their bite, but they also provided the picture of a man who went at his work with extraordinary integrity. In one of the last letters he wrote to Dana, CF declared: "I've never envied those dear old preachers who always jockey for the easy places and took the path of least resistance and finally ceased to breathe long years after they had ceased to really live." Perhaps only after CF was gone could his son uncoil his complicated feelings about the father who never quite reconciled himself to Dana's decisions, but who also never relinquished his affection (the word Dana used) for his wayward boy. Just two weeks before he died, CF wrote his son: "You write such nice talking letters almost like having a brief conversation with you except that they're too short."

Dana said no more about his father in his journal, but of course letters from his family commemorated the epic event of CF's passing: "I've all but worshiped him despite his faults," Wilton wrote to Dana. Charles wrote and reminded Dana of their wonderful days in Rockdale fishing with their dad—an utterly fearless man, Charles said, and a man of great faith precisely because he was such a sinner. Like Wilton, Charles thought his father "truly was a great man." David wanted his older brother to know that although CF might have concealed from Dana how "very proud" he was that his boy was "getting ahead to some extent in his chosen profession," he "put you up to me as an example of what determination and hard work will do." All the brothers contributed to the medical and funeral expenses.

When Dana resumed writing in his journal on March 26, *Lucky Cisco Kid*, the third in a series of pictures starring Cesar Romero, had completed shooting under the "ineffectual and emasculated direction of 'Lucky' [H. Bruce] Humberstone (who in private is a 'good guy')." Cesar Romero "was nice but not exactly cordial during last week or two," Dana reported. "Did a lot of riding, played a lot of 'hearts'—neither won nor lost much." As in *Sailor's Lady*, Dana had a decent amount of screen time, but this formula feature hardly challenged his talent. He plays tough talking but inadequate Sergeant Dunn, who always loses out to the Cisco Kid. Humberstone (1901–84), known chiefly for the Charlie Chan series, often puts Dana's character in the middle of the action—literally in the middle—with nothing to do. Dana sounds a little like Dan Duryea, but the role of Dunn has none of the humor or edge that made Duryea such a screen presence in the 1940s.

The review in *Variety* (May 23, 1940) echoed Dana's opinion of Humberstone. *The Hollywood Reporter* on the same day mentioned Dana but concluded, "[I]t is still too early to report on his screen possibilities." In both *Sailor's Lady* and *Lucky Cisco Kid*, he was playing well behind the male leads as characters, with quite limited emotional and mental ranges. Sergeant Dunn had comic possibilities the director did not exploit, and Scrappy Wilson had only two notes: sour and sweet.

Dana's brief remarks on these undistinguished films mark the end of his journal, save for a page on which he practices a flourishing signature—as if he is indulging himself in dreams of stardom that will require an apposite autograph. He continued in his letters and in interviews and personality profiles to account for his career, but he had apparently arrived at a stage that no longer required the validation of his journal, which seemed all about getting to his goal. No matter how unsatisfactory his pictures had been so far, he had traveled an enormous distance from the $10 a week bus-driving job he had taken just after arriving in California. In his journal entry for February 1, 1940, he notes: "Whom should I run into today on the set but Vivian Dubois, a girl who used to ride my school bus back in 1931. She didn't know me but remembered me after I introduced myself."

Norma wrote to Dana in July to say how pleased she was to see him in *Lucky Cisco Kid*. She understood better than anyone except Mary what it meant to him to appear in a picture. His voice came through beautifully, and she had only one piece of advice: He photographed better without a hat.

By the time Norma had seen *Lucky Cisco Kid*, Dana had completed work on *Kit Carson* (released August 30, 1940), playing Captain John C. Fremont, second lead to Jon Hall in the title role. On location in Kayenta, Arizona, in late May, Dana wrote to Mary describing the "mad scramble at the box every day when we come in and your letters pep me up like nothing else in the world." After a tiring trip from Flagstaff on a herky-jerky train that kept making stops and adding cars, he was enjoying rides on a "beautiful black horse that is as frisky as any I've ever seen." He seemed more at ease than on his previous pictures, playing cards with cast and crew and describing some horseplay on the set. "The powers that be seem to think my work is allright and have taken the trouble to say so," he noted. He had decided not to accompany the cast into town for a Memorial Day (then called Decoration Day) spree: "They'll probably all get drunk as hell and I don't like to do that when I'm working." The scenery was stunning: "El Capitan rises sheerly about 2000 ft or more from the floor of the valley and is in the shape of a gigantic cathedral spire. It is positively magnificent in its coloring and lordly solitude." Not so the dirty, dour, bedraggled Indians on a reservation where the picture was shot. Other than a trading post and a few small houses, there was not much to see. In close quarters, the stars complained about having to share tents: "Jon Hall acted babyish and got what he wanted. I said nothing and got as good accommodation as any." But sand got into everything because of the high winds. For entertainment they watched a Gene Autry production, "the corniest bit of picture making I've ever seen. We all just howled." Dana had obtained a baby prairie dog for David: "The natives tell me they make wonderful pets." He mentioned notes from Aggie and David and that "Gramp" (William Murray) had undergone serious surgery and "would appreciate your dropping in just to say hello."

Mary's letters made a "banquet of reading" that the camp envied, and Dana promised to keep writing himself so that her replies continued. Did she, by the way, cook up the fan letter he had received? He called it a "work of art." "I've had a lot of fun out of it," he assured her. "The gang thought it was wonderful." He was lonesome, he told Mary, "I'd give one of my beautifully straightened teeth for a look at your wonderful smile and those love-laden eyes—not even to mention the feel of your arms about me."

Mary answered his call, and after her visit, he wrote, "Ever since arriving here there has always been the desire to have you share the beauty. Somehow there just isn't the pleasure in anything that is there when you are with me!" This would become a refrain in letters to her from wherever the movies sent him. "In only a few months I have come to depend on you for everything—even my enjoyment of nature." He was cordial but taciturn on movie sets, but far happier at home. "Sometime when I'm a big star (like Jon Hall)," he joked, "we will have a tent all to ourselves and you can stay as long as you like." The society of movie sets almost never engaged him, so that when he told Mary "I don't think other people even know what real love is," he was expressing more than just a longing for her. It was essential to his own nature not to invest his feelings in these "other people" who took the unreality of movie making so seriously.

Kit Carson contains a good many action sequences, and evidently Dana did not work with a stunt double: "I fell off my horse in the midst of 15 or 20 charging mustangs but had the presence of mind enough to lie still and so escaped unhurt. They were shooting to scare the horses and believe me, they did. Mine just jumped right out from under me. But I got right back on and did it again." George Seitz, a versatile director of B movies, handles the action sequences well, although he does not do much with the awesome landscape, except for panoramic shots of stunning rock formations towering over valleys traveled by the wagon train headed for California, guided by Carson and Fremont. Jon Hall was just then coming into his own as the hero of action adventure films. Dana does not seem to have thought much of Hall in their second film together. Both actors were straitjacketed by parts that had long-haired Hall, dressed in fringed buckskin, playing the drawling, informal scout whose every other word seems to be "reckon," and Dana, in short curly hair and attired in an immaculate uniform, performing as the ramrod soldier who stiffens at every departure from decorum.

Kit Carson did not make Dana Andrews a star, but it established him as a second lead and at least a contender for leading roles in other B pictures. More importantly, the picture featured the sort of honorable character that Dana Andrews would come to personify. The reviewer for the *Hollywood Reporter* (August 27, 1940) rightly deplored the film's uninspired cinematography, inept screenplay, and Hall's perfunctory performance, while noting that "among the principals, Dana Andrews comes close to drawing top honors."

When *Kit Carson* came to Huntsville in October 1940, Norma and her mother invited Dana's mother and sister Mary to a showing. Mary wrote to tell Dana about how his friends all turned out to see the picture. He stole the show, and everyone admired his good looks, Mary reported, not to mention his acting. Norma was just as excited about his performance and enjoyed watching his mother take it all in. Dana was beginning to get letters from people who knew him when. "You probably don't remember me but our family went to the Baptist church where your father served as pastor. . . .You used to fascinate me by putting a wire in your mouth & bringing it out the back of your head; in your ear & out your nose," wrote Rosene Cagle Temby.

CHAPTER 9

Fox
1941–44

IT WOULD BE several months before Dana would appear in another film. Tired of waiting for screen roles, he joined Eighteen Actors, a group of Pasadena Playhouse regulars that included Victor Jory, Byron Foulger, and his wife Dorothy Adams, as well as Mary Todd, who performed in small cast plays sometimes at the Playhouse and sometimes on tour. Playhouse actor Oliver Prickett recalled that they were "just great . . . These were old friends, and they just got together and formulated this thing. . . . They would do it on, say, Friday, Saturday and Sunday; over a weekend they would stage a production. They didn't have any monetary interests other than keeping their heads above water. . . . you can imagine it was quite a session to determine the next play that they would do. But it was a fun, extracurricular type thing. We were as proud of them as of anything."

A good role in an A-film still eluded Dana Andrews in spite of his diligent and praiseworthy work. Never very good at coping with downtime—he always had to be doing something that demanded his entire concentration—Dana turned to gardening, cultivating azaleas, gardenias, and camellias, among other flowers, and trucking in soil, compost, and other amendments, as he did during his stay with the Murrays. As any serious gardener knows, planting and transplanting, deciding which varieties work best in various locations, can be an all-consuming and deeply satisfying activity. Gardening means constructing your own world and exercising complete control over you own domain, not an option otherwise available for a contract actor who had to take what was offered. Hours working in a garden are dream-like in their intensity, and they provide a grounding experience not available on a studio lot. Dana's letters home to Mary convey just how temporary picture making seemed, however pleasurable the change of scenery and the camaraderie of sets.

Making pictures was hard work, to be sure, and he enjoyed that aspect of the business, but it was also boring and exhausting—not only because of the early calls, but also because of the tedium of repeated takes that depended on *everything* (the actors, the lighting, the sound, the cameras, and often the weather) synching together. Watching an incompetent or at best uninspired contract director work with contract actors on a B picture demoralized Dana, and he let his disappointment show to Ida Zeitlin, for example, when she did her profile of him for *Modern Screen*.

For nearly three years (1941–44) Dana would appear in a motley assemblage of roles that rarely required much from him. During this period he was often depressed about his career, even though in the eyes of other actors his steady diet of parts and split contract with Goldwyn and Fox put him in an enviable position. He loathed the demeaning role of an on-call actor. What kind of world was Dana building for himself? Isn't that what his father had wondered? Well, at least Dana could plant himself in the firm soil of his garden. Even better, there was Mary to josh him out of his dour days, telling him that both of them had invested far too much already for him to quit. And behind her were Twomey and Wardlaw, not only still high on Dana's future, but expecting to *collect* on it. Their hopes were never merely mercenary, but capitalizing on their stake in Dana meant their vindication. The money, Dana well knew, had to be made—not only out of gratitude and fairness to them, but as tribute to the faith they had put in him and that he had put in himself. At a time when he had almost nothing to show for himself, they had placed their bets in the high-risk world of Hollywood.

In retrospect, it seems like a strange concatenation of forces, personalities, and events: this Texas boy striving to achieve the Horatio Alger myth of success and fathered by a man who believed in the doctrine of justification by faith; the businessmen who believed in a return-on-investment economy; and a factory-like motion picture production system that used actors like interchangeable parts and, yet also created "stars." The actors who survived and even triumphed (like Gary Cooper and Humphrey Bogart, two of the stars Dana greatly admired) cultivated in both their acting styles and their off-screen lives a deep reserve that restored some semblance of integrity—even though, they, too, performed their share of run-of-the-mill roles.

Thank God for Mary. Holding on to her meant holding on to a dream that often appeared evanescent and receded farther with each do-nothing performance. "I don't know if I would have given up my career," Dana told reporter Jack Holland, "but it would certainly have been easy for me to toss things overboard without her constructive confidence." No one else—certainly not those directors and producers—could be trusted. Not Allan Dwan and Edward Small (the producer of *Kit Carson*) who had touted their star-making powers. Not even the legendary John Ford, director of *Stage Coach* (1939), the film that made John Wayne a star, and the Henry Fonda star turn, *The Grapes of Wrath* (1940), could deliver. He cast Dana in *Tobacco Road*, his first A-list picture, and said: "You look very good. The studio'll be interested in you after this," although the result was merely second lead in a tawdry Technicolor B film, *Belle Star*, starring Randolph Scott.

In *Tobacco Road* (released March 7, 1941), Dana plays Captain Tim Harmon, a peripheral character in a beautifully photographed but dull version of Erskine Caldwell's best-selling novel and Broadway sensation. The main problem is the script, which bowdlerizes the raunchy Deep South lingo that regaled New York audiences and novel readers. In Depression-era Georgia, the Lesters are about to be thrown off their property because their landlord, Captain Tim, has lost his land to bank foreclosure. Even so, Captain Tim cheerfully provides some help to the struggling family in the form of money for rent and seed. Although Dana is cast in a paternalistic role, he avoids any hint of condescension, delivering his lines with persuasive affection and familiarity. A still from the film shows Dana, nattily dressed in a suit, gripping a picket fence and smiling broadly. This man *knows* and cherishes the Lesters, while understanding their failings. When the patriarch's wife asks if it is all right to buy some snuff with the Captain's money, the Captain replies, "If snuffs gonna help you to get Jeeter to work Ada, get all you want." As film critic Bernard Dick observes, Dana does his last scene beautifully, showing compassion toward Jeeter, but not indulging him. "He gives Jeeter a chance to reclaim his property . . . although we know it will never happen. The final scene is one of great poignancy, and Andrews is the catalyst, without whose blend of sympathy and firmness the ending would never have had such an emotional impact."

In *Belle Star* (released September 5, 1941), Dana has his first romantic scene with Gene Tierney. He looks dashing in a Ronald Colman sort of way, playing Union officer Major Thomas Crail. He is in love with Belle Shirley (Tierney), the sister of his friend, Ed Shirley (John Shepperd, aka Shepperd Strudwick). The South has lost the war and Ed returns to tell Belle that Missouri must accept the Union victory. The rebellious Belle will have none of it, although she softens when Crail, who courted her before the war, gently tries to reconcile her to defeat even as he woos her. Dana has his suave and debonair moment, murmuring to Tierney, her back to a sheltering tree, that his blue uniform almost looks grey in the moonlight. This romantic scene had no off-screen counterpart. During shooting, Tierney suffered from an eye ailment that became so severe there was talk of replacing her. Dana liked her well enough, but he felt only compassion for a co-star whose physical and mental problems would multiply in the course of her career.

Dana's Major Crail is another version of the John C. Fremont character in *Kit Carson*, although the sufferings of the Civil War are reflected in Crail's reaction to Belle's hard feelings: Why shouldn't she reject defeat since "we both fought for what we thought was right." Dana delivers the line with delicate force, which is perhaps why James McKay notes in *Dana Andrews: The Face of Noir* that this nuanced performance contains a trace of the "troubled" character that Dana would hone in later roles.

Most reviewers barely noticed Dana's performance. They gave him, at best, a few lines of commendation, spending most of their copy on Gene Tierney, whom they hailed as an upcoming star. *Belle Star* would not be worth this much attention, except that it drove home to Dana just how shameful and slapdash a product Hollywood could put together. While not offering an explicit comment on the film's derivative and racist plot, which had slaves speaking in hushed and adoring tones about Belle, a knock-off of Scarlett O'Hara, he expressed his distaste by simply treating the picture as beneath contempt. What did he get after John Ford had praised him? *Belle Star*, Dana told Ida Zeitlin, as if just the title of the film said it all.

The film's director, Irving Cummings, mainly known for action pictures and musicals, told him, "You're a good actor. I'm going to tell Darryl about you. They should give you a lead." And Zanuck was impressed with Dana's performance, giving him a starring role in *Swamp Water*, originally intended for Henry Fonda. First, though, Dana would have to turn in another small supporting performance in Howard Hawks's *Ball of Fire*, which provided him with about four weeks of work in September 1941.

According to Dana, Hawks specifically requested him: "There's a boy I want," the director told Goldwyn. "He's a nice boy," Goldwyn said, "but he can't play gangsters." The undeterred Hawks got Dana anyway. Why Goldwyn said Dana could not play such parts is not clear, except that in Hollywood actors were quickly typed. Dana had already been slotted into roles that gave him the second lead, which meant he remained a noble contender but in the end would lose the girl. Goldwyn could be a shrewd observer of talent, forecasting that Ronald Colman and Vilma Banky, at the early stages of their careers, would make a sensational starring team. But he could also blunder badly, trying for years to make a star of Anna Sten, a Russian beauty the producer believed he could make into another Garbo, before abandoning his futile campaign amid much joking about Goldwyn's Last Sten.

In *Ball of Fire* (released December 2, 1941), Gary Cooper plays Bertram Potts, a professor who falls in love with nightclub singer Sugarpuss O'Shea, played by Barbara Stanwyck. Dana appears in four scenes as Joe Lilac, the gangster Sugarpuss is supposed to marry. Lilac, with a cigarette nearly always in his mouth, mocks the district attorney's threat to put him in the specially designed 20,000-volt electric chair, mildly inquiring, "AC or DC?" Lilac is silky smooth whether he is talking to the police or to the professor. He can get mean, turning his cigarette into a missile by flicking it at a table of professors who are helping Bertram harbor Sugarpuss. But Lilac keeps his cool—hardly breaking the elegant line of his superbly tailored suit—even when he punches Professor Potts with a straight left.

Sugarpuss no longer finds Lilac's brand of dapper thuggery appealing. She prefers the maladroit professor, with his sincerity and endearing inexperience as a lover. Dana's Joe, by contrast, is all show, with a veneer of manners he drops whenever his vital interests are affected. Students of acting ought to observe how comfortably Dana fits into his expensive clothes, exuding the elegance of power and the arrogance of good looks. The picture's denouement features a fight in which the deftly jabbing Lilac is overcome by Professor Pott's clumsy windmill attack.

Dana loved to watch Gary Cooper, the epitome of underplaying, work. Lewis Milestone in his unpublished autobiography remarks that you could watch Cooper all day and swear he was not acting and that nothing good could come of it on screen. But then the camera caught every nuance of his performance. On set, Cooper seemed even more listless when he was not acting. Cooper had a motto, Dana later told his son-in-law, Tim: "Never stand when you can sit. Never sit when you can lie down." Dana said Cooper was always leaning on something; he would drape himself on whatever was nearby.

Dana's brief but strategically placed scenes elicited few comments from reviewers. Louella Parsons, always kind to Dana, called him a "very good looking boy and an excellent actor and will go far." That Howard Hawks, already celebrated for pictures such as *Scarface* (1932) and *Bringing Up Baby* (1938), insisted on using Dana showed the director's confidence in a young actor who could bring the right light touch to the role, with an interpretation quite independent of the Cagney/Bogart school of gangster performances.

Dana modeled his character on Bugsy Siegel, whose paramour, Virginia "Sugar" Hill, appears in the film as a showgirl as a result of ingratiating herself with Goldwyn. Siegel was a natty dresser and cared about appearances, emphasizing that only "class" counted. His carefully combed hair, hand-tailored suits, and silk shirts are copied in Dana's meticulous portrayal. Siegel hung around Hollywood and even dreamed of becoming an actor. Dana met him once at the Formosa, where many movie actors dined and drank. As his daughter Kathy recalled:

> Dad met all sorts at The Formosa and other spots. Staying out late and meeting well-known people, including notorious ones, in interesting lines of work other than his own came with that territory. He had access to them once he, too, was well-known. I'm sure that that was an important, intriguing part of the nights out. He would not have sat on a stool and chatted with the bartender all night or sat stoically sipping on a drink. He wasn't simply seeking drinking companions. There were times when he was looking for excitement or relief from boredom.

At the Formosa, conveniently located across the street from the Goldwyn Studios, Siegel kept an upstairs office and ran a bookie operation.

Dana's performance is the thrilling perfection of a persona that Siegel had labored over for years. He worried about his thinning hair and tried all sorts of thickening agents. Did Dana tell Siegel about Hess's Hair Milk, the product the actor used to enhance the luster of his own healthy-looking hair? (Goldwyn used to tease him, wondering aloud if Dana's coiffure had been produced with an eggbeater.) In *Hollywood Babylon*, Kenneth Anger reports that Siegel attended the premier of *Ball of Fire* and socialized with Dana, Howard Hawks, Gary Cooper, and Barbara Stanwyck. A few years later, Dana would tell Mary that he had a gun he needed to return to Siegel.

Dana had now performed well for two A-list directors, John Ford and Howard Hawks. And yet neither Sam Goldwyn nor Darryl Zanuck seemed prepared to cast him in an important role in an important picture. But so much of the machinery of Hollywood studio production was like work on prototypes that in their final form result in outcomes that no producer, let alone an actor, could foresee. While Dana worked his way through a frustrating series of small parts and second leads, the scenario churning process at Fox was moving toward a denouement that would provide the actor with the most satisfying experience of his career. He would be working not only with a world-class director and actors, but also with material that came close to articulating his own spiritual autobiography. If no other picture—even far more successful ones—ever gave Dana Andrews quite the fulfillment of *Swamp Water* (released July 24, 1942), it is because he never again had a role that so perfectly expressed what he once had been and what he had wanted to become.

Dana was still standing in line behind stars like Gary Cooper and Henry Fonda, the latter now in consideration for the lead in *Swamp Water*. *Swamp Water* had first appeared as a novel serialized in *The Saturday Evening Post* in November and December 1940, when it intrigued Julian Johnson, a Fox associate producer. The studio bought film rights for $15,000. Set in the enchanting but also forbidding Okefenokee swamp in southern Georgia, the story featured characters that were, said a Fox staffer reporting to Zanuck, "primitive people—people who live close to nature—people whose passions flare and subside with equal violence. There is something fascinating about these people—something electric in the atmosphere. It is a natural story, there is nothing forced or phony about it." Just so, since the novel had been written by Vereen Bell, a Georgia journalist saturated with the lives of his swampland characters. Kenneth MacGowan, another Fox producer, and Dudley Nichols, one of the studio's top writers, agreed with Julian Johnson's judgment, but only if the plot of this picturesque story were made more melodramatic. Otherwise, as another producer put it, Fox might make only "a very fine small picture." A week later Zanuck responded to Julian Johnson's summary of reactions to the novel, saying it was a story that "grows on you" and that the chief character, Ben Ragan, "is a natural for Henry Fonda." Zanuck also realized that Ben's dog, Trouble, "is almost human," and would provide a key element in making the audience care about Ben and his world. Usually quick to suggest ideas for a treatment and screenplay, on this occasion the studio head depended on Nichols to write a piece of pure cinema that would not waste "an inch of film," but with the "smell of earth and lifeblood in it."

By May 1, 1941, Nichols, after consulting closely with the novel's author, had a first draft continuity script to show Zanuck. The novel's villain, Tom Keefer, a murderer who had taken refuge in the swamp, seemed "too obvious" and was softened, but also given more nuance as a natural philosopher, changes that would suit Walter Brennan quite well. The novel was also fitted with a Hollywood happy ending. On May 28, Zanuck gave an enthusiastic go-ahead to Nichols's screenplay, mainly advising that the plot be tightened and the action condensed. Dean Jagger, the star of *Brigham Young* (1940), was up for the lead as was Dana, who was scheduled for an "exhaustive test." What finally led to Dana's casting is not clear, although in retrospect the role seems the one he was born to play.

Four months earlier, Jean Renoir (1894–1979), acclaimed director of *Grand Illusion* (1937) and *The Rules of the Game* (1939), arrived in Hollywood ready to work for Twentieth Century-Fox. He had barely escaped from Nazi-occupied France, but was already taking English lessons, reading Fox scripts, and urging Zanuck to let him film an American subject because he dreaded "directing sequences with moustached policeman and gentlemen in velvet jackets and imperial beards parading against a bogus-Montmartre, bogus-cafe background." Alexander Sesonske notes in a meticulous study of the picture that Renoir, trying to bring his son Alain to America, may well have been attracted to *Swamp Water* because of the fraught relationship between Ben Ragan and his father, Thursday, a conflict that is also what made the picture so significant to Dana Andrews.

Renoir liked Nichols's script and Zanuck's proposed cast, although he expressed his disappointment at not working with Tyrone Power, who the director admired as both an actor and a man. "I do not say this in disparagement of Dana Andrews, whom I know too little through his brief performance in *Tobacco Road*, in which he was excellent," Renoir wrote Zanuck on May 23. Three days later, Zanuck replied that Power was not right for the role: "His voice is a quality voice and every effort we have made in the past to adapt it to backwoods requirements has completely failed." Dana was, in Zanuck's words, the "new boy" and would be a "sensation in the film. He is an outstanding actor and is now giving a wonderful performance in BELLE STARR . . . and unless I am seriously mistaken, this is the next big star on the lot." Renoir soon became Dana's champion, later claiming he had discovered this new star—perhaps because at the last minute, Zanuck proposed replacing Dana with Shepperd Strudwick (he had played Belle Star's brother), and Renoir successfully argued Dana's case

Like Dana, Renoir was no fan of studio-produced films or, for that matter, of California, which the director called "a sort of desert, artificially irrigated." The deal making and fidgeting between projects disturbed him, and he pressed Zanuck to give him *Swamp Water*, which Renoir wanted to film far from the Fox lot. A wary studio head assigned Irving Pichel, a Fox producer to supervise dialogue and permitted some location shooting in Georgia, but he told an incredulous Renoir that most of the picture would be made in Hollywood, where a "perfectly fine swamp" would be constructed. Renoir was learning just how tightly controlled a world he had signed up for, and chafed against it much as Dana had done. Dana truly respected only a handful of directors, and Renoir was one of them.

Both Renoir and Dana enjoyed the liberation of their June 1941 jaunt to Waycross, Georgia, where they filmed the swamp scenes that make the opening sequence of the picture so enthralling. On June 25, the *Waycross Journal-Herald* interviewed Dana shortly after his arrival: "'It's my big chance,' laughed young Andrews a bit groggy after his first plane trip but fascinated by it all to such a degree he hadn't been able to sleep." Dana explained his father had been a minister in DeFuniak Springs, Florida: "'That,' he drawled, 'should be a good start.' He is by the way a cousin of Senator Andrews of Florida, a fact of which he is justly proud. He is conscientious and wants to do an honest to goodness sincere portrayal of the character," the newspaper reported.

Dana loved to listen to Lem Griffis, subject of a *Life* magazine profile, and to absorb the swamp denizen's corny tall tales, taking in the "wild and deceptively dangerous" environment "too beautiful for words." On a day his stunt double had all the work, Dana decided to go fishing. As he wrote to Mary on June 28, "a big alligator nosed up by my boat and swelled out and 'blew' at me. They do that to try to scare you away. I hit at him with the paddle and he went under." Just such an alligator can be seen early in the picture gliding past a moving boat. In his letters Dana seems not to have wanted to worry Mary over the risks he was taking. In fact, he fell into the water eleven times while learning to pole a boat. Dana was the only cast member sent to Georgia, and he quickly developed a friendship with Renoir. The director remembered struggling in his uncertain English with a local girl standing in for Anne Baxter. When the girl rushed her scene, Renoir shouted "Miss, wait a little," but his "wait" sounded like "wet," and when the embarrassed stand-in turned to Dana to ask, "Does he really want me to?" Dana replied, "These foreign directors sometimes have strange ideas." It was wicked, but Renoir recounted the scene with relish in his memoirs.

Dana was pleased with the cast, especially Walter Huston. Indeed, in Raymond Durgnat's description, Huston's character is a ringer for Charles Forrest Andrews: "A dour, unforgiving spirituality looms in the face of Ben's father Thursday." Dana had qualms only about Virginia Gilmore, who would play Mabel, Ben's first sweetheart. Dana looked forward to meeting Vereen Bell the next day. "I'm beginning to talk like a native and even they think I must come from this part of the country," he reported. At the same time, away from home his anxiety and longing for Mary intensified. He closed his next letter, "Darling, I love you and miss you like a man would miss his sight."

Meanwhile, Renoir was describing "a land where nature is at the same time soft and hostile." He wanted the whole film to reflect that paradox, although, in truth, only the initial and closing sequences approximate the director's vision. Too many close-ups and reaction shots, mandated by Zanuck, ruined the director's shooting style (long takes with deep focus shots and a mobile camera). Renoir's art clashed with Zanuck's commercial sensibility, which demanded shot and counter shot in rapid succession. The studio head wanted less emphasis on different camera angles and fewer dolly shots; otherwise, the film would go way over its modest budget ($601,900). In Alexander Senonske's terse summing-up, the picture does indeed seem a perversion of Renoir's style, instead favoring the Hollywood way: "a stern father who cannot express his love for his son; a brave and just young hero who must win his independence; an innocent man wrongly condemned who becomes a second, more understanding and more articulate father figure; two women—one sexy, self-confident and perfidious; one pure and lowly but spirited, who is surprised that someone would love her."

Whatever disappointments Renoir experienced, he told Nichols, "I got good performances from Dana Andrews and Anne Baxter." Zanuck concurred, noting that Dana's work was "sincere, particularly in his light moments when he is allowed to smile and be relaxed." Like Norma, Zanuck thought Dana looked much better without a hat. The rapport between Dana Andrews and Anne Baxter, playing Julie, the downtrodden daughter of Tom Keefer, the picture's putative villain, is palpable, the product of an off-screen affinity that Dana rarely experienced with his leading ladies. For the first time, Dana had a script and enough screen time to develop a character that liberated him from the stifling roles that had demoralized him.

But for Dana Andrews, *Swamp Water* represented more than deliverance from Hollywood formulae. When Hannah, Thursday's wife and Ben's stepmother, remarks that the "funny thing about you men is that you won't let on to each other how you feel," she articulates the trouble Dana had with his own father. Like CF, Thursday expresses his love in stern commandments, forbidding Ben to enter the swamp in search of his dog and ordering him to return home within two days. Refusing to abide by his father's decree, Ben angrily leaves home only to encounter Mabel, his girlfriend, who marvels that Ben and his father could get into such a terrific fight over a dog. If the overt plot of *Swamp Water* is simplistic Hollywood fare, the subtext is not. It concerns the overbearing Southern male world that drove Dana at an early age to confide in Norma, and that drives Ben to find the right girl to share his own way of becoming a man.

The next long sequence of shots show Ben alone in the swamp, poling his boat along the mirrored surface of the water. When Ben sounds his hunting horn and hears the baying of his hound Trouble, he plunges right into the water. Here Renoir's mobile camera tracks man and nature, interacting in this soft yet hostile environment without a word. As Ben moves forward, the vegetation thickens, and he leaves behind the world outside the swamp. Ben returns home with Trouble after a long sojourn in the swamp with Tom Keefer, who indeed does become a kind of second father to him, teaching Ben the ways of the swamp and revealing the perfidy of a society that could turn against an innocent man. But Ben's own father, although relieved to have his son home, denounces his disobedience. Their argument is not remarkable for its dialogue, but rather for the force and deeper register of Dana's voice. When Ben declares to Thursday, "I'm my own man," he does so in a baritone that is a good octave below what can be heard in Dana's earlier performances. All those years of singing lessons pay off in this scene. The drop in Dana's voice signals his character's depth of feeling, a guttural assertion of his own authority.

Cast out of the house like CF's prodigal son, Ben is without a family to support him and is naturally drawn to the picture's other outcast, Julie. Anne Baxter (then only eighteen) plays Julie with the tentative, darting elegance of a deer. Indeed, as the abused servant of a storekeeper, she seems barely human to the other characters. Only Ben speaks up for this dirty-looking girl who consorts more with cows than she does with people. Ben is attracted to her, as he is to Trouble, because both are creatures who remain apart like Tom Keefer, who regards the swamp as another world.

Why Dana disliked Virginia Gilmore is not clear, but her character, Mabel, stands for everything he loathed about the coercive way society treats individuals. Mabel, like Ben's father, wants him to behave by conventional rules. But after returning from the swamp with marsh animal hides to sell, Ben announces that there is no one in the town he will have to say "sir" to anymore. Mabel rejects such "big talk" and Ben's plan to return to the swamp. She wants Ben to conform to a conventional courtship, while he wants to live by his own rules. Dana plays Ben as a risk taker who will make money his own way and establish his own kind of respectability.

Since Mabel has arranged for another man to take her to a dance, Ben shows up with the unspoiled Julie, who is grateful for his attention and protection. He has bought her a new dress for the occasion, but she does not know how to dance, and keeps bumping into Mabel and her partner. Not yet his own man, Ben is daunted by his father's presence, especially when Thursday points out that Ben has not owned up to bringing Tom Keefer's daughter (Ben introduces her to Thursday as Julie Gordon). Ben's declaration of independence, in other words, is as difficult to achieve as Dana's own, since the both actor and the character he plays still wanted, in some measure, to defer to the very communities they could no longer comfortably inhabit. Ben cannot, like Tom Keefer, simply reject a corrupt society and seek the solitude of the swamp; on the contrary, he must find a way to live with the world that bore him without compromising what he wants to become. And so must Julie, who Hannah teaches to dance. In a later scene Julie dances a graceful solo that foreshadows her reunion with Ben after he has absolved himself of accusations that he has collaborated with Tom Keefer in stealing a hog and proven, as well, that Tom Keefer is not a murderer.

Swamp Water, in true Hollywood fashion, makes Ben the hero though his discovery that others have committed the crime Keefer was tried for before he escaped to the swamp. Thus Ben restores Tom to his daughter and to society, even as he redeems society by obliging the community to acknowledge its injustice to Tom. Ben is also reconciled to his father in an earlier scene in which Thursday stops a group of men from torturing Ben, plunging him under water in an effort to make Ben reveal Tom Keefer's whereabouts before anyone realizes Tom is innocent. Back home, Thursday nurses his son and tells him there will be no more disputes between them. Such scenes are too neatly resolved, of course, but Walter Huston's performance exudes the yearning attachment that is apparent in CF's last letters to Dana.

Dana was thirty-two years old during the filming of *Swamp Water*, a good decade older than the character he plays, and yet even in close-ups his animated face seems to reveal a boy just entering his adult years. This is the Dana of 1931, still uncertain but on his way to discovering what it is given him to do. Dana was no method actor, but in *Swamp Water* he had a part that compelled him to draw on his own experience.

Dana's mother loved the picture because her son set an innocent man free, although she squirmed a little in the love scenes when Dana's kisses seemed too long. Charles summed up just how close to home the picture had come:

> Dear Carver,
> "Swamp Water" was a masterpiece of its kind and you in it were preponderantly Carver as opposed to Dana. But perhaps I should explain. Your performance was nostalgically reminiscent of the erring but lovably human Carver, the object of my ill-concealed adoration from boyhood. While in "Ball of Fire" you were distinctly the Dana Andrews of Hollywood—cosmopolite, suave gentleman, and perceptibly in process of becoming a finished (polished) actor. Both performances gave clear evidence of progress both in grade of pictures and quality of acting.

The authenticity that Renoir, Walter Brennan, Anne Baxter, and Dana brought to the film made it a box office success, especially in the South. Brennan loved to tell stories "by the hour," Dana told Clyde Williams, and the two actors formed a friendship that became part of the rapport their characters share in the picture. Renoir had taken John Ford's advice and had used many of Ford's actors—including John Carradine and Ward Bond, who had already appeared with Dana in *Kit Carson* and *Tobacco Road*—to create an impressive ensemble, praised by reviewers who otherwise thought poorly of the picture's sentimentality and "hokum." Several reviews singled out Dana's performance. The *Motion Picture Herald* called him a "new star." The *Hollywood Reporter* hailed him as emerging from the picture with "commanding personal honors." And John Hobart in the *San Francisco Chronicle* observed that Dana had secured his "first real part . . . and plays it with a maturity of understanding that should establish him right away as one of the best younger actors in Hollywood."

A disappointed Dana did not see his stock rise much. Indeed, he called his next assignment, playing brash and dashing journalist Bill Roberts in *Berlin Correspondent*, "a stinker." In the half dozen or so movie magazine articles that appeared after Dana's breakthrough role in *Laura*, *Berlin Correspondent* (shot in May and June and released September 11, 1942) is not even mentioned. His Clark Gable mustache looks tacked on. Co-star

Virginia Gilmore (Mabel in *Swamp Water*) plays Karen Hauen, a Gestapo employee Roberts falls in love with. She speaks with an American accent, and nothing in her manner or tone is even faintly Germanic. Improbability follows improbability as Karen rejects her Gestapo fiancé and races in a car to successfully rescue Roberts, who has been in a concentration camp because he has engineered the escape of Karen's father, who spied for the Allies. The film is on a par with that offensive television series *Hogan's Heroes*. It is also a ludicrous rip-off of Hitchcock's *Foreign Correspondent* (1940). Director Eugene Forde, best known for his Charlie Chan pictures, is stymied by static cinematography that is the diametrical opposite of the mobile camera work in Hitchcock's stirring work. The best that can be said for *Berlin Correspondent* is that it contains some well-executed comic scenes, a rarity in a Dana Andrews picture. To the bumbling Nazi spy who has trouble keeping up with him, Roberts turns and says, "For a moment I thought I lost you. Come on—let's go!" It is a funny moment, epitomizing Dana's perfect grasp of his character's brisk and business-like sense of humor.

Berlin Correspondent moves right along for seventy minutes of silliness and stupidity, which perhaps makes it an overlooked camp classic. Recent viewers have found the picture entertaining, making allowances for its role as an American propaganda picture made in the aftermath of the Pearl Harbor attack.. However much he derided this work, he gives an engaging performance. The *Hollywood Reporter* (August 18, 1942) praised Dana's "easy assurance" in a "tight melodrama you will enjoy." *Variety* (August 13, 1942) was just as complimentary, although the *New York Herald Tribune* reviewer judged the picture implausible and synthetic, and Thomas Pryor in the *New York Times* called it "cheap melodrama" unworthy of the "fight to stamp out in Germany today [what] is too terribly real and vital to our future existence."

Dana was fortunate in his next role in *The Ox-Bow Incident*, a literary and film classic that he always cited as one of his proudest achievements. Shot in thirty days in the early summer of 1942, this art western had an unlikely director, William Wellman, who scorned pretensions about movies as art. Clint Eastwood remembered his impressions of Wellman as a director who shot his films like a commando raid, which actually served the director well. Wellman was a contract director, but as critic Frank Thompson observes, Wellman sometimes made pictures "for himself." In this case, he made one that constituted a stirring scrutiny of male bonding codes and perversions of justice that is worthy of Fritz Lang's haunting noir cinema. Every producer in Hollywood had turned down

The Ox-Bow Incident (which cost Wellman only $500 to acquire) except for Darryl Zanuck, the only one with enough nerve to film "an out-of-the-ordinary story for the prestige, rather than the dough," the director said. Nominated for best picture, *The Ox-Bow Incident* lost the Academy Award to *Casablanca*.

The Ox-Bow Incident is often treated as a suspense picture, as though the three men accused of rustling and murdering rancher Larry Kinkaid are not found to be innocent until after they are hung. The lynchers learn from the sheriff, who arrives too late to save the unjustly condemned, that Kinkaid is wounded but alive and the rustlers have been apprehended. I have not spoiled the picture for those who have not seen it because it is clear from the start that the vigilantes are acting upon nothing more than rumor. They are motivated by feelings, not facts, by prejudices, not perceptions. Indeed, the last third of the picture is an extended comment on the folly of this organized mob. No one needs to wait until the end of the story to realize that Arthur Davies (Harry Davenport) represents the correct minority opinion that no punishment can be meted out for a crime that has not been established. In other words, *The Ox-Bow Incident* is a due process Western.

Dana's first scene occurs as Major Tetley (Frank Conroy), who is heading the vigilante expedition, arrives at a promontory. Perched atop this rise, the riders appear huge in the foreground, the result of a low angle shot that shows them peering down into the ox-bow, a depression in the land that is lit by campfire. Believing they have found their cattle rustlers, the men divide into two groups, presaging the internal conflict that emerges when they split over whether they should hang the three suspects on the spot or return them to town for trial. They descend slowly into the pit of their desire to punish the men who are presumed to have murdered their neighbor. Tetley calls a halt as his contingent comes to ground nearly level with the campsite. The camera slowly pans left to right and rests for just a moment on the prone figure of Donald Martin (Dana Andrews), then cuts to Tetley, who signals his men forward, with the group dividing once again as they veer off in opposite directions from a huge oak tree that is the scene's focal point.

Never before had Dana's appearance in a picture been so carefully choreographed and dramatically structured. Wellman, whose work Dana had admired since he had first run *Wings* on a projector at the Dorothy Theatre in Huntsville, Texas, had now placed Dana precisely in the world of cinematic art that had been his destination for nearly two decades. During breaks in the filming, Dana had done the unusual, talking with cast and crew about his own technical feats, synching sound recordings to the shots and scenes of silent film. Like Wellman himself, Dana could visualize the devastating impact of those low angle shots, and the diagonal composition of two descending lines of men on horseback riding toward the doomed Donald Martin. These vigilantes are full of conviction and so loom large in their own eyes, yet they are also vultures preying on fellow creatures, helpless and taken unawares on the ground. When Tetley shouts, "Get Up!," the camera first alights on Juan Martinez (Anthony Quinn), whose cunning smile suggests deceit; then on Alva Hardwicke (Francis Ford), who responds to the gun pointed at him by covering his face with a blanket; and finally on Martin, sleeping soundly and enjoying the rest of the innocent, a slight smile on his face.

Dana is shot from above with Gil Carter (Henry Fonda) towering over him, gun in hand. In close-up, Dana swivels his head slightly left, then right, facing his accusers while the camera shoots him straight on—as if to show every side of the man who is plainly baffled by this ambush. "This is a posse—if that means anything to you," says Carter. In a high angle close-up shot, the startled Martin (only the campfire lights his face) blurts out, "But we haven't done anything," flicking his eyes, and moving his head ever so slightly to the left and right to again take in his accusers. His subtle gestures and barely visible eye movement reveal in almost microscopic fashion a man genuinely caught unaware. His incipient dread is detectable only when frames of film are slowed and repeatedly shown, reinforcing the kind of scrutiny Dana schooled himself to observe in the silent era.

Tetley is shown intently watching each man's face as his weapons are confiscated. And yet he does not see what is made plain to the movie audience. A reverse high angle shot of Tetley's son stooping to collect Martin's gun segues to Martin, who makes eye contact with the boy as soon as the two are on the same level. Martin smiles at the young man, who smiles back. This is the moment when Dana establishes his character's innocence. The next shot, a profile portrait of the stony-faced Tetley that emphasizes his hawk-like features, suggests he cannot see Martin's humanity. Then the two flanks of the posse rush in on horseback to corral the three alleged murderers. Martin looks both ways, demanding to know the charges against him. Rustling? That notion amazes him, and his face seems to open up in wonder. But when murder is mentioned he blanches and swallows hard, his eyes opening wider to take in the implications of the accusation. He stares straight ahead, suddenly immobilized by the very thought of the crime, until he mutters an assurance to

"Dad" (as he calls his older companion) that there must be some mistake. When the posse proves unreasonable—refusing to check out Martin's story—Dana's jaw juts out firmly, and his mouth becomes a tight line, as if to confirm Martin's conclusion that it is pointless to say more. But when a posse member starts swinging a noose, Martin swallows hard again and explains that the cattle in his possession have been purchased from Kinkaid, although Martin has no bill of sale. That is enough for the vengeance-seeking mob.

Because of this rush to justice, objections to hanging Martin and the others, however, begin to emerge from Arthur Davies and Gil Carter. Martin's eyes blaze as he projects his outraged innocence, which those prejudiced against him wildly misinterpret as "cool" deception. When Davies expresses his belief in Martin's innocence, Martin's smile reveals a fleeting hope, which is immediately dashed by Tetley, standing firm in more statuesque profile shots accentuating his aquiline nose. Martin finally bows his head and loses his composure, a humiliating sight that is unbearable to Carter, who tells Tetley that if there are any doubts, then Martin and the others need to be taken into custody and tried in a proper court. Finding his voice again, Martin brands his interrogation a "filthy comedy," and his outburst is rebuked with a slap from the deputy sheriff. Martin holds his head high when he refuses the deal Tetley offers: Tell them who killed Kinkaid, and they will let Martin go. "None of us killed anybody," Martin affirms in a profile shot that firmly establishes the rugged, terse, nobility that emerges in Dana's best performances. In response to Martin's plea, Tetley gives Martin some time to compose a letter to his wife, saying drily he does not want to give anyone "cause for complaint."

As the posse settles down to eat in a party-like atmosphere, Martin covers his face with one hand, agonizing over what to say to his wife. Running his fingers through his hair, Martin seems to unravel. But when Davies tries to show Martin's affecting letter to Tetley, Martin, overhearing them, jumps up and strides into the center of the screen, protesting: "What right have you to show him my letter!" This violation of privacy—really of his final moments—strikes at the core of Martin's manhood, and his outrage overcomes even his terrible fear of death and worries over what will happen to his family. "It's none of these murderers' business!" Martin cries, denouncing the cruelty and levity he has heard while writing to his wife. Martin becomes, in fact, the very picture of probity that results in Carter's realization that an innocent man is about to be hanged. When Martin demands that Davies return the letter to him, Davies points out that Martin's wife will want the letter to show to his children. "I'm sorry," Martin says, as if he had done an injustice to Davies. This unbearable scene is abruptly ended when Martinez tries to escape and is recaptured. Then Martin, in a three-quarter profile shot, watches the posse line up on opposing sides, for and against delaying judgment. The look Dana gives is one of expectation, neither hope nor despair, but rather intense concentration

Martin is the very picture of aroused integrity and seems to motivate Carter to stride into the center of the scene and the film frame, deliberately crossing by Tetley and joining the small band of men who have decided they cannot hang Martin. But not enough men choose the side of innocence, and the camera returns to Martin, who swallows hard again, recognizing his fate. The camera pans from Martin's point of view to the faces and figures of the merciless men, thus making his plight the viewer's own. Carter, Davies, and Martin's five other defenders, their backs to the camera, also become, like the audience, spectators at a hanging. Tetley asks Martin—now sitting in abject misery and shot in a left profile close-up that emphasizes his dishelved hair and discomposure—if he has any last messages. Martin, slightly trembling, can only shake his head.

This part of the film, intricately and reverently edited, is a crucifixion scene. Indeed, one shot places Martin against a rail bisecting a tree that forms a cross. Given two minutes to pray, Martin drops to his knees, bows his head, grips his hair, and then rises to ask Davies to get word to Martin's wife and make arrangements to care for his family. Proclaiming his innocence once more, Martin declares these men simply want to punish someone for what they have lost. It has nothing to do with justice. Martin suffers a final indignity when he is punched for speaking out and struggles against the mob subduing him. Martin's last word is his wife's name, "Miriam." This is a modern passion play that is nevertheless medieval in its almost formulaic quality, even while Wellman's direction and Dana's acting never forsake naturalism. Donald Martin is not merely a type of innocent man, but a very particular person finding his own way to grapple with injustice and death. Almost as shocking as the lynching itself (shown only in shadows), the group demonstrates an inability to recognize Martin's individuality and to sort through their own prejudices in order to discover who he really is. That obtuseness explains why it is so terrible that Davies cannot get anyone—not even the sympathetic Carter—to read Martin's letter to his wife. A perverse and willful desire to murder these men prevents their persecutors from even considering the letter as exonerating evidence. And Carter, having come this far, cannot confront his own shame.

Through his superb acting, Dana makes Martin a witness to his own character—and to the dignity of a human being violated. This was the actor's breakthrough performance, demonstrating that he was ready for even more ambitious parts. "A heart-wringing performance by Dana Andrews as the stunned and helpless leader of the doomed trio [of lynching victims] does much to make the picture a profoundly distressing tragedy," wrote Bosley Crowther (*New York Times*, May 10, 1943). Later (January 2, 1944), Crowther cited Andrews as one of the contenders for the New York Critics best actor award.

Why did Wellman and Fonda—both creators of positive American myths—choose to do this picture, despite knowing it was sure to be a box office failure? It was hardly the kind of upbeat fare available in wartime comedies and even in battlefield epics. Indeed, *The Ox-Bow Incident* was a rebuke to the rah-rah spirit of the times, which seemed to promote far too many self-congratulatory stories about American virtues. Wellman later told Clint Eastwood the picture's failure to do good business was Mrs. Zanuck's fault:

> Everyone at the studio was proud of the movie, but when Darryl screened it at home his wife said: "But this is terrible! How can you let them lynch Dana Andrews and Anthony Quinn?" The rumor spread that the movie was jinxed. So it only got a limited release. It was only when the movie was praised by French critics that Fox tried to run it again in New York.

Did "Wild Bill Wellman" want at least one picture that showed a side of himself he otherwise carefully concealed? Dana liked to tell a story about doing a climactic scene, when, in the midst of a noisy set, he asked the director if he could have some quiet time to work himself up to a proper pitch. Wellman, known for his raucous and even belligerent behavior on movie sets and for badgering actors, shouted: "Everybody quiet! The son-of-a-bitch is about to act!" The business of movie making and the art of acting made for strenuous moments at times, even for an actor like Dana Andrews who did not indulge in the pretensions of method actors or hold up productions to prepare for his scenes. Dana later called Wellman a "two-fisted sort of man," who told him that he joked on the set in order to prevent Dana from giving a hammy performance. Wellman and Dana also argued over the scene in which Donald Martin tears up. "Dana, dammit, *a man* won't cry here. Don't do it!" Dana objected: "You're wrong. A man in Martin's situation, about to be hanged for a crime he didn't commit and with a wife and two little children back home, *would cry*. Martin's no stoic." After a dozen retakes, Wellman conceded his actor's point. So much for those critics of Dana Andrews who have said he could only play stoics.

Dana believed Wellman had produced a beautiful film, but that like most directors he was just part of the Hollywood machine. Actors, too, were part of the assembly-line approach to picture production. Both Wellman and Fonda were taken prisoner by Zanuck, who exacted promises from them to work in inferior films as recompense for the unremunerative *Ox-Bow Incident*. Similarly, Dana next saw service not in another superior role, but instead reported for duty in another pedestrian second lead: this time in *Crash Dive*, shot in the summer of 1942 at the New London, Connecticut, submarine base and released December 23, 1943. He plays a submarine commander who loses the girl (Anne Baxter) to Tyrone Power, playing Dana's chief executive officer with all the savior-faire of a movie idol. Except for a few action sequences that entitled the special effects team to an Academy Award, the picture—made just before Power joined the marines—is forgettable. Dana, now the father of two children (Kathy was born on July 10, 1942) was, for the moment, excused from military service.

For an action picture, the shooting was uneventful—except during a scene when the submarine Dana was commanding became the target of a navy cruiser that began bearing down on him. A signal went out that Dana's sub was shooting at a hulk dummied up to look like a real boat. "They [the cruiser] were coming down with blood in their eyes and might have destroyed us until we explained what the hell we were doing. . . . It was a pretty scary moment there," Dana told Clyde Williams. Dana always seemed lonesome away from his family and compensated by writing love letters to Mary and calling her when he had a moment: "I mustn't think about it too much or I'll go crazy; I'm a sex-starved maniac on top of everything else, you know. It's a good thing I'm working hard every day—if you know what I'm driving at—and I think you do," he told Mary. After a long day on his feet doing "crash dives" and "battle surfaces," he went to dinner and then to bed. He liked the shots they were getting—"lulus"—declaring, "I'm getting to be an old hand at this." He had put nine-year-old David in charge of the garden. "Tell David I'm very proud of him for caring for the flowers so well and that I'll bring him something interesting for being such a good boy." This was the world that ultimately mattered to Dana: "I'm a lost pidgeon until I'm with you again," he wrote Mary. He stayed in bed, faking illness to avoid a public appearance and worrying that the shrubs at home were not getting enough water and that the lawn was unmowed. Sometimes he got so worked up he was on the "verge of sitting down all by myself and crying just for one touch of your soft, luscious lips!"

Dana did not write home about his nights out with sailors, one of whom, Gordon Howard, later wrote a reminiscence of their carousing, when "you said that you couldn't get drunk in this climate—well Dana, if you weren't high that night then you never will be." "Gutz" wanted Dana to know that all the gang said "hello." Dana was reaching a point when references to his drinking would become much more frequent.

Shortly after the film was released Dana received a letter that reminded him of just how far from "home" he had traveled. "Soon after that first sight of you [in *Crash Dive*] my work—oil scouting—took me thru Huntsville and I called on your mother," wrote an old friend, who signed himself only as "Macon":

> She, of course, was awfully proud of you and told me about the other boys too. It had then been about 17 years since you-all left Uvalde and I was a little surprised she remembered me. That I should remember the Andrews is not so surprising though. What a colorful family! Do you remember Fred McKenzie & his gang of outlaws? Levy Old whom Fred killed? Jake & Lee Schwartz? The Ku Klux Klan? Those were hectic days in Uvalde's history with your dad, fiery and fearless, enemy of Catholicism and the things for which the "antis" stood. I was only about 7 or 8—between Ralph & Charles—but all that stands out vividly even now.

That world was indeed vivid, *real*, in ways the pretend world of Hollywood could never be, no matter how much of an "old hand" Dana would become.

Louella Parsons gave the picture her usual enthusiastic send-off. In the *New York Times*, Bosley Crowther noted Dana's "second lead charm," but also observed that the picture had "no more sense of reality about this war than a popular song." Other reviewers rewarded Dana with honorable mention as Power's worthy rival and noble commanding officer, who does not let his disappointment in love interfere with their mission to blow up a Nazi naval base (an improbable but nonetheless exciting commando raid never actually attempted in the North Atlantic theater of war). Naturally Tyrone Power and his on-screen romance with Anne Baxter received most of the attention, even from Dana's son who said, "Well, Dad, you were pretty good and all. But that Tyrone Power—wow! What a man!" Responding to the DVD release of *Crash Dive*, reviewers on the Internet movie database imdb have praised Dana's projection of "resolute dependability" in what is virtually an animated recruiting poster for the naval war effort. Those bored with this picture directed by journeyman Archie Mayo may agree with one imdb wag, who remarked that it was too bad that they could not get Anne Baxter into the submarine.

Tyrone Power left for active duty after the completion of *Crash Dive*, and Dana expected be drafted. He did not share the urgency of stars like Jimmy Stewart or Clark Gable, both single at the time, to enlist. "Our lives are pretty much in a turmoil these days," he told Charles:

> Isn't it a crying pity that change has to be accomplished so violently? I'm sure that we'll never know such happy days as we have known ever again. Things may resolve into some semblance of order before we're gone but it appears that it will be a different kind of order—less heart and more regulation. Guess I'm a progressive who has become a little conservative. It makes me a little sad to think most of our way of life is fast going—never to return. The mellow old age I have planned for us suddenly seems most uninteresting. I find myself all keyed up with the radio and headline jitters—wanting to get in the thick of it—live today, tomorrow may be your last, drink, joke, etc. There's bound to be a terrific reaction when this is over.

In a fit of nostalgia for his Texas days, he acknowledged that Hollywood seemed cold and calculating:

> Just when I'm beginning to be successful here, I begin to hate the place. I never get any rest, never any peace of mind or rest for contemplation—even for writing letters. If it weren't for Mary, who is wonderful, I'd be like the rest of the Hollywood gang: shallow, position conscious, pleasure-seeking, money mad maniacs. Sounds like my Hollywood lot is not a happy one, doesn't it? Just feeling a little that way tonight.

Charles Forrest Andrews could not have composed a better screed against Hollywood. But it is doubtful that his restless son could have sat still for long without a role. He wanted to stand out and be a player, which is one reason why the character of Kolya Simonov in *The North Star* (released November 5, 1943) appealed to him. He wrote to Charles about meeting Lillian Hellman: "[S]he's okeh, but definitely pro-Russian if that matters. My part is not so big—but good."

Kolya is a bombardier, proud of his military process, and devoted to his family and his land. He lives in a Disneyland Soviet village in the Ukraine that is first bombed and then occupied by the German army on June 22, 1941, the first day of Hitler's invasion. Hellman, an extravagant admirer of the Soviet Union, blamed Samuel Goldwyn and *The North Star*'s director, Lewis Milestone (acclaimed for his work on *All Quiet on the Western Front* [1930]), for botching her screenplay with ridiculous song-and-dance routines that made a mockery of her effort to show the "courage of a people who had been presented to two generations of Americans as passive slaves."

Other than peasant costumes, haircuts, and thatched roofs, no effort is made to make the village or the people seem Ukrainian. Hollywood shied away from the foreign even when the subject was foreign. But the fault for film's failure is also Hellman's. Despite six months of reading Russian novels and translations of *Pravda*, she admitted: "I'm just no good at writing about people and places I don't know about." The point, really, is that Goldwyn wanted a product that Americans could identify with: Ukrainian peasants should be made to seem not much different from rural Americans. The Ukrainians just sang more and believed in collective farming and were devoted, like Kolya, to serving this new, vigorous Soviet Union that had risen out of revolution (the word is never used). The U.S.S.R. was now an American ally, and Hellman, Goldwyn, Milestone et al. were doing their part to promote the war effort.

If Dana did not find this picture especially embarrassing, it may be because Hellman's conception of his role arose out of what she knew best: the drama of family dynamics. He undoubtedly enjoyed the early scenes when, as Kolya, he teases his younger brother, Damian (Farley Granger) at the dinner table, and when Damian overturns Kolya's bed when he is late for breakfast. As Kolya, Dana is a young man with ambition and style, and with a personality that is bigger than his village can contain. Kolya is not a rebel—indeed he is strongly rooted in family and village values. And yet, like the young Carver, he wants more from the world than his provincial surroundings can offer. Kolya, as Dana plays him, is more than a stock character and more than just a stalwart Soviet citizen. When Kolya tells old fashioned Clavdia (Jane Withers), a young girl who idolizes him, that she is a throwback to the past and that he represents the new age, he does so with an amusing, lighthearted tone that tempers his youthful arrogance, making him seem less doctrinaire than determined and engaging. Kolya's criticism of Clavdia is also a flirtation. Dana felt at home in this sort of role, as he did with Ben in *Swamp Water*.

Dana's character goes out in a blaze of glory, taking over the controls from a pilot who has been shot. As he dive-bombs the plane to his death, he declares: "This is going to be for my father [killed in the German attack], for me, for my village, and for people I've never seen. Those are big words. I guess I'll have to stand by them now." Those words, said with quiet conviction, would have made the scene less histrionic but more effective. But the Hollywood script required that he raise his voice and shout: "I'm coming down, and it's going to hurt you. And I'm coming down just where I want to. Because I'm a good bombardier and a good pilot too!"

The North Star marked the first film appearance of seventeen-year-old Farley Granger, "giddy with excitement" that he should triumph in an audition for the formidable Lillian Hellman, "wreathed in clouds of cigarette smoke," and the ramrod straight Goldwyn staring at Granger with his "ball-bearing" eyes. Lewis Milestone, called Milly by his friends, broke the tension with a smile and a wink. Granger went to work on Anne Baxter and Dana. "She treated me like a kid brother," Granger noted, "something Dana never did even though I was playing his kid brother." Granger describes a taciturn and grumpy Dana, line-perfect but definitely not interested in socializing on the set, in contrast to the "warm and supportive" Walter Brennan. When Granger confided his concerns about Dana to Milly, the director told him: "Dana's just hungover and trying to get it together each morning, and it don't help that you're the good looking new kid on the lot, either."

Dana's drinking—if not a problem during the workday—had nevertheless become obvious. A pestering neophyte could not have been welcome early in the morning, especially to an actor just coming into his own after more than a decade of struggling to find his métier. That such a big break should come to someone as young as Granger could well have made Dana resentful. Past thirty, Dana may also have been looking over his shoulder even before he attained his first major starring role. Susan Andrews notes that there were actors her father liked "as actors, and those he didn't. He didn't like John Wayne, nor seem to respect Burt Lancaster or Kirk Douglas and I think he was jealous of Gregory Peck and didn't highly regard him either. He liked Anthony Quinn as an actor, Bogart, Gary Cooper, Cary Grant, 'Hank' Fonda, and, as you know, Ronald Colman: well, the ones that weren't a threat to him, I notice."

The North Star was an expensive production costing more that $3 million, with sets by the renowned William Cameron Menzies, cinematography by James Wong Howe, and a very able and accomplished cast that included Walter Huston and Erich von Stroheim. The picture received six Academy Award nominations and mixed reviews. *New York Times* critic Bosley Crowther objected to the operatic style of the picture's first part. In the *Nation*, James Agee deplored the "beautified" village scenes, stock characters, and glossy camera work.

While *The North Star* did nothing for Dana's career, his immediate future seemed secure when Milestone decided to cast him as the lead in *The Purple Heart* (released February 23, 1944). The picture is based on the famous April 14, 1942, Doolittle raid on Japan four months after the bombing of Pearl Harbor. Colonel James Doolittle led a force of sixteen bombers, launched from the aircraft carrier USS Hornet in the Western Pacific, a feat that astounded the Japanese, who never imagined that such huge planes could take off from aircraft carriers. This desperate but vital effort to boost American morale also sought to demonstrate Japanese vulnerability. The raid displayed American ingenuity in modifying heavy planes for seemingly impossible service so far away from an American base. Since medium bombers could not safely land on the flight deck of the Hornet, the mission mandated the planes land in China, where, it was hoped, American airman would be rescued by Chinese forces allied with the US. All but eleven crewmen returned from the raid. Three died, and the Japanese captured eight others after they crash-landed planes running low on fuel. These eight men, all of whom had volunteered for the raid, were tortured and tried for war crimes. Three Americans were executed, although the details of their trial and execution (by firing squad) were not made available until the war ended. Darryl Zanuck, Milestone, and the Fox production team had to invent courtroom and interrogation scenes based on censored and sketchy wartime reports.

Dana is the "skipper," Captain Harvey Ross, of an army air force crew, all of whom are outraged at their treatment as war criminals rather than prisoners of war (the Japanese allege the Americans bombed civilian targets). One by one, the men are subjected to psychological and physical abuse that results in mental trauma (one man becomes virtually catatonic), broken limbs, and in the case of the crew's youngest member, loss of speech (his tongue has been cut out). Dana personifies the stalwart, decent American hero, refusing to give information to the enemy. In a

1958 interview recorded for the oral history collection at Columbia University, he explained the film's importance in his career:

> Mr. [Spyros] Skouras the head of 20th Century Fox, chairman of the board, once told me this, after it had happened. The picture that made me what is called a star, he told me once at his house in Mamaroneck, was *The Purple Heart*. Well, this was rather surprising to me. I knew it was a pretty good picture, but it was a war picture and very similar in some respects to *30 Seconds Over Tokyo*, and so didn't receive great national acclaim in *Life* magazine or something. The reason for that was that the part I played in this was a captain in charge of a whole group of men, and it was a very kindly treated character. The women all over the country, whose men were away at war, identified their husbands as being that sort of a man. For some reason, this made a terrific impression on them. There was no romance in it at all. There was not even a woman in it. There was a very short little flashback, I think about 30 seconds, of my being back home. But this was the picture that he said put me over.

Dana's character heroically keeps his unit together in their cell, dealing with each man's concerns but also demonstrating their common purpose, which is to deny the Japanese knowledge of their bomber base. Dana Andrews has often been labeled the movie star as "ordinary guy." Certainly he plays a down-to-earth, sturdy, everyday man's man in this movie. He is upright, brave, and angry, but above all beautifully composed. He has the posture of a hero, and posture—as he often told his daughter Susan—is vitally important in putting yourself across.

Several features of Dana's performance are worth noting. He never lectures his men; instead, he reassures them with a steady gaze and a smile. When he is interrogated by a Japanese general and refuses to divulge any information, he hovers over the general's desk, leaning slightly forward, and then nonchalantly twirls his cap twice. The movement does not look showy (Dana's hand hardly moves as the cap is pitched a few inches in the air); rather, the gesture is quietly expressive of a man who cannot be cowed by threats. Dana's popularity undoubtedly stemmed from his quietly confident articulation of core American values. When one crew member announces that he will tell the Japanese what they want to know in order to end their ordeal, the skipper tells his men that Sergeant Clinton (the youngest among them, played by Farley Granger) can say what he wants if he can square it with his conscience.

The skipper's unwillingness to force unity here, and his respect for the individual, make this the picture's crowning moment. And yet Dana utters the line mildly, almost impassively, not only calming his agitated crew, but motivating Clinton's decision not to tell the Japanese anything.

Dana discovered his new status aboard a train in the company of such stars as Betty Grable, Tyrone Power, and Joan Fontaine, as well as Hollywood columnists and critics—all assembled to attend the premiere of Zanuck's *Wilson*, which the producer considered the "benchmark film of his career." At a civic luncheon in Wahoo, Nebraska, Zanuck's hometown, Andrews's appearance was greeted with an ovation. Reviewers had the same reaction: "Dana Andrews is magnificently congruous as the leader of the bomber crew," the *New York Times* critic declared. "*The Purple Heart* establishes Dana Andrews, who scored highly in *The Ox-Bow Incident*, as one of the year's most promising young actors. His portrayal of the leader of the captured aviators is both convincing and restrained." (*Life*, March 13, 1944).

More than any other director, Lewis Milestone understood Dana's evolving screen personality: A decent, sensitive man with a quiet kind of heroism, deeply aware of his fellow man's strengths and weaknesses, his vulnerabilities and worries. Few directors took an interest in actors as persons they would befriend. Few develop a persona based on the level of trust and affection that Milestone would capitalize on with a "reserved twinkle," said film critic Otis Ferguson, who watched the director in action: "He is the kind of director it is a pleasure to see working, and apparently a pleasure to work with." Dana later provided an example of why his collaboration with Milestone worked so well:

> In *Purple Heart*, there was a scene at the end where they walk out the door. In the script it says, "So they walk out the door"—presumably to be executed, which they were. He suddenly said, "I want a shot of them coming down that long corridor." You know, Mr. Milestone and I worked this out together. I had heard, in some dramatic radio presentation about the Air Force, the Air Force song ("Wild Blue Yonder") played almost as a funeral dirge, because great tragedy was involved. So I said, "Why don't we do that?" He said, "That's a good idea, but I'll tell you what we'll do." (This is how we worked this out together.) "We want this to end on a note of triumph, so we'll start it out this way, and then we'll cut to these faces as they march along. 'All right, we're going to die, but let's die for a reason'—like this."

This really gave the music department a time, because to change the tempo of the music, which had been prerecorded, was a job. They finally had to go back and rerecord the music, which cost them quite a bit of money because they had to have another music session—to do it to our footsteps. Milly said, "I can't have the scene go to the music; I have to have the music go to the scene." So we started out at a very slow pace and worked this up, and it ended right on rhythm.

Milestone not only cast Dana in four pictures, the director advised Dana on his career-making role in *Laura*. As Milestone told interviewer Tay Garnett:

> I cast everything, carefully and meticulously. I take a long time to find the right person even for the smallest bits. I talk the role over with my actors again and again, sometimes for days. I lay the basis in conversation, for what is to follow. By the time we get on the set, the actor will know what I want of him and why. And if I have been any good he will want the same things I want.

In *Include Me Out: My Life from Goldwyn to Broadway*, Farley Granger confirms Milestone's expert reading of actors, noting that the director overcame a few "wary looks" from actors when he proposed they share one large dressing room near the set of *The Purple Heart*: "As usual, Millie was right. We quickly became a band of brothers." The results for Granger were especially gratifying, since Dana became "my big brother" and "could not have been warmer" after the picture wrapped. The Milestone method produced utterly convincing ensemble performances in *The Purple Heart* and *A Walk in the Sun* (1945), which also seem to have had a powerful impact on director Henry Hathaway when he cast Dana in *Wing and a Prayer* (1945). Other directors, such as Jacques Tourneur and Otto Preminger, who also employed Dana in several films, have Milestone to thank for discovering and nurturing the distinctive Dana Andrews style of underplayed nobility.

James Agee, noting that *The Purple Heart*, essentially a "Japanese atrocity picture," observed that the film was "much more controlled than it might have been." Agee gave the credit to Milestone's "direction, his best in years," because it was "unusually edged, well organized, and solidly acted." His verdict seems right, despite the opinions of later critics, who have deplored the film's jingoism, racism, and fanciful use of Chinese actors to depict Japanese culture. On April 14, 1944, the *Hollywood Reporter* noted that the picture's box office receipts had already recouped production costs.

When Aggie saw *The Purple Heart*, she shed tears. Dana's brothers were not sure what to make of his success. Wilton still wanted to call him Carver. Billy, the youngest, seemed bent on following Dana into the acting profession, reported sister Mary. Dana's mother was reading about him in movie magazines. Brother John provided the fullest analysis of Dana's place in the family:

> Since childhood "Carver" has always been a mysterious quantity to me, and someday I'd like to get to know you as a real brother not as a movie star who bears the family name and drops in for a "hello" and "goodbye" every two or three years and writes maybe once a year. When we were in Madisonville you were in Huntsville, when we moved to California, you stayed in Texas, for a brief period you seemed like one of the family and then swoosh, we left for Texas in a cloud of dust and you became again the unknown quantity. I know your life and outlook is quite a bit different from mine due to your work but that shouldn't sever the kindred feeling. I hope that being constantly in the public eye will not deaden innate sensibilities in you, common to all the Andrewses. Old C. F. might have been narrow and provincial in religion and moral conviction, but he had one of the sharpest minds I've come across and nothing (or very few things) that he wanted to become a part of him ever slipped by. Much of what he had has been passed down to us with unpleasant edges honed down. You got much of his drive and independence of spirit as well as love of fine things; I got what humility he and mother together mustered (perhaps too much) plus a longing for great things backed by a hard head.

After a visit to Dana, in October 1944, John wrote that "glamorous Hollywood" had not spoiled his brother, whose cozy home and delightful children convinced John that Dana had created a happy home.

That home in Sherman Woods, located at Sepulveda and Ventura boulevards, had just been built. In the "$17,000 range," with a Williamsburg Colonial design, it featured living and dining rooms "grouped about the garden." "Oak-studded Sherman Woods in the San Fernando Valley," as a newspaper account put it, "is becoming more and more the home of celebrities and the choice for permanent residence of discriminating families seeking the quiet exclusiveness of suburban living." As of August 10, 1944, Dana's accountant, Vernon Wood, estimated his client's net worth at about $50,000—with only mortgage payments and taxes as outstanding liabilities. It had taken Dana five years to pay off Twomey and Wardlaw, but he estimated that they had enjoyed a 300% return on their investment. Dana himself kept running totals of his income from picture making in account book ledger paper, starting with his first forty weeks working for Sam Goldwyn at $150 a week for a total of $5,450.00. By the end of 1940, he had earned another $8,063.53, jumping to $12,429.69 in 1941, $20,000 in 1942, $30,000 in 1943, and $40,000 in 1944.

Such are the absurdities of the Hollywood production system that Dana next appeared as a "stooge" (Dana's word) for Danny Kaye, playing the hypochondriacal draftee Danny Weems in a Samuel Goldwyn musical, *Up in Arms* (released March 27, 1944, just a month after *The Purple Heart* appeared). Dana plays Joe Nelson, the straight man and still point around which Kaye frenetically dances and sings, supported as well by singer Dinah Shore, who plays Virginia Merrill, a nurse in love with the hypochondriacal draftee. Weems, in turn, is in love with Mary Morgan (Constance Dowling). This Technicolor musical, in which Dana does not sing, featured the Goldwyn Girls, the producer's answer to the famous Ziegfeld Girls, who parade aboard the navy ship carrying Danny and Joe off to war. Dana would later say that he never made a point of telling studios he could sing, precisely because he did not want to get stuck in more musicals like *Up in Arms*.

Dana has nothing to do in this picture except smile and laugh at Danny's antics and to romance Mary (who loves Joe, not Danny), setting up the denouement in which Danny finally realizes that Virginia is the girl for him. An extraordinary dancer who could sing tongue-twisting lyrics at a phenomenal rate, the effervescent Kaye dominated the screen to the delight of his ecstatic fans and to the enervation of everyone else. As James Agee concluded, "[E]verything depends on whether or not you like him. I do." Reviewers found the film entertaining, and it made money for Sam Goldwyn, who saw in Kaye the perfect replacement for Eddie Cantor, whose films, long a Goldwyn mainstay, were yielding diminishing returns.

Dana had a much better part as Lieutenant Commander Edward Moulton in *Wing and a Prayer* (shot before *Laura*, but not released until March 14, 1945), leading a squadron of fighter planes attached to an aircraft carrier that is part of the buildup to the decisive battle of Midway, a turning point in the war when the US regained its supremacy at sea after the Pearl Harbor disaster. This was one of Dana's favorite roles, one that he ranked above his performance in *Laura*. Compared to his portrayal of Captain Harvey Ross in *The Purple Heart*, Dana's work in *Wing and a Prayer* seems subtler—or perhaps it is just that he is playing a man who has seen more war than Captain Ross and is consequently more circumspect about his reactions. Serving under harsh Flight Commander Bingo Harper (Don Ameche), Moulton bears down hard on a pilot who recklessly lands his plane on a carrier deck. But Moulton also treats another grounded airmen with just the right amount of discipline and respect, fostering good morale.

Don Ameche remembered a pleasant movie set in which the actors reminisced about their pre-motion pictures lives, with Dana regaling the cast with stories about working in a gas station. Veteran director Henry Hathaway remembered Dana's no-nonsense professionalism: "Dana had a quality. I'll tell you one thing he had like nobody I've seen in my life. Drunk or sober, he comes in, in the morning and they're making him up and he'd say, 'What do I do today?' And you say, 'Do this.' And he'd look at the script and he goes out . . . and never misses a word."

Some of the credit for the excellent ensemble acting is probably due to Darryl Zanuck, who favored character development and action sequences over attention to plot (there is almost none here, since the picture is all about the slow, agonizing buildup to the destruction of the Japanese fleet at Midway). As Zanuck put it in one of his memos, "[O]ur story is our characters." Fox already had in the can "magnificent" stock footage of actual battle scenes that would give the picture "full authenticity and integrity," Zanuck noted. Against this broad canvas of war, Dana's customary minimalism—allowing the camera to observe him in action—is especially effective in scenes where Harry Morgan, with his distinctively gruff voice and extroverted behavior, acts as the perfect foil for the quiet authority Dana brings to his character.

Accounts of Hathaway's career often overlook this film, as well its vital place in Dana's drive to stardom. What everyone working on this picture found appealing can be summed up in Zanuck's comment: "We do not have any old props to fall back on to help us when the scenes run thin. Nobody is going to turn out to be somebody else's brother in the last reel. This thing has got to stand on its own feet. . . ." The writer, Jerome Cady, had captured the demoralizing period right after Pearl Harbor, the "Where is our Navy?" complaints. "The audience will feel that it is being let in on a secret, that it is being taken backstage and told at last the answer to what we were all asking in early 1942," Zanuck argued. From the start, Zanuck saw Moulton as "someone like Dana Andrews, although possibly the role may not have enough color in it to permit the casting of someone as important as Andrews. In the present script the character is indefinite. When we introduce him we say the he is tough on his men, yet nowhere in the entire story does he do anything to indicate this toughness." Rewrites under Zanuck's guidance would give Dana just enough material as was suitable to an actor who never liked to overplay his parts. As Zanuck put it, Moulton "is never soft, but more like a devoted coach . . . His men worship him, and he gets results even though he is not exactly the perfect Squadron leader." Indeed, just as Zanuck proposed, the picture focuses on "two philosophies of discipline," which the studio head compared to Howard Jones of USC, a man "who never called a player by his first name, who never even nodded to them when they were off the field, who even insulted them, and yet got great results in the playing field . . . and Rockne, who was almost a daddy to all of his players." Dana, however, never indulged in the sentimentality that is suggested in Zanuck's comment on Rockne.

By December 14, 1943, Cady delivered a rewritten script that was becoming specifically tailored to Dana's talents, a sure sign that he was an emerging star with a screen persona. Dana also benefited from Tyrone Power's absence owing to military service. The character of Scott Hallam, a movie star who has joined Moulton's crew, is played by William Eythe, who bore a slight resemblance to Power, but who had very little of Power's charisma. Dana's best scene occurs when Bingo Harper interrogates Hallam about the position of Japanese airplanes that have attacked him after the American planes returned to the aircraft carrier. Harper hectors the confused Hallam, while Moulton calmly asks questions about altitude and other factors that might yield important information. The scene includes shots in which other crewmembers reveal their fear, express their bravado, and vent their frustrations and disappointments while Moulton does his duty. He is eager to join the fight against the Japanese, but he maintains a composure and sensitivity (he feels the pressure, too) that no one else aboard ship is able to summon up. Although the script would go through several more rewrites, expanding and contracting the details about Dana's character, in the end Moulton emerges as quintessential Dana Andrews: reserved but also commanding and engaging, the very image of authority—but without the prickliness and pomposity that makes the dour Don Ameche character so hard to take.

To this day, commentators on *Wing and a Prayer*, even when they commend Dana, fail to see how remarkably nuanced his performance is. What would it take to rescue him from the fate of a second lead in second-rate pictures? Virginia Zanuck and Lewis Milestone had the answer.

CHAPTER 10

Laura

1944

LIKE *CASABLANCA*, which seemed a mess while it was being made, *Laura* is an accidental masterpiece. Make a list of what can go wrong with a picture, and *Laura* fits the bill: miscasting, poor direction, interference from producers, script problems, wrong musical score—even the portrait of Laura, painted by director Rouben Mamoulian's wife, was scrapped after producer Otto Preminger took over as director and had a photograph of Gene Tierney touched up to look like a painted portrait. All this and more stood in the way of what became a cinema classic and an indelible image in Hollywood film: "Dana Andrews being beguiled by the portrait of Laura," as David Thomson writes in *The Whole Equation: A History of Hollywood* (2005). "[O]ne of the great moments of postwar American cinema," write Borde and Chaumeton in the first book to give a name to what Hollywood did not yet call "film noir." Indeed, to know the history of how *Laura* came to be is to understand the whole equation: how Hollywood worked in its heyday, and how Dana Andrews finally snared stardom.

The picture opens with the portrait of Laura and the film's haunting theme, composed by David Raksin (who worked on this mournful music over a weekend after he learned his wife was leaving him). Director Otto Preminger first wanted to use Gershwin's "Summertime," and then Duke Ellington's "Sophisticated Lady," neither of which evokes the yearning swell of Raksin's unforgettable melody, expressing not only detective Mark McPherson's anguished but muted love for Laura, but also Waldo Lydecker's frustrated, unrequited passion and Shelby Carpenter's hope that Laura will not reject him despite his failings. Hedi Lamarr rejected the starring role in *Laura*, later saying she had read only the script and not heard the score. In fact, none of the actors heard it, since it was added after the picture wrapped, and it came, as Vincent Price recalled, as a wonderful and welcome surprise. The song, played strategically throughout the picture, is made to seem like a melody that is already a part of the world the characters inhabit. It became a hit when Johnny Mercer composed lyrics for it, and it remains not only a classic but the very epitome of longing and wistfulness. It can be heard, for example, in *Bus Stop*, when Bo (Don Murray) falls in love with his "angel" Cherie (Marilyn Monroe).

Laura is each man's ideal beloved—the very picture of his desires—as the film signals in its first frame when the music and the portrait simultaneously materialize. The initial credits, reading from top to bottom, list Gene Tierney, Dana Andrews, and Clifton Webb, followed in the next frame by the title "Laura by Vera Caspary." The novel and its author are given pride of place before the next frame adds Vincent Price and Judith Anderson to the cast, followed by the credit for the screenplay, by Jay Dratler, Samuel Hoffenstein, and Betty Reinhardt, a composite crew that eventually developed a story—much worked over by Darryl Zanuck—that no one was certain would work. This stately roll out of film credits slowly reveals the full portrait, making it the focus of intrigue even before the action begins. The actors' performances—as good as they are—benefit significantly from the mystique created around this image of a beautiful woman, enclosed in a gilt frame and flanked by sconces suggesting the sumptuousness of a world that (as the next frame announces) is "produced and directed by Otto Preminger."

As the screen goes black, the first voice heard is Waldo Lydecker's, delivered in Clifton Webb's effete, melancholic voice, which begins, "I shall never forget the weekend Laura died," making an immediate connection between the portrait and the death of a beautiful woman—the subject Edgar Allan Poe declared the most poetical in the world. Rudy Behlmer, in one of the most notable studies of the picture, observes that Laura is the name of Petrarch's beloved and has become the symbol for a "spiritualized passion for the unattainable." Vera Caspary denied she had the fourteenth-century poet in mind, but her Laura is inescapably linked to her literary avatar. The first image visible in a darkly lit room is a sculpture, an Asian-looking, upright figure with an impassive expression, its left hand raised in an open palmed peaceful gesture. This museum piece, ensconced in a niche, is suddenly seen in bright light that reveals glass showcases of precious objects. The camera slowly pans across the shelves to an ornate standing clock, part of a luxuriously appointed apartment. The Laura theme music takes on the quality of retrospection as Lydecker explains that he was just about to write the story of Laura's horrible death when "another of those detectives came to see me." Mark McPherson, standing across from Lydecker's impressive built-in bookcase, is suited up with the standard fedora and cigarette, the very model of the 1940s detective.

Laura's elaborate two-minute setup easily surpasses in intricacy any other sequence of film in which Dana had appeared. He later said his role would have made any actor a star, a claim that sells his performance short but also reveals his extraordinary grasp of picture making. He understood that *Laura* built a frame not only around Gene Tierney, but around his character, amplifying postures and gestures that would subvert Lydecker's assertions that McPherson has no depth, no texture, no subtlety that an aesthete like Lydecker or a woman with exquisite tastes like Laura, can appreciate.

From a half-open door, Lydecker watches McPherson walk to a wall displaying masks from different cultures (European, Asian, and perhaps African) and study them. He is a detective casing a joint, but he is also a connoisseur—a notion that never occurs to Lydecker, and one not usually associated with McPherson's type or with film noir, which so often features a tight-lipped detective who talks tough when he talks at all. The first of several slight smiles breaks up Mark's impassive countenance as he turns at the sound of the clock striking and walks to look at it (the second time this timepiece is shown, establishing its importance in the story about to unfold). Then McPherson walks to one of the glass cases, slides a door open, and picks up a glass piece for closer examination. Why? The piece cannot possibly contribute to solving his case. Lydecker warns the detective to be careful because the object is priceless. This moment deftly signals that there is more to McPherson, an aesthetic sensitivity that Lydecker fails to perceive. Indeed, the decadent world Waldo Lydecker represents is a kind of anthropological curiosity to the wryly-observant McPherson. His slight smile reflects confidence—even the superiority of a sensibility trained to scrutinize the habits of others. Could just any actor have played McPherson with the finesse Dana Andrews shows in this opening scene?

A swish-pan mimics McPherson's sudden swerve to take in the sybaritic Lydecker in his marble tub, a typewriter perched on a tray. This scrawny, emaciated figure seems sunken in what he calls a "lavish" bathroom, beautifully appointed with a glassed in bookcase, a vase of flowers at the end of the tub, and other features that make this a sitting room and study as well. In spite of his wealth, Waldo's wizened figure suggests an austerity that accords well with his aloof manners and acerbic tongue.

Darryl Zanuck had not wanted to use Clifton Webb, a Broadway song-and-dance man on the level of Fred Astaire but no movie star. Webb had appeared in a few silent films and then spent a few fruitless years in Hollywood waiting for a role. Zanuck wanted Laird Cregar, who had been brilliant as Ed Cornell in *I Wake Up Screaming* (1941), framing another man for murdering Vicky Lynn (Carole Landis) whom Cornell lusts after. Also, Cregar had played Sheridan Whiteside in *The Man Who Came to Dinner* and was said to have been as good as Monty Wooley (also considered for Waldo Lydecker), the actor famous for this signature role (based on the *New Yorker* writer and radio raconteur Alexander Woollcott, who also served as a model for Lydecker). Better to have this known quantity, Zanuck reasoned, than take a chance on Webb, whom one producer cautioned against because "he flies," a coded way of saying Webb was a homosexual. But Otto Preminger was not bothered by Webb's effeminacy; indeed, he may have regarded it as a good way of playing off Mark McPherson's masculinity. At any rate, Preminger argued that choosing an actor who played villains would destroy the whodunit aspect of the picture. The determined producer disobeyed Zanuck by shooting a screen test with Webb and proving to the annoyed studio head that Webb was right for the part.

Zanuck wanted John Hodiak, the romantic lead in *Lifeboat* (1944), to play Mark McPherson. But Dana started campaigning for the role the day Lewis Milestone gave him the script for *Laura* on the set of *The Purple Heart*. Although Milestone turned down the assignment when Preminger offered it to him, Milly told Dana the role would make him a star. Dana later told Rudy Behlmer that he got Hedda Hopper to plug him for the part in one of her columns. Fortunately, Zanuck's wife, Virginia, who brought her son to the set of *Wing and a Prayer* so he could play around the navy planes, saw Dana in action and remarked, "I never thought of you as a leading man, but as a character type. But I've seen a different side of your personality today." Dana explained that he had been obliged to play such parts credibly, so that his losing the girl to Jon Hall, Randolph Scott, and Tyrone Power was believable. Of course, he would play a leading man's role differently. "You really believe that?" Virginia asked. "Of course," Dana replied. Two days later Preminger called him: "Dana, I don't know what happened, but Zanuck says you have the part in *Laura*."

Jennifer Jones turned down the part of Laura, and Gene Tierney told Zanuck, "Who wants to play a painting?" She would be taking a risk, she thought. Both Clifton Webb and Dana Andrews were "regarded as gambles," she notes in her autobiography: "Andrews was unproven as a leading man. Webb had never made a movie, but had spent his career on Broadway, and had an image that was, well, prissy."

When McPherson takes out his notebook and completes one of Lydecker's prepared sentences, the detective adds, "Why did you write it down? Afraid you'd forget it?" His question is delivered like repartee in a drawing room scene, which could not have been sustained with the three-hundred-pound Cregar, who's sheer bulk would have projected menace. Lydecker wants to dance around McPherson, believing that he is much more nimble than a clumsy cop, whom he now orders to hand him his robe. The camera cuts to a smirking McPherson, who notes that Lydecker is on the list of suspects because his writing reveals a fascination with shotguns, the type of murder weapon used in this case. For the first time, the detective takes out his little box game, a baseball diamond with metal balls that have to be jiggled into the bases—like slotting suspects into the right places. This little game also contributes to our sense McPherson's composure and concentration. With typical obtuseness, Lydecker asks, "Something you confiscated in a raid on a kindergarten?" Focusing on the game allows McPherson to ask a direct question without looking at Lydecker: "Were you in love with Laura, Mr. Lydecker?" Then the detective looks up and asks, "Was she in love with you?" The suspect replies that she considered him the "wisest, wittiest, the most interesting man she ever met." She also thought him, Lydecker continues, the "kindest, gentlest, most sympathetic man in the world." Was he? the detective asks. "McPherson, you won't understand this," Lydecker concludes, but he did try to become the man she believed him to be. "Have any luck?" asks the detective. "Let me put it this way," Waldo rejoins: "I should be sincerely sorry to see my neighbors' children devoured by wolves."

McPherson agrees to Lydecker's proposal that he accompany the detective on a round of interviews—an improbable development that nevertheless prolongs the pleasure of watching these two actors jousting. A camaraderie of competitors ensues: Lydecker delights in denigrating McPherson, who contently amuses himself with carefully watching Lydecker. The actors, in fact, fell into a comfortable dynamic off set as well. In his autobiography, Webb describes his first day on the set, sitting in a tub, when "a young man came up to me and made himself known. He was Dana Andrews. He was very friendly and put me at my ease. I was naturally nervous, but trying to appear completely detached. I sat in that bloody tub for two days in hot water, until at the end of the day I had shriveled like a prune." Looking at the rushes, Webb felt like vomiting. He looked like Gandhi: "After it was over Dana saved my life with a big swig of bourbon. The first shock of seeing myself had a strange effect on me, psychologically, as it made me realize for the first time I was no longer a dashing young juvenile, which I must have fancied myself being through the years in the theatre." Movies themselves are, of course, a mirror, and before that first scene in *Laura* ends, the stark contrast between Lydecker and McPherson, seen in a mirror, reflects the animosity Lydecker feels for the young detective who has taken an interest in Laura.

The friendship between the actors continued after the picture was made. Webb sent a note to Dana on May 5, 1947, after both had become stars, that reveals a good deal about their rapport:

> Just in case, dear boy, you may feel all hot and slightly bothered with a violent desire to vomit, on the 13th of this month it will simply mean that your vibrations are at an unusually high pitch for the simple reason that this is the day I am arriving at Pasadena complete "en suite". I shall proceed in an armored car to a tiny villa that I have taken in Bel Air. . . . I am informed by my tiny spies that it is "all too" so I expect to be very happy. I shall also expect you to give up your entire time to me from that date on.

Saying he was very busy, Webb closed the letter with his "fond love" to Dana and Mary and with the words "Quand meme, Clifton." As writer Eric Karpeles pointed out to Dana's daughter Susan, "This was the life-long motto of Sarah Bernhardt, and Webb would have been channeling her as a final witticism to this note about the wretched excesses of celebrity, the cocooned world of privilege she sometimes, but not always, inhabited." Dana and Webb shared a disdain for Hollywood pretension that Webb like to parody. But the generous Webb exhibited none of Lydecker's jealousy.

Clifton Webb's contributes far more to *Laura* than his performance. For all his seeming haughtiness, he loved to encourage young actors. In his autobiography, Webb reports that Dana "became very clothes conscious after he had seen the clothes I had worn in *Laura*. He asked me, 'What is the matter with my suits?' And, I told him they weren't the clothes of a gentleman, much too exaggerated, which I found was the trouble with tailors in California. They looked more like zoot suits." Clothes would remain important for Dana; they became a feature of his style that his daughters would often remark upon.

Susan suggests that Dana may have played up to Webb because Dana knew Webb was attracted to him. At one point Webb said, "Shit, or get off the pot," meaning that Dana should make up his mind about whether he was attracted to Webb. They remained friends but no more than that. Similarly, Vincent Price recalled that Webb took an interest in him—as Webb did in Marilyn Monroe, James Dean, and other rising stars of a later generation. On the set of *Laura*, Webb's encouraging presence meant a lot, since the actors were under tremendous pressure. Zanuck was still fretting about the cast and the director. Dana may have already resorted to heavy drinking mode, while the high-strung Webb relied first on amphetamines to boost his energy, and then on sleeping pills to get some rest.

Dana's role in the picture was now in flux, as he explained many years later in the oral history he recorded for Columbia University, and as he repeated to film historian Rudy Behlmer:

> I talked to Mr. Preminger and Mr. Mamoulian for some time about the character, and they wanted to do this in a different way. What conversations they'd had between themselves, I don't know, but they were in agreement in talking to me that they wanted this character played as though he were a student of criminology from Yale or Harvard or something like that, and not at all the hard-boiled detective that you generally see. But this was something that I think Mr. Preminger wanted to be different, in this respect—to blaze a trail. This was very interesting to me, too. I didn't know how it would come out, but I knew what they meant and, having been a college man, I had some idea of how college men conducted themselves.

After two weeks, Zanuck reviewed the rushes and was upset. He summoned Dana to a meeting with Mamoulian and Preminger and proceeded to explain that the part should be played along the lines of Pat O'Brien's performance in *Broadway* (1942). Apparently, Preminger seized the opportunity and agreed with Zanuck, saying, "Why, that's what I was telling Rouben." Dana remembered that Mamoulian "became livid and said, 'That's a lie. You did not! You explained to me that you wanted this man played in the other way.'" As a big fight developed, Dana, who could not affect its outcome, secured Zanuck's consent to be excused.

Zanuck fired Mamoulian, and Preminger took over direction of the picture. Notorious as an autocrat who ordered actors around, he even managed to alienate the easy-going Dana, who told Rudy Behlmer about a futile call he made to Sam Goldwyn to get removed from the picture. "Just do what I tell you," Preminger told Dana, but Dana had trouble dealing with a director who even specified which way his finger should be turned. "Don't bother me," the director said. "Look here I can stay as long as you can," the actor replied. So they sat it out, with neither man giving way. Two hours later Mary visited the set and wondered why her husband was not working. "We're having a little disagreement," he told her. Then Viennese-born Preminger walked over and said, "Dah-na [he was never able to pronounce the actor's name properly], we are acting like children." Dana agreed. "Now, what is it you want?" the director asked. The actor explained himself and, in Dana's words, "it was patched up." He now reverted to playing the hardboiled detective, although vestiges of that more literate character seem to glimmer through his performance. As usual, Dana's fellow actors found him, as Vincent Price put it, "easy going."

Preminger's postmortem version of Mamoulian's firing alleges that the "performances were appalling. Judith Anderson was overacting, Dana Andrews and Gene Tierney were amateurish, and there was even something wrong with Clifton Webb's performance." Preminger cites a telegram from Zanuck calling Dana "'an agreeable schoolboy' who was not tough enough for the role of the detective," and that is why Zanuck had wanted Hodiak. This Otto-to-the-rescue redaction of what happened is hard to challenge, since Mamoulian refused to offer a rebuttal. For certain, the Preminger takeover disturbed the cast, who had enjoyed working with Mamoulian. Preminger admits in his autobiography that only Clifton Webb trusted him—perhaps because Webb had always been Preminger's first choice, and only Webb's close-ups survived the pillaging of Mamoulian's footage. Judith Anderson balked at Preminger's suggestions. "We were all on edge," Anderson told Behlmer. But Gene Tierney suggests in her autobiography that this mixture of second choices—"me, Clifton, Dana, the song, the portrait"—worked because "the ingredients turned out to be right. Otto held us together, pushed and lifted what might have been a good movie into one that became something special." Vincent Price pinpointed Preminger's contribution, suggesting that Mamoulian "had no concept about these kind of upper class scum people. Otto gave our characters a feeling of evil underneath this sophistication, a facade these high society people had." Preminger, who lived much of the time among the Broadway theater crowd and directed plays there, later told Price's daughter, "Rouben only knows nice people. I understand the characters of *Laura*. They're all heels, just like my friends."

As with *Casablanca*, the actors also had to adjust to script changes, as Samuel Hoffenstein, Betty Reinhardt, and other uncredited writers revised the Jay Dratler version Mamoulian had rehearsed with them. Dana was asked to record voiceover narration, which would have been faithful to the novel but disastrous for the picture. So much depends not on what the detective says, but on the audience's reading of his understated performance, which is more palpable than any words could be. When the screenplay was adapted for The Lux Radio Theatre (aired February 5, 1945), the whole effect of McPherson's powerful but tightly controlled feelings is ruined when Dana verbalizes his character's longing for Laura. In the film, he becomes, like Laura, a canvas on which the viewer's emotions are projected. As Tierney insisted in her autobiography, it was not her performance but the portrait of Laura—that is, the movie's idealization of the character—that counted. Tierney also recorded a voiceover for the picture, but it, too, was fortunately cut in the final edit.

Presumably the first two weeks of work had to be reshot before filming the next sequence, in which McPherson interviews Ann Treadwell (Judith Anderson), the older woman in love with Shelby Carpenter (Vincent Price), Laura's fiancé, who lopes into the room looming very large and tall in a generously cut double-breasted suit. Glib and soft-spoken Shelby, Lydecker's rival, is rather surprised that McPherson does not interrogate him, except for asking Carpenter about the music played at the concert he attended the night of Laura's murder. Like Lydecker, Carpenter tries to manipulate the detective, offering to show him the location of the key to Laura's country home, which McPherson wants to search.

At Laura's apartment, Lydecker berates McPherson, who looks at Laura's portrait and says "not bad," while calling her a "dame." Waldo, noting that the portrait painter was in love with Laura, asks McPherson if he has ever been in love. "A doll in Washington Heights once got a fox fur out of me," McPherson answers in classic film noir mode. "Ever know a woman who wasn't a doll or a dame?" Lydecker wants to know. "Yeah, one," answers McPherson, continuing to chew his gum. He plays a record, which reprises the film's theme song. "Sweet if not exactly 'classical,'" Carpenter intones. Here he falls into McPherson's trap. The concert Carpenter says he attended did not play Brahms (as Carpenter reported) but Sibelius, the detective notes. An embarrassed Carpenter confesses he fell asleep and did not hear the music. McPherson tells him not to worry about it. A perfectly reasonable explanation, the detective suggests, adding, "I fall asleep at concerts myself." This line seems like a throwaway, but it invites the question: Does McPherson attend concerts, and if so, then there is indeed more to this gumshoe than either Lydecker or Carpenter suspects. Catching Carpenter in his second lie, McPherson points out that the key in Laura's bedside table was not there when the police did a thorough search of the apartment. Suddenly Carpenter drops his silken voice and smooth manner to say rather grimly that he did not want to tell the detective about the key in Lydecker's presence. Sitting in a chair and playing with his baseball game, McPherson allows the two quarreling men to reveal more about themselves. What at first seemed odd—having the suspects in effect tail the detective—becomes his sly, efficient way of observing them in action. When Carpenter and Lydecker almost come to blows, the detective intervenes. An exasperated Lydecker says that he wishes McPherson would quit playing with that game because it is getting on his nerves. "I know," the detective replies, "but it keeps me calm"—the first indication that, for all his nonchalance, this cop has to restrain his own turbulent emotions in this highly wrought *haut monde*.

In almost every change of scene, Preminger finds a way to introduce the "Laura" theme music—this time scored for violins playing in a restaurant, as Lydecker and McPherson dine at the very table where Waldo spent many quiet evenings with Laura. In effect, the scene now pairs detective and suspect, each devoted to her in his own different way. In a long flashback, Lydecker explains how beautiful Laura, naive and new to New York, introduced herself to him, persuading this celebrated writer and radio personality to endorse a pen her firm is selling. He then takes her up, Svengali fashion, as his creation, while making sure that every rival for her affection is exposed as unworthy of her—until she falls for the soignée Shelby. In effect, Lydecker retails Laura's biography, providing McPherson with an intimate picture of a woman every man wishes to possess. It is Lydecker's conceit that only he loves Laura for herself, when, in fact, his narrative reveals him to be a collector who treats her as his ultimate treasure.

Immediately after this intense overview of Laura's life, McPherson returns to her apartment, spending hours looking at her possessions, going through her drawers, reading her letters and her diaries. Bessie (Dorothy Adams), Laura' maid, enters and is aghast at this invasion of Laura's privacy. She is contemptuous of cops, but McPherson likes her anyway, no doubt enjoying her refreshing candor after talking to the sarcastic Lydecker and the duplicitous Carpenter. McPherson's affectionate treatment of Bessie may have been influenced by the friendship between Dana and Dorothy, both of whom had worked at the Pasadena Playhouse.

The detective, feeling more pressure than he has yet to acknowledge, is relieved to deal with the forthright working-class woman who, it turns out, really did love Laura for herself. He relishes her remark that she has been brought up to spit when she sees a cop. "Okay, go ahead and spit, if it will make you feel better," he tells her. When she declares that Laura was "a real fine woman," something "you cops," she says, "would not know anything about," an earnest McPherson replies, "But you do." Bessie's worship of Laura has its impact on the detective, who begins to drink more after another round of interviewing suspects.

He remains in Laura's apartment, staring at her portrait. He loosens his tie, sits at her desk, picks up her letters and fans them against his hands. Pacing through the living room, he enters her bedroom, touches a silk scarf in a dressing table drawer, opens a perfume bottle and smells it, opens a closet door, runs his hands through his hair, fans the letters again, then exits to the living room, where he pours himself a drink from the liquor cabinet, making himself at home. He walks to the portrait, raises his glass as if to toast her, then drops his head—almost as if expressing a sense of loss. The buzzer sounds, interrupting this reverie. It is Lydecker, who makes explicit the detective's growing obsession with Laura by noting that McPherson has put in a bid to purchase Laura's portrait. "It's none of your business," the detective replies testily, avoiding his interrogator's glance by concentrating on his baseball game. "It's a wonder you don't show up with flowers and a box of candy," Lydecker needles. "Drugstore candy, of course," he continues. Then Lydecker asks if McPherson has imagined asking Laura to marry him, taking her to the policeman's ball, and so on. "I see you have," Lydecker observes, as McPherson turns away and shakes his game in frustration. As Waldo exits, he warns his prey that he may end up in a psycho ward as a novelty, a patient who has fallen in love with a corpse. The mournful strains of "Laura" play, while the detective drinks himself into a maudlin mood before collapsing in a chair by the fireplace. He looks around, apparently feeling lost, looks again at the portrait, and falls asleep.

McPherson's drug-induced sleep is in effect an overdose that marks the death of the pre-Laura Mark McPherson, who awakes to the baffling realization that his dream has come true. Laura appears before him, an apparition that causes him to rub his eyes in startled disbelief: Like Hermione in *The Winter's Tale*, a work of art has come to life. "You're alive," he says, gaping at her in wonder. After initial explanations, he reverts to detective mode, saying someone has been murdered in her apartment, and he wants to know who had a key. "Nobody," she gasps, thinking, most certainly, of Carpenter. McPherson vows he will find the murderer, and then his face softens as he says she should get out of her wet clothes. He watches her move toward her bedroom. He seems about to smile, but his countenance remains unreadable except for the heightened alertness in his fully opened eyes. He is thinking about his case. When Laura returns, he buttons his collar and straightens his tie. He listens to the explanation of Laura's long weekend away from town (Friday to Monday night) and her discovery of a dress that belonged to Diane Redfern, a model who has a figure and a hairstyle similar to Laura's. The dialogue becomes heated when McPherson accuses Laura of covering up a crime to protect Carpenter, who had been having a tryst with Diane Redfern. The detective seems on the verge of making his interest in the case entirely personal, asking Laura if she loves Carpenter so much that she would lie for him. To Laura's vehement protestations, he replies mildly, "I suspect nobody and everybody. I'm just trying to get at the truth." An offended Laura notes that he has looked at things she never meant anyone else to read. He apologizes, saying, "strictly routine, really." Yet he cannot help smiling when she tells him that during the long weekend she decided not to marry Carpenter.

As soon as McPherson leaves the apartment, however, Laura forfeits the detective's trust by immediately calling Carpenter, prompting McPherson, who is listening on a phone tap, to say, "Dames are always pulling a switch on you." The detective follows Carpenter, who confesses that he is removing a shotgun from Laura's country cottage because he suspects her of the murder. It gets worse for Laura when McPherson discovers that the radio she said had not been working—establishing she did not know about Redfern's murder—switches on without a problem.

The next sequence of scenes shows McPherson gauging the reactions of the principal characters when they first catch sight of the resurrected Laura. McPherson is disgusted to learn that Shelby and Laura seemed to have resumed their engagement in order to cover up for one another. But in fact Laura's attachment to Carpenter ends when she realizes that he does indeed believe she is the murderer. The sordid world he represents is driven home to Laura when she encounters Ann Treadwell, who says she believes that although Carpenter did not commit murder, he is, like herself, perfectly capable of the act. "Are you as interested in McPherson as he is in you?" Treadwell asks, advising Laura that the detective is a better choice for her. Carpenter is no good, but he is what

Treadwell wants. Neither she nor Shelby is a nice person, she admits, but she knows how to take care of him. And indeed, the rather masculine, severe-looking Ann is a perfect protector for the fey, hapless Shelby.

Back at the party organized to celebrate Laura's return, McPherson answers a phone call, then says he is about to bring in the murderer. In a parody of the whodunit, he walks toward Carpenter, then Lydecker, before turning on Laura and saying, "All right, let's go," as Bessie screams "No!" When Carpenter tries to interfere with the arrest, McPherson punches him in the stomach, revealing for the first time just how much he loathes the idea of Shelby as Laura's suitor.

In the police station interrogation room, the detective shines a powerful light on Laura, trying to read the truth in her features. She has some explaining to do—about the radio, for example, which she had a workman fix. He looms over her, sits on a desk, turns off the light at her request, and turns his body towards her, his face only inches from hers. To his considerable relief, she calls the engagement merely a ruse to protect Shelby—or so Laura thought, until she realized he believed he was protecting her. You can practically feel McPherson's pulse racing when he blurts out: "Are you still in love with him?" The detective has been holding his breath and relaxes when she says, "I don't see how I could ever have been." But Laura is angry that McPherson has dragged her to the station house when he has not even booked her and never really believed in her guilt. She suddenly softens when he tells her that he needed official surroundings to remove the last bit of doubt. "Then it was worth it, Mark," she says, using his first name for the first time. They exchange a knowing look, sharing a powerful rapport in a scene impossible to re-create now in a world that is so informal and explicit.

The picture moves swiftly to its denouement. Mark returns Laura to her apartment, where the chiming clock signals the clue the detective has been seeking: Lydecker visits Laura, who has apparently told him of her love for Mark, so that Waldo—now pacing toward the clock that is a replica of his own—must once again convince her that such a mate is unworthy. She relives the dreamy moment when she came back to town and discovered Mark waiting for her, while telling Waldo she never wants to see him again. Waldo exits, predicting a "disgustingly earthy relationship" for Laura and Mark. "All I need is the gun," Mark says, discovering a shotgun in the clock. He then explains how Waldo, mistaking Diane Redfern for Laura, unloaded both barrels of the shotgun into her face, then hid the gun and concealed himself in the hallway as Shelby arrived at the crime scene. "I knew it," Laura says, "but I didn't want to believe it." Mark returns the shotgun to the clock, and the couple kisses for the first time. Mark is off to arrest Waldo, telling Laura not to open her door and that the clock and weapon will be picked up the next morning. The clockwork plot results in Waldo's return to the crime scene, having never left it because he has again hidden in the hallway—waiting for Mark to leave so that he can retrieve his gun and this time murder Laura for good. And he almost does, failing only because Mark and his men arrive just in time to shoot the murderer, whose last words are to Laura: "Goodbye, my love."

Laura, on first release, was only a modest hit, and a not a big award winner—although it did receive several Academy Award nominations, including one for Preminger as best director. But the picture was built to last. It presents such a fully realized world in Joseph LaShelle's deep focus cinematography (which did win an Academy Award) and its distinctive characters. Tierney's Laura has an openness and freshness she never loses, no matter how she becomes mired in the creepy and calculating confines of Manhattan society. Price's Shelby Carpenter is weak but so charmingly attentive to women that it is no wonder they succumb to his flattery. Webb's Waldo Lydecker is refreshingly candid about his snobbery and does not pretend to say or to do anything that does not suit his elitist sensibility. Dana's Mark McPherson is a workingman's hero with a romantic soul—and even a sense of style (look at the cut of his suits and his posture) that is extraordinarily appealing in a democratic society that craves distinctive individuals with integrity and down-to-earth manners. This wonderfully realized ensemble of characters overrides any number of plot contrivances and improbabilities. Vincent Price considered it the best picture he ever appeared in: "Not pretentious, very simple, just brilliant."

Laura once and for all settled the issue of Dana Andrews's status as a leading man. The *New York World Telegram* critic, who had been following Dana's career closely, observed that the actor had "consistently outdone each of his successive performances. . . .The smoldering force with which he plays the detective leaves one pretty sure that the chain of topping himself will be broken in this picture . . . unless he turns out to be just about the finest actor of our time."

But stars do not do it alone. They need vehicles that are built around their strengths as persons and performers. In Dana's case, *Laura* coupled his understated acting style with that inherent nobility of character that makes Mark McPherson stand out from the deceitful male beauties and Svengalis of a fashionable society. Laura appeals to him because she, too, has that same air of purity. He affects a cynicism that protects his chivalric desire to deliver her from the wiles of Waldo Lydecker and Shelby Carpenter. In Molly Haskell's felicitous phrase, Dana's character becomes "Laura's true knight." In every great role after *Laura*, Dana's characters would struggle to maintain the authenticity and genuineness that makes Mark McPherson so appealing.

    The only surprise for a biographer of Dana Andrews is that he did not express more affection for the role that made him a star, especially since that role gave him the satisfaction of exposing phonies. In the phony world of Hollywood, here he had the opportunity to play a character very much like himself. Dana was, after all, no more impressed with Hollywood glamor than Mark McPherson was with Manhattan elegance. A somewhat disconcerted Dana Andrews was now playing in a different league—as he confessed when Clifton Webb spotted him standing alone at a party. In Webb's autobiography he recalls asking Dana, "what was the matter. He startled me when he said, 'I didn't realize that one doesn't get asked to a party like this unless they make a thousand dollars a week or over.' This rather stunned me because I didn't realize that one's social position was rated by their weekly paycheck."

Charles Forrest Andrews and Annis Speed shortly after they were married, c. 1905. Courtesy Dana Andrews Collection.

Dana, c. 1925. Courtesy Aimee Abben.

The Andrews Brothers: Ralph, John, Harlan, Wilton, Dana, David, and Charles, c. 1921–22. Courtesy Angela Fabry.

Norma Felder, *Alcade* yearbook photograph, Sam Houston State University, 1928. Courtesy Sam Houston State University archives.

Janet Murray, David, and Dana, c. 1934. Courtesy Aimee Abben.

First Baptist Church, Huntsville, Texas (c. 1925), when Charles Forrest Andrews became pastor. Courtesy Times and Places Collection, #511, Walkercountytreasure.com, Huntsville Art Commission, City of Huntsville, Texas. 4/22/2009, accessed 11/14/2011.

Dana in Austin, Texas, before leaving for California, c. 1929. Courtesy Dana Andrews Collection.

Dana in Huntsville, Texas, bank, c. 1927–29. Courtesy Sam Houston State University archives.

Mary and Dana at the door to their first home on Doheny Drive, c. 1939. Courtesy Dana Andrews Collection.

Dana starring as George Washington in *Valley Forge* (1939), a Pasadena Playhouse production. Courtesy Huntington Library.

Dana in a Pasadena Playhouse production, c. 1937–39. Courtesy Dana Andrews Collection.

Mary and Dana's early days together, c. 1937. Courtesy Dana Andrews Collection.

Early portrait shot, c. mid-1930s. Courtesy Dana Andrews Collection.

Mary and Dana get married (Dana was growing a beard for his first picture, *The Westerner* [1940]). Courtesy Dana Andrews Collection.

Dana in a Pasadena Playhouse production, c. 1937–39. Courtesy Dana Andrews Collection.

Studio Portrait Shot, c. 1939.
Courtesy Dana Andrews Collection.

Noir portrait, c. early 1940s.
Courtesy Dana Andrews Collection.

Portrait with Hollywood-enhanced cleft chin, c. 1939. Courtesy Dana Andrews Collection.

Dana (Captain Harvey Ross) in *The Purple Heart* (1944). Courtesy Dana Andrews Collection.

Dana (Joe Lilac) slugging it out with Gary Cooper (Professor Bertram Potts) in *Ball of Fire* (1941). Courtesy Dana Andrews Collection.

Dana (Joe Lilac) in *Ball of Fire* (1941). Courtesy Dana Andrews Collection.

Anne Baxter (Julie Keefer) and Dana (Ben Ragan) in *Swamp Water* (1941). Courtesy Dana Andrews Collection.

The three accused cattle rustlers and murderers: Anthony Quinn (Juan Martinez), Dana (Donald Martin), and Francis Ford (Halva Harvey) in *The Ox-Bow Incident* (1943). Courtesy Dana Andrews Collection.

Anthony Quinn (Juan Martinez), Dana (Donald Martin), and Francis Ford (Halva Harvey), the accused cattle rustlers and murderers, are confronted by Henry Fonda (Gil Carter) and Frank Conroy (Major Tetley) in *The Ox-Bow Incident* (1943). Courtesy Dana Andrews Collection.

Dana (Mark McPherson) interrogates Gene Tierney (Laura) in *Laura* (1944). Courtesy Dana Andrews Collection.

Clifton Webb (Waldo Lydecker) is interrogated by Dana (Mark McPherson) in *Laura* (1944). Courtesy Dana Andrews Collection.

Gene Tierney (Laura) finds Dana (Mark McPherson) in her apartment in *Laura* (1944). Courtesy Dana Andrews Collection.

Gene Tierney (Laura) learns that Dana (Mark McPherson) is investigating her "murder" in *Laura* (1944). Courtesy Dana Andrews Collection.

Gene Tierney (Laura) reacts to Dana's (Mark McPherson) revelation that someone has tried to murder her in *Laura* (1944). Courtesy Dana Andrews Collection.

Dana (Eric Stanton) marries Alice Faye (June Mills) in *Fallen Angel* (1945). Courtesy Dana Andrews Collection.

Director Jacques Tourneur with Dana (Logan Stuart) in *Canyon Passage* (1946). Courtesy Dana Andrews Collection.

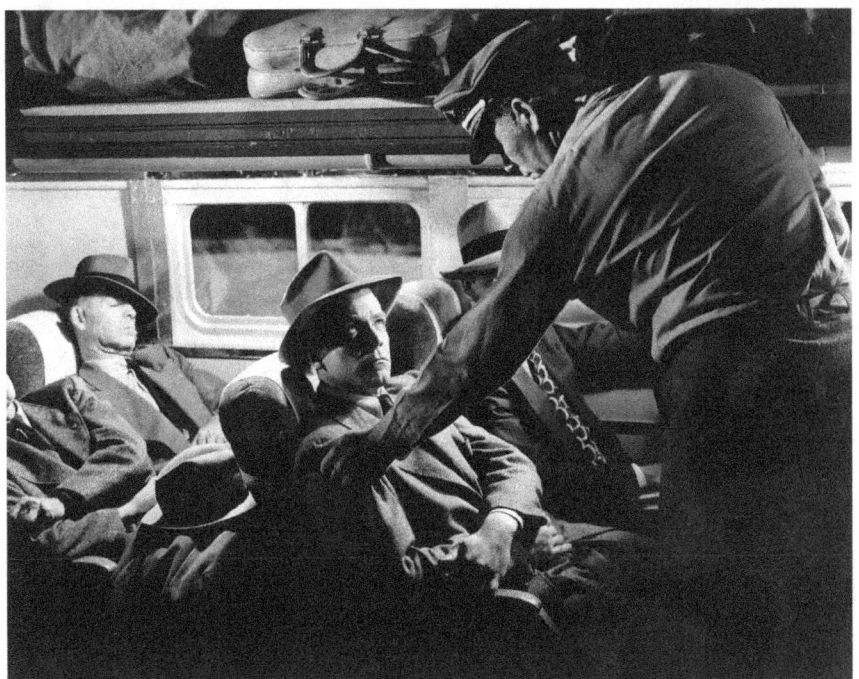

Dana (Eric Stanton) in the opening scene of *Fallen Angel* (1945). Courtesy Dana Andrews Collection.

Linda Darnell (Stella) meets Dana (Eric Stanton) in *Fallen Angel* (1945). Courtesy Dana Andrews Collection.

Teresa Wright takes care of Dana (Fred Derry) after he experiences a nightmare about the war in *The Best Years of Our Lives* (1946). Courtesy Dana Andrews Collection.

Dana (Corporal Tyne) takes over leadership of his platoon when Private Porter (Herbert Rudley) has a breakdown in *A Walk in the Sun* (1945). Courtesy Dana Andrews Collection.

Dana (Fred Derry) on his way home after the war in *The Best Years of Our Lives* (1946). Courtesy Dana Andrews Collection.

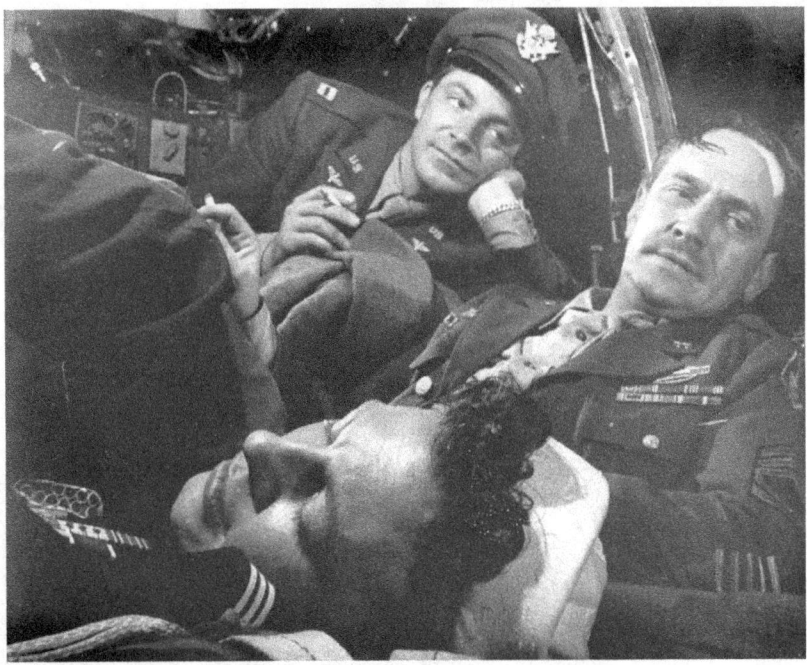

Dana (Fred Derry), Fredric March (Al Stephenson), and Harold Russell (Homer Parrish) flying home after the war in *The Best Years of Our Lives* (1946). Courtesy Dana Andrews Collection.

Joan Crawford (Daisy Kenyon) and Dana (Dan O'Mara) in *Daisy Kenyon* (1947). Courtesy Dana Andrews Collection.

Dana (Henry L. Harvey) in *Boomerang* (1947). Courtesy Dana Andrews Collection.

Dana (Mark Dixon), Gene Tierney (Morgan Taylor), and Bert Freed (Paul Klein) in *Where the Sidewalk Ends* (1950). Courtesy Dana Andrews Collection.

Director Elia Kazan, Dana, and a script supervisor on set of *Boomerang* (1947). Courtesy Dana Andrews Collection.

Toluca Lake house backyard, c. late 1940s. Courtesy Dana Andrews Collection.

David, Steve, Mary, Kathy, Annis, and Dana, c. 1947. Courtesy Dana Andrews Collection.

Dana on the bowsprit, c. 1950.
Courtesy Dana Andrews Collection.

Dana on the *Katharine*, one of his three
sailboats, c. 1950. Courtesy Dana Andrews
Collection.

Charles and Billy (Steve Forrest) on board, c. late
1940s. Courtesy Dana Andrews Collection.

The *Valeehi*, Dana's 80-foot sailboat, c. 1950s. Courtesy Dana Andrews Collection.

Dana and Mary playing backgammon, with their dog, Michael, beside them, c. 1950s Courtesy Aimee Abben.

Dana on the set with Susan, Steve, Kathy, and Mary, 1950. Courtesy Dana Andrews Collection.

Father and son celebrating at the Copacabana, c. 1958. Courtesy Dana Andrews Collection.

Dana's photograph (c. 1950s) of Minnie Carter, who took care of him and his children. Courtesy Dana Andrews Collection.

Dana and David, c. late 1950s. Courtesy Dana Andrews Collection.

Walter Matthau (Gentleman Caller), Mary (Laura), June Walker (Amanda), and Dana (Tom) in *The Glass Menagerie*, 1952. Courtesy Dana Andrews Collection.

Kathy, Dana, Mary, and Susan on the set of *Strange Lady in Town* (1955). Courtesy Dana Andrews Collection.

Mary and Dana at their home in Weston, Connecticut, during the run of *Two for the Seesaw*, 1958. Courtesy Dana Andrews Collection.

Mary and Dana in their happy dinner theater period, 1970s. Courtesy Dana Andrews Collection.

Dana in the 1970s, one of his family's favorite photographs. Courtesy Dana Andrews Collection.

Steve Forrest and Dana Andrews, c. 1960s. Courtesy Dana Andrews Collection.

Dana directing his granddaughter Abigail to look at the camera, 1975. Courtesy Dana Andrews Collection.

Dana with his grandson, Matt, 1975. Courtesy Dana Andrews Collection.

Matt, Abigail, and Ilena, Dana's three grandchildren, c. 1972. Courtesy Dana Andrews Collection.

CHAPTER 11

Stardom
1944–45

EVEN BEFORE *LAURA* COMPLETED PRODUCTION, the change in Dana's status was signaled in the September 1944 issue of *Modern Screen* with a profile titled "The Guy Next Door: The Star Nobody Knows." The piece opens with an anecdote about a "swank Hollywood premiere" where Dana was told to get his own car because the attendant did not recognize him. The unassuming Dana did not complain or reveal who he was because this sort of thing happened to him all the time.

Accurate or not, such stories established a truth about an actor who did not present himself as "grand and glamorous," but as an "easy going, unaffected, down-to-earth guy." He is pictured as such: shaving, eating breakfast, relaxing with Mary and Kathy, and gardening. *Laura*, the article announced, would probably be his star-making breakthrough after more than a decade in Hollywood and appearances in sixteen pictures. Too many costume epics and uniforms had hidden his leading man looks, a problem the smartly tailored role in *Laura* would now remedy. The article describes how Dana junked his wardrobe and ordered a dozen new, well-made suits tailored to the studio's specifications.

The veracity of movie magazines, designed to publicize all things Hollywood and in league with actors who sought to promote themselves and their studios, is questionable, yet in this instance *Modern Screen* seems close to the truth. In the article, he is quoted as saying: "Just because I have a job that ballyhoos me is no reason to think I'm superior to anyone else." Indeed, the article describes his early years in Texas and his attraction to motion pictures, and it reveals that his attention to acting—watching the same performances again and again—made it seem like a job he could learn and perfect, and not the actions of "gods and goddesses strictly from Olympus." After a quick rundown of his struggling years in Hollywood, the profile concentrated on Dana the family man, again in terms remarkably close to the truth.

That these early articles about Dana are not more fanciful is probably attributable to his utter lack of interest in creating a romantic myth about himself. Unlike Raymond Burr, for example, he did not invent a war record (which, amazingly, no one ever checked), or create, like Marilyn Monroe, a melodrama out of his childhood. Love affairs, bad boy behavior of the Robert Mitchum sort—often the staples of movie magazine stories—simply had no place in his biography. Dana worried about his wholesome image only in so far as it might cost him dramatic roles. He continued to keep his singing voice a secret, although that did not prevent his casting in a Rodgers and Hammerstein Technicolor musical, *State Fair* (released August 30, 1945), a starring vehicle for nineteen-year-old Jeanne Crain, just as *Up in Arms* had been for Danny Kaye. But at least in *State Fair* Dana plays the romantic stranger who sweeps farm girl Margy Frake off her feet. As a bonus, he is not saddled with chaperoning Dick Haymes, a superb singer but no actor—and certainly not convincing as Wayne, Margy's hick brother. Dana did not have to appear in production numbers with nothing to do, and he is dubbed singing for only one brief scene on a carnival ride. He later said he could have handled the song but preferred to give the work to someone else.

The picture counts in a biography of Dana Andrews only in so far as it contributes to the evolving persona of a movie star. James Agee reported that *State Fair* was "lacking any real delicateness, vitality, or imagination, and painfully air-conditioned-looking, for a bucolic film." The critic singled out Dana, Crain, and Harry Morgan for their "nice performances" in a "good-natured and pleasant" production. Dana arrives as Pat Gilbert, Mr. Handsome, in the life of Margy Frake, who is stuck with a homely suitor—who she immediately forgets after a roller coaster ride that leaves her clinging to the dapper Pat. He is the perfect gentleman, even when they pass through a dark tunnel at the end of the ride. He shows his press pass, telling the attendant that he wants another ride, and he smiles when Margy properly departs, silently declining his implied invitation for another go around. But she is obviously smitten, as she gazes back at the roller coaster, only to be startled by Pat's teasing voice, "Feel safer down here?" He describes the way her hair bouncing up and down attracted him, and as she gapes at him, he says: "Now it's your turn to say something." But she does not know him, Margy replies. "That can be arranged," Pat counters smoothly, making you wonder about this slick sophisticate's interest in her. His sporty fedora and well-tailored suit signal urbanity. He pitches their mutual attraction as a lark. It will be fun to get to know one another, and then if they break up, there will be no hard feelings. Finding his proposal irresistible, she joins him on another ride that has the effect, of course, of throwing her against him once again.

A wonderful sequence has them walking around a merry-go-round without no dialogue, the camera tracking their developing romance. During scenes of them climbing a hill outside the fair, Pat quickly sketches in his biography: the work as a journalist that has made him familiar with seemingly every big city amusement park. He works on a Des Moines newspaper but has bigger ambitions. This down-to-earth charmer suits Dana Andrews far better than the working class stiff he impersonates in *Up in Arms*. Not even the girls who call out to Pat unduly disturb Margy, since Pat tells her they are just part of his "racket" as a newspaperman. Later, when they are lying on the ground, the reformed rake admits that he would be no good for her. But, reclining and looking up at her, he says, "Of course, you'd be awfully good for me"—a line that clinches his hold on her. "I couldn't marry anyone but you," she blurts out, as she turns to go back to the family trailer.

Margy can think of all sorts of reasons why her family would not appreciate Pat, but he waves them all away, saying he has a hard time understanding himself. He has, in other words, the disarming appeal of Dana Andrews, persistent but so easy on the eyes that Margy finds him irresistible. Wilton was fond of saying that Dana was as popular with the boys as with the girls. He was never arrogant and yet so self-confident that he just drew people to him. Margy need do nothing about their meeting, Pat tells her. After all, he is a journalist and knows how to find the right people at the right time. In fact, the picture does a splendid job of featuring Dana's leading man strengths, his Clark Gable-like belief in himself, even as every other male in this musical is struggling to find his true love—even the prize hog, Blueboy. Wisely, the film never allows Pat to meet Margy's family, since Pat is a dreamboat in a world elsewhere that Margy's family, absorbed in culinary and hog raising contests, are not prepared to confront. Margy and Pat sing no duets, a welcome respite since Dick Haymes is singing his heart out for Vivien Blaine, playing band singer Emily Edwards. Pat breaks his date with Margy to catch a last-minute flight to Chicago to audition for a big job—his own column—and leaves her to return home forlorn from the fair. But Pat returns to reclaim Margy and the adventurous idea of faithful love he embodies. In a perfect ending, she answers his phone call and drives off in a neighbor's truck to greet him and join Pat on his return to Chicago.

This Technicolor fantasy shot on Fox sound stages is important because it shows what Dana could do in the role of charming leading man, a type of extrovert that is the opposite of Mark McPherson in *Laura*. That Dana could play outgoing types so well surely helped him get more important roles in films like *Daisy Kenyon* and *My Foolish Heart* (playing Walt Dreiser, Susan Hayward's lover), even though his major impact on the screen is associated with his enigmatic characters. Walt Dreiser and Pat Gilbert have an edge, a slight cynicism about them that becomes fully developed in Dan O'Mara, the adulterous attorney in *Daisy Kenyon*, and in Dana's role in his next film with Otto Preminger, *Fallen Angel*.

Although Dana described his work with Preminger as close and productive, he did not want to do *Fallen Angel*. As written, his part does seem to lack credibility, since his character, Eric Stanton, has to go through considerable contortions before redeeming himself. Even worse, the script's depiction of small town life was unconvincing to Dana, whose character goes to work for a medium, Professor Madley, played by John Carradine. To have a séance "in front of a village and tell what the secrets of the village were" seemed preposterous, Dana told interviewer Allen Eyles. No one would come to such a meeting. In this case, however, perhaps the actor was distracted by knowing too much about small town life, since the séance is really just a transitional scene, the focus of which is on Dana's character, pinioned between the two women he is courting. Dana's demand for verisimilitude missed the point, since Carradine is there as a foil to Dana, who discovers he cannot perpetuate the kind of con that the medium happily practices in every town he visits.

Dana may have been reluctant to play Eric Stanton because Dana had what he thought was a better role. The Fox legal files reveal that he was considered for the part of Richard Harland, a novelist who becomes the obsession of Ellen Berent in *Leave Her to Heaven*, a Technicolor film noir based on a best-selling novel that would have teamed Dana once more with Gene Tierney in another story of romantic obsession. *Fallen Angel* turned out to be a much better picture, but judging only by the scripts, it is not surprising that Dana might have regarded Preminger's black-and-white production as inferior to *Leave Her to Heaven*, which burnished Cornel Wilde's leading man aura.

Dana had several conversations with Preminger about Stanton, a drifter, who gets booted off a bus when he does not have the fare to continue on to San Francisco. Stranded in small-town Walton, this glib con man talks his way into a hotel room and employment with the shady Professor Madley. Stanton, with only a dollar left, heads over to the "one-arm lunch wagon," as the reviewer in the *Hollywood Reporter* (October 10, 1945) labels it. The grim, stripped-down feel of the joint makes the word "diner" sound too grand. The dreariness of this setup is relieved a few minutes later when Stella (Linda Darnell) arrives in sensational style. A bell jingles, signaling her appearance in a beautiful ensemble: wide-brimmed hat and exquisitely tailored jacket and skirt. With her dark hair and sensuous features, she is the epitome of a film noir femme fatale, who leads with her shapely right leg, then sits down, crossing her legs, and massages one of her sore feet. A stunning beauty, Darnell began modeling at the age of sixteen, and this experience shows in her flashy entrance. She had already co-starred with Tyrone Power in several popular pictures. I doubt anyone had to tell Linda Darnell that just by taking off her shoe she could make a man want her.

Stella has returned from an outing with a man who promised marriage but reneged. She arrives tired and exhausted, just like Eric. Soon Eric decides he must have her. But Stella is wary. She goes out with Eric, but she is scornful of his vague promises that he will get the dough to set them up as man and wife with a family, which is what she wants. He is sincere, but Stella is the wrong woman for him. She is too jaded and just plain weary of hearing all the promises men have made to her. Eric implores Stella to believe that he has never felt this way about a woman before. He is, in fact, a man who does not know his own mind. He is ready to drop the pretenses and poses of a PR man, but he his own worst enemy. He tries to prove himself to Stella by marrying June Mills (Alice Faye), who has an inheritance he plans to grab, then get a divorce and marry Stella. What woman would fall for that scheme? Certainly not Stella, who points out that June—even if she has been deceived—has the ring on her finger. Where does that leave Stella?

Then Stella is murdered, and Eric becomes one of the suspects. He decides to run away. To his amazement, June decides to go with him to San Francisco—an offer he can't refuse because he still wants her money, which has been banked there. June, it turns out, is no dupe. Although Eric does not marry her for love, she perceives in him an incipient integrity that no one else—certainly not Eric himself or her older sister Clara (Anne Revere)—recognizes. Clara, who has herself been deceived by a husband who absconded with her inheritance, rightly suspects Eric's mercenary motives. But June, refusing to give way to cynicism, rejects Eric's evaluation of himself as a failure unworthy of a second chance. She remains open hearted, gradually breaking down his resistance to her and making him realize that Stella may have been his obsession, but any relationship with her would have lasted only a few weeks. June, on the other hand, is (to use the language of the time) for keeps, and Eric is the fallen angel she is able to redeem. Accepting him in his fallen state, she provides him with the opportunity to forgive himself and to fall in love with her.

The novel the picture is based on is narrated quite crudely by Eric Stanton himself. Marty Holland's prose is atrocious, and Eric is a cliché of no redeeming interest. What shape Harry Kleiner's script was in when Dana first read it is unknown, but the picture that resulted is magnificent, culminating in one of Dana's greatest performances, made possible by Alice Faye's faith in him—the same faith that June has in Eric.

To hear Dana Andrews tell the story of *Fallen Angel* in his Columbia University oral history, the picture was a disaster. It is true that the picture did not succeed at the box office, and that (with some notable exceptions) critics have not rated it highly, but in this case the actors, the director, and the picture itself have been done an injustice. Dana called the picture "pretty bad," adding that it put Alice Faye "out of business." He felt so adamant that he risked a suspension, one of those unpaid enforced holidays that actors took when they refused a role the studio assigned to them. Dana still worked in a period when a suspension meant that time was added on the traditional seven-year contract. So if he took, say, a six-month suspension, his contract would be extended to seven years, six months. On the advice of his agent and attorney he reluctantly agreed to appear in the film, but he continued to wonder why Faye did so:

> I had long conversations with her, and I found out later why there was pressure for me to do the picture: it was because Alice, who had been semi-retired, said unless she found something she wanted to do she wouldn't do it. Well, Alice was a big box-office draw for 20th Century Fox, and they didn't want her idle. So they sent her every script that came in, practically, hoping she'd find something interesting she might like to do. Well, this little story came along. She had seen *Laura*, and she liked me in this part. It was a good part—almost anybody could have done it. She said, "I'll do this one if you can get Dana Andrews." This I didn't know. So this is why it happened.

Faye had been trapped in popular Fox musicals—exactly the fate that Dana had dreaded should he be typed as a singer-actor—and was hoping that *Fallen Angel* would be her breakout picture. What she saw in *Laura* was an actor who could play conflicted feelings, exactly what the Eric Stanton role called for, and, of course, after *Laura*, Dana was hot.

Even during the making of the picture, Dana did not grasp what was happening:

> There were long conversations I had with Miss Faye, when I said, "Why did you ever do this?" "Oh, you wait and see, this is going to be great, it's terrific." As it turned out, Linda Darnell was the best thing in the picture, and the scene I had with her was the only good thing in the picture—at least it was showy. When she [Faye] saw the picture, she made the statement, "I'll never do another picture." And she hasn't since then. When she saw it she knew it was bad, but she didn't realize it while she was making it. She was really in tears.

Upset at Zanuck's editing of the film to feature the sexy Darnell, Faye wrote an "unprintable" note to the producer, vowing never to work for him again. She never did, although she did return to the screen a few years after Dana recorded his oral history. Many of her favorite scenes in *Fallen Angel* had been cut, but her performance remains intact. She overreacted and never seems to have realized that, in the end, the picture is hers. She owns it. More to the point is Faye's tribute to Preminger, who was notoriously hard on actors but who also, as Faye confessed, "got a lot out of me . . . I was proud of the performance I turned in."

For all his misgivings, Dana gave Preminger no trouble at all, always arriving on time, knowing his lines, and knowing exactly what he wanted to do with the part. David Raksin concurred, calling Dana "a man's man, a great guy really, and so easy to worth with. At Fox he was one of Otto's favorites." Preminger saved his rages for Linda Darnell, far less experienced and confident than Dana and Alice Faye. Years later Dana was still grousing, never realizing how right he was for the role. Preminger "didn't understand why I didn't like it. I said, 'In the first place, I don't think it's a picture for Alice Faye, but besides that, I don't like the part for me. I don't like the picture. It's terrible. It's in bad taste, it's unbelievable. I just can't see it at all.'" Dana had a blind spot—perhaps because he did not like Alice Faye, who seemed to have become obsessed with him. Charles's wife, Jeanne, remembered that Faye tried to call Dana several times, and that he left messages saying he wasn't at home.

It is disappointing to hear Dana talk like Darryl Zanuck or like any producer who types actors, thinking he knows what they are capable of.

Dana, who rarely took much interest in his fellow actors, did not realize that Alice Faye was ready for a huge shift in her career. She was getting too old to play ingénues and wanted to extend her career by playing more serious parts. Nobody but Otto Preminger seemed to realize as much. He assembled a first rate cast and the same crew that had worked on *Laura*. Sometimes Otto the autocrat really did know more than his actors. He lost interest in the picture after it was made and hardly mentions it in his autobiography, although to critic Gerald Pratley, Preminger admitted that years later he got "very involved" in watching the picture on television and called it "an interesting film."

It is more than interesting; it is *engrossing*. And in bad taste? Dana sounds like Charles Forrest Andrews. Yes, there is a sordid quality to the picture's milieu, but in truth it is no tawdrier than *Laura*'s Manhattan, and Eric is not repellent (a word reviewers used for the characters in *Fallen Angel*) in comparison to, say, Shelby Carpenter. When Dana's daughter Susan commented in the opening scene for the DVD reissue of the picture, she noted the parallel between her father arriving in California with next to no money and Eric's plight. Both, I might add, were seeking a new life and very much on their own. To be sure Dana was no con man, but why he could not make the connection is puzzling. On screen, the affinity between the man and the role is obvious.

Fallen Angel is set in dingy small town America at the end of the war, so it lacks the glossy veneer and escapist appeal of *Laura*, but that grimy atmosphere is transfigured in a moment of cinematic magic when June, sitting in her shabby San Francisco hotel room, quietly waits for Eric's return. In a ten-second close-up, as the camera moves in on her, the look of wonder, of expectation—but also of uncertainty—is utterly believable as Faye exposes her character. This moving scene is what makes her ultimate union with Eric possible—and then *necessary*. It is the acting, not the script, that does it. Failing to see the skill in Faye's wonderful performance is the only explanation for Dana having labeled the story "unbelievable."

To do justice to *Fallen Angel* requires, close inspection of the two actors who served one another so well and yet did not realize what they had achieved in performances as remarkable and as seemingly "impossible" as the story the picture has to tell. *Fallen Angel* represented a challenge to Dana that he met admirably well. He simply concentrated his force on Laura, but now he had to handle two women, who speak to two very different sides of Eric Stanton's character: the man who knows he is a fraud, and the man who (deep down) wants to expose that fraud. Dana plays glib charm and furtive decency equally well, and the role continues his refinement of characters divided against themselves.

Preminger's lighting scheme draws on the traditional tropes of film noir, especially the alternation of light and dark. The effect is achieved through careful use of light filtered through venetian blinds, a staple of the genre and here present in the greasy spoon. But symbolic use of the interplay of light and dark is also present in transitions between scenes, so that Eric's romantic night on the beach with Stella segues to his sunny afternoon visit to the church, where he accosts June, setting in motion his plot to marry her for her money. As Susan Andrews notes on the DVD edition of *Fallen Angel*, her father approaches the church with an erect posture that was a very deliberate part of his identity, and one that the costume designer, Bonnie Cashin, emphasized by always putting him into suits with ventless jackets, emphasizing the straight, pillar-like deportment that suggests a rectitude that Eric's actions do not yet convey. Eric has, in other words, conned himself, thinking he is not worthy of anything more than a scheme to bilk a woman out of her money.

The first scene in the church establishes June's character. She is not as young as Stella, or as experienced. She is a mark for a con man, but she is not gullible or worshipful of this handsome stranger who gets the organ music she is playing wrong. It is not Brahms but her own composition, she says, correcting him. Her cool manner suggests that she knows he is feeding her a line and cares nothing about music. But he does it so charmingly that she is intrigued. As they walk out of the church and cross the street to her home, Eric grabs June to get her out of the way of a passing bicycle, signaling his first involuntary effort to protect her—his prize and also (although he does not yet realize as much) his salvation. He has already begun to work on her, teasing her about her absorption in books, accusing of her of being afraid to live. He is already implicitly offering her adventure and escape from her overbearing sister. But she counters that Eric, who admits he never reads, cannot know about life without the experiences that books offer. Indeed, Eric is afraid of the truths that book contain. "You know that's quite a mind you have there, Miss Mills," Eric admits. "You mean for a girl in a small town," she retorts. "Must be the books, huh?" she asks. "Must be," he replies evenly. Between them, in fact, they make a whole, although neither of them understands, as yet, their compatibility. June brings out qualities in Eric he has not acknowledged to himself. June, in fact, is Stella's superior in every way except for raw sexual power. It is already obvious that she is no pushover, just as it is obvious that Eric will have to work for his money. He tells the impatient Stella as much, which is why she decides she cannot wait for this drifter with big plans but no follow-through. But June can afford to wait; indeed, she has been waiting for someone like Eric all her life. "You're afraid to step out of your tower," Eric taunts her, and smiles as he turns away after securing a date with her. He believes he has goaded her into his trap.

Eric Stanton is not that far removed from the worldly Pat Gilbert in *State Fair*, except that *Fallen Angel* refuses to gloss over the male lead's chicanery. It takes no effort to like Pat, but because he is doubtful about himself, Eric makes us work for it. David Thomson's comment on Dana Andrews as actor and man seems procrustean, but it fits Eric's own performance: "Andrews could suggest unease, shiftiness, and rancor barely concealed by good looks. He did not quite trust or like himself, and so a faraway bitterness haunted him." Was this role too close for comfort?

When Eric promises a life of cities and stardom ("Miss June Mills, woman of the year") she is beguiled by this vision of greatness—much as Dana Andrews was on his trek west. But Eric is, in fact, a quitter, having left New York City and his dreams, becoming the kind of embittered failure Dana's family feared might result from his wanderlust. June never believes that she has the musical talent to justify Eric's bogus praise, but she is enamored of his style, which is such a contrast to Clara's constricted sphere of possibilities. But Eric feels caught in his own trap. Returning to June's home, where he sits in an ornate Victorian living room, he is visibly uncomfortable as Clara latches on to the couple, presuming they will want her to be their "guest" in their married home. When Eric rises stiffly from the sofa, he rotates his right shoulder as if trying to relieve the strain, even as he is playing the happy newly married husband. It is the kind of physical business Dana might well have picked up from Ronald Colman in a picture like *Lady Windermere's Fan*. (Expressing his discomfort in this silent film, Colman as Lord Darlington tugs at his cravat wondering how he is going to get out of a situation he is caught in with another man's wife.) The structure of Eric's plot is beginning to disintegrate, and he is having trouble holding himself together. Many students of Preminger's films have noted his long takes and refusal to break up action with fast cuts. Here cinematographer Joseph LaShelle, a holdover from *Laura*, follows Eric as he paces the room, unraveling moment by moment in Dana's exquisitely poised performance.

A similar scene occurs when June accompanies Eric to San Francisco. He storms out of their hotel room, angry because she suggested that he is acting like a guilty man and that he should return to Walton to clear himself of the murder charge. She does not try to follow him. June never clings to Eric, never suggests that she is entirely dependent on him. His return to the room suggests, in fact, how much he needs her. She is in the shower and asks him to hand her a towel, and then a few moments later, her robe—just the kind of service a husband performs for his wife and that she expects. The matter of fact tone that June takes indicates her refusal to make a frenzied drama out of Eric's predicament. When she emerges from the bathroom, Eric presents her with a toothbrush and a book, and she smiles in pleasure at the husbandly gesture, which, he admits, is his way of apologizing for rudely walking out on her. Imagine Eric buying a book for Stella! Such scenes are so natural and so right that they seem anything but the impossibility Dana deemed them. He may have thought he was just giving Preminger a professional performance, but in retrospect such moments appear to be pure art.

This tender moment is broken up by June's first expression of anger when Eric starts to run himself down. She wants him to stop talking about the money he married her for. "All I know is that I love you, I love you," she says, collapsing into his arms. Rather than suggesting weakness, June's cry shows how much she wants him. This act is a stunning revelation to Eric, who stands there holding her, perhaps realizing that his original motives no longer matter. He holds her face in his hands and kisses her passionately. Then he gives an unsparing account of his "batting average," hitting home runs (starting a successful PR firm) but always, in the end, striking out. "But why go on?" he adds. "I want to know everything about you," June says, quietly but emphatically. He calls himself a washout at thirty. How could Dana not have thought of himself at almost the same age, at the very moment he wanted to quit acting, when he was, in fact, on the verge of success. This is exactly Eric's nadir, when he calls himself a failure, but paradoxically wins June and a new life. She tells him he is not finished. He says he is tired, "with a million jobs behind me." This is exactly what Dana used to say when he described to his daughter Susan that perilous period before his big break.

June finally asks Eric if he loved Stella, and he has to admit he did. But "that's all over too," he marvels, describing his obsession as though it belonged to another life. Did any actor in Hollywood know more than Dana Andrews about what it felt like to be obsessed with one woman and unable to look at others, and then have to put that obsession behind him? The psychological dynamic of this picture suits Dana so perfectly that I have to wonder if he did not want to do it for that very reason. It is painful for Eric to recount the last ten years of his life and to surrender himself to June. But self-acceptance results in Eric's redemption, just as the initially reluctant Dana gradually gravitated to Mary and rejuvenated himself.

Eric still resists June's suggestion that they return to Walton, and he still does not understand why she does not leave him. "Because you are my husband, and I am your wife," she says quite simply. "Right out of a book," he says wearily, implying that what she says is unreal. "You're tired," she says, inviting him to bed. She recites a poem about a fallen angel, about the human fall from grace. Exhausted, Eric says, "Go on," drawing strength from the bookish June. "Love alone can make the fallen angel rise," she intones. "Sounds good," he says, falling off to sleep. It is a slumber that will result in his rebirth, signaled by the next scene. Light pours through a window overlooking the Golden Gate Bridge just after June finishes the poem, which ends, "For only two together can enter paradise," words that linger over the segue to the next day.

The picture wraps quickly. June is detained for questioning by cops, who spot her entering the San Francisco bank where she is about to withdraw money for Eric. Then he returns, having figured out that the violence-prone ex-cop, Mark Judd (played with sly menace by Charles Bickford) is the murderer. Setting up a confrontation in the greasy spoon with Judd, Eric exposes the guilty man in a setup he has worked out with the cops, and then rides away with June who is, appropriately enough, at the wheel.

Unfortunately, Faye's fears about how her work in this picture would fare have often been realized. Borde and Cahumeton in *A Panorama of Film Noir* do not even mention her in their description of *Fallen Angel*. Unable to understand the intricate transitions in the psychology of the characters, they charge the film with becoming "bogged down in inane concessions to morality." But *Fallen Angel* ought to be regarded as Otto Preminger's triumph over the production code—not for violating its sanctions, but for honestly creating a story that did not need the restraint of censorship. Critic Jonathan Rosenbaum is right when he notes that Preminger's "narrative lines are strewn with deceptive counter paths, shifting viewpoints, and ambiguous characters who perpetually slip out of static categories and moral definitions." Critics have noted the parallel with *Laura*, which similarly revolves around obsession with a beautiful woman and her murder. But *Fallen Angel* blows apart the romanticism of *Laura* and presents a more mature, nuanced view of human motivations and love in a flawed world. More scenes with Alice Faye would have made the film more digestible for those needing time to adjust to the way she wins Eric, but the additional material would not have made this film a greater work of art. What a pity that it was not honored as such when it appeared—and what a pity it remains largely unheralded for its considered reading of human relationships.

World War II is not even mentioned in *Fallen Angel*, although it is there in the background: when Pop, the owner of the greasy spoon, tells Eric he has no meat, and at a dance, where men in uniform lead their ladies in the traditional way, one arm extended, while Eric hugs Stella, their arms close to his chest. Dana was still subject to the draft (he was classified 1A), and his certificate of fitness deemed him "physically fit, acceptable for general military service" on January 12, 1945. Some reports suggest he had been ruled ineligible for the draft because of a physical disability. Fan magazine shots of a bare chested Dana do show a concave chest, which has been associated with heart murmurs and decreased lung capacity, but Dana left nothing in his papers that indicates he was excused from military service on medical grounds. Mary told her children that their father was never called up because by the time they were ready to take a fit man with children, the war had ended. By then, Dana was the father of three children: David, Kathy, and Stephen, born on December 15, 1944.

Dana surely knew that this was the time to capitalize on his opportunities, although his hectic schedule had more to do with the Goldwyn/Fox sharing agreement than any decisions on his part. Dana's brother John wrote to say he was gratified to read articles praising Dana's acting and no longer simply gushing over his rise to stardom. Dana was already thirty when signed to his first contract, and well into his thirties—not old by Hollywood standards—before he won his first starring role. Clark Gable did not catch on until he was thirty, and Humphrey Bogart did not become a leading man until he was forty-two. But stardom could be evanescent. Fashions changed. Certain periods favored certain actors, and the war gave breaks not only to Dana, but also to Van Johnson, Robert Mitchum, Victor Mature and others, while Gable and Stewart, for example, were in the service. Like other stars, Dana did his part entertaining serviceman. Bette Davis, one of the organizers of the Hollywood Canteen, sent him a thank you note, and Dana kept letters from servicemen expressing gratitude for the time he spent with them at his home and out drinking.

Of all the war films Dana appeared in, *A Walk in the Sun* (released December 25, 1945) is the most distinguished. *A Walk in the Sun* is director Lewis Milestone's troubled tribute to America's fighting men, and his only picture that rivals his greatest anti-war work, *All Quiet on the Western Front*. Just as the director had remained remarkably faithful to Erich Maria Remarque's classic work, so now he carefully followed the tersely presented action of Harry Brown's novel in a war movie that seemed so authentic an army general told Dana, "That's the best goddamed Army picture I've ever seen. Somebody in the army must have made it." Dana plays Sergeant Bill Tyne, part of a platoon that has seen action in the invasion of Italy and is assigned to move inland from their beachhead to assault an enemy stronghold: a well defended farmhouse. These are not the noble airmen of *The Purple Heart*, the gallant naval heroes of *Crash Dive*, or the gung-ho carrier crew of *Wing and a Prayer*. These are battle-hardened grunts, cheerfully cynical about their mopping up operation, veterans fighting exhaustion and enervation. When their leader succumbs to what then would have been called a nervous breakdown, Tyne takes over. He does so quietly, and with the same unassuming power that Dana demonstrated in his earlier roles—but this time in the context of a heightened realism that makes the war much less of a romance and more of a gritty act of survival.

The picture's most memorable sequence features Tyne crawling toward the machine gun nest in the farmhouse. Filmed intermittently from his point of view, the landscape whirls in and out of focus as the exhausted soldier presses on. In earlier close-ups, Milestone makes maximum use of Dana's fabled minimalist acting. The camera concentrates on his face, the eyes staring ahead, the mouth fixed in a straight, determined line. Milestone uses Dana's visage to reflect the platoon's varying emotions: anxious perseverance and anticipation of atrocities to come, but also unfathomable openness to the moment itself, which manifests as an unblinking mask of a face. Unlike the other soldiers, however, Dana's character does not indulge in sarcasm or petty sadism. He treats the men democratically, recognizing they have different uses and will be responsive to his firm direction. When a skeptical solider asks, "Why me?" Tyne responds, "Why anybody else?"

Howard Barnes's *New York Herald Tribune* review is typical of the positive critical response to the picture and to Dana's performance, praising the "quiet intensity" of a "knowing actor." Later critics have faulted the film's use of balladry to narrate the action, as well as the highly stylized dialogue that James Agee deplored. But perhaps more significant is a war veteran's memory of watching the film in a hospital in Atlantic City in 1945. Many of the soldiers were amputees used to deriding Hollywood war picture heroics, but they watched *A Walk in the Sun* in stunned silence. Years later, this same veteran watched the film again, suddenly aware of the absence of four-letter words and of the fact that the soldiers were speaking in blank verse. Rather than rejecting this literary conceit, he actually thought the language elevated the picture's truthfulness.

Some vets did write to complain about inaccuracies: bunching the men together; Dana's failure to take the ammo clip off a fallen soldier; walking on an open road when cover was available; and the failure to search two captured Italian soldiers. But other vets understood the requirements of dramatic license and the need to situate the men close together in order to deliver the film's dialogue. Dana thought the authenticity of the film derived from its documentary feel. He called Milestone "a poet with a camera" who knew exactly when to cut to close-ups of the actors' faces.

Dana was very proud of the film and his performance. He was in tears at the premiere in New York City, as the *New York Sun* reported on January 11, 1946. In an interview for the paper, he praised the Russian-born Milestone: "Milly, it seems, is the kind of director who actually asks for an actor's advice instead of giving him orders.... He's not only the finest director in Hollywood. He's one of the grandest people. I've worked with him so much now, and we see so much of each other, that I'm beginning to get a Russian accent." Dana also described the night before the harrowing assault on the farmhouse was shot:

> Stephen made his appearance in the world. I drove my wife to the hospital, had a flat tire on the way, but finally managed to make it in good shape. Then I spent the rest of the night pacing the floor in true worried-husband fashion and never did go to sleep. Those circles under my eyes were no make-up job or good acting on my part, they were Stephens's contribution to realism!

Production files for the picture show that while Milestone considered different actors for various roles, Dana was the only actor he wanted to play Sergeant Tyne.

Norman Lloyd, who played the wise-guy Private Archimbeau in *A Walk in the Sun*, was a fit ninety-five and still playing doubles tennis when I interviewed him about Dana and the picture. Responding to one of my letters, Lloyd called Dana "a prince among men," an epithet that could just as well suit Dana's character in *A Walk in the Sun*. Lloyd, an original cast member of Orson Welles's Mercury Theater, is a veritable historian of the New York stage and Hollywood. "There was one beautiful guy," Lloyd told me, reminiscing about Dana. "This was a man you could trust." They became friends. Lloyd remembered visiting Dana at his home, driving there with Lewis Milestone, to pick Dana up for the day's shooting. Like many others, Lloyd remembered not only his friend's extraordinary ability to memorize lines quickly, but also his astonishing drinking: "Dana could drink a fifth of bourbon, and it meant nothing. He did not become inebriated." But getting up the next morning could sometimes be a problem. "I remember little Kathy running out to the limo saying, 'Daddy is still asleep.' And Milly who loved Dana, said, 'It must have been Jack Daniels.'" Milly told Kathy to wake up her Daddy, and she eagerly ran into the house to do so. "Dana emerged. He looked ready to run a quarter mile race. He looked just great," Lloyd said, laughing. The phone rang, and while Lloyd answered the call, his wife, who had been watching us, said, "You are talking about someone we dearly loved."

Dana's drinking never affected his performance. *Never*, said Lloyd, who marveled at the way Dana could take a page that rewrote his lines, go to his trailer, and emerge fifteen minutes later with a perfect rendition of the scene. "He was so good, oh God, they didn't know how good he was," Lloyd said, as though he were delivering an elegy. "What he gave you was bigger than acting. It was only what the man can give you. It's some kind of marvelous quality of person, which he had. . . . Dana was the kind of guy you knew you could trust, *immaculately*. His acting was very direct and simple. No curves. To me he was the most American actor of his time. Always, they talk about Jimmy Stewart. But Jimmy Stewart got cute, I think. He got self-conscious."

"Mannerisms," I interjected.

"Dana, never," Lloyd declared. "Dana was forthright. He was from Texas, right?" "Right," I said.

"But he could have been from any part of the country," Lloyd insisted. "I never thought of him as a Texan. . . . He had great strength. His father was a minister, right?"

"Right," I said.

"I often wonder," Lloyd mused, "if we could get ministers that pure, then religion would be all right—as Dana was. . . . When it came time to cast the hero of *A Walk in the Sun*, Milly went to Dana," Lloyd said, as if no other choice was conceivable.

I had just watched *A Walk in the Sun* and wanted to test my reactions on Lloyd:

ROLLYSON. There's a wonderful scene when Dana takes over, when the sergeant cracks up. And it's just before that climactic scene when they are going to charge the farmhouse. Dana is addressing the men just as the sergeant before him did. Dana's words are the same: "This is a bad situation. It stinks." Everybody agrees. He looks at these men, and it's the most natural gesture in the world—because everybody is exhausted . . . and he puts his hand to his helmet and just shoves it up slightly. There is so much in that moment.
LLOYD. Oh yes.
ROLLYSON. He's expressing their exhaustion at the same time as he is leading them.
LLOYD. Perfection. Instinct. Because Milestone never . . . He'd just let Dana be Dana.

Milestone's genius, as Lloyd saw it, was to pick Dana to play in situations that the director had an affinity for: a group of men under stress. The director knew how to stage such scenes and to react to them—but as for the acting itself, that was entirely a matter for the actors to sort out.

The straightforward, even-tempered demeanor of the man and the actor that Milestone admired is also what made the two men friends. The sociable Milly was a frequent guest in the Andrews home, a fairly unusual practice for an actor who did not spend much time with his Hollywood associates away from movie sets. Few directors and few actors ever got to know Dana well. Even Norman Lloyd mentioned that Dana never talked about his children or his family. But Milestone was, in Dana's words, a drinking buddy and raconteur: "He taught me more about people than [he knew] long before I was in motion pictures. He told me all kinds of stories about great characters, like Douglas Fairbanks, Sr., and Charlie Chaplin." And Dana wanted his family to know this intriguing man. Critic Otis Ferguson described Milestone in motion: "rather burly . . . with thinning sandy hair and heavy eyelids, a manner that is not so abrupt as decisive. . . . He is a little short in the legs and walks with a sort of sidewise throwing motion of the feet, rolling a little and talking gaily." Norman Lloyd admired Milly's "great Tartar face."

Jean Renoir, Lewis Milestone, and now Jacques Tourneur joined that small group of professionals Dana brought home. Tourneur cast Dana in an unusual western, *Canyon Passage* (shot in the summer and fall of 1945, and released September 30, 1946), a neglected masterpiece. Set in the small mining town of Jacksonville, Oregon, in 1856, this Technicolor western uses cinematography that runs counter to the vast horizontal landscapes of Hollywood big budget productions. Jacksonville is jammed into the mountains and hemmed in as well by hostile Indians. Dana plays Logan Stuart, a restless, ambitious general store owner. Although this film seems a world away from film noir, Tourneur exploits his friend's enigmatic quality. Every scene between Dana and his co-star, Susan Hayward, is charged with sexual tension, even though Dana's character is a man on a mission—not solving a crime this time, but instead attempting to build a life for himself in a community where the law hardly operates and the settlers succumb to a herd mentality.

Logan Stuart is the lone individualist—but not in the usual western way of, say, Gary Cooper in *High Noon*—an entrepreneur who has to live among and do business with men suspicious of his desire to better himself. In a stunning scene reminiscent of *The Ox-Bow Incident*, Stuart stands up to a mob ready to lynch a man accused of murder. While film critics have praised this film, they have said little about Dana's crucial performance—perhaps because critical acclaim for films like *The Ox-Bow Incident* and *The Best Years of Our Lives* has crowded out any awareness of yet another superlative but understated performance. Biographers of Susan Hayward rush past the film in their eagerness to recount her later, Oscar-worthy roles, apparently unaware of just how well her pairing with Dana works in this picture.

In Tourneur's version of the noble hero, Dana's Logan Stuart does right by his friend, George Camrose (Brian Donlevy), a poor businessman with a fatal penchant for gambling, loaning Camrose money to cover his huge losses and defending him when he is accused of murder. One look at the heavy-set Brian Donlevy, and you know he will not be able to hold on to his intended, Lucy Overmire (Susan Hayward), who has the spunk of a Scarlett O'Hara. One look at homebody Caroline Marsh (Patricia Roc), and it is apparent that she won't want to trail after the restless Logan, who is courting her. How Lucy could ever have favored Camrose is a mystery, unless she mistook his sedentary habits as a promise of domestic bliss and supposed the peripatetic Logan is not ready to settle down. Donlevy, who had to be cinched up for his romantic roles, has the girth but not the gravity demanded of a true hero. He is the ostensible leading man, since he has assigned Logan the job of retrieving Lucy from Portland while Donlevy is off on another futile quest to strike it rich with a gold claim. The steady-as-he-goes Dana is obviously attracted to Hayward, but he holds his horses and does the honorable thing by escorting her home.

But the feckless Camrose, who continues to lose thousands of dollars gambling, runs off after he is accused (rightly, it turns out) of murdering a man for his gold. Camrose is conveniently killed by one of the townsmen. Meanwhile, Caroline turns to another suitor (Stuart's rival) just as Stuart returns to his burned-down store (Indian retaliation for the murder of an Indian maiden by a devilish white man, Honey Bragg) and to Lucy, who rides off with him to begin another life and a new business.

Honey Bragg, the appropriately named villain, is played by Ward Bond, who has a huge barroom fight with Dana in which, after much pummeling and chair breaking and glass crashing, Dana emerges triumphant, beating the town bully. Dana and Bond knew each other well, having appeared together in *Tobacco Road*, *Kit Carson*, and *Swamp Water*. They got carried away in the fight scene and actually drew some blood. "Bond came at me a little too fast—got his timing wrong—and when I socked hard with my fist he didn't roll," Dana told a reporter for a Cleveland newspaper. "Just took it solid right on the mouth. The doc fixed him up with six stitches. Then—in the very same 'take'—Bond shoved me against a barrel so hard I had to have four stitches taken in my head." Dana leaned over to showed his scar to the reporter. Reviewers liked the picture's brawling realism.

Bond, one of John Wayne's cronies, did not see much of Dana after a few years—in part because Bond became one of those chauvinistic conservatives that Dana despised. As Kathy put it, "Dad used the word reactionary as if it meant ax murderer." When Ronald Reagan later ran for governor of California, Dana showed Kathy a picture of Reagan's house in a magazine. The picture showed a black jockey figure in front of the house. Reagan would have to get rid of that now, Dana said. "Dad said life was simple for Reagan: He only had to look at the world from one point of view. Dad did something rather similar, from the opposing side. He found it disgusting when former Democrats from modest backgrounds made a lot of money and became Republicans."

In *Canyon Passage*, Bond plays not merely a killer, but a rapist. Although his crime is never labeled as such (the Hollywood production code forbid showing the rape), it is clear that his leering at a young Indian woman leads to murdering her and to the ensuing Indian massacre of whites. Bond's character, in other words, not only stands for the outlawry of the Old West, but also the rapacity of the frontier mentality—rarely explored with such honesty in Hollywood westerns. Dana's Logan Stuart is a hero not merely because he is good with his fists, stands by his friends, and believes in fairness and justice, but also because he is self-controlled male and man of integrity in sexual matters as well—a character type Dana developed further when he played Fred Derry in *The Best Years of Our Lives*.

Dana hardly raises his voice in *Canyon Passage*, even when his character is upset with the townspeople and berates them for wishing to see him beaten in a fight with Bragg. Stuart even reprimands Lucy, who is seen enjoying the fight. When she tells him he should have killed Bragg because now Bragg will never let Stuart alone, Stuart replies that he only fought Bragg because he did not want the bully to take over the town. The blood lust that Lucy and the others have shown disgusts him. It is rather like Ashley Wilkes rebuking Scarlett O'Hara.

And, in fact, Susan Hayward had auditioned for the coveted role in *Gone with the Wind* when she was only nineteen, attracting the attention first of producer David O. Selznick, and then of Walter Wanger, who had her under personal contract when she appeared in *Canyon Passage*. Born in Brooklyn as Edythe Marrenner, Hayward, like Dana, grew up dreaming about acting in pictures, worked hard on erasing her accent, and schooled herself by watching Ronald Colman, her favorite movie star ("an object of special adoration," as biographer Gene Arceri puts it). "Elegant, gentle and world weary though he was, perhaps the most appealing thing about him to the Brooklyn girl was the beautiful way in which he spoke English, turning words into music." On movie sets, Hayward was all business and rarely socialized with cast members or her directors, many of whom found her aloof and even hostile. She seemed, like Dana, put off by Hollywood glamour, even though her own physical appearance—especially her luxuriant red hair and well-proportioned body—typed her as a screen siren on the verge of stardom when she appeared in her first film with Dana.

The convergence of Jacques Tourneur, Dana Andrews, and Susan Hayward is one of those remarkable and yet untold events in the history of Hollywood film. The credit may, in part, be due to independent producer Walter Wanger, who later cast Hayward in her Academy Award winning performance in *I Want to Live* (1958). More intellectual and cosmopolitan than most Hollywood producers, a man of "impeccable taste, manners, and sophistication," Wanger appreciated Hayward's independent streak and realized that the studios had overlooked a significant talent. In the beginning, though, Hayward did not understand that Tourneur's refusal to shoot close-ups of her was right, since he was deliberately de-emphasizing the overstated romanticism of the typical Western. In other words, Hayward was enough of a Hollywood prima donna to complain to the director that the audience would not be getting "what you pay me for." Wanger, too, was worried about the paucity of close-ups, even though, in general, Tourneur's direction delighted him. Misunderstanding both the director and Dana, the producer called for more anger from Dana in the bar fight scene. Tourneur resisted, noting that only at important story points would he resort to close-ups. To appease the producer, however, the director shot more close-ups, many of which were later cut in the final edit.

Dana, on the other hand, never complained about lack of close-ups or watched himself in the daily rushes, which he found distracting because they made him self-conscious. As he later said in his Columbia Oral History interview, he approached his parts as a writer, not an actor, and always regarded his roles in the context of the whole picture. He told Virginia Zanuck: "Wouldn't it have been silly, in *The Ox-Bow Incident*, if I'd acted like Errol Flynn and said, 'All right, boys, hang me, but you'll find out you're wrong.' This would have made me look like a hero or a silly leading man, but it would have ruined the story."

Critic Robin Wood mentions Tourneur's "reserve," a quality that translated into pictures with long fluid takes and long shots, compositions which in *Canyon Passage* often make the movie look like a painting. The underplaying of his actors amidst the lush Oregon foliage—such a change from the arid atmosphere and florid performances in most Westerns—complements Tourneur's penchant for approaching genres as an outsider and an observer, to use Wood's words. Not even the perceptive Wood, however, saw that Wanger and his actors shared a similar detachment from Hollywood histrionics that makes the scenes between Dana and Hayward, for example, such a pleasure to watch. The couple rarely touches, let alone embraces. The fun is literally in the way they look at one another, affectionate and appraising and tantalizing. It is as if Tourneur turned to this page in the novel *Canyon Passage* (written by Ernest Haycox) and said to his leading actors, "Just play this":

> She sat across from Stuart, pleasant still; she was aware of her surroundings and occasionally her eyes show curiosity and some vagrant thought stirred her face. Then he found her attention on him, once more with its deep and well-guarded interest. Sometimes warmth lay between them, strong and unsettling, and his own expression would sharpen; and at times like these the bare repose of his face would break, giving way to smiling restlessness. It was these times when she looked at him most observantly, trying to read him.

As Wood says of the character Dana plays, he is "committed chiefly to the preservation of his own independence." Even at the end of the picture, Lucy has to politely ask him if she can join him on his trek to start a new life and business—an ending, by the way, that is superior to the novel's, which is much too explicit about Logan's and Lucy's feelings for one another.

Milestone had identified and exploited a vein of nobility in Dana's character, and Preminger probed Dana's brooding conflicted sensibility. Tourneur, building on their work, captured the actor's romantic and yet reserved allure. There is no point in Susan Hayward attempting to seduce Dana's character, which explains why she seems to settle in the first part of the picture for the available if stoutly second-rate Donlevy. As Logan Stuart, Dana will eventually come round to realizing he cannot resist his attraction to Lucy Overmire, but only after he has explored every other possibility. The beginning of their relationship is rather like Dana's with Mary: not love at first sight, but a gradual building up of attachment based on his keen observation of her character and person. Westerns, as Robin Wood reminds us, are simply not made this way. Again, the subtlety of approach has to be credited, in part, to Wanger, the producer who put all these elements into play. *Canyon Passage* represented a departure from the usual run of Westerns, and reflects the producer's desire to create more sophisticated work within the constraints of the studio system. As he declared in his statement to the Office of War Information seven months after Pearl Harbor, he struggled with the "problem of motion pictures and mass enlightenment."

Still not in the canon of great Westerns, *Canyon Passage* nevertheless remains a contender. John Wakeman's *World Film Directors* singles out Dana in "one of his best roles," noting that the picture was "warmly received on release for its pace, gusto, and almost documentary evocation of frontier life," and that "its reputation has continued to rise." Dana, who usually mentioned *The Ox-Bow Incident* as a source of special pride, did not give himself enough credit for his contribution to *Canyon Passage*, "one of the greatest Westerns," as Tourneur's biographer, Chris Fujiwara, claims. Squeezed between *Laura* and *The Best Years of Our Lives*, *Canyon Passage* has been overshadowed—and so has Dana's resistance to studio star making. He wanted, of course, the fame that would lead to better roles, but he dreaded being stereotyped and shoehorned into other Mark McPherson-like parts that would inhibit his development as an actor. He said as much years later when reminiscing about this period in his Columbia oral history interview.

Jacques Tourneur did not film Dana Andrews like a movie star. Chris Fujiwara's description of the director's shooting style helps explain why: "an actor's body is oriented screen left, with only his or her face turned toward the camera, to interact with someone in the foreground or in the off-screen space behind the camera. Logan is posed and photographed in this way," enforcing "our sense that the people in the film are not fully understandable, that they have something to conceal (the sinister interpretation) or simply, and more generally, that they live in a world of which we can see only fragments, often from oblique angles." It is precisely Tourneur's restraint that Dana admired, finding in the director not merely a congenial professional, but a friend to Dana's way of working, to his reticent way of approaching the world. Tourneur exemplified an extraordinary degree of integrity not readily available to an actor who wanted stardom on his own terms. Thus a film like *Canyon Passage* spoke to Dana's evolving sense of himself as man and actor.

On August 18, 1945, after location shooting on *Canyon Passage* wrapped, an item appeared in the *Los Angeles Times*: "Dana Andrews in Lockup for Stone Throwing." He had evidently been out with a few servicemen drinking. "It's all just a misunderstanding," the article quoted Dana. "I was driving Lt. Normis home and my car stalled near Sgt. Collani's house. I knocked at the door to see if I could use the telephone, but nobody answered. Then I threw some pebbles at the window hoping to wake them up so I could call a garage." A cop arrived and called for a car to arrest Dana and his companion. Whatever the truth of this incident, it is the first sign that Dana's drinking was beginning to be a problem—as it was for other stars like Joan Crawford and Susan Hayward, who sought to relax and relieve stress using intoxicants. "Success is a frightening thing," Dana later explained. "There are tremendous demands put upon you, and it's never anything you can feel or touch. Success is intangible, and when you achieve success, you begin to worry that the success won't last, that it's all going to be some isolated, fragmentary moment in your life."

Before beginning production on his next film, Dana wrote a long letter on December 20, 1945, to his youngest brother, Billy, a survivor of the Battle of the Bulge (December 16, 1944–January 25, 1945), Hitler's surprising and desperate last effort to break through the Allied line and stop the advance into Germany itself. Billy was still in the army, convalescing after an operation, and Dana wanted to catch him up on family news, including telling him that their mother seemed happy living with him. "She is healthier than I have seen her for a long time and her only worry is about her youngest lamb being away over there among all those foreigners—and sick too." Annis would return to Texas, still feeling it was home to her. Later Kathy and Susan would enjoy her stays with them, but David found her harder to take.

David was now a precocious twelve-year-old. He could be a little hard to handle and was at an age when he was prone to act out—at least that is the impression conveyed in one of Aggie's letters. She remained deeply devoted to her grandson and intensely concerned about his education and upbringing. She wrote him a long typewritten letter about an altercation the boy had had with "Grandmother Andrews," as Aggie called Annis. Aggie reminded David of what a lovely home and family he had, even if he was sometimes unhappy: "I know there are times when you feel the world is all against you and everybody is unfair and unkind and so on. But when you feel that way just stop and ask yourself, what you have done to make it so?" Annis only had his happiness in mind, Aggie pointed out: "She is very kind to you. She wants to do the right thing by you." After much advice about proper deportment and cleanliness, Aggie signed herself with much love and then added, "I AM COUNTING ON YOU 100%."

In her profile of Dana for *Modern Screen*, Ida Zeitlin put an amusing, positive spin on concerns over David:

> The only trouble they ever have with three-year-old Kathy is when they reprimand David. The two form a mutual adoration society— a kind of Benevolent Protective Order of Andrews. Kathy's been known to shake a protesting finger at her parents. "You mustn't *talk* to David like that. David's a nice *boy*—" Which of course breaks them up and plays hob with the discipline.

In fact, David seems to have resented Kathy, although neither his parents nor Kathy understood the depth of David's adjustment problems until much later.

Shortly after Zeitlin's piece appeared in November 1945, Dana described the "picture business" for Billy, accurately reflecting just how busy he had been "appearing before cameras or radio microphones, coming home, having a drink, eating dinner, putting the children off to bed, going to sleep, and doing the same thing all over the next day." Dana did not dwell on his radio work, where he reprised his roles in radio productions of indifferent quality. "This life is not as simple as quite a lot of people apparently think—at least I would judge so by the way that they ask you for your time and money. However, it is a bed of my own choosing and I cannot say that I'm unhappy with lying in it." Of his recent roles Dana discounted *Fallen Angel*: "I cannot honestly say that I think much of it." But he praised *Canyon Passage*, relishing getting the girl, the "gorgeous" Susan Hayward, in a Technicolor production that "should reach an entirely new audience for me—which is the reason I chose to do it." Dana ended his letter with the hope that Billy would come to live with him and Mary for a while when he returned to the United States, even suggesting: "I don't know if the idea ever occurred to you but I have often thought that you might like to work in some branch in this foolish business that I am in." Dana had heard from his sister and mother about Billy's performances in plays while still in Texas, and of all his brothers, Billy was certainly the handsomest. Billy had already appeared uncredited as a sailor in *Crash Dive* and would go on to star in pictures and television series as the actor Steve Forrest.

Dana's success in the picture business is evident in his change of agents. Charles Feldman, who paid off Dana's earlier agent, Lew Golder, was a much more influential Hollywood player, one who "knew how to talk his [Goldwyn's] language." Feldman's clients included Howard Hawks, John Wayne, and many other Hollywood legends. Goldwyn was pressing for a new contract. Dana was now a firmly established A-list actor, as signified by the agreement he signed with Goldwyn on October 25, 1945, which specified the following payment terms: $2,500 per week during the first year; $3,000 per week the second year; $3,250 per week the third year; $3,500 per week the fourth year; $3,750.00 per week the fifth year. After five years, Goldwyn had the option to extend the contract another two years, paying $4,000 per week for the first extended year, and $4,250 per week for the second extended year. The contract included twelve weeks "leave of absence" or vacation. With no options clauses, a no lay-off clause, and the right to do two independent productions, Dana believed that his new deal would yield "in the neighborhood of a million and a half." Even with the heavy taxes imposed during the war years and the expenses involved in operating his new home at 4310 Arcola Avenue in North Hollywood, Dana's accountant Vernon Wood estimated that the actor would "save net, after all charges, $50,000 a year." Perhaps owing to his new sense of financial security, Dana had purchased the *Vileehi*, an eighty-foot Auxiliary Ketch built in 1930 for $30,000 on April 20, 1946.

The Goldwyn deal had not been easy to make, taking, in fact, seven months to complete. After *Laura*, Goldwyn and Dana had discussions about a $500 per week raise once the wartime wage freeze was lifted. When Dana's agent asked for much more, an apoplectic Goldwyn accused Dana of reneging on their oral agreement. "Sam," Dana said. "I studied business law in college, and I know that an oral contract is no good after a year. You've forgotten what you said. I may have forgotten what *I* said. Neither one of us would have a case in court." Goldwyn shouted that he felt entitled to slap Dana's face. Dana, acting more calmly than he felt, replied: "You go ahead and slap me in the face. I promise you I won't slap you back." Then the actor got the full Goldwyn treatment, one of his patented tirades:

GET OUTA MY OFFICE! I'LL NEVER SPEAK TO YOU AGAIN! I WON'T TALK TO YOUR AGENT! DON'T WRITE ME LETTERS! DON'T CALL ME ON THE TELEPHONE! I'M THROUGH WITH YOU! AND WHEN I'M THROUGH WITH YOU, YOU'RE THROUGH!

This was not an idle threat. Goldwyn did jettison actors, but only after their box office appeal diminished or they simply became so uncooperative (as would be the case later with Farley Granger) that the exasperated producer cut them loose from their contracts. But Dana was still a hot property, and he had never given Goldwyn any trouble. Besides, after years of seeing Fox benefit from its contract with Dana, Goldwyn finally had found a role in one of his own prestige projects, *The Best Years of Our Lives*, which would fulfill the producer's hopes for him.

CHAPTER 12

The Best Years of Our Lives
1946

ON APRIL 15, 1946, Dana began fifteen weeks of work on the most important picture of his career, *The Best Years of Our Lives*. William Wyler directed this celebrated postwar film about returning serviceman trying to adjust to home life. Dana's performance as Fred Derry, a bombardier, has been much admired, especially the scene in which he crawls into a junked bomber and relives, through the intensity of his facial expressions alone, the ravages of war. It was apparently Sam Goldwyn, who wanted to use as many of his contract stars as possible, who insisted that Dana appear in the picture. "William Wyler didn't want me," Dana later told an interviewer. But on the first day of shooting, after an early scene with Harold Russell, the director called Dana over to him, and said:

> "What happened to you! You're a very good actor!" I laughed and said, "Willie, thank you very much but I've made 20 pictures since I first saw you. Why, if I hadn't improved somewhat, I'd be a pretty stupid actor." In his mind, it was practically yesterday—he'd been in England all during the war with the Eighth Air Force.

Wyler had no trouble telling Dana what he wanted in the actor's culminating scene inside the bomber. As Dana recalled to Clyde Williams, the director looked at the script and said:

> Well, this fellow, this is a scrappy guy. But this plane, it was torn down and this engine, it was torn down. And the fuselage. So I pulled myself up, and I went up into the nose of the plane, and I was looking down as though I were at 50,000 feet . . . He explained

to me what he thought I would be thinking about, back when I was in France, so I got a faraway look in my eyes as I could get.

An excerpt from the "cutting continuity" reveals how much the director came to rely on Dana. The excerpt shows the intricate interplay of mobile camera work and actor, between long shots, medium shots, and dissolves or cross-fades, in which one shot seems to bleed into another so that both seem momentarily present. Greg Toland's deep-focus cinematography makes the background and foreground, and the interior and exterior of the world that confines Fred, crystal clear. Dana realized that his character would be the still point of this panorama, as the world comes to him, so to speak, in the crucial seconds of his crisis, when he seems to have nowhere to go, with no job and no beloved . He is in the graveyard of his own hopes. A winner of the Distinguished Flying Cross, he walks out to the wrecks of bombers and crawls up into one of the plexi-glass ball turrets, quite literally the belly of a bomber, which poet Randall Jarrell compares, in "The Death of the Ball Turret Gunner," to a mother's womb, with the bombardier compacted into this small sphere, "six miles from earth, loosed from the dream of life." All alone in a killing machine, Fred Derry contemplates his fate, which is like a propellerless plane, devoid of any forward motion. The close-up shot does not occur until the end of the sequence, when all the machinery of motion picture making—of reverse, low, and high angle shots—depends on what the actor does with his face.

Dana himself did not realize how well he had done until he saw the completed picture in a movie theater. Mary remembered he had "tears in his eyes" and that he said, "Oh, if I had only known how good this was going to be, I could have been much better." Mary disagreed. If Dana had thought of himself as working on a great picture, he would not have been as good—presumably because he might have been less spontaneous. Dana conceded her point. On the day of the shoot, Wyler deliberately told his actor very little about the effect he wanted to create. Yet Dana projected an indelible image, one belonging to a new kind of male movie star in postwar America, "who could show his weaknesses and feelings without apology."

Derry is the key figure in the *The Best Years of Our Lives*, linking the stories of his fellow servicemen: Al Stephenson, a banker (Frederic March), and Homer Parrish (Harold Russell), a physically disabled sailor. Through his involvement with Stephenson's daughter Peggy (Teresa Wright), Derry, who had been a soda jerk before the war, exposes class differences that the war and the camaraderie of returning servicemen only temporarily suspended.

Wyler worked seamlessly with celebrated cinematographer Greg Toland, whose deep-focus cinematography permitted actions to occur, seemingly, on two planes, rivaling the kinds of shifts in perspective that novels can so deftly accommodate. In a much discussed bar room scene, Wyler pits overbearing Al against the stalwart Fred, the former telling the latter to stay away from his daughter. As Homer talks with his buddy, Butch Engle (Hoagy Carmichael), seated at the piano, Derry is shown in the background calling Peggy to break off their budding relationship. The physical space between the scene's two foci mimics the social and psychological distance between Stephenson's world and Derry's. Derry must somehow bridge this gap with Peggy's help. And at the end of the picture, it is evident that this couple will make some kind of future together, their two-shot (looking across the room at one another) occurring even as Homer and his devoted fiancé, Wilma (Cathy O'Donnell), are married.

At the picture's beginning, on the plane that brings the men home, Al is nonplussed as he watches Homer use the hooks that replace his hands. Fred, for his part, seems unfazed by his new friend's handicap. On the set the seasoned Fredric March, star of *The Dark Angel* (1935) and *A Star Is Born* (1937), seemed unnerved by Russell, who had lost his hands in a wartime accident and had never before acted in a picture, but who was remarkably poised and adept with his hooks. March, who won an Academy Award for his performance, warned Russell about scene stealing and keeping those hooks out of sight while March delivered his lines. Dana and Mary (who watched part of the production) were amused at March's tendency to ham it up. "He was inclined to overplay," Mary told Clyde Williams. "Wyler would say, 'Just give me 10% of that Freddie.'" But Dana appreciated March, remembering his wonderful sense of humor. Dana, who did not receive even an Academy Award nomination for what is arguably his best performance, helped Russell rehearse. That the neophyte actor won an award while he was ignored never seemed to trouble Dana, his daughter Susan recalled, although an anonymous advertisement in *Variety* complained: "I would surely like you to watch 'The Best Years of Our Lives' one more time and tell me what Dana Andrews has to do to win an Academy Award."

Teresa Wright recalled the day Dana did not show up on the set. He had been drinking:

They had to go find him, and we had to wait. They discovered him at some motel and brought him to the set and fed him a lot of coffee. He could work but he was having a hard time.

We were doing a scene that we started the night before. It was when the three guys come home—they've been out drinking—and they take Fred Derry home by car. Unfortunately, Dana hit his head getting out of the backseat. It was an accident. But Willy [Wyler] said, "Hey, that's good. I like that. Do it again." And that went on and on for about twenty-five takes. Dana was not going to complain. He just kept hitting his head harder and harder. I just cringed.

Dana almost never complained on sets about anything. Did he feel, in this instance, that he had no right to object to the retakes? It was not unusual for Wyler, a perfectionist, to shoot a scene many times. Norman Lloyd liked to tell the story about an actor whom Wyler put through the torture of many takes. "Willy, what do you want?" the exasperated actor asked. "Better," Wyler said. Wright wondered whether Wyler had a sadistic streak. And yet Wyler and Dana had such good rapport, she emphasized: Wyler "*loved* Dana." In an interview with Clyde Williams, Dana himself described Wyler's reaction to his drinking:

> "Dana, can I talk to you for a minute?" He said, "I'd like to ask you to do something for me. It may sound a little strange." He said, "When you have had as much to drink as you had, apparently, last night, before you come to work, do me a favor,"—do *him* a favor! [chuckles] He said, "Just call in sick, so you don't have to come in and we can do it some other day." But he said, "Yesterday, you have very obviously—you had had—a long night the night before." And he said "It [day's rushes] weren't terrible. We can use it." But he said, "It's not your best work." And he said, "If you'll do me a favor and when you happen to have one of those nights, just call in early in the morning. You don't have to call me or anybody. Just call in and say you're sick. And then we'll just shoot around you. You don't have to worry about that. We'll get you another day." Well, the way he did that, I decided, well, I decided. I never had another drink while we did that picture. I mean the *way* he did it. No criticism or anything. Just do me a favor.

There came a point, however, when Wyler decided he could no longer employ Dana in subsequent pictures, Susan Andrews said.

When I asked biographer, Donald Spoto, a friend of Teresa Wright's, about her reaction to Dana's drinking, he replied:

> Yes, Teresa did mention Dana's drinking during Best Years—but as always when she mentioned human frailty, it was with the most enormous kindness and compassion, especially because she was so fond of him and enjoyed working with him. Like Spencer Tracy, Dana—perhaps no more than two or three times during the entire production of BEST YEARS (as did Tracy, during their work on *The Actress*)—simply vanished for one or two or three days, and the company had to work around the absentee alcoholic. At the time, almost nothing was said above a whisper here or there, and when Dana returned, everything resumed with his usual amiability and professionalism.

Wright loved Dana, as she confided to Spoto. No romantic liaison developed between the two stars, but their friendship flourished on a production "characterized by a congeniality and dedication rare in Hollywood history," Spoto notes. Dana remembered Wright as "very quiet, intelligent, deep." They worked together easily and pleasantly. He admired her emotional restraint.

Samuel Goldwyn, who regarded the film as the apex of his career, won his first Academy Award for the picture. He had worked hard to make *The Best Years of Our Lives* great. The producer engaged distinguished novelist MacKinlay Kantor to write a story about returning serviceman, and Kantor produced an epic blank verse novel placing Fred Derry at the heart of the story. Renowned playwright and screenwriter Robert Sherwood, a Goldwyn mainstay, adapted the novel for the screen, transforming Fred into a more nuanced character, only hinted at in Kantor's lines about his character's "jaunty weariness / That could be taut when life demanded it." Kantor's characters are still in the war, but Sherwood's are shown after the heroics are over, when wearing a uniform is no longer uplifting, only a reminder of what is *over*. Wyler, who had returned from filming the war nearly deaf after his missions aboard bombers, worried about whether he could recapture his pre-war glory as the director of *Wuthering Heights* and *The Little Foxes*, to name just two of his many successes. His uncertainty, as he later told interviewers, enhanced his ability to direct a film about characters who doubted they could adjust to civilian life.

Dana's description of Wyler's working methods reveals how attuned the actor was to the entire production, not just the part he had to play:

He will do a scene over and over and over again, and I think sometimes he doesn't know exactly what he wants—in opposition to some directors I know that do know exactly what they want, and their minds aren't malleable to accept something that might even be better. I think that he's waiting to see what develops, which is more or less a rehearsal type of creation right there before your eyes. And when he gets it, he knows immediately. He's been criticized by a lot of actors I know, who say they don't think he knows, and that Take 2 might be as good as Take 26. This is not so. When it does happen, he knows it's there. But sometimes he doesn't know how to explain to the actor what he wants, and sometimes I think he himself doesn't know exactly. But when something does happen that's acceptable—print it. He'll take maybe one more, for safety, trying to do the same thing.

What Dana brought to the direction of pictures is evident in his description of the scene shot in Peggy's bedroom, where she has tucked him into bed after a night of carousing with her father and Homer. Wyler shot over a dozen takes designed to dramatize Derry's distraught condition, his restlessness and reliving of his war experiences. But somehow, none of the business the director invented quite captured the authenticity everyone wanted the picture to embody. Dana recalled the way Wyler would say "once more" through his gritted teeth so quietly you could hardly hear him. Finally Dana said:

> Mr. Wyler, the man has probably been rolled a few times; not knowing where he is, he might immediately reach in his pocket to see if his money is there. We can put over the idea that he doesn't know where he is and doesn't have any idea what has happened. So he said, "Let's try that." We did it that way, and boom, that was it. We printed that. That is a little spot in the picture that people always mention when they talk to me about the picture.

Dana's great performances are built on such quiet but telling moments. All those Depression-era jobs before he became a success, all those nights out on the town with sailors and soldiers during the war, are channeled into Dana's magnificent portrayal of Fred Derry, a workingman's hero with class, one of Thomas Jefferson's natural aristocrats, the paradoxical paragon of a democratic culture.

When Derry returns home to Marie (Virginia Mayo), his dishy and unfaithful wife, he finds her suggestion that he parade around in his uniform distasteful. The war has shattered his provincial psyche and made it impossible for him to remain with this crude and brash woman whom he impulsively married. Similarly, when he visits his parents, their home—not much more than a shack—is startling compared to Al's posh apartment and even Homer's decidedly middle class home. Fred's life before the war obviously ran on a very narrowly gauged track—the only possible explanation for his involvement with the flashy and superficial Marie. Fred loves his parents, but he can't wait to get out of their claustrophobic sphere.

That Derry becomes identified with the national purpose, and with American pride over the outcome of the war, is evident in the scene where he socks a guy who comments cynically on the servicemen's sacrifices. Derry lashes out, partly in a frustration that the other returning veterans share. The world has changed, and although they have made their contribution to that change, the transition to a postwar economy and culture is unnerving. Al Stephenson drinks too much and perplexes his bosses at the bank by giving a loan to a veteran who has no collateral. But Stephenson argues the man's experience is his collateral. Similarly, Derry—who cannot return to his job at the soda fountain counter and is uncomfortable as a sales clerk under the supervision of a kid who has no idea of what Fred has experienced—will eventually realize that his bombing missions are his collateral. They will be a pledge, so to speak, of his dedication to work in an aircraft junkyard, salvaging his life as he salvages the planes.

Archer Winsten, movie critic for the *New York Post*, wrote to Dana on November 13, 1946, about the "variety, deep conviction, and power" of performances in *Best Years*, *A Walk in the Sun*, *Canyon Passage*, and *State Fair*, which should have earned Dana consideration for the New York Film Critics best actor award. "Unfortunately, it [Dana's performance] is unspectacular. The very thing that makes it real and good also limits its chances to win an award. It is the big, bravura, knock-em-dead performance that usually wins," the critic noted.

Dana and Mary traveled to New York for the premier of *The Best Years of Our Lives*, beginning the first extended break from picture making under his new contract. David was left behind so as not to interrupt his schooling. Aggie wrote Dana about an excited David looking forward to joining his parents for a skiing holiday in Vermont as soon as school was over. Aggie added: "I marveled many times at how you could keep up the pace you were going and still carry on successfully. Of course you know that the fact you said you were 'on the wagon' was the *very best* piece of news I could ever hope to receive. I pray you have the courage to stay on it. I am sure it will not be easy in your 'hectic business called the cinema.'" In fact, the period of sobriety did not last long.

CHAPTER 13

The Name above the Title
1947

WITH SUPERB PERFORMANCES in *Boomerang* (released April 27, 1947) and *Daisy Kenyon* (released December 25), and the hoopla over *The Best Years of Our Lives* (the most successful picture since *Gone with the Wind*), Dana Andrews reached his apotheosis—signified by the appearance of his name above Henry's Fonda's in the credits for *Daisy Kenyon*. Dana would land other good roles before the decade ended, but in terms of sheer star power, he had reached the acme—although he did not see it this way. Indeed, like other stars he often felt thwarted by the very system that had built him up. The eat-your-heart-out aspect of stardom leaves you feeling you should be a contender for *every role* you fancy. You resent other stars getting in your way, especially the new ones who have not paid their dues. That you have makes you believe the industry owes you one—more than one, in fact.

On November 30, 1947, Dana turned to the drama section of the *New York Times* and read an article by Tennessee Williams entitled "A Streetcar Named Success." The article told the story of a man who could neither accept nor enjoy his success—in this case, the overwhelming acclaim for *The Glass Menagerie*: "I sat down and looked about me and was suddenly very depressed." It got worse when Williams had to deal with friends who knew him when: "I soon found myself becoming indifferent to people. A well of cynicism rose in me. Conversations all sounded like they had been recorded years ago and were being played back on a turntable. Sincerity and kindliness seemed to have gone out of my friends' voices. I suspected them of hypocrisy. I stopped calling them. I stopped seeing them. I was impatient of what I took to be inane flattery." After underlining the first three sentences of the above passage, Dana wrote at the bottom of the paragraph, "I know what he means." Now that Dana had it made, he was afraid of what he had made. "Security is a kind of death," is the other underlined passage in the Williams article, at the end of which Dana wrote: "Keep this!" Later Dana's friend, Irving Rapper, introduced the actor to the playwright, and Williams spent a day on Dana's boat.

Dana was now a player and behaved like one. His income for 1948 was over $155,000, and the next year jumped to over $215,000. By the end of the decade he had made nearly a million dollars. He was earning $5,000 for each radio appearance. His nemesis now was Gregory Peck (1916–2003). For a Twentieth Century-Fox publicist, Dana listed his greatest disappointment as not getting the leading role in *Gentleman's Agreement* (1947), a landmark social issues film directed by Elia Kazan and featuring Peck as a character who poses as a Jew in order to expose anti-Semitism. Dana could not get Sam Goldwyn to buy the rights; Dana did not look Jewish, he was told. He also totted up losses to Peck for *Keys of the Kingdom* (1944) and *Twelve O'Clock High* (1949). In the former, Peck played a priest in China with the kind of moral authority that Academy voters like, earning for his debut performance an Oscar nomination. In the latter, which resulted in another Oscar nomination for Peck, he plays General Frank Savage, tasked with rejuvenating a demoralized bomber crew. It was a role Dana probably thought he owned and that might well have earned him the recognition Peck received.

In *Boomerang*, shot in the first part of 1947, Dana was cast in a good, if decidedly less flashy social issues picture directed by Kazan. Playing the crusading district attorney Henry L. Harvey was an attractive role that showed off Dana's strength. Harvey is a man of integrity under fire from a corrupt political machine that would just as soon railroad an innocent veteran into a murder rap. As film critics Adam Garbicz and Jacek Klinowski note, Dana's character is the "first of those Kazan heroes who fight uncompromisingly for the ideals of justice and democratic humanism."

Students of Kazan's career like to retail an anecdote that Karl Malden, who played a cop in *Boomerang*, told about the director's concern over Dana's drinking. The director, trained in the New York school of method acting, believed that the best performances came from actors caught at their most vulnerable moments—when they could not rely on proven techniques and mannerisms, but would have to respond to some new stimulus. Dealing with Dana, an actor who did not like to reveal much about himself or his methods on a movie set, the frustrated Kazan decided to play a trick that would shake up his star. So he rewrote a courtroom speech and delivered it to Dana the morning after one of his star's all-night drinking binges. Malden said that Kazan wanted to teach Dana a lesson. Malden also notes that Dana was a "lovely man"—which I take as code for an actor who did not exhibit the kind of *sturm und drang* Kazan believed was required for a first-rate performance. The director probably expected some kind of uproar over this last-minute substitution of a new "hefty block of dialogue" that Dana would have to master with a hangover. Certainly stars have walked off productions and indulged in tantrums after much less provocation than Kazan proffered. But Dana just said, "Give me twenty minutes." Malden admitted he relished watching the flummoxed director, as Dana delivered a letter-perfect speech for the picture's climactic scene. "Dana was one of the few actors I have ever seen who was able to pull off that kind of memorization, sober or otherwise," Malden concludes. The scene lasts far longer than most single takes in Hollywood films and is a testament to Dana's domination of the screen even when there is no action, close-ups, music, or any of the other sorts of accompaniments used to bolster a performance.

Richard Schickel, Kazan's biographer, supposes that the director was trying to get a jaded actor, a wooden performer, to liven up. Schickel says the scene that Dana did so well is just what bad actors, used to histrionics, can pull off in courtroom scenes, since lawyers are such bad actors anyway. If there is a more preposterous account of a superb piece of acting, I have yet to come across it. How could Dana be prone both to woodenness and then to overacting? You only need to read Malden's full account of Kazan's perverse behavior in *When Do I Start?* to see how badly Schickel misreads this episode. James Agee deemed *Boomerang* "notable for Dana Andrews's best performance to date."

Dana was far more experienced than Elia Kazan in filmmaking. As Dana told Allen Eyles, "This was Mr. Kazan's third picture and he was still mixed up on camera angles. He used to say, 'Print it', you know, and the script girl would say 'You can't print that, you've got it on the wrong side, the camera has to be over here.'" What may have bothered Kazan more than anything else is that he had an actor who could remain so unflappable no matter what the director did. In *Kazan on Directing*, Kazan calls Dana "actorish" and "not a real lawyer"—whatever that means. But almost in the same breath, Kazan contradicts himself, remarking, "There was very little you could do with Dana Andrews. He'd come to work, and we'd roll him out. His style was okay in that movie because he was playing a lawyer, and essentially there wasn't supposed to be much going on inside him." It would seem there was not much Dana could do with

Kazan, a director who had his own preconceptions and believed every role had to have something personal at stake. No wonder Dana preferred the company of actors like Laurence Olivier, who just got down to work and did not worry about the connections between his psyche and his part.

Kazan's cruelty and the sort of sadism practiced by William Wellman, William Wyler, Henry Hathaway, and Otto Preminger did not impress him. Dana had a quiet authority that *bothered* these in-charge individuals, directors who believed they had to control the conditions in which actors performed, in contrast to Lewis Milestone and Jacques Tourneur, who sought to create environments in which the directors and actors collaborated in achieving the highest art. Otto Preminger told Dana that there could only be one boss on a movie set, and that movie making was not a democratic enterprise. Dana just did his work, later telling Clyde Williams that Preminger was "a pretty fair director, but he was a son of a bitch." When Mary added that "Preminger wasn't nice to anybody but the stars," Dana said, "I couldn't stand that bastard." "He was nice to you," Mary reminded him. "He was nice to me," Dana agreed, "but I didn't like the way he treated other people." Mary said, "Dana was very friendly with everybody." "I didn't get 'stuck up' because I became a star," he noted.

CHAPTER 14

"What Is This Thing I Do to Women?"
1947-50

IN LATE FEBRUARY 1947, Otto Preminger called Dana "unofficially" to discuss *Daisy Kenyon* and the role of Dan O'Mara, a manipulative but ultimately decent and even noble attorney vying with Peter Lapham (Henry Fonda) for Joan Crawford's affections. The director then sent the script to Dana, who called Preminger a few days later. Dana was not enthusiastic about the story or the role but would do it if nothing better turned up. He later told interviewer Allen Eyles that he thought the story "soap-opera-ish." Dana cancelled two appointments with his agent and Preminger to discuss the role and then called to say he wanted to be considered for the other male lead, even though the director believed the part of Peter less desirable. They agreed, however, that if Preminger could not find another Dan, then Dana would do it.

The studio tried without success to get Walter Pidgeon, then Joseph Cotten, and even Wendell Cory to play Dan, while engaging Henry Fonda to play Peter. With advance publicity for the picture already underway, Dana was informed of the decision to cast him as Dan. At a May 12 lunch with Preminger, Dana asked to be excused from the picture, but the director insisted he could not do without Dana and would not go ahead with the production. Dana then said he could not perform the role for "personal reasons which he asked Mr. Preminger not to quote to the studio," according to Fox executive Lew Schreiber—who explained the situation to the studio legal counsel, George Wasson, who, in turn, asked Sam Goldwyn to remind Dana of his contractual obligations. Dana's agent, Charles Feldman, a Hollywood powerhouse, advised his client to do the picture, and, accordingly, on May 15, Dana wrote to Darryl Zanuck affirming Feldman's message to the studio head that their contract player would comply. But Dana was clearly upset and seemed to imply that Preminger had taken advantage of him: "In the future I shall not under any circumstances discuss parts or pictures except through my authorized representative. . . . I shall not appear in any picture until I have officially accepted the role in it. No acceptance by me of any role shall be official unless such acceptance is in writing signed either by me or by my authorized representative."

Correspondence in the Fox legal files suggests that after Henry Fonda signed on, the part of Peter was built up considerably, and that Dana wanted the final draft to look more like the first script he had been shown. But he may also have been concerned about Joan Crawford, a complicated, vexing sort of leading lady. "She overdramatized everything," Dana recalled. Mary, who saw Crawford in action at a cast party, called her "neurotic." "Yeah, she was," Dana agreed. Somehow Crawford would have to fit into an Otto Preminger production, which could be a trial even for the easygoing Dana, although he holds his own with Crawford and Fonda as part of a love triangle. Dan O'Mara commandeers the career girl, Daisy (Crawford), even as he maintains the façade of a happily married family man. Like Eric Stanton in *Fallen Angel*, Dan is driven to abandon his spurious life by sheer hypocrisy and self-disgust. He seeks Daisy's approval by forsaking his fashionable Manhattan law practice and defending a US citizen of Japanese descent who has been unjustly deprived of his land while he is off fighting in Italy. That Dan does not get the girl in the end is predictable, given Fonda's earnest, self-assured character. And yet this ending is disappointing, since Dana definitely makes Dan the most dashing male on the scene.

This film is superior to most of Dana's later work, which strives to maintain his romantic aura with inferior scripts. Crawford called her costar "an underestimated actor who wasn't fully appreciated because his style was to underplay, which is so difficult." It is not surprising that Dana would want to play Peter—not only because Peter gets the girl, but because the part played to Dana's strengths, as it did to Fonda's. Both actors were adept at playing characters with innate integrity and strength who manage to remain sensitive and vulnerable. It is easy to see Dana and Fonda switching roles in *The Ox-Bow Incident*, for example. Fonda recognized his affinity with Dana, telling Mary at a party that he had secured certain roles that would otherwise have gone to Dana. In this case, however, Dana did not begrudge Fonda because he had such profound respect for Fonda's talent.

In spite of Dana's qualms, *Daisy Kenyon* was a trouble-free production with none of the fireworks usually associated with a Preminger picture. The director was working with seasoned pros on a June 16 to August 12 shooting schedule that came in on budget (just under $2 million) and wrapped two days early. In his autobiography, Preminger briefly mentions *Daisy Kenyon* as a pleasant experience, and to Gerald Pratley in *The Cinema of Otto Preminger* he claimed he could remember nothing at all about the production. But *something* happened—that much is clear from the Fox legal files, which make for intriguing if murky reading. On August 13, the day after the picture wrapped, Dana was asked to do publicity stills with Crawford. This would mean, however, taking a day out of his six-week vacation period. The studio warily sounded out Dana, perhaps worried that his earlier resistance to doing the picture would result, now, in insistence on his contractual rights. But in the words of a Fox executive, "Dana explained he was perfectly agreeable to coming in without it interrupting the vacation period and said that this was a personal thing between himself and Joan Crawford." As usual, Dana was not revealing much—although in an interview with Clyde Williams, Dana and Mary tried to explain what happened at the post production party when Crawford, who had had more than a few drinks, suddenly disappeared:

> MARY. Dana found her, and he said, "Joan, what's the matter? You know, we need you to be the hostess" and all this, and "everybody's been wondering what's happened to you. What's the matter?" She looked at Dana with those big eyes, you know, and she says, "Don't you know?"
> DANA. [Laughs] Oh, my God . . . And I never was sure whether she meant that she had something for me or—Henry.
> MARY. But she finally came back [to the party], and she was ok.
> DANA. She was a character. She really was a character. That kind of thing happened two or three times.

Dana believed Crawford was insecure, one of those Hollywood types who got her start at a very young age, and now at forty-three worried about her place. The men on the set used to joke with him, saying they wondered if Dana ever dreamed as a boy he would be playing opposite Crawford, who had begun in pictures as a flapper and re-invented herself every time fashions changed. Mary, a big admirer of Crawford—and apparently not concerned about the actress's interest in her husband—noted that Dana, thirty-six during the making of *Daisy Kenyon*, was not much younger than his co-star. But she had become so "ladylike in her speech," Mary noted, and "careful to have this mask-like face—closeups through gauze...." Lady-like or not, Crawford seemed determined to have an affair with one of her leading men. She tried to get a rise out of Henry Fonda, so the story goes, by presenting him with a jewel-encrusted jockstrap and asking him to model it for her.

What Dana ultimately thought about his role in *Daisy Kenyon* is hard to determine. Clyde Williams tried to get him to discuss the "mean" side of the characters Dana played in *Fallen Angel* and *Where the Sidewalk Ends* (1950), but Dana merely said these were parts that as a contract actor he could not refuse. In other words, the biographer could not get his subject to brood about the brooding characters he portrayed and the extent to which they might have drawn out aspects of his own personality. It is tempting to think that perhaps Dana's drinking dissolved—at least temporarily—any reckoning with himself, with that uncomfortable feeling that Eric Stanton tries to shake off when he shrugs a shoulder, and that Dan O'Mara hopes to disguise by winning cases, placating his fractious wife Lucille, and romancing the demanding Daisy. But Dana's Dan has a power and authority attributable not only to good looks and a successful law practice, but also to Dana's absolute command of his movie star aura, a glamour that Preminger knew how to exploit better than any other director. As Chris Fujiwara puts it in *The Life and Work of Otto Preminger*, the camera moves with Dana, showing the power of this man (and his character) to cross thresholds—Daisy's apartment, his home, and his law offices—with an elegance rivaling the aplomb Clifton Webb exhibits in *Laura*. And to make such a comparison is to record, of course, just how good an actor Dana Andrews had become. Dan O'Mara is grace personified. Fujiwara calls *Daisy Kenyon* the "culmination of what might be called Preminger's Dana Andrews series. The value of Dana Andrews in Preminger's films comes from his supercivilized nature, his smoothness and glibness, his imperturbability (which serves, of course, as a provocation to perturb). Dan O'Mara has perfected the ability to ... to make himself liked, to claim unobtrusively the right to control situations..." This is not a bad description of Dana Andrews, either. Fujiwara might have added, however, that in just a few years, Preminger's *Where the Sidewalk Ends* would serve as witness to the disintegration of that polished persona. All of the performances in *Daisy Kenyon* are superb, but the picture did not do that much business in its first release, except perhaps to enhance Dana's prospects as a leading man.

Much closer to Dana's own world than his romantic leading man roles was his performance as a lobster fisherman in *Deep Waters* (released May 26, 1949), co-starring Jean Peters as his love interest and Cesar Romero as his fishing partner and sidekick. The film was based on Ruth Moore's best-selling novel, *Spoonhandle*, set on an island off the Maine coast. Dana wrote a friend that the book "might make a fairly good little motion picture," although he did not think it was a great story. It is, in fact, dull, centering on the efforts of Dana's character, Hod Stilwell, to adopt the orphaned Donny Mitchell (Dean Stockwell) and rescue him from the state reformatory, while winning back the heart of Ann Freeman (Jean Peters), who fears the sea that has taken the lives of so many fishermen.

Dana always looks comfortable playing working class and down home types, but here his Hollywood-smooth voice detracts from his characterization. He simply does not inhabit his character with the kind of regional authenticity that distinguishes *Swamp Water*. A few reviewers praised his reserved kind of eloquence, Dean Stockwell's understated and beguiling performance, and the single action/adventure scene when Hod rescues Donny from a capsized rowboat. But under the conventional direction of Hollywood veteran Henry King, *Deep Waters* has little else to recommend it. The radio drama version of the picture, with Ida Lupino sounding more attractive than Jean Peters, did not otherwise improve on this slight story.

The location shooting did Dana good, however, serving as a kind of vacation owing to his love for the water. This was a period of sobriety as well, as he told Mary and his brother Charles, who said he, too, was on the "water wagon." Away from the hothouse pressures of Hollywood, there would be less call for alcohol as a relaxant. Dana enjoyed the local clam and lobster chowders. He relished going out even in rough seas with lobstermen and eating a sample of day's catch right on the boat. "It's a simple kind of bedrock life for a change and I like it," he wrote Mary. His first letters to Mary in late September emphasized the "proud, thrifty, and industrious" people, but by the end of his stay they had become rather off-putting to his still Southern sensibility: "Their much praised independence is carried a little too far I think, and becomes nothing short of insolence."

Dana's letters home asked about the children, of course, but were filled with expressions of how much he missed Mary: "It makes me giddy right now to think about that wonderful sinking feeling I get in my stomach when I look into your eyes and then press your lips to mine, taste your mouth and caress you—I'd better stop before I go too far and work myself into a state. I love you!" And she kept up her part, sending within a week three letters that made the cast and crew envious, Dana told her, as he retreated to his room to read and re-read her sweet words.

He spoke amusingly of wanting "everything that is you & me to be community property." He was not, however, above teasing Mary, telling her about a little party with a couple of young women, one of whom seemed to tremble when he came near her. "What is this thing I do to women?" he asked. But in the same letter, he closes with, "I sing to you in the bath and out on the boat and my heart sings to you always and everywhere."

Dana's work at Fox after *Daisy Kenyon*, *The Iron Curtain* (released June 16, 1948), is a rather dreary semi-documentary based on the story of Igor Gouzenko, a code clerk in the Russian Embassy in Ottawa, a defector who exposed a Soviet spy ring. Dana plays Gouzenko without an accent or any distinguishing features, really, except for a certain formality of speech, rigidity of gesture, and a shorter than usual haircut. These effects are meant, apparently, to evoke a dour, austere Russian who rejects the advances of an embassy femme fatale and gradually warms up to the West, forsaking his comrades in order to provide for his faithful wife (Gene Tierney) and family and enjoy the free world. Ben Hecht's tendentious script was Darryl Zanuck's answer to complaints that he exposed American corruption in films like *Boomerang*, when he ought to attack America's adversaries. So he assured anti-Communist zealot, Hedda Hopper, that he would take care of her concerns: "If we do not succeed in showing to the world the advantages of the American way of life, then somebody will probably come forth with another way of life that may impress the peoples of all countries more, and then all that we fought for in this war will have been lost." Later Zanuck would write a letter to the *Chicago Tribune* protesting an article accusing him of supporting leftist causes: "I produced the first anti-Communist picture made in Hollywood, namely *The Iron Curtain*."

Not even teaming up with Lewis Milestone in *No Minor Vices* (released November 12, 1948) reversed the downturn in Dana's performances. Milly presented the idea of the picture, a farce about art and modern psychiatry, to Dana over dinner. Dana would play a rather smug child psychiatrist and Lilli Palmer his devoted wife, who almost succumbs to the charms of Louis Jourdain, playing an eccentric painter. It sounded *"great,"* Mary later told Clyde Williams. It would be independently produced by a company Kirk Douglas and some other actors were forming, the short-lived Enterprise Pictures. A wonderful storyteller, Milly had Dana hooked. "We used to go and look at the rushes, oh, we thought, oh, we thought this was so funny, and, oh, 'Great idea!'" Mary said. Then, at a preview, Mary watched the audience and realized that "all of these things we thought were so funny, we had seen . . . " Dana interrupted to say, "They didn't get it at all. Hah!" Mary agreed: "It didn't work."

The "bitchy" Lilli Palmer, as Mary called her, was miscast and "too serious, Germanic." In other words, Palmer lacked the light touch that Mary would have given the role (although she did not say so to Williams). In fact, Palmer is painful to watch because she is trying so hard to play screwball comedy. Palmer was upset because her husband Rex Harrison was having an affair with actress Carole Landis, who committed suicide on July 5, shortly after *No Minor Vices* wrapped. Norman Lloyd, who played one of Dana's colleagues in the picture, remembered Palmer coming to work with a face "battered by tears." Mary also thought the writing did not live up to Milly's story telling. Perhaps—although Dana, too, lacks the light touch needed for this kind of satire. As one imdb viewer suggested, this attempt at a wacky take on the worlds of psychotherapy and painting might have been redeemed by Cary Grant, who could deliver absurd dialogue with an amused self-deprecation that seems beyond Dana's range.

In truth, *No Minor Vices* would have been good enough for a television skit compressed into less than an hour. Of all Dana's pictures, it transferred best to radio in the truncated version broadcast February 22, 1951, on *Screen Director's Playhouse*. With a condensed plot and lines delivered to a live audience, both Louis Jourdain and Dana seem sharper than in the screen version.

Dana had better leading ladies but also hackneyed scenarios in his next three pictures, in which he starred opposite Merle Oberon (*Night Song*, released April 26, 1948), Maureen O'Hara (*The Forbidden Street*, released May 3, 1949), and Susan Hayward (*My Foolish Heart*, released January 21, 1950). All three films were remarkably similar romantic tear-jerkers, with Dana playing, respectively: a blind, bitter but brilliant pianist brought back to life, so to speak, by a beautiful beloved; a double role as a charming but alcoholic artist who dies young and is succeeded in his wife's affections by a dead ringer, a barrister who rescues her and makes a success of their puppet show; a dashing but doomed World War II airman whose lover spends her life mourning in an alcoholic rage.

The Dana Andrews of these films is a Hollywood fantasy—especially in the role of Dan Evans, the morose classical pianist who has to be guided back to good spirits by a smitten socialite (Merle Oberon), who is instrumental in restoring his sight and orchestrating his triumphant return to Carnegie Hall. As Oberon's biographers, Charles Higham and Roy Moseley state, the picture promotes the "ennobling power of love." Dana enjoyed working for director John Cromwell, an actor himself, and with Oberon, whom he invited on one of his sailboats (he now had three). Only a handful of his Hollywood cohort (Anne Baxter, Harry Morgan, and Jacques Tourneur) made it aboard. Kathy, then about five, stepped on Merle Oberon's face during the actress's only appearance on deck.

Like Joan Crawford, Oberon seems to have wanted Dana. Higham and Moseley report that a disconcerted Dana had to put up with Oberon's "moderately subtle advances," even as her husband was photographing them. Dana cancelled more than one lunch once he understood his co-star's intentions. He was more comfortable with the guys, showing no interest in the tony social set that surrounded Oberon on screen and off. Later, in an interview with Clyde Williams, both Dana and Mary would make a point of this aspect of Dana's makeup. He liked the camaraderie of men on movie sets and steered clear of the romantic affairs that many stars felt entitled to. For Dana, the pleasure of learning the fingering for his takes at the piano under the supervision of Artur Rubenstein and working with Cromwell compensated for the trite plot. Dana's performance hurt him with at least one British critic, Richard Winnington, who ridiculed the story and lamented that Dana "managed to exist as a very satisfying actor in some of the best films of our times until stardom hit." Now he had "acquired heart-throb status and is apparently ready for anything."

About the only good thing in *The Forbidden Street* (British title *Brittania Mews*) is Dana Andrews, according to his co-star, Maureen O'Hara, who offers him a tribute in her autobiography. The picture upset Dana because he was dubbed, negating his carefully cultivated British accent, which—had it survived the editing process—would have made for a striking performance, as he reappears in the second part of the film as an American.

The Forbidden Street's director, Jean Negulesco, recalled that the "critics crucified us." He wrote to Darryl Zanuck: "I liked the cast, I like the story, I thought I did my best. I promise I'll make it up to you somehow." The studio head replied: "Who the hell do you think you are, playing the hero like that? I okayed the picture, I bought the book, I okayed the cast, I saw the rushes and approved them. Sure, you made a mistake, but so did we."

Dana and Mary did enjoy their time in England, where the picture was shot. They were away from home from early June to Christmas, leaving behind infant Susan, born January 29, 1948. Susan bonded with Minnie, who told Susan she cried when her parents returned to take care of her. Who were these white people? Minnie's importance, as Dana's children attest, cannot be exaggerated, and she deserves her own paragraph and more. Dana's meticulousness amused her. She pointed out that even when he was drunk he made sure to fold his clothes neatly. In Kathy's words, "Minnie wrapped her big arms around herself and rocked back and forth, laughing until tears ran down her face when she told stories about his behavior. She could predict his every move. She was with him during his best days and his very worst, years later. She could read him beautifully. In certain ways, she knew him better than anyone. And had his back always."

Years later Susan thought that in going to England her mother had to make a sort of "Sophie's choice": whether go on location with Dana, taking Kathy and Stephen, or to stay behind to care for baby Susan. England was still experiencing postwar food shortages, a daunting prospect. But more importantly, Susan believes, Mary did not want her husband to go abroad alone. And judging by the forlorn letters he would often send to her while on location, Mary's anxiety is understandable.

Dana gave an interview to Louella Parsons, saying Sam Goldwyn warned him to watch what he said. "I made a vow not to touch one drop of liquor while I'm in Europe, and I like being on the wagon so much I may stay right on it. I feel if you are in control of yourself, it's easier to say the right thing." Goldwyn was right to be concerned. Before the trip to England, the *Los Angeles Examiner* (January 12, 1948) carried the headline, "Dana Andrews Ends Night in Jail on Drug Charge," with a photograph of him laughing and pointing his finger through the bars of a jail cell. He was quoted as saying to the police, "You can't arrest me. When I appear in court I will be sober, so how can he [the judge] decide whether I am drunk now or not?" Talking loudly he refused to get into the police car. What happened next is not clear, except that he spent four hours in jail and was bailed out by his attorney.

Dana was more or less dropped into *My Foolish Heart* as the guy that got away. The film was a hit, if not the Academy Award-winning vehicle Susan Hayward hoped for, and it has been much derided for its sentimentalization of "Uncle Wiggily in Connecticut," the J. D. Salinger story on which it is based. Dana liked the director, Mark Robson, but Robson later disowned *My Foolish Heart, Edge of Doom* (released August 3, 1950), and *I Want You* (released December 23, 1951), calling all three "awful" films, made during "one of the worst periods of my career." They were all part of Samuel Goldwyn's postwar decline, which was mainly caused by his selection of bad scripts that not even the best actors and directors could surmount. This demoralizing string of failures that provoked a determined Farley Granger, one of Dana's co-stars, to break his contract with Goldwyn, also precipitated the decline in Dana's own work.

Dana's next two pictures with Mark Robson were disastrous. In *Edge of Doom*, he plays a saintly priest, and in *I Want You* he appears as a rather bland World War II vet dealing with his younger brother's reluctance to fight in the Korean War. Dana's career suffered because Goldwyn lost his fabled "touch," as his biographer Scott Berg illustrates with an anecdote about the producer's anger over the abysmal advertising campaign for *Edge of Doom*. "I don't know what's the matter with you," he told his staff. "This is a simple story about a boy who wants a fine funeral for his mother, so he kills a priest." Hearing himself sum up the preposterous plot, Goldwyn then said, "Let's not spend another dime."

Unlike Farley Granger, who had several angry confrontations with Goldwyn, Dana, the producer thought, was a good sport about the postwar string of studio bombs. The producer did not seem to appreciate that Dana, like many contract actors, resented the rigid regime that put him in pictures he would never have chosen on his own. Producer and actor did not normally socialize, but Dana recalled for Goldwyn biographer Carol Easton the time when his agent told him that Goldwyn felt hurt that he had not been invited to the actor's tenth wedding anniversary. But Sam never invited Dana to his parties, so why should Dana invite Sam? the actor asked his agent. A few days later, Sam's wife Frances, a fixture on the Goldwyn lot, approached Dana with an invitation to a dinner party with some important guests, including Benjamin Fairless, the president of United States Steel. Dana's description of the party speaks volumes about what he thought of Hollywood and its pretensions:

> There were only ten people. The Firestones, Hedda Hopper, Anatole Litvak [a distinguished director who had just made *Sorry Wrong Number* with Barbara Stanwyck], Mr. and Mrs. Fairless and Mary and me and the Goldwyns. Then I realized that Frances thought she was gonna give me and Mary a great treat by having us meet the Benjamin Fairlesses. Well, when I walked in the room, he got up and walked over to me and said, "Well, Dana! It's been a long

time!" Frances was absolutely stunned! I've known Ben for years! Leonard Firestone said, "Mr. Andrews, my name is Firestone. I'm in rubber." As though you didn't know a god damned thing! Then Goldwyn was telling Ben what a model husband and father I'd been kept my skirts clean and all, and I said, "Sam, what about the time I got picked up for drunk?" He said, "Vell, you know, ve all make mistakes." We were never invited back again.

Some of Dana's acting out is probably attributable to his drinking, but it was also undoubtedly a result of his disgust with such ostentatious entertaining.

Dana's comments to Easton, delivered in the 1970s, are essential to understanding what happened to him in Hollywood. He had left Texas to become his own man, to pursue, the Horatio Alger dream of becoming a success. But you cannot become a success in Hollywood on your own terms—certainly not as an actor, but really not as anyone. Even studio heads like Louis B. Mayer were in hock to the money men in New York, and Goldwyn was forever fighting with United Artists and other distribution companies that could make or break a picture by how high or low it was placed in the exhibition chain of releases. As a result, Hollywood bred insecurity—as Easton herself discovered when Goldwyn's associates shied away from her. They did not want to alienate *anyone* who might have some sort of power over them: the ability to get good parts, to secure financing for a production, or to blackball them, as Goldwyn himself had done with certain actors.

Dana fulfilled his contractual obligations, but he not would pretend to like it. Easton, who met Dana only once, keenly understood. Actors are not always so articulate, but Easton let Dana speak for himself, and the result is an extraordinary assessment of Goldwyn and, in effect, a revelation of the actor's own insight into the Hollywood psyche:

An actor, if he is any good, *must* be self-absorbed; his instrument, which is himself, requires constant attention, and leaves no time for probing the motivations of other people. But Andrews' *observations* of Goldwyn's behavior were thoughtful and right on.

"He was indomitable, as far as never giving up. He would spend loads of money trying to prove an unprovable point. Like trying to prove that Virginia Mayo was a great actress. Everybody talks about the 'Goldwyn touch,' but Mr. Goldwyn made a lotta bad pictures. I was in a couple of 'em. People say Sam Goldwyn had immaculate taste. I don't think so. He *tried* to find out what *was* good taste. He asked a lotta people. A lotta time he'd ask the wrong person, and he'd *believe* them! Because he was *not able to discriminate!*

"I always called him Sam. But when he would say, 'Dana, I love you like my own son!'—look out! Like the time he came to me in my dressing room, when I was making *The North Star*. There was this girl that he wanted to put in a musical he was going to make, but he wasn't happy with her test. He told me that this girl was crazy about me, and if I would be nice to her—that is, have an affair with her—it would make her a lot more confident. I laughed! He said, 'She's in love with you! She told me so!' I said I'd heard about producers doing these things, but I never believed it. He said, 'If you tell this, it's a lie and I never said it.' He turned around and walked out."

Easton, not used to this sort of candor, describes herself walking out "into the sunlight feeling grateful, disoriented and depressed."

CHAPTER 15

Hollywood Fights Back
1947-57

ON NOVEMBER 2, 1947, right after returning home from shooting *Deep Waters*, Dana appeared on the second of two live radio broadcasts, both titled "Hollywood Fights Back." The project had been organized by the Committee for the First Amendment, headed by Humphrey Bogart, Gene Kelly, and other stars, who assembled a delegation of actors to fly from Hollywood to Washington, D.C., to protest the House Committee on Un-American Activities (HUAC). HUAC was investigating the dissemination of communist propaganda in the movies, claiming a communist cabal had infiltrated the ranks not only of writers, but also of directors and actors. At first, the studios felt inclined to put up a fight. After all, Hollywood had done its part at the bidding of the Roosevelt administration, producing anti-Nazi films such as *Confessions of a Nazi Spy* (1939) and *Berlin Correspondent* and pro-Soviet ally pictures such as *Mission to Moscow* (1943) and *The North Star*.

Whatever legitimate anti-communist sentiment HUAC espoused was quickly compromised by attacks on films like *The Best Years of Our Lives*, which, in HUAC's view, were subversive insofar as they undermined American morale at a time when the nation confronted the Red Menace. The story of veterans having trouble adjusting to postwar America offended certain congressman. Republicans like Richard Nixon and Joseph McCarthy would shortly lead a charge against Democratic administrations allegedly soft on communism, provoking many Democrats and others (including some Republicans) to suspect that HUAC intended an all-out assault on Roosevelt's New Deal.

In one respect, *The Best Years of Our Lives* was prophetic about the Cold War that would soon subsume Hollywood and the nation. In the film's fight scene, a soda fountain customer reads a newspaper headline ("Senator Warns of New War"), and then turns to Homer and, in front of Fred, says that Homer lost his hands in a sucker's war: "We let ourselves get sold down the river. We were pushed into war. . . . The Germans and the Japs had nothing against us. They just wanted to fight them Limeys and them Reds. And they would have whipped them too, if we didn't get deceived into it by a bunch of radicals in Washington. . . . We fought the wrong people, that's all." Fred reacts to this profound insult to his wartime service with his fists, knocking the man down and losing his job. "Them Reds," in other words, were the real enemies.

Dana enthusiastically joined the "Hollywood Fights Back" broadcasts, with their spirited early opposition to HUAC—called the "UnAmerican Committee." On the October 27 program, each star spoke no more than a few sentences, beginning with Judy Garland's salvo: "I've been following this investigation, and I don't like it." Gene Kelly followed her blunt opinion with a pointed question addressed to those who had seen *The Best Years of Our Lives*: "Did you desire to overthrow the government?" Director John Huston noted that in its nine years of existence HUAC had produced only one piece of legislation, which was denounced by the Supreme Court. Danny Kaye quoted FDR's statement that HUAC was just a headline-grabbing committee that ought to be abolished, and Marsha Hunt noted that Wendell Willkie, FDR's Republican opponent in the 1940 election, had rejected HUAC as inimical to the democratic process. Producer Walter Wanger quoted a *New York Times* editorial deploring HUAC's equation of any kind of criticism of America with subversion. Richard Conte, who had appeared with Dana in *The Purple Heart* and *A Walk in the Sun*, observed that several reactionary figures and groups like Gerald L. K. Smith and the Ku Klux Klan supported HUAC. Robert Ryan, who starred in *Crossfire*, a film attacking American anti-Semitism directed by Edward Dmytryk (later blacklisted) accused HUAC of "dragging people through the mud of insinuation and slander." Myrna Loy, who had played Teresa Wright's mother in *The Best Years of Our Lives*, accused HUAC of violating the First Amendment by trying to force witnesses to testify about their political beliefs and convictions. In an especially telling moment, Bogart asked, "Is democracy so feeble that it can be undermined by a look or a line?" HUAC had not produced any tangible evidence that American democracy had been subverted, he concluded. William Wyler expressed his doubts that he would have been able to make *The Best Years of Our Lives* in "today's climate. They [HUAC] are making decent people afraid to express their opinions." The director added, "They are creating fear in Hollywood. Self-censorship will paralyze the screen." He worried that the idea of what it means to be American would have to conform to

HUAC's dictates. Fredric March, whose provocative scenes in *The Best Years of Our Lives*, where bankers argue about granting loans to returning veterans, asked: Who is next? Would schoolteachers or ministers be told what the proper way to be an American was? "They are after more than Hollywood," March contended.

In the second program, aired a week later, Myrna Loy reported a rising tide of indignation—expressed in commentaries, letters, and telegrams—against the committee. She was one of just a few hundred people fighting for freedom of expression and conscience, "[B]ut we are part of a landslide of opinion against what is happening in that committee in Washington," she declared. "You don't have to be in Hollywood to come out fighting against the UnAmerican Committee," urged Douglas Fairbanks, Jr. Publisher Bennett Cerf summed up the group's sentiment succinctly, calling HUAC "fascism in action." He was expressing, in fact, the postwar fears of many liberals, who believed that a brand of American fascism might indeed overcome democratic institutions.

In this heady moment of aroused dissent, a truly historic and defining turning point in Hollywood history, Dana Andrews, a board member of the Screen Actors Guild (SAG), took a stand, saying in a firm crisp voice:

> The UnAmerican Committee have recessed because they think they have got what they were after. Censorship. Blacklists. People fired from their jobs, and a blanket of fear smothering free speech, free thought, and free motion pictures. Mr. Thomas's [HUAC chairman] last words were a threat: "Hollywood better clean house. We're not through." Far from intimidating Hollywood, Mr. Thomas got these words from Mr. Samuel Goldwyn, executive producer of the picture, *The Best Years of Our Lives*: "I defy anyone to point out a single thing in any picture I have made which could justifiably be called subversive or UnAmerican by anyone, including very publicity hungry, self-righteous would be part-censors who have appeared before the committee. While many of us have been trying to build up an appreciation of America through this far reaching medium of entertainment I regret to say that the Committee seems to have been doing it very best to undermine these efforts of our industry."

Goldwyn, always an independent and even cantankerous holdout in dealing with his fellow moguls, stood firm against HUAC and was disappointed when he was not called to testify before the committee.

Attacking the screenwriters in hearings that turned into shouting matches proved to be a better ploy for HUAC, since the unfriendly witnesses—now called the "Hollywood Ten"—made a spectacle of themselves. Their self-righteousness seemed, to some Americans, as worse than that of their interrogators. Public opinion began to tilt toward the notion that perhaps these unfriendly Hollywood witnesses were hiding something, invoking constitutional protections simply to disguise disloyalty, rather than speaking forthrightly about their politics.

Actress Marsha Hunt pinpointed the moment when Bogart et al. began to realize they had lost the battle in the court of public opinion:

> On the flight back to Hollywood, we were, I think, subdued, kind of shaken by what we had witnessed and heard in the hearing room, by the ridicule and suspicion that the press afforded us. When we returned to Hollywood, The Hollywood Reporter and people like [columnist] Hedda Hopper wrote that "they ought to be asked the $64,000 Question." Were we then, or had we ever been members of the Communist Party? Far from being offered thanks for defending our industry, we were suddenly controversial ourselves, and under suspicion.

Historian Larry Ceplair explains, "[A]gents were summoned to the major Hollywood studios and practically ordered to tell their clients that the studios would no longer tolerate public stances by performers on political issues deemed to be detrimental to the film industry. The Committee for the First Amendment collapsed in the wake of these open threats."

Untainted by associations with the left-leaning New York theater crowd, Dana did not have to worry about his own employment in motion pictures. Even so, his forthright support for the First Amendment reflected his own growing disaffection with that other end of Hollywood—soon to be represented by Jack Warner, Ronald Reagan, William Holden, Adolf Menjou, Robert Taylor, and Gary Cooper—who cooperated with HUAC, giving the committee a kind of cover to press on with its probe of subversives in the motion picture industry. Just how much public sentiment had swung in HUAC's favor is reflected in Humphrey Bogart's recantation of his protest trip to Washington, calling it "ill-advised" in "I Am No Communist," a March 1948 *Photoplay* article, in which he also said he had been "duped." Such words, of course, played into HUAC's charge that Hollywood itself had been bamboozled into purveying communist propaganda.

Between November 1947 and March 1948 something like a seismic shift occurred in Hollywood. On November 25, Eric Johnston, head of the Motion Picture Association of America (MPAA), publicly declared that the Hollywood Ten, cited for contempt of Congress, had by "their refusal to stand up and be counted for whatever they are," performed a "tremendous disservice to the motion picture industry and to the cause of democracy." Ring Lardner, Jr., one of the Hollywood Ten, was off the Twentieth Century-Fox payroll by November 24. At SAG's annual meeting, the membership approved a resolution calling for all SAG officers to "sign affidavits that they do not belong to the Communist Party." An appalled Charlie Chaplin told a London newspaper, "Hollywood is dying," adding that he was making plans to "end my days" in another country.

In late November, top studio executives met in New York and agreed that in the future they would "not knowingly employ a Communist or a member of any party or group which advocates the overthrow of the U. S. government by force or any illegal methods." On December 3, MGM mogul Louis B. Mayer convened a joint meeting of the boards of directors of SAG, the Screen Writers Guild, and the Screen Director's Guild, along with members from the MPAA. In effect, Mayer was laying down the MPAA law to the talent guilds. The Hollywood Ten could remain employed only if they took an oath affirming they were not communists. "If action had not been taken by the industry itself," Mayer explained, "federal legislation would have undoubtedly been the result." His statement was not surprising in a business that already self-censored through the production code, preferring that means of stifling itself over government-prescribed curbs on free speech. The only leeway the MPAA policy offered was Mayer's comment that each studio head would make his own decisions "regarding employment of any person."

Mayer emphasized that he was not endorsing HUAC's actions, but in the view of the three hundred to seventeen vote in the House of Representatives to uphold the committee's contempt citations of the Hollywood Ten, it would do great injury to the industry to affront public opinion, which Mayer believed supported Congress's decision. Dore Schary, known for being more liberal than his fellow producers, opposed a blacklist, but he added that the actions of the Hollywood Ten had "impaired their usefulness to the industry." The courts, however, would have to determine whether these writers' civil rights had been violated. Walter Wanger, who had appeared on the broadcasts attacking HUAC, nevertheless now spoke in favor of the MPAA policy, noting that the "general public feels that anyone who is a Communist is an agent of Russia."

That Mayer had Schary and Wanger speak out in support of the MPAA's position suggests how it was. Mayer, Schary, and Wanger all averred this position had not been adopted precipitously. But it was, of course, and the MPAA feared that perhaps the talent guilds would not go along, which is why the independent and highly respected Wanger was used to warn the unions not to issue any statement criticizing the producers' policy. At this point, Ronald Reagan suggested that each guild board meet separately "for a few moments in order to formulate the exact questions which they wished to ask."

After the joint meeting reconvened, Reagan began by asking about the mechanics of determining "who is a Communist." There were no mechanics, Mayer replied; individual studio executives would make the decision. Director George Stevens then voiced his union's support of the MPAA and agreed not to make a statement without conferring with the MPAA and the other unions. Reagan, saying the SAG board would have to meet to discuss the MPAA policy, then asked the essential question: "What is the actual difference between the firing of the ten men and the existence of a blacklist?" Dore Schary repeated that, rightly or wrongly (it was a matter to be determined by the courts), the men had lost their jobs because they had undermined their usefulness to the industry.

After much discussion of other questions, this fraught situation was clarified: In effect, anyone accused of communist affiliation who did not publicly deny it would be dismissed from employment. This was *not* the position the producers had taken before or during the hearings, but as Dore Schary observed, not only had public opinion swerved toward supporting HUAC, exhibitors were putting pressure on the studios to adopt the new policy. To skeptics who voiced concern during the meeting as to why the industry should heed the hysteria of the moment, Wanger replied, "[I]t is entirely evident at this time that the public is very opposed to anything they consider Communistic." As a result, the MPAA felt it had to take pre-emptive action before pictures were boycotted and protests organized that could damage business. The MPAA believed, in Mayer's words, that it was protecting everyone. As long as a studio employee renounced the Communist Party, he could remain or be reinstated in his job, said Joseph Schenck. Other producers agreed. The meeting adjourned with the understanding that no one would talk to the press and that some kind of public relations committee representing the industry should be formed.

On December 8, 1947, SAG president Ronald Reagan welcomed Dana and Van Heflin, newly elected board members, to their first meeting.

Present also were William Holden, Walter Pidgeon, Olivia de Havilland, Edward Arnold , Richard Carlson, Dan Duryea, Boris Karloff, Lloyd Nolan, Larry Parks, Tyrone Power, and Anne Revere. Reagan reported on the December 3 meeting. Executive Director of SAG Jack Dales, Jr. had given board members an "intelligence report" on the "aftermath of Washington Red Hearings," noting that it was the first time in motion picture industry history that the governing boards of the three talent guilds met jointly with the producers. Dales's report also pointed out that Attorney General Clark had branded seventy-eight organizations as subversive groups, including the Hollywood Writers Mobilization For Defense, People's Radio Foundation, Joint Anti-Fascist Refugee Committee, and the Civil Rights Congress. These were so- called Communist Front groups, established in the 1930s as part of the anti-fascist movement that included many liberals, some known as fellow travelers because they worked with and, in some cases, condoned the policies and practices of the Communist Party. Many SAG members had signed petitions and joined protests sponsored by these organizations, especially during the Spanish Civil War (1936–39), when Hitler and Mussolini sent munitions and other aid to the fascist rebel leader Francisco Franco, who successfully overturned the duly elected Spanish government, itself supported by Stalin and a group of international volunteers, including American citizens who formed the "Lincoln Brigade." Inevitably, then, the politics of liberals and communists intersected during this period, and now what had seemed fairly innocuous matters—signing a petition, attending a communist-sponsored meeting—had become grounds for declaring someone "guilty by suspicion."

Dana, entirely absorbed with his acting career, was not a "name" that any Communist Front organization would want to feature in newsletters, pamphlets, and other literature. But many of his colleagues in the industry, including some who had appeared in pictures with him, had reason to worry. That their primary concern, in many cases, was antifascism, not pro-communism, meant nothing to HUAC, which only absolved individuals who were either entirely free of any communist taint, or who were prepared to expunge that taint in a public ceremony of recantation, naming others involved in communist-sponsored activities. In other words, HUAC had developed a ritual of public purgation, so that recalcitrant witnesses—like the Hollywood Ten—were made to seem like obstructionists who sought to obfuscate the committee's investigations.

So place yourself with Dana at this meeting. He was sitting beside actors who had to wonder how much of their own political pasts might seem problematic in this new climate where they would have to prove their loyalty. As the meeting minutes indicate, Reagan presented a substantial five-paragraph statement he wished the board to consider adopting. A four-hour discussion ensued, focused on his principal points: 1. SAG opposed communism and members of the Communist Party because the latter remained loyal to the party's dictates. Indeed, SAG had passed a rule that all SAG officers and board members had to execute an affidavit swearing that they were not communists; 2. SAG deplored the producers' inquiry into the political affiliations of employees, although SAG also sympathized with the producers' "dilemma" as members of an industry so vulnerable to public opinion and political interference; 3. SAG did not want to protect communists but cautioned that the "pressure of fear" could harm American liberties; 4. SAG now was included in the producers' dilemma, having to "make of ourselves lawmaker, judge and jury and to take punitive measures in direct contravention of the law"; 5. SAG proposed leaving the investigation of subversive individuals to law enforcement agencies; to do otherwise was to "adopt communist methods as a means of defeating Communism." Reagan's proposed SAG statement was remarkably similar to the "Hollywood Strikes Back" broadcasts, except that he had removed the sarcasm and direct attacks on HUAC. It was a masterful political statement because it essentially expressed regret that SAG should be put in such an "untenable" position. He had removed any trace of self-righteousness that might alienate HUAC and its supporters.

Several board members, however, argued against issuing any statement, since no actors had as yet been affected by the producers' policy. Any SAG statement would only further publicize the problem the producers had already made into a front-page story. Others believed Reagan's statement could be interpreted as a defense of communists. Still others believed a blacklist was already being established. Reagan apparently did not address the issue of the blacklist directly, but he did say it was SAG's responsibility "to protect actors who are being discriminated against by the public without any evidence that they are Communists." Laurence Beilenson, one of SAG's founders and its attorney, cautioned members that this was one of those periods in American history when hysteria ruled, but that after some reflection the American public always repudiated reactiveness His comment seems to have provoked another member to say that if SAG did not issue a statement, it would be tacitly accepting the producers' policy. Many members shared Reagan's discomfort at the idea that SAG would, in any respect, be charged with investigating and determining the loyalty of its own members. Several motions brought Reagan no closer to gaining approval for his statement. Dan Duryea's motion that another special meeting should be called for December 12 was, however, "unanimously carried."

What did Dana make of these proceedings? Like most SAG board members, he is not identified with any of the positions articulated in the minutes. He also witnessed another prolonged board discussion on December 12, the upshot of which was a motion, unanimously carried, that SAG draft a letter to the producers essentially reiterating the points Reagan had made on December 8. Reagan, George Murphy, Laurence Beilenson, and Buck Harris were delegated to draft the letter. This maneuver apparently satisfied a SAG board reluctant to make a public statement at a time when the other industry unions had not decided on a course of action.

In effect, for all its concerns about a blacklist, SAG did not take a public stand against it. A SAG press release on January 15, 1948, reported that members voted 1,307 to 157 in a mail referendum that all officers, directors, and members of guild committees must sign individual affidavits swearing that they are not members of the Communist Party. Behind the scenes, SAG lobbied on behalf of actors like Lionel Stander accused of Communist affiliations. Board minutes for January 19, 1948, reported that Stander remained employed, but he would soon join the increasing ranks of blacklisted actors.

As early at 1946, the FBI contacted Ronald Reagan in an effort to determine what he knew about SAG members who took the Communist Party line. The FBI may also have contacted other board members, including Dana, who could not have told them much, but who might have, for their part, learned something from the FBI. Alexander Knox, who played Woodrow Wilson in Darryl Zanuck's biopic and first met Dana on the Fox lot in 1945, reported cryptically that Dana told him about two FBI employees who said they were listening to Knox's speeches. Why, they did not say. The only reason the baffled Knox could only think of for such surveillance was his appearance at the Hollywood Bowl for a program commemorating Franklin D. Roosevelt. My Freedom of Information Act request for Dana's FBI file resulted in a Department of Justice response indicating there was no extant record of contacts between Dana and the FBI.

By 1951, after another round of HUAC hearings, SAG issued a statement saying, in effect, actors were on their own. SAG opposed a "secret blacklist," but "if any actor by his own actions outside of union activities has so offended American public opinion that he has made himself unsalable at the box office, the Guild cannot and would not want to force any employer to hire him. That is the individual actor's personal responsibility and it cannot be shifted to his union." On May 28, 1951, Anne Revere, a board member who had been in the room with Dana in that December 3, 1947 meeting, addressed the board to explain her HUAC testimony. She had signed a non-communist affidavit in good faith but had decided to invoke her Fifth Amendment privileges to avoid testifying against others. "In consideration of the foregoing, and of her own altered status in the motion picture industry, Miss Revere stated that she felt her presence on the board of Screen Actors Guild was no longer proper and therefore tendered her resignation," which, the board minutes recorded, was duly accepted after she left the meeting. Dana was not there. If anyone said anything at this sorry moment in SAG's history, the minutes did not acknowledge it. The confident voices of "Hollywood Fights Back" were silent.

Who is to say what this kind of capitulation to public opinion did to Hollywood? HUAC's anti-communism campaign happened to coincide with a downturn in movie attendance, occasioned by the advent of television. Even Sam Goldwyn had to abide by the blacklist, if only tacitly. Louis B. Mayer made it clear that he disapproved of HUAC but was making the best of a bad business. Dana was not part of the special committee, set up by the SAG board on March 3, 1952, to look into the Communist Party connections of its members—exactly the sort of witch hunt Reagan had opposed in 1947. Anne Revere was placed on a list of those condemned as "present or past Communist Party members who refused to state whether they have been members of the party." On July 15, 1957, Revere replied in a letter to SAG: "The Guild not only failed to use its power on behalf of its members, but went on record as supporting the Un-American practice of blacklisting." SAG Executive Secretary Jack Dales answered her: "This chasm between your belief and ours (moral duty vs. legal defense) remains as deep as ever and is quite untouched by the decision to which you refer."

SAG's rebuff of Revere occurred in a period during which infiltration of the highest levels of government and communist espionage became a pressing public issue. On January 21, 1950, a jury found Alger Hiss, a former State Department official, guilty of perjury—that is, lying about his involvement in spying for the Soviet Union. And on August 17, 1950, Julius and Ethel Rosenberg were indicted for their part in a Soviet spy ring alleged to have stolen the secret plans for the atomic bomb. Hiss went to prison, and the Rosenbergs were executed.

Dana never got over the traumatic period of the blacklist and would often talk about it, as his daughter Susan recalls: "He hated HUAC. My dad was a 'card carrying member of ACLU' and proud of it. A party member, he was not. A union man, yes, through and through." Postwar America transformed itself into what historians have called the national security state, expanding the role of intelligence agencies such as the CIA and the FBI. Dana starred in *I Was a Communist for the FBI*, a series of seventy-eight episodes broadcast between March 30, 1952, and September 20, 1953, over six hundred radio stations. Although based on the memoirs of Matt Cvetic, an FBI informant for nine years, the programs were independently produced without the cooperation or sanction of the FBI. Each episode became an adventure story, with Cvetic always at risk of having his undercover work exposed. At the same time, however, this work took a toll on Cvetic, leading him to resent both the Communist Party and the FBI. His inner torment helped to elevate this radio serial above the commonplace anti-communist propaganda of the period. Remaining true to himself becomes as much a theme in Cvetic's work as does the focus on subversives infiltrating American institutions and attempting to sway public opinion in favor of Soviet inspired initiatives and policies. To deceive his own family and others about the true nature of his work was profoundly disturbing to Cvetic and exactly the kind of vexing dilemma that would appeal to a card-carrying member of the ACLU.

CHAPTER 16

Period of Adjustment
1950–53

DANA'S ROLES IN the early 1950s provided him with little opportunity to utilize the nuances he had perfected in his best work, although two pictures from this period trade on the ennobling courage that made him one of the silver screen's most decent and desirable leading men. In *Sword in the Desert* (released October 3, 1949), he appears as a cynical ship's captain who comes to adopt the cause of Jewish refugees on the way to Palestine. Appearing as another ship's captain in *Sealed Cargo* (released May 19, 1951), Dana played opposite Claude Rains, playing a villainous Nazi agent whose nefarious plot Dana's character exposes and thwarts.

Otto Preminger's Fox production of *Where the Sidewalk Ends* (released July 7, 1950) broke Dana's string of mediocre pictures. His role as detective Mark Dixon invites an obvious comparison with Mark McPherson, especially since Dana is again cast with Gene Tierney as his love interest. Indeed, Dixon seems like a McPherson who has met his Laura when it is almost too late. Dixon is McPherson five years later, brutalized by his job. He is getting a reputation in the department for roughing up perps. When he accidentally kills a suspect who has attacked him, he panics and attempts to conceal the deed, using his expert knowledge of criminal behavior. Although *Where the Sidewalk Ends* lacks *Laura*'s gloss, Dana's gritty performance is mesmerizing. His character's inhibitions become the focus of the picture, as he attempts to open up under Tiernery's wide-eyed gaze. Imogen Sara Smith calls his acting a "tour-de-force of slow-burning pain and agonized intelligence," his best performance. Other critics have lauded Dana's convincing portrayal of a ruthless but vulnerable character. Like McPherson, Dixon is hard to read, an impassive, taciturn, and fascinating study in the enigma of human identity.

The Frogmen (released September 8, 1951), marks Dana's slide back into the position of second-lead. He plays the reasonable, duty-bound hero opposite by-the-book commander Richard Widmark, playing a role remarkably similar to Don Ameche's dour officer-in-charge part in *Wing and a Prayer*. Dana did well in semi-documentaries (this one was an adventure story about a navy team of underwater demolition experts) but both his performance and the picture lack the power of *The Purple Heart*. In this Cold War period, the risks and dangers were real enough, and yet *The Frogmen* lacked the kind of urgency and sense of camaraderie that had Lewis Milestone so deftly created earlier.

From Norfolk, Virginia, where the picture was filmed, Dana sent a reassuring letter to Mary on December 18, 1950, saying the Navy brass did not seem all that thrilled to meet movie stars, "but the wives are just a little batty. I drank eight or ten coca colas and stood up for three hours without a rest. When they all began to get loaded (including our Mr. Bacon) I pulled out as gracefully as possible, went to a show by myself, then called you." Drinking cokes did not last. By September 1951, Dana was in Hartford, Connecticut, undergoing treatment for alcoholism at the Institute of Living. Established in 1922 as one of the first mental health centers in the United States, the institute is situated on thirty-five acres designed by the famous landscape architect Frederick Law Olmstead, and is now part of Hartford Hospital, specializing in the treatment and research of behavioral, psychiatric, and addictive disorders.

Dana first wrote to Mary from the institute on September 11:

Darling:
It was so nice to talk to you last night—it always is. And I always get a kick out of the kids. Sue—Sue was really trying to find out why I hadn't kept my promise to come home in "a little while"—or was it, "pretty soon"? I guess it's hard for her to understand why I stay away. It makes me feel good to know that they want me back, anyway.

Dana was not an abusive alcoholic. A few drinks relaxed him, but he could not stop at a few drinks. He just got happier and wobblier—and, at times, tiresome.

He was a hard man to treat since the enforced leisure of a sanatorium bored him. He tried to occupy himself with the Dave Brubeck record Mary sent, and he listened to the radio and played the occasional game of canasta. He had tried to amuse himself at a party for the patients, but he found it a chore dancing with other women, some of them "real lulu's. . . . If we had some booze we could have made everybody happy and really fixed things up—but really!" He was worried about his older son:

> Keep working on Dave and see if you can get him to write to me. Have you heard anything further from Margo? I wish I could be there to talk to the teachers about a curriculum for David so that he could get as much as possible that will help him rather than a lot of stuff that he will never be able to use.

Dana impressed on his doctors that he was "by nature a family man" and wanted to be released as soon as possible. He had not yet realized the progressive nature of alcoholism, or he would not have been so shocked at the arrival of a patient—a psychiatrist, no less—who had to be given glucose intravenously. "As bad as I was, I was never as bad as most of the people who are here," he wrote Mary. Not yet.

The letter Dana wrote Mary the next day suggests he had plenty of time to think about the life he had arranged for himself:

> In lieu of being able to sit down with you and tell you in the way I would like, I am going to try to put down here how much I appreciate the way you have taken all the job of handling the household, taking care of the children, getting all the gear together to send to me, etc. It's probably a good thing that you have something to do but maybe this is just a little too much. I am sure you must [be] pretty tired at the end of the day when the children have all gone to bed—and there is no husband to put his arms around you and kiss you. What a contrast to me. I am not tired at all because I have not done enough to keep a child occupied for two hours at the end of a day but I sure do miss not having some one to put my arms around and love. It's bad, bad, bad!

This last comment implies what Dana would say in so many words in his letter of September 18. He was losing his self-respect and feeling cooped up with losers (he never uses this term, however). It was also rather frightening: He had just heard that one of his fellow patients had relapsed only a week after his release and was on intravenous feeding. Dana's affable roommate, Russ, had been in treatment for over four months. Although Dana did not say so, he was part of a group of rather hard cases. That he pitied the others so much suggests he could not quite see how much he shared their plight. When let out for dinner at a nearby restaurant, Dana Andrews hated to be recognized as Dana Andrews: "I get that same old ga-ga treatment; I get so damned tired of it I could spit in their faces." Maybe so, but it is hard not to suppose that star treatment reminded him that he was *somebody*.

Back home, Mary was awakened one night by a call from a drunken sailor, who got the phone number from another drunken sailor. As Dana told his wife:

> [I]t appears that they sort of pass it [their home telephone number] around; at least that has happened quite a few times. I can only say that this is just some of my past sins revisiting me. When I look back at some of those escapades, they all appear tremendously childish and a complete waste of time that could have been spent in much more enjoyable and rewarding ways.

Repentant alcoholics can talk a good game, and here is what Dana said he learned from his stay:

> I have just learned that a majority of the people who become abnormal drinkers are superior in intelligence and are almost always introverts. They generally set rather high standards for themselves and those about them, not to mention the world and people in general; and when the cold facts of reality and the imperfections of themselves and others around them become too much for them to bear, they seek some way of evading reality. . . . The goal of therapy for such a person is to reeducate him to face reality.

Re-education involved a rather formidable reconstruction of the psyche and of behavior. He should not resist thinking about the urge to drink, but to consider the consequences of drinking—the ill effects that would soon overcome the "childish enthusiasm" that swept over him in alcoholic waves.

By September 22, Dana believed he could get "the best" of his drinking, although he admitted, "I have had this feeling before, so I must watch that it doesn't subside." All he could think about, really, was getting home. The letters are not convincing. Dana was sincere enough, but as he came to realize after another twenty years of failed treatments and resolutions to get better, sanatorium solutions did not work for him. Changing his habits, working on his state of mind, did not, in the end, mean a damn thing. He just had to make up his mind to quit. Quitting—not how, not why, not when—but *now* would be the solution. So Dana took his medicine, went home, and went back to work.

In *Assignment Paris* (released September 4, 1952), the nation's rather demoralized postwar mood is reflected in Dana's role as Jimmy Race, a brash reporter who thinks he can penetrate the Iron Curtain to get the story about an American imprisoned for espionage without doing damage to himself. In fact, the picture ends with a ravaged Race, having been tortured by his communist captors, returned to his newspaper colleagues in a mental stupor. It is a scene that graphically shows how much had changed in ten years for Dana and for his characters, who could no longer outwit enemies with panache.

Cutting himself loose from Goldwyn in the spring of 1952, Dana would find it increasingly difficult to secure worthy leading man roles in good pictures. The studio system was breaking up, a process hastened by a Supreme Court decision forcing the studios to divest themselves of the theater chains that ensured a steady market for their product. Dana described the consequences in his Columbia oral history interview:

> I was built up as a star, because the studio could so build me up because they had theaters. And whether the theater managers wanted me or not, they could depend on a certain amount, almost enough to pay for the picture, in the way of playing time in the USA, that would get them back their money, because they could say, "This is what you're going to have."

Stars could ride out their failures—at least to a certain extent—until the 1950s, and though stars remained important in the business, an individual actor like Dana, without a studio, was at risk of being replaced by a new generation of stars acting as independent agents and securing their own financing—so long as they could prove, like William Holden in *Picnic* (1955) and *The Bridge on the River Kwai* (1957), that they were big box office.

Dana had turned to the theater in the summer of 1952, touring the East Coast in a production of *The Glass Menagerie* playing the narrator, Tom, to Mary's Laura, his crippled and introverted sister. June Walker as their mother was joined by Walter Matthau as the "gentleman caller." The *New York Post* critic reviewing Dana's performance recommended more theater work to develop "vocal variety, body movement, interpretive power, poise and ease," but William Hawkins in the *New York World-Telegram* praised Dana for his composure and vigor, which made his stage presence as magnetic as his screen persona. It was an especially harmonious production that Kathy remembered fondly; she loved this new experience of joining a traveling troupe. Matthau may have had a crush on Mary, but he was a godsend for other reasons. He kept cast and family together during those nights when Dana got into trouble. On August 11, 1952, Dana was arrested and fined $5.00 in the Waltham, Massachusetts, district court for drunkenness and using profane language. An article appearing in the *Fitchburg Sentinel* on August 12 implied that he had been so disoriented that he was not sure how to contact Mary and had become irate. Such incidents, though, could still seem manageable for a performer with tremendous recuperative powers.

From time to time Dana tried television, which allowed for greater expression of his talent than pedestrian movie scripts. Usually, though, he appeared in very narrowly focused family dramas with constricted plots that catered to the small black-and-white screen. His wonderfully resonant voice was well suited to radio, and yet his performances in that medium were usually routine. He could not have had much respect for the radio drama scripts. They usually truncated screenplays like *Daisy Kenyon, Night Song, My Foolish Heart,* and *Where the Sidewalk Ends* into an hour-long rush, making huge jumps in character motivation and plot. Trite music was usually employed for awkward transitions, and breaks between the first and second acts were devoted to touting products like Lux soap, which nine out of ten Hollywood stars swore they applied every day. And then, an always affable-sounding Dana would appear in a "curtain call" with his co-stars, talking about his love of sailing or touting his most recent picture. The original radio dramas he appeared in, such as *Weather Is a Weapon* (aired May 14, 1945), covered events like the Battle of the Bulge in simplistic plots devoid of character development, and inspirational dramas such as *My Six Convicts* (aired October 20, 1952), a psychologist's account of his dealings with prison inmates, were marred by sentimentality. In *One Foot in Heaven* (aired July 27, 1953), he played a Methodist minister, who resembles CF only insofar as he is restless and on the move to form new congregations and build new churches. Dana co-starred in this Lux Radio Theatre presentation with his brother Billy, now an established actor named Steve Forrest who became Dana's only true male confidante. Somewhat more appealing is Dana's role as a scientist trying to repel a Martian invasion, an updated version of H. G. Wells's *War of the Worlds* (aired February 8, 1955), shifted from London to southern California.

Dana worked incessantly, and sailing remained his only real recreation. As Billy put it, Dana would wake up in the middle of the night thinking about his sailboats. Dana and his youngest brother bonded at sea, as Billy watched Dana's whole-hearted commitment to his enthusiasm and came to understand a brother who had been "eaten with ambition" all his life. And yet for all Dana's self-assurance and quick judgment, Billy sensed self-doubt, which is perhaps the key to Dana's successful portrayal of characters like Mark McPherson, strong personalities that nevertheless seem vulnerable.

In an undated letter Mary wrote to Dana, then on a six-week sailing trip, expressing her own understanding of why her husband sailed:

> I keep hoping that you're having a wonderful time and that you get rested and stimulated too. I think a man like you needs to get away from the confinement and pressure which our modern civilization inflicts on you. A tussle with the elements now and then and the ever-changing quality of the sea should do something for that restless feeling you get.

That "tussle with the elements" reminded Mary of an article, "Safe and Insane," by Philip Wylie in the *Readers Digest*. A popular writer of the 1940s and 1950s, Wylie campaigned against what came to be known as "Momism," a theme in *While the City Sleeps* (1956), one of Dana's most provocative pictures. Wylie worried about fencing children in, Mary said, quoting Wylie: "The life of a child ought to be a process of adventure, experience, and exploit. Only thus can he achieve self-reliance and independence. But instead of aiding this process we shield and protect our children from the facts of life." Mary concurred, although she also believed they needed to "learn discipline and to live within the confines of civilization." The wording is revealing, since it echoes her own characterizations of Dana's need to escape conformity. Both she and Dana were trying to strike some balance in childrearing and in their own lives.

In another letter from this same period, written from Palm Springs on hotel stationery, Mary tells Dana: "Kathy is as interesting as ever and I am happy to see that she is more independent of me than she used to be. I'm with her so much when I'm 'alone' at home. I was happy that she made no fuss when I left and I told her that I would be gone for several days." Steve, Mary assured her husband, "has the cowboy craze already and wants to go out and hunt a wolf." Mary, too, needed to get away, but said, "I've had a good rest and I'm tired of resting now." Like Dana's letters, hers were full of endearments: "Darling, you know how I miss you! I got to thinking about you last night and I couldn't sleep." Her closing words reveal why their marriage worked: "I can't tell you now much I'm looking forward to being with you again, but I'm happy that you are doing what you like to do."

And what about David? He was a bright, inquisitive boy, but somehow a vague sense of unease about him comes through not only in Mary's letters, but also in Aggie's. One of David's teachers told Mary that he had "certain basic problems to work out. She says he still is not very truthful in 'small things' with them." The other boys and girls liked him and looked on him as a leader. And he continued to be immersed in his love of music. Kathy, Steve, and Susan, as she grew up, got along fine with David, and yet they never seemed quite comfortable with him. Dana, who had left David in his earliest years in Aggie's care, never quite established a rapport with his oldest son, no matter how much he loved him and included him in family affairs. David can be seen in many of the family celebrations and playtimes that Dana filmed. He is much older than the other children, and although a sequence of shots shows him affectionately holding his baby sister Kathy, inevitably he cannot participate in the other children's activities.

With his appearance in *Elephant Walk* (released April 21, 1954), playing opposite Elizabeth Taylor (replacing Vivien Leigh) and Peter Finch, Dana had the best opportunity to revive his flagging career. But the sudden death in January 1953 of his brother Charles, the younger brother who worshipped Dana, sailed with him, drank with him, and identified most closely with Dana's ambitions, left him inconsolable. On his way to shoot the picture in Ceylon (Sri Lanka), he wrote Mary from the Dorchester Hotel in London: "[I]ts just horrible to be here where nobody is close enough to be of much help. . . . I am so depressed I can't eat anything or think of anything but the horrible fact of his death." Producer Irving Asher did his best to comfort Dana. So did Peter Finch. Charles was only forty-two.

Although Dana does not mention it in his letters to Mary, he began to drink heavily, perhaps for the first time allowing his malady to show in his work. Jeanne, Charles's widow, who knew Dana extremely well, said she could identify the scenes in which he is drunk, although the telltale signs (the drooping eyelids Kathy noticed) are not apparent. Elizabeth Taylor, perfectly punctual and professional, helped Andrews with his scenes. Some scenes are shot with Dana's back facing the camera, supposedly to cover up his ravaged appearance. Yet on screen he seems to manage all the "business" of his role as overseer on a tea planation, including bounding up steps and riding a horse. His own 16-millimeter film shows him fit enough to mount an elephant. Dana, seated with his back to the elephant's head, neatly swivels around and seems ready to ride. Other shots show him riding horses with his usual grace and cheerfully walking along with Peter Finch. And yet such footage obviously gives the lie to some essential truths. That Dana nearly ruined his reputation with the production company, Paramount Pictures, is indisputable. Dana had to do considerable special pleading before Paramount agreed to employ him again.

The production company would not let Dana go home for his brother's funeral, and that denial may have started him drinking after a period of sobriety. Finch, another hard drinker and a man who could handle a horse as well as Dana, became a buddy; the two later formed the "Fuck You Club" at the El Adobe, a restaurant across the street from Paramount Studios. Like Dana, Finch got his start in the theater and became a protégé of Laurence Olivier, who also became one of Dana's favorites. All three actors did their time in Hollywood but scorned its spurious practices, like giving an interview to Hedda Hopper. On location, Dana did so, managing to reserve his criticism and playing up the prankish elephants and noisy crows.

Mary heard reports only of an enchanting Ceylon, where Dana shot his own pictures—both stills and films—of a brilliant green and "many-shaded" land, full of the frangipani and bougainvillea that grew in a "wonderful climate." The tea plants looked like gardenias, and the garden-like tea plantations were breathtaking to behold. Huge crows flew into his room and ate breakfast leftovers, flying off with toast and huge slices of papaya. Tell the children, Dana wrote Mary on January 28. But he carried around his thoughts about Charles like a "huge hunk of lead" in his stomach. What kind of a God could Dana possibly believe in? he wondered. "I just feel kind of dead myself," a lonely, grieving Dana told his sorely missed wife. In spite of the lush and enchanting surroundings, he could not throw off his depression.

One of the disappointments of *Elephant Walk* is how little is made of Ceylon other than to display its scenery and its ornery elephants. No sense of Ceylon's culture and politics is allowed to distract from the banal story of an oafish master, John Wiley (Peter Finch), stupidly supposing a young woman, Ruth (Elizabeth Taylor), will be able to adjust to life in a palatial plantation home and the society of her husband's carousing male friends who amuse themselves by playing polo on bicycles. Into this disgusting spectacle strides Dana as Dick Carver, described as "always late"—a way of suggesting how tiresome he finds this male carnival. Indeed, he has given his notice and will be off to Paris soon. Then he meets the stunningly beautiful Ruth and begins to court her. Called Wilding in the Robert Standish novel on which the picture is based, Dana embodies the novelist's depiction of his character's "easy assurance of manner, his good clothes and his carefree, reckless brown eyes, which seem to see everything." In his first scene with Taylor, Dana shoots her a long, yearning stare. His devouring look is never matched by Finch, even though as the tea planter wins back his wife in the end. As in *Daisy Kenyon*, Andrews may lose his love interest, but he creates a far more fascinating character than the film's stolid leading man is able to sustain.

The real misfortune of *Elephant Walk* is not that Dana was drinking, but that his role was thrown away in the script. An actor who looked upon his roles like the writer who created them could only have been dismayed at the way he became a prop, losing Taylor in the end because she admires the way Finch rouses himself to combat a cholera epidemic. Conveniently, elephants demolish the plantation home so that Finch can tell Taylor they will build a new home elsewhere. This disappointing denouement leaves Dana's character stranded with not much to do other than console the leading lady. Such a poor recompense for an actor's talents might also have made him want to drink.

Writing to Mary on February 8, 1953, Dana accurately predicted the outcome of the picture:

> Leslie Storm has arrived from England to rewrite some of the dialogue which certainly is needed. I hope she can make the scenes live a little more than they now do as otherwise I think we will have a pretty corny picture. It would be such a shame to go to all this trouble for the background and have nothing in the foreground. . . . we are all depending on a rewrite to make the picture believable.

Whatever Storm did, it was not enough. *Elephant Walk* received mixed reviews. It was an A-list, Technicolor picture that kept Dana near the top—but nearly tipping over into lesser pictures and performances. In the *New York Times* (April 22, 1954) Bosley Crowther called Dana's performance "pompous," which is perhaps unfair but also a signal that he was beginning to become a little orotund in those later scenes when he is trying to woo Ruth away from her domineering husband. On the other hand, James Agee believed it was Dana's "strongest performance in several years."

By late August 1953, Dana was in Africa, filming *Duel in the Jungle* (released August 21, 1954), in which he plays an insurance investigator who believes that one of his firm's top clients has faked his own death in order to collect on a $2 million policy (suspiciously making his aged mother the beneficiary). Writing from South Africa, where part of the film was shot, he told Mary he did not think much of South Africa: a "flat and parched looking" land. And what a corny lot: "They are terrific movie fans but such *squares!* They knock at my door at all hours to get autographs and all want to know 'How do you like our country?' What can I say?"

Unfortunately, *Duel in the Jungle* was an equally corny picture, with Dana (Scott Walters) winning the love of Marion Taylor (Jeanne Crain) after proving to her that her fiancé, Perry Henderson (David Farrar) is a fraud, willing not only to bilk an insurance company but murder its investigator as well. The picture does a better job of showing off wildlife than does *Elephant Walk*, but it is even more ridiculous than its predecessor in making Dana behave like an action adventure hero, who not only apprehends Henderson but dives into alligator-infested waters to retrieve the criminal and bring him to justice. The dopey denouement is accompanied by a ludicrously triumphant musical score. Dana did not have to play a second lead—he is in almost every scene—but it is no wonder that he groused about his fans when he was appearing in such tripe. Getting lions and cheetahs to perform for a picture proved daunting, and the finished product is rather shoddy, with the actors' proximity to the animals largely a result of obvious cinema fakery: one animal shot, one reaction shot, and so on. When a career begins to go south, dull scripts usher it downward.

Why did Dana take on such roles? He wanted and needed to work. No actor of his age and experience could afford layoffs. He worked for himself and for his family. Sometimes, he admitted to Clyde Williams, he just wanted to say "fuck it" and do a perfunctory job. But his letters to Mary during this period suggest that no matter how silly the vehicle he was still behaving professionally, going to sleep early and getting the job done, putting in days that stretched from 5:30 a.m. to 6:30 p.m. Some days Dana was too tired and depressed to write—quite an admission for an energetic man with an indomitable constitution. But he apparently did not succumb, like at least some of the cast and crew. George Marshall, a journeyman director who had occasional hits like *The Blue Dahlia* (1946) and "the gang at the hotel get pretty tight before dinner most every night and its pretty boring for me," Dana admitted. "They become so silly and childish that I just can't bear it. When I go off to my room they all think I'm snooty or just plan anti-social." Dana felt just plain stuck and promised his wife "never again." He simply could not divert himself like other men. "If I were of a different nature it wouldn't be so difficult as there is plenty of 'nooky' around but that wouldn't satisfy the need. Marlene Dietrich is quoted as saying, 'A man is attracted much more by someone who is interested in him than by the most beautiful legs in the world.'" He needed Mary, in other words, to lavish his affection on, "someone . . . not just excited physically or selfishly agitated about your money, position, or any other material or possessions." He admitted his need for "sexual release gets pretty desperate at times but that need is insignificant in comparison to the need for your love and affection."

By October 10, Dana was relieved to be back in London and to hear Mary's voice on the phone. He wanted to believe that the remaining shooting schedule would be more business-like. "I only hope the picture doesn't show how little thought has gone into it." After the staging a few fight scenes at the Elstree studios that left him worn out and sore—especially after much rowing, diving, swimming, and drenching in the action scene plus sessions of shooting stills—Dana looked forward to returning home. The best offer he had was from Columbia to do *Three Hours to Kill* (released November 4, 1954), a "medium good Western for $50,000 + 17 1/2% of profits," he reported to Mary. He thought of holding out for something better, but at least it would mean he could work close to home. "<u>Home</u>! what that word means to me now. I love you my sweet, sweet girl. More than ever." Other than a few erotic dreams and daytime fantasies, life was just a bore without her.

CHAPTER 17

Home and Abroad
Dr. Jekyll and Mr. Hyde
1953–57

KATHY REMEMBERED HER FATHER'S return as a nice period, when he would come home for lunch while shooting *Three Hours to Kill*: "He liked to have us at the table with him when we weren't at school in the summer." They ate in the little breakfast room with sunlight streaming in through the branches of a big walnut tree. Dana bought the home at 4310 Arcola Avenue in Toluca Lake in 1946, shortly after he signed his new contract with Goldwyn. Built in 1937, the five thousand square foot home with six bedrooms and five baths is "an important character in the internal movie of my childhood," Kathy says. "It had a wonderfully warm personality and it was carefully chosen to be what Dad wanted for himself and his family. Not Beverly Hillsy." Or as Shirle Duggan puts it in "Casual Grace," (April 13, 1952, *Los Angeles Examiner*), "the home had none of the tinseled glamour or baroque elegance once associated with homes of screen star citizens." Kathy later described the entrance as having "two car-width white wooden gates, one at each end of the lot. Dad called it Normandy style."

"Casual Grace," provides a panoramic picture of a twelve-room, two-story house, one that Susan and Kathy expanded upon in their vivid recollections. From the outside, you approached a rose-beige stucco facade with white trim, and saw a roof with wooden shake shingles. A large blacktop area between the garage and the back door was big enough for badminton and bike storage. Inside, Dana's favorite room, the den, was almost as large as the living room, and had dark oak walls and furniture with nicely carved patterns and beige carpeting. Dana usually sat there in his favorite leather chair with ottoman. The rarely used living room had lighter and more formal mahogany furniture, with forest green walls that seem to glow. It had floral print draperies, a monotone loveseat, two wing chairs upholstered to match, a raspberry-and-white striped sofa set before a handsome bay window, and a rose marble fireplace. Copper, brass, and antique pewter Dana had acquired while doing *The Forbidden Street* gave the ensemble the look of an English countryside home.

In Dana's wood-paneled study upstairs his desk had everything "just-so in the drawers," Kathy remembered. "If anyone borrowed and returned his scotch tape or scissors, he knew it. Everything in its place, always the same place." He filled his bookcases with leather-bound classics, such as Balzac. "They represented something important to him," Kathy said. "Also some plays, Steinbeck, a Hemingway or two, some books on navigation and tying knots, a much-used dictionary, a Kipling book he could quote from flawlessly." Mary and Dana's bedroom had a fireplace (one of three in the house) and red quilted satin bedspreads. Dana's dressing room had two closets with everything categorized by style, length, and color. His shoes, many English bench made, were precisely arranged, as was every item in his dresser and built in drawers. No shoe was ever missing a shoetree. And cuff links were in boxes, arranged perfectly. No one tidied these things up for him. Before Dana went out, he would buff both his nails and his shoes.

A screened-in terrace with wrought iron furniture looked out on sweeping lawns. The article describes "two acres of attractively landscaped grounds which create a pastoral setting of charm and beauty," to which Susan adds:

> GREAT GROUNDS, WITH A BIG GRASSY HILL WHICH WE ALL ROLLED DOWN THOUSANDS OF TIMES—pool added at the bottom in roughly 1954. Large black walnut trees. Dad probably had almost 100 rose bushes and knew the names of all of them. They were set out in a grid next to a large iris garden done the same way. In between the two was play equipment—a high slide, painted dark green, built by JW Todd [Mary's father]. He also built parallel bars where Susan broke her collarbone. He also set up a fenced in compost yard.

"Susan's right," Kathy confirmed:

> The gardens were really something. Dad had worked out a bloom schedule so that as the Iceland poppies at the top of the hill faded, something else was budding. The two gardeners were either full

time or close to it. Except for planting seeds with us once or twice, Dad didn't work in the gardens, but he was very hands-on with planning them. . . . I planted a maple sapling from a soup can and it's now enormous on Google Earth! It was a prize at the St Charles Fair. Dad didn't like the spot I chose at the top of the hill in a sunny, well-edged bed, but he let me leave it where I'd planted it. There were many separate parts of that yard. I remember the house and gardens like a safe little kingdom. I'm really not going over the top on that.

They loved that house. "Who wouldn't?" Susan said. "It felt safe, warm (I can't help returning to that word over and over) and absolutely family-oriented. It would have been fine for entertaining, but they didn't do much of that at all. Very little was fragile. It was kid-friendly." Michael, the cocker spaniel, completed their household, although he was really Dana's dog.

Dana was happiest at home with his kids. Kathy remembered meals when her young brother Stephen, "lively, playful, silly, and funny," made faces at her across the dinner table "while showing me (and only me) a mouthful of chewed food. If I whined about it or started to cry—because I knew he'd get away with it . . . parental eyes turned to him, and that angelic half smile sunk my case every time. Then he'd lift a devilish blond eyebrow at me, unnoticed by all but me again." Stephen's antics were on display when his father lovingly filmed his son making several headfirst show-off dives into the pool. Dana had a powerful need to record his family life, showing everyone with their Christmas presents, children playing in the yard, and domestic scenes of Annis with Susan, who was especially close to her grandmother.

The Toluca Lake house had a four-car garage. Gertrude and William, a couple that helped manage the household, had the space on the right, and David had the space on the left. Gertrude and William had a Cadillac, and David had a white Jaguar XK120. "My parents joked about having the modest cars in the middle," Kathy said. David had inherited some money from Aggie, and there was not much Dana could do about his son's extravagant habits. The neighbors regularly complained about David's speeding. He used to drive Kathy very fast along Mulholland Drive, all the while giving her advice about when to let up on the brakes and to accelerate for control just before a corner. He sped up when they hit water so that the car would spin or the rear wheels would swing around. Kathy remembered a few too many of his more daring moves later when she learned to drive. She appreciated her father's methodical way of teaching her. "He was wonderful, really," Kathy said. "He and David were opposite extremes as drivers. Dad was never an aggressive driver. David was a daredevil, but highly skilled."

For Kathy, her father's *presence* in that home remains palpable. When she sat on his lap or he put his arm around her, she would listen to the sound of his deep, smooth voice. He kissed the back of her neck when her hair was pulled up and Mary smiled, "eyes and all," Kathy said: "She loved the way that he was crazy about their children. I think it's such a memorable experience for me because there was so much interaction." They read *Pat the Bunny* together, and the experience was more of a game than of a story: "Feel Daddy's scratchy face" was written on a page with a sandpaper patch. "I'd end up feeling my own daddy's face, which wasn't scratchy at all and usually smelled like lavender. He liked us to touch his face after he shaved," Kathy recalled.

Precise pronunciation was a mania: "He often corrected the grammar of a speaker on TV," Kathy said. "He corrected ours, too, sometimes including a lengthy explanation. Dad instructed my friend Paula, at great length, on the correct (French) pronunciation of chaise longue as opposed to the Americanized chaise lounge. He stressed that it meant long chair. He enunciated 'shez lawng' repeatedly and practically held us captive until she performed satisfactorily." No one was exempt. "My friends kind of liked it, though we'd fall down laughing with exaggerated versions of his already exaggerated corrections once he was out of earshot," Kathy said.

If Kathy had problems with homework, her Dad helped out. He said, "Make the problem simpler, solve that, and then do the hard one the same way." The technique worked well for her, and now, a teacher herself, she has taught the method to students and their parents. Dana used to ask Kathy to pick any number, tell him to add a certain number, subtract another one, and then to hold it in her head. Later that day he'd ask her to divide the number by something, double it, multiply it by a certain number, then hold that in her head. This exercise was performed over the course of about three sessions, Kathy said:

> I clearly remember standing outside with him under one of our walnut trees and he told me what my number was. I couldn't believe it. He said it wasn't magic. I kept asking "How did you do that!?" I don't recall if he told me what he had done or I figured out that he had multiplied by 0 at one point and then he gave me a few numbers after that. He could be playful that way.

Kathy's memories of her father reveal a man so attached to his home that it is little wonder the world of studio politics and on the set love affairs never attracted him:

> There's a picture I love somewhere, from a movie magazine, of him in his pajamas, holding me in the air in my robe and slippers, on his bed with the rose red quilted satin bedspread. He liked to have his children curled up next to him. Stephen's sweet vision of them night sailing together with his head resting on Dad's lap is perfect. If you asked each of us separately how we picture ourselves with our father, there would be touch involved for sure. Riding on his shoulders, holding hands, sitting in his lap. While his presence and his touch made his children feel secure as young children, I believe that ours did the same for him. His siblings helped each other weather whatever came along, probably often through touch. I know that he shared a bed with Charles, He loved holding his family and being held. Whenever he hugged Mom, it lasted a long, long time.

Returning home from location shooting was always an event, almost a movie production. Dana wanted his whole family to be waiting at the airport. Those were the days when people dressed up for travel and even to pick up travelers. Dana took *a lot* of luggage wherever he went, and all of those bags had to match and be in perfect condition. He tipped very well, and the skycaps all knew him. It became challenging for Mary to round everyone up for the big airport greeting as the children got older. "We started wondering why he had to have the brass band treatment every time," Kathy recalled:

> Mom said that it meant a lot to him and it did. She worked hard at not disappointing him and took care of what mattered. He gave it all back to us later, when we grew up and arrived at LAX with our own children. He was always waiting at the gate, beaming, greeting us with wide open arms and what must have sounded like a stage voice, "Darling!" (though it was simply his voice). He never failed to demonstrate in a big way, in a public way, at the airport, how important we were in his life.

Making a drama out of his domestic life—staging scenes, so to speak—became a lifelong occupation. He even had family members redo entrances so that he could get a better shot with his camera. Not everything was stagy, of course, but he was prone to record his life in takes in a way that could sometimes try his family's patience. The Toluca Lake house was a self-contained world that Dana had deliberately set off from his workaday routine. "People have said to me that it must have been really something to grow up in Hollywood, but I don't feel as though I did," Kathy noted.

The Toluca Lake house was more than a sign of Dana's success. It embodied a way of living over which he had virtually complete control. Like other well-off stars, he had help: two gardeners, a nursemaid, a housekeeper, and so on. He loved being served and installed a buzzer so that drinks and meals and snacks would appear at his call. But there was nothing peremptory about this setup. He simply thought it a pleasant and elegant way to live and would get irritated if Mary got up to get something or the children forgot to use the elaborate intercom system he installed.

Of course, Dana had done his share of menial labor, and this experience led him to formulate a view of life he passed on to his children. As he told Kathy, not only does everyone deserve to be treated decently—period—but failing to be open to the possibility that we can learn from almost anyone would be a mistake. Kathy remembered a conversation with her father after she told him about a semantics class at USC. The discussion was about how certain words and ways of naming people's jobs tend to carry judgmental views of intelligence and value in society. "He's dating a waitress," for example, which that the woman has lower status than the man. Kathy and her dad discussed that topic extensively that day:

> I realize that my attitudes toward people that I meet in many different settings are influenced by those kinds of conversations with my father. He talked about how he was the same man he had been before anyone had heard of him, and how he commanded respect that hadn't been his at all in those different early jobs. If he had been good in a picture, fine, but was he a worthless human being before that? If you could have seen him talking, however briefly, to the man he bought a newspaper from on the street in New York or the man who checked his oil at the gas station in Toluca Lake, you'd know right away what I mean.

In some ways, life with Dana was not so different from what other families experienced in the 1950s. If they were out, he always wanted to rush home to watch *The Jackie Gleason Show*, and he would spend hours laughing at the down home humor of Andy Griffith's comedy records and the albums Mel Brooks and Carl Reiner produced. Jonathan Winters was another favorite.

Kathy remembers that during one stretch of filming *Three Hours to Kill*, her father had "a prominent noose scar on his neck at every lunch." He was playing Jim Guthrie, who barely escapes hanging for a murder he did not commit when his fiancé, Laurie Mastin (Donna Reed), fires a gun, momentarily stopping a lynch mob and allowing the innocent man to drive off in a horse-drawn wagon with the noose still around his neck. Guthrie returns three years later to confront his accusers and discover who the real murderer is. The picture has quite a following and draws admiring notices for its taut structure and Dana's performance as the wronged hero, which reminds viewers of *The Ox-Bow Incident*.

But with some significant exceptions, Dana's pictures after 1954 lack not just good scripts but basic veracity and credible co-stars. Jeanne Crain (in *Duel in the Jungle*) seems nothing like a South African secretary, and in *Three Hours to Kill*, soon-to-be-television star Donna Reid appears helpless without modern appliances. But Greer Garson is by far the worst example of inauthenticity, doing her star turn in a Technicolor dud, *Strange Lady in Town* (released April 12, 1955). She is supposed to be Dr. Julia Winslow Garth, a doctor from Boston who travels to Santa Fe in 1880 to join her soldier brother and to escape the male chauvinism of her East Coast colleagues. Garson does nothing to modify her movie star voice and mannerisms to suit her character. Even while working long hours as a doctor in primitive conditions, she remains fresh and always smiling. Sounding like a lady of the manor, Garson displays a stunning wardrobe to show off her impressive figure and is surprised to learn that the West is also infected with misogynists like Dr. Rourke O'Brien (Dana). It takes nearly an hour of running time before she meets her match in Dana, who clearly relishes his role, which allows him to give voice to politically incorrect opinions with savoir-faire.

There are two reasons to watch this movie—or rather two minutes of the movie that ought to be included in a documentary about Dana Andrews. First, there is Dana Andrews teaching Greer Garson how to sit on a horse: "Your seat is mainly a question of balance. You've got to learn the trick using your knees—like this," he says, adjusting her right leg. "I think I get the idea," she responds drily. "Another thing, to turn a horse you don't use the bit," he says, moving her hands from side to side with the reins. "Sit up straight," he commands, slapping her on the rump.

"Try not to look like a sack of potatoes!" To her startled gaze, he replies, "You know, I think you're going to be all right. You've got the hands for it. You've got the legs. Yes, you certainly have got the legs," he eyes her appraisingly. "Look, before we get too deeply involved in my anatomy, suppose we take that ride," she says, cutting off his commentary. It is a delicious moment—two stars having fun. Second, when the couple stops after the ride, Garson gets off her horse stiffly, as Dana begins to romance her:

> GARSON. Don't let yourself get carried away. You know, the wide open spaces, the drumbeat of hoofs, the wind in our faces. You know the poetic approach.
> DANA. Poetic? That's like cutting good whiskey. Personally I like mine *straight*.
> GARSON. Like what straight?
> DANA. The relationship of the sexes.

Dana does these scenes without the affectations that ruin Greer Garson's performance. The difference between these two stars was evident to Ralph Pease, who watched them appear on stage at the Austin, Texas, premiere of the picture:

> Garson was a literal chatterbox, looking lovely and charming and gracious and very, very confident.
> Andrews, on the other hand, seemed shy, hesitant, almost embarrassed by his presence. He spoke simply and directly to the audience about the making of the film, rather than about himself.
> When they were finished, I felt that we had seen Garson perform. I felt that we had met Andrews, and that he was not unlike the roles he played.

The Dana Andrews that Ralph Pease describes also appears in *Smoke Signal* (released March 1955). Piper Laurie, his co-star, is a much better actress than Crain, Reed, or Garson. Or is that she is just spunkier and seems less movie-starish? She is a more credible love interest for Dana, who plays Brett Halliday, wrongly suspected of treachery because he has sided with the Indians against his fellow soldiers. Halliday is a perfect fit for an actor portraying the wronged hero again, this time in director Jerry Hopper's marvelously composed action sequences on the Colorado rapids.

In her memoir, *Learning to Live Out Loud*, Piper Laurie recalls her excitement at the prospect of co-starring with "one of my idols from adolescence." Laurie had watched *Fallen Angel* "at least six times," waiting for that moment when Dana kissed Linda Darnell, their lips parting slightly. Laurie and her girlfriend thought they saw him put his tongue in Darnell's mouth: How daring and provocative! Laurie remembers her limousine driving up to the circular drive of the "glamorous looking" Toluca Lake house. After waiting a half hour, a stunned and disappointed Laurie watched her hero being delivered to the car and deposited next to her, slumped over. He did not sober up until their plane landed for location shooting in Utah. And yet they worked well together. He always knew his lines and was on time. But then he would show up at her motel after the day's shooting, asking, "Will you come with me and help me find a drink?" With no bars nearby, she dragged Dana to her room. "Then an amazing thing happened," she recalls. "He began to recite the most beautiful poetry—biblical poetry, long Shakespearean soliloquies. For at least two hours, I was spellbound. Finally he had recited himself sober enough to get himself back to his room." The next morning Dana arrived at the set with apparently no recollection of the night before, so hung over the prop man connected him to an oxygen tank. This fixed him up, Laurie notes: "[H]e was suddenly transformed into the terrific actor he really was." Gradually, Dana took an interest in her, and they became friends. He would repeat his after-hours recitals, which she found touching. "None of this was the relationship I had fantasized, but in a way it was better," she concludes.

Comanche (released March 1956) gets an honorable mention in Bob Herzberg's *Savages and Saints: The Changing Face of American Indians in Westerns* (2008) as "well produced and directed and presenting a sympathetic view of Native Americans." But Herzberg also notes that the "usual contrivances pop up," including a lame love story involving Dana as Jim Reed (a scout) and a Comanche captive, Margarita (Linda Cristal). Speaking of Cristal, one imdb wag quipped: "for acting less wooden, watch a cigar store Indian." Drunk some of the time, the susceptible Dana had an affair with his co-star.

Dana shot a good deal of film on the *Comanche* set, where it is apparent he did not have much to do other than play around. Cristal appears in several close-ups, rather self-consciously playing to the camera. He was infatuated with her, but neither in these "candid shots" nor in the picture itself does she exhibit much talent. The affair with Cristal did not receive much notice in the US, but it became a staple of the Mexican tabloids (the picture was shot in Durango). Dana was so far gone at one point that in a telephone call home he tried to convince Mary she would like Linda. Mary left for Mexico to do damage control, as her daughter Kathy put it, stopping at Saks for a few snazzy nightgowns:

> As far as Dad ever falling for anyone else, it never happened. No question. I'd bet my life on that. I'm sure Mom never doubted that he was crazy about her, and he never tired of telling people how amazing she was and how fortunate he was. It was a given that he would say that at any opportunity. He meant it, but also went a little overboard saying so. I mean she could come home from a trip to the market and he'd hug her and say "My darling!" Not exactly fake, but . . . well, overboard. I'm quite sure that she never considered any woman a serious rival.

Mary knew she was the essential ingredient. Kathy again said it best: "Dad was a great father in many ways, but having him without her? We would *all* have gone up in flames." Dana spent many hours filming Mary. Of all the family members, actors, and friends that appeared before Dana's camera, Mary stands out as the star. Her poise, unaffected manner, alertness—and what can only be called "sparkle"—are wonderful to watch. Footage of Mary in close-up that Dana took sometime in 1953 lingers on her smiling face as the sun and shadow move across it. If this had been a screen test—which is what it looks like—she would have gotten the job.

Spring Reunion (released March 1957) teamed Dana with Betty Hutton (far more subdued than in her 1940s heyday) in an inconsequential story about a high school reunion. Forty-seven, Dana was playing a thirty-three-year-old in a role that his fans like because he seems so "real" and matter-of-fact—and that his critics decry because he seems to have so little affect. The best moment in the picture comes when Dana has an opportunity to deliver a speech about the attraction of the sea for a man never quite comfortable on land. He seemed to have a good time singing the picture's title song on the Perry Como Show, a stodgy program that was also a throwback to 1940s entertainment. For certain cinemaphiles such television shows and pictures help fill a nostalgia quotient.

Of an entirely different order are Fritz Lang's final two American pictures, *While the City Sleeps* (released May 30, 1956) and *Beyond a Reasonable Doubt* (released September 5, 1956). Dana felt comfortable with Lang and even described him to Clyde Williams as a friend. Although Dana certainly saw the director's dictatorial side, the two got along in much the same way as Dana did with Preminger: "I didn't want to take his directions as to what he wanted until I could ask him questions and *then* get him to tell me what he wanted so that I could understand—instead of the way he said it [as orders]," Dana told Clyde Williams. Lang repeated in countless interviews that he allowed Dana to play roles his way and would not dream of interfering unless he thought the performance was just plain wrong. At any rate, in Fritz Lang, Dana had a world-class talent, renowned for his work on *M* (1931), *The Woman in the Window* (1943), *The Big Heat* (1953), and many other pictures. The two men seemed to appreciate one another. They did a silly promotion piece for *While the City Sleeps*, in which Lang jokes about working Dana to a frazzle twelve hours a day, and Dana gallantly replies that directors work harder than actors because of all the pre-production planning. Dana shows a rifle to Lang, who says, "Very good, Dana, to shoot actors who don't know their lines." Dana just laughs.

The plots of both Lang pictures, especially on first viewing, seem improbable—especially in the latter work, where Dana as writer Tom Garrett fabricates evidence incriminating himself in the murder of a burlesque dancer. His plan, instigated by his prospective father-in-law, a newspaper editor opposed to capital punishment, is to expose a zealous prosecutor who manipulates circumstantial evidence to obtain his convictions. But Lang's low budget pictures blithely employ contrived plots because, as critic Robin Wood suggests, the director is more interested in a "concept" than in verisimilitude. The two pictures with Dana form part of Lang's newspaper noir trilogy, which began with *The Blue Gardenia* (1953), a film that attacked the sensationalism of American media and its corrupt practices as exemplified by columnist Casey Mayo. Dana played Mayo on the Lux Radio Theatre (November 30, 1954), although Lang cast Richard Conte as the lead in the picture. Lang's switch back to Dana Andrews, then going through one of his worst alcoholic periods, seems a deliberate assault on Hollywood itself and its halcyon heroes.

While the City Sleeps benefits from a first-rate cast, including Vincent Price as Walter Kyne, the playboy heir of Kyne Enterprises, a publishing empire. His role is a reprise of the feckless Shelby Carpenter, although this time the effete male is cunning enough to set up an inner office rivalry: Which one of his recently deceased father's newsroom editors will break the case of the lipstick killer and be put in charge of the flagship paper, *The Sentinel*? Only Edward Mobley, a Pulitzer Prize-winning journalist and a television commentator, played with panache by Dana, refuses to compete. He is happy doing his own work and romancing his much younger fiancé, Nancy Liggett (Sally Forest). But Mobley is drawn into the world of office rivalries because he cannot resist the importuning John Day Griffith, the managing editor played with appropriate crusty charm by veteran character actor Thomas Mitchell. Griffith is an old school journalist and as such appeals to Mobley much more than the oily advertising chief, "Honest" Harry Krizer (James Craig), who schemes to win by having an affair with Kyne's wife, played by the alluring Rhonda Fleming, and the suave but utterly decadent Mark Loving, delivered with his customary smug sarcasm by the inimitable George Sanders.

Unlike nearly all the other pictures in Dana's post-1940s career, this cast has marvelous chemistry, which then is superheated by Ida Lupino, playing gossip columnist Mildred Donner. Donner is Loving's paramour, whom he employs to seduce Mobley just after the latter appears on television to address the lipstick killer directly, describing the criminal and his motivations so accurately that the journalist startles the murderer, who is watching Mobley's performance. Mildred's job is to get Mobley drunk (not a tough assignment for a man who is seen drinking all the time) and learn all she can about the case.

Lang never commented on Dana's own drinking, but he took advantage of it by having a drunk play a drunk. Gene Fowler, Jr., credited with editing the picture, described Dana as reporting to the set with hangovers so terrible that shooting began at about eleven a.m. after innumerable cups of coffee. Producer Bert Friedlob became so worried he had an assistant follow Dana around. In one harrowing incident, Dana is supposed to have taken off fast in his car and then executed a sudden illegal U-turn across a highway dividing strip, successfully eluding his pursuer, who did not want to participate in a high-speed chase. On another occasion, he did not escape. On December 29, 1956, Dana was arrested for drunk driving after ramming the back of another vehicle stopped at a red light. The police report stated he was driving erratically. He paid a $263 fine and was also sued by a passenger in the other car, who was awarded $5,000 in damages.

The bar scene between a drunken Dana and the seductive Lupino, who places her mouth around a cigarette with exquisitely broad suggestiveness, is better than any other single piece of acting in any post-1950 Dana Andrews picture. How this scene got past the censors I cannot imagine. The film's producer wanted to cut the scene, but Lang insisted on it, and after a preview audience laughed and applauded it, the grumbling executive had to relent. Dana Andrews and Ida Lupino were friends off screen, and their utter ease with one another contributes to this pleasurable duet.

In order to catch the killer Mobley is willing to put his fiancé in harm's way. Mobley knows how to catch the killer because he shares some of that criminal's sociopathic personality. Like the killer, for example, Mobley undoes a lock to gain entrance to his fiancé's room after he has bidden her good night. Mobley is, in other words, just as manipulative as the next man in this picture, but Dana plays his character with a decadent charm that outdoes even George Sanders, who, it turns out, has been played by Mildred, who gets exactly what she wants: a better position at the paper. Lang cynically bows to Hollywood conventions, though, in making sure that Edward Mobley, the charming dipsomaniac, does not make the ultimate surrender to Mildred Donner's enchantment. He remains true to his Nancy and comes out in better shape than anyone else. The film's denouement is actually so preposterous that it has to be regarded as the first of Lang's two goodbyes to a Hollywood whose conventional happy endings and good guys finally drove him away.

As Edward Mobley, Dana Andrews returns to his nobler self, reprising the abiding message of nearly all of Dana's great roles, and the biography that Hollywood created by developing that side of his character. The unspoken message of Dana's best performances, even in the mediocre films of the mid 1950s, is that he can he do it again: provide a satisfying performance and redeem himself. Dana has a moment in *Beyond a Reasonable Doubt* that calls for the kind of subtlety that harkens back to *Laura*. Sitting in the court room listening to testimony that is going to convict him of murder, writer Tom Garrett exhibits just the faintest smirk, a sign of his (to that point) well-concealed arrogance. Presumably his facial expression is connected to his anticipation of the after-trial scene, when his soon-to-be father-in-law, Austin Spencer (Sidney Blackmer), will come forward with evidence that will exonerate Garrett and humiliate the confident prosecuting attorney. Garrett still faces execution, however, because Spencer dies in a flaming car crash that destroys the evidence proving Garrett's innocence. Then, in yet another last-minute twist, Spencer's statement explaining the ruse he concocted with Garrett is discovered, and Garrett is set free. Utterly relaxed in the company of his still loyal fiancé, Susan (Joan Fontaine), Garrett then makes the fatal mistake of mentioning the dead woman's first name in such a familiar tone that Susan realizes he is, in fact, the murderer, whom she must turn over to the police.

Lang himself thought that so many twists at the end of the picture were preposterous and that audiences would not accept rooting for the hero, only to discover that he is the villain. But the director said he had no power to change the script. Dana, too, thought the script took one turn too many. And yet, his smirk as the picture reaches it climax is its most telling moment, revealing a man who thinks he can get away with anything: a writer who believes he can put over any plot he devises, a writer who puts off marriage to his fiancé—first in order to finish his novel, and then to join Spencer in her desire to fool the prosecutor. One momentary smirk is perhaps too little to pin a whole picture on—and yet, how else to read Tom Garrett? He puts himself entirely at the service of his story—as a good actor should, as a good writer must—except that in this case the writer believes he can even commit murder in the service of his ambitions. Tom Garrett, in this respect, is the culmination of Dana's restrained characters, all of whom have their secrets, but none as monstrous or as egotistical as Tom Garrett's. His willingness to murder a blackmailing woman simply so that he can expunge an embarrassing past and marry well and further his career is a shocking counter to the roles Dana usually played, since Tom Garrett's real offense is that he could be so ignoble.

It is doubtful that such an interpretation of *Beyond a Reasonable Doubt* would be apparent on first viewing. Indeed, it does not seem to have occurred to Dana, his director, or his co-star. Joan Fontaine told biographer Patrick McGilligan that Dana's "alcoholic haze added a further layer of insincerity to the film." *Beyond a Reasonable Doubt* is one of those pictures which demands to be seen, again and again, because every move that Garrett makes becomes the subject of minute scrutiny the second time around. The ending of *Beyond a Reasonable Doubt*, in other words, is all about returning to the beginning. The preposterous plot does not matter because, at bottom, the picture is not really about journalism, the criminal justice system, or the death penalty so much as it is about the writer's (and the actor's) mentality and his desire to create his own reality.

In the same league as Lang's masterpieces is Jacques Tourneur's *The Night of the Demon*, a.k.a. *The Curse of the Demon* (released in July 1957), a horror cult classic that is about the very nature of reality itself. Dana's levelheaded, straight-ahead style of acting serves him especially well in the role of psychologist Dr. John Holden, a no-nonsense investigator of the occult. A believer in science, he has little patience with the shenanigans of magician and wizard Dr. Julian Karswell (Niall MacGinnis), although as their titles indicate, the two men are experts in their respective fields. The unflappable Holden has to reckon with forces he cannot account for, but he never relents in believing in his own rationality, refusing to be intimidated by Karswell's menacing tricks. In the end, though, he admits there are powers that reason alone cannot fathom or control. Heroes in horror movies are usually histrionic in the Vincent Price mode, so the sobering conclusion of *Night of the Demon*, when Holden says that in some instances it is better not to know, is especially welcome. As critic Raymond Bellour puts it, "Dana Andrews gives Holden that square-shoulderedness, that distant allure, that barely expressive look, the manner of keeping his thoughts to himself and of believing without believing (just like a spectator) that make him into one of the strongest actors of a certain type of American cinema." Dana would, however, succumb to overplaying a mad Nazi doctor with a bad German accent in *The Frozen Dead* (released November 1967).

Dana had trouble remaining sober during the making of *Night of the Demon*, although his co-star Peggy Cummins still refuses to comment on his drinking. She had been on the Fox lot in the 1940s when they were both contract actors, and, like Norman Lloyd, she treated Dana with a kind of reverence. "Dana was a remarkable actor—brilliant, absolutely brilliant," she said. She did not claim to know him well, saying he was quite reserved. She describes an atmosphere that is diametrically opposed to the one that others working on *Night of the Demon* remember. Her Dana Andrews knew his lines and was never less than a consummate professional. The contradictory testimony concerning what happened on the picture suggests the Jekyll and Hyde behavior that bifurcated Dana's life.

What he was like when drunk is glimpsed at the start of a publicity campaign for the picture. Introduced to witchcraft scholar Dr. Margaret Murray, then ninety-three, Dana embraced her with a kiss on the cheek and with the greeting: "You old son of a witch." Tony Earnshaw's *Beating the Devil: The Making of The Night of the Demon* relies on Hal Chester, the film's producer, who clearly detested Dana and did not like the film's director much, either. Dana became infuriated because Chester, "a real little schmuck," kept interfering with Tourneur's work, especially by insisting that the demon be shown, thus destroying the director's desire to make fear of the supernatural a palpable and yet unseen phenomenon. Chester told Earnshaw that when Dana arrived to do the picture on October 18, 1956, he stepped off the plane and fell down a flight of steps. Mike Frankovich, then head of Columbia Pictures in Europe, said, "This is your star." Chester did not want him, but it was too late to make a change. Earnshaw interviewed a crewmember who supported Chester, saying Dana's woozy first take was always a disaster, but he'd get it right by take four. Dana would stay up all night, for several nights running, Chester remembered. And he was probably telling the truth, since Dana's own family saw him do exactly that. Chester sent a doctor to examine his star. Why did he drink so much, the doctor wanted to know. "Because I like it," Dana answered. "It's bad for your health," the doctor said. "You think so?" said Dana, grabbing the doctor's arm. "I've still got black and blue marks on it. He's as strong as a bull," the doctor told the producer. Chester also described a scene in which police showed up on the set after an incident in a nightclub, where Dana punched a performer and threw her into the orchestra. To prevent his star's arrest, the producer promised his insurance company would pay damages, and the complainant was bought off with "a couple of thousand pounds."

Dana had never before behaved badly on a movie set, but according to Richard Leech, who played a police inspector in the picture, the star "was a frightful nuisance." Leech remembered a raucous argument between Dana and an assistant director, who tried to get the actor onto the set. The director kept saying, "Come on, Mr. Andrews, you're paid to turn up," to which Dana, clearly drunk, replied, "No, fuck off." But then Chester does not come off much better in Leech's testimony: "The producer was a nasty little bit of work. . . He was a very bumptious little bugger, rather full of himself."

This characterization is rather telling. Both of Dana's daughters remember that their father and mother used to talk about "little people," by which they meant small-minded individuals. Chester represented not only what Dana hated about the picture business, but also about anyone who seemed petty and lacked any discernible style or integrity. In other words, Chester was everything Dana detested. "By drinking as he did Dad said *Fuck You*. He just did. Plain and simple," Susan said. "But when he got sober, he knew that was not a logical or rational response and he pulled it together enough to nobly carry on and go to that side of his character that was responsible, and, yes, prided himself on "'being somebody.'" But to be somebody and yet also be subjected to Hal Chester was infuriating.

How much Dana's drinking affected his performance in *Night of the Demon* is debatable. The keen-eyed Chris Fujiwara mentions only a "process shot of Andrews getting out of a car in front of a hotel, in which his delivery is noticeably slurred and unsteady." In the dozens and dozens of enthusiastic comments in the imdb user review, Dana's drinking is rarely mentioned even as background information.

Accounts of Dana's appalling behavior on *Night of the Demon*—Peggy Cummins's valiant disclaimers notwithstanding—now made him a risky actor to employ. Dana admitted as much when he wanted the starring role in *Zero Hour* (released through Paramount Pictures, November 13, 1957). In the picture's production files, Dana's representative (unidentified) notes:

> He knows that he caused you a great deal of trouble on "Elephant Walk" and he knows well that Paramount is reluctant to use him again. He has told Harold Rose, his agent and friend, that he is going to show all of us, and, most particularly, you, that he can deliver with his full talent and his full attention. We have been with him several times now, in discussing the picture, and he looks very fit.

Paramount took a chance. As a former World War II pilot tortured by memories of bombing missions—even as he is called upon to take over a commercial airliner after the crew is disabled with food poisoning—Dana is riveting. The close-ups on his tense face, reminiscent of the bombardier scene in *The Best Years of Our Lives*, reveal a fine piece of acting. Both the picture and Dana's work received rave reviews. But *Zero Hour* was a black-and-white low budget picture that got lost among the blockbuster Technicolor extravaganzas that Hollywood confected in the 1950s to compete with television

Similarly, *The Fearmakers* (released October 1958), is a fascinating failure that did not find an audience. Dana's last collaboration with Jacques Tourneur, the picture fails not for lack of ambition, but for attempting too much. It tries to cram in an exploration of postwar politics, Communist subversion, and the commercialization and packaging of American culture—all of which Dana, as Captain Alan Eaton, a Korean War veteran and a victim of communist torture, confronts when he tries to resume his role in a public relations firm that is exploiting the uneasy climate of the Cold War.

Zero Hour and *The Fearmakers* proved to be only a respite. Dana resumed his alcoholic decline during the production of *Enchanted Island* (released November 8, 1958), a lamentable adaptation of Herman Melville's *Typee*, filmed in Acapulco. The producer sued Dana for $159,769 for breach of contract, citing twenty times when Dana was not able to work because of "self-induced intoxication." He was supposed to be playing a "healthy, robust character," a sailor, in fact, but he had become involved in "insulting, offensive and abusive" encounters with Mexican citizens. Although Dana denied the charges, reached a settlement with the producers, and eventually completed the picture, it marked a sad and shocking turn of events. *Enchanted Island* was no good. The director, Alan Dwan, had directed Dana in *Sailor's Lady*, another rather lame effort, and that circumstance could not have lightened the actor's load. Dana had come full circle, and for what? He had lost the "willingness to play the game to win," his daughter Susan believed.

CHAPTER 18

Sobriety
1958–64

SUSAN, THE YOUNGEST of Dana's four children, grew up when her father was on a downward slide. "Sometimes my friends would come over when my father was drunk, even passed out. I would cope by just walking them around the situation. What else could I do? Since my father was an actor it would be in the paper in a fan magazine with a picture of him drunk. I couldn't hide it." He would rifle through the refrigerator and leave everything on the floor. Stephen, who loved to watch his charismatic father light up a room, was devastated to see him lose control. After a few drinks Dana was wonderful; after a few more, he was a drag. He got sloppy. Mary drank with Dana sometimes. Susan remembered going to the cabana at the Toluca Lake house pool and seeing a man passed out on the floor. She ran to her mother in alarm. Mary said, "Oh, darling that's okay, it's just Sydney Chaplin." This reaction was typical of her family, Susan said. "The other side of being on the floor," Susan added, was a classmate's letter about the time Dana visited the Rio Vista school: "I remember when your father came. And he was wearing a trench coat and a fedora, and everybody was just so excited to see him. And he was such a nice man.' It always made me proud," Susan said.

After the fiasco of *Enchanted Island*, a doctor told Dana for the first time that he would die if he did not stop. That dire warning had its effect, and Dana began a period of sobriety that lasted until 1964. Susan remembered her dad on a camping trip "in good shape," treating her bee sting with tobacco, an old country remedy. The bee had been attracted to the sardines and saltines they were eating, food Dana had liked as a boy. Her father was always busy making movies, so this trip stood out. He could revert to the country boy Susan liked watching in *Swamp Water*. "I think that the memorable moments with my father . . . would always reduce down to the time when he wasn't needing to be somebody he wasn't, when he could just be himself . . . and give his attention to us. Any child wants that," Susan told Clyde Williams.

Resuming a stage career was also a tonic. TV producer Fred Coe had seen Dana in "The Right-Hand Man" on *Playhouse 90* (aired March 20, 1958), considered the best live dramatic series on television. Dana played a big-time Hollywood agent modeled, he told Clyde Williams, on Charles Feldman and others Dana had known. Unfortunately, Dana's live performance does not seem to have been recorded, a misfortune since he regarded his work on *Playhouse 90* as one of the highlights of his career. Coe needed a "name" to replace Henry Fonda, then co-starring with Anne Bancroft in the Broadway production of *Two for the Seesaw*. Coe believed Dana would work well with Bancroft and director Arthur Penn, both associated with the Actors Studio and method acting. Henry Fonda had little patience with method actors, but Dana got along well with them as he proved while working with Elia Kazan, and his staple of mainly method actors. Unlike Fonda, who could seem quite aloof to his fellow actors, Dana enjoyed getting to know the people he worked with. His daughter Kathy remembered how eager her father was to work with the best people so that he could be his best. "He wanted to know and found out things about their childhoods and backgrounds and approaches to their work because he was interested, never because he wanted to be their friend, at least not socially." She remembered her father taking her to dinner at Jean Renoir's house: "While Dad seemed comfortable enough talking with him, I know that he would have much preferred *working* with him."

From July 1958 to June 1959, Dana returned to form playing the lead male role in *Two for the Seesaw*. "I was looking for a kind of revitalization," Dana told Lillian Ross:

In the movies, I had been a leading man, and in movies a leading man is usually a man who can do no wrong. I was expected to play pleasantly, to play pleasingly, to play a good man who is always victorious over evil. I've always thought of it as being a boom-boom-boom actor. I'd outshout, outfight, outcharm, out-everything everybody while acting. Meanwhile the real acting parts were going to the character actors. After all those years in movies, my senses as an actor were dulled. On the stage, it was up to me to hold the interest of the people out there in the audience. I wasn't expected to boom-boom-boom away. I was expected to *act*. That one thing made all the difference. Everything was before me, and the possibilities were endless.

Dana's aria of self-revelation is both exhilarating and chilling. He had come to New York at the same time as Marilyn Monroe, in fact, and for the same reason: to renew himself, to get in touch with that aspiring actor who had told a Hollywood talent scout twenty years earlier that he wanted to be a "character lead." He wanted the best of both worlds, something that very few actors in the history of Hollywood have been able to win

As Jerry Ryan, a Nebraska attorney, Dana was called on to portray a man going through a difficult divorce while also adjusting to a new life in New York City. In the city, he meets Gittel Mosca (Anne Bancroft), an aspiring dancer. They fall in love, although Jerry cannot overcome a still powerful attachment to his marriage. Gittel, for her part, has never found a man she can trust, and she is unsure of Jerry. Their separateness and isolation is reinforced by a stage set divided between her apartment and his. This schematic play types Gittel as the giver (many men have taken advantage of her) and Jerry as the taker (back home his father-in-law set up both his practice and his home). Jerry is struggling now to live on his own. In a sense, so is Gittel, since she wants a life independent of the men who relied on her.

In Jerry, Dana confronted a difficult acting problem. How to make the complaining male sympathetic and give him color and warmth? Henry Fonda had quit the role in disgust after six months. He did not like his character. Jerry is forever talking about how he had it made back in Nebraska but could not remain beholden to his overly protective wife and her father. Dana could certainly have identified with the plight of a man who does not want to rely on his wife's wealthy family. And to work at a role in which he would not be simply the handsome, noble leading man appealed to him. Yet the play's bleak ending, which places Gittel exactly nowhere, while Jerry decides to return to Nebraska, is unsettling. On the one hand, the play offered Dana the opportunity to overturn all those factitious happy Hollywood endings, but on the other, what kind of resolution could he offer in a drama that seems so unresolved?

Critics generally credited Dana as a worthy replacement for Fonda. Whitney Bolton of the *New York Morning Telegraph* believed Dana had mastered his role. In the *New York Post*, Richard Watts, Jr. also lauded Dana's assured and attractive performance, although the critic thought the actor gave a harder edge to his character, thus losing "some of the disarming quality of his predecessor's portrayal." It is, of course, hard to be sure so many years later, but it would seem that Dana did not want to add too much of his movie star luster to a character who was not supposed to be all that likeable. He may well not have wanted to turn Jerry into another one of those Darryl Zanuck creations that won over the audience by giving them a rooting interest in the hero.

Returning to the stage was not easy, even though Dana had occasionally done so, playing with Mary, for example, in a touring production of *The Glass Menagerie*. But those fitful forays did not measure up against the kind of scrutiny of his own work he conducted during the year-long recovery of his talent. Not merely dedication to his profession, but dedication to himself is reflected in his statement to Ross that he "didn't miss a single performance—not even one time when I had a temperature of a hundred and three." He watched himself grow on the stage and felt that after a year he had just begun to understand what the author meant his character to be:

> When I started out in the play, I was overemotional. Because I was playing the part of a self-pitying man, I had a tendency to whine. My wife pointed that out to me, and I found that if a man feels sorry for himself, he doesn't have to whine to show it. I stopped whining at once. It's not difficult for me to hide emotion, since I've always hidden it in my personal life. What is difficult is to convey feelings in a quiet and reserved way.

Of course, in Dana's best screen roles, before his persona congealed, he had done just that: conveyed the quiet and reserve of a man full of feeling. But he had relied on the camera to pick up that reticence. "The camera is so close. It sees so much and shows so much. It picks up every little thing you do with your eyes and mouth," he told Ross. While Dana had used that instrument to his advantage, it had also made him passive, an object onto which the audience projected its feelings. On stage he had to find his audience and project his character.

During his time on Broadway, Dana's family moved to a house in Connecticut with a pond in the backyard and a tennis court. This was a happy period, Susan recalled, and there were trips to the city and meals at the Algonquin Hotel—"a very important place for Dad," who often spent a night or two there every week. The bellmen and operators knew the Andrews family, and they were well taken care of by Ben and Mary

Bodne, who then owned the famous writers' hangout, located not far from where Lillian Ross occupied an office at the *New Yorker*. When Stephen ran away from home, he turned up at the Algonquin. "The kitchen knew exactly how Dad liked his scrambled eggs—loose, but a specific kind of loose," Kathy said:

> Late at night, the waiter would bring one coupe aux marrons and one zabaglione to our table. Dad loved those desserts! The Algonquin was as close to a club as he ever had. It was connected to working, though—important—and it was family-owned then. He wouldn't have seen the point in belonging to a club and just stopping by . . . for what?

Susan loved going to the play, listening in the lobby and restroom for comments about her father, going backstage to visit him, kind and happy, and then moving on to Sardi's. "He was a success on Broadway, he was very proud of himself. And he was able to show us around New York and feel proud and show us," Susan told Clyde Williams. Dana took the train to New York every day. "Everything became normalized," Susan said.

Back in California, Dana cashed in on the vogue for aerial disaster pictures playing an airline pilot who collides with a navy jet fighter, flown by the doomed Dale Heath (Efrem Zimbalist Jr.) in *The Crowded Sky* (released September 2, 1960). John Kerr, who played Dana's co-pilot, remembered Dana's calm, methodical, and professional behavior. He saw no sign of drinking and, in fact, was surprised to learn later that Dana was an alcoholic.

Dana then tried to repeat his Broadway success in *The Captains and the Kings*, based on the life of Admiral Hyman Rickover and his struggle to get the navy to build the first nuclear submarine. The out of town reviews in Philadelphia were promising. In the *Wall Street Journal* (January 4, 1962), Richard Cooke praised Dana:

> [T]he very model of fanatical dedication, his jaw set like the proverbial steel trap, his hands briskly rattling papers, his voice barking orders or telling subordinators to get out that report, even though it is near midnight. This Mr. Andrews does very well, and when called upon to display the softer and more intimate emotions as upon the occasion when the death of his subversive son is discussed, he performs just as ably.

But the writing let Dana down, Cooke suggested, when the play degenerated into lofty sentiments that ill suited his plainspoken character. The play failed to find an audience and closed in less than two weeks.

Shortly after the close of *Two for the Seesaw*, Dana read William Nickerson's book, *How I Turned $1,000 into a Million in Real Estate—in My Spare Time*. Like Napoleon Hill's books about how to become a success, Nickerson's self-help guide appealed to a man who felt stymied and sought a new avenue of endeavor and achievement. Fixing old properties, trading up, and taking a profit was the formula Dana said he followed. He had bought, fixed up, and sold an apartment building, making a $150,000 profit, he told reporter Charles D. Davis, Jr. Dana liked to talk about all the money he made in real estate deals, but his family saw little evidence of it.

Dana sold his Toluca Lake home in 1962 and bought land in Palos Verdes, close to the Chadwick School, which Stephen and later Susan attended. Dana and Mary became consumed with planning their dream home while living in apartments in Redondo Beach during the construction period. The new property was at the top of a hill and had huge windows providing spectacular views of the coast and the Pacific across to Catalina, as well as rolling hills below. The panorama gave Dana the feeling of a sailor looking out to sea. According to his neighbors, he was a "very kind, gracious and gregarious man—and, of course, ruggedly handsome." Susan and Stephen spent their teenage years in this house, as Kathy was heading off for college, and David was away working at radio stations. They were old enough to find their father a trial at times. He enjoyed reading whole articles to anyone who happened to pass by. He could give an article a real workout. "As teenagers and older, we became quite adept at taking alternate routes through the house when he was reading. Or zipped past, rolling our eyes and laughing silently at the one who got nailed. There was no escaping . . . he'd have been insulted," Kathy said.

From 1960 to 1964, Dana made no pictures, except for the mediocre *Madison Avenue* (released January 7, 1962). He received $50,000 for six weeks of work on a deeply disappointing project that he hoped would be the *Mad Men* of its day. Dana owned a part of the project and starred as Clint Lorimer, an advertising executive bent on proving that he is a better man than the men who fired him. Unfortunately, the script bogs down with the predictable complications of Clint's romances and realization that there is more to the world than advertising. The picture has none of the edginess of *Mad Men*, or the understated acting that makes Don Draper so effective as an enigmatic hero—one who recalls Dana Andrews in his prime. (Indeed, Jon Hamm is probably the one actor today who could play Dana Andrews.) Dana needed better co-stars than Jeanne Crain and Eleanor Parker. He was miffed that Joan Collins and legendary model Suzy Parker turned down the two female leads, which did not have enough screen time. "Their psychology is all wrong," Dana complained, pointing out that "some of the best roles from a dramatic standpoint are not the longest ones by any means."

Dana also got stuck with a director on the decline—actually, a director who delivered only one outstanding picture, the provocative film noir *I Wake Up Screaming* (1941). Director H. Bruce Humberstone had also achieved popular success with the Charlie Chan movies in the mid-1930s, but otherwise he had served as a hack for Goldwyn and other producers, directing Dana, in fact, in *Lucky Cisco Kid*. Humberstone proved incapable of perking up a script that actually paid scant attention to the business of advertising, concentrating instead on attacking corporate America.

Dana did good work in television in the early 1960s, appearing on episodes of *The Twilight Zone*, *The General Electric Theatre*, *The Barbara Stanwyck Show*, and *Alcoa Premiere Theatre*. In "Crazy Sunday" (aired September 26, 1961 on *The Dick Powell Show*), Dana appears as Nat Keough, a wry screenwriter who advises Joel Coles (Rip Torn) on his first assignment for an award-winning director, Miles Calman (Barry Sullivan). The writing and cast for this one-hour drama, derived from an F. Scott Fitzgerald story, are a cut above most of the television fare Dana was usually offered. He plays what Gore Vidal liked to call the "wise hack," a sardonic yet sensitive observer who narrates the story as well as becoming a witness to Coles's fumbling efforts to become a Hollywood player. Dana plays his character straight—not as a caricature of a Hollywood sell-out, but as a man who still insists there is an integrity in his work, which Coles dare not denigrate without compromising himself. Indeed Keogh, like Dana, preserves some modicum of integrity by attending the important parties but standing somewhat aloof, doing enough to honor his commitments but not ever giving himself up to the dreams that Hollywood sells. It is a poignant performance, especially since Dana has the advantage of playing off a very young and already superbly subtle Rip Torn.

Dana's performs a similar role in "The Last of the Big Spenders" (aired April 16, 1963 on *The Dick Powell Show*) as Paul Oakland, a renowned writer of the 1940s now in decline. Of that decade, Paul will later say to his estranged son Nick, "I should have perished with it." Paul invites Nick, played by a very young Robert Redford, for a visit. The two have not seen one another in twenty years. A wary, resentful Nick, brought up by his divorced mother, does not make it easy for his father to achieve some sort of reconciliation, even though Paul tries to level with his son: "I'm a splendid hack, sonny boy." It is not a word to look down on, he assures his son. Paul has pride in his professionalism and calls himself a man who knows his craft and works at it, but who no longer has anything special to say. Paul drinks too much but is not apologetic about it. When Nick accuses Paul of abandoning him, Paul retorts that Nick's mother left because she could not take the self-absorption of a writer's life. An especially telling moment occurs after a party, during which Nick challenges his father to an arm wrestling contest. Paul is still quite strong but cannot conquer his son, who seems to have wanted all along to humiliate his father. But as they return home, Paul walks in, maintaining that perfectly erect posture that is no different from the Eric Stanton stroll in *Fallen Angel*. Paul's dignity recalls what Hollywood and a generation of moviegoers admired in Dana Andrews. But the moment is in character—an actor working at his craft—personifying a father maintaining his fortitude in the presence of his scornful son.

Dana's own biography fitted well with his role. When Nick first appears and looks over his father's living room, he sees photographs of Paul and his second wife, which are, in fact, pictures of Dana and Mary sailing. Dana was no method actor, but he wanted Mary's picture on the set. She was the core of his life. What they had was so romantic and dramatic, Dana's son Stephen told me, that it was "never to be repeated." This is what Paul Oakland tries to tell his son: that Paul's second wife had given him the gift of a kind of devotion and love that Paul's first marriage (like Dana's first marriage) simply could not deliver. Did Dana also draw a parallel with his son David, who in his earliest years saw his career-driven father only fitfully and was brought up by his grandparents? Dana worked at having a good relationship with his first-born son, but somehow it never quite jelled between them.

Dana's relationship with teenage Stephen also had its complications: "1963 would have been about the time of the most fractious period in my relationship with dad," Stephen wrote, "graduating high school, serious girlfriend (later wife), lots of buddies down at the beach (probably as close as a white boy from Palos Verdes could get to being in a gang)."

Dad was drinking, and then he tried not to drink. He'd be very cranky. He was feeling bad about a lot of stuff. His career wasn't going well. He would do these things that I'm sure his father did to him—like "MOVE THAT PILE OF WOOD FROM HERE TO THERE." It would take you all day. And then he'd say, "ALL RIGHT. MOVE IT BACK." That was the point at which we broke, the point at which you say, "Okay, Dad, that's it. You don't get to tell me anything anymore." I just lost it. I went after him, "YOU THIS, YOU THAT!" My whole family was standing there and thinking, HE'S STANDING UP TO DAD! I was crying. It was a total, convulsive moment for me.

Kathy was not there for the explosion, but she remembers hearing about it: "When Dad strongly disagreed with us, he tended to make a dramatic but silent exit and head for his downstairs study, feeling outnumbered. When I was older, it became very pleasant to have almost any kind of discussion with him. He probably felt that I was no longer in danger. Whew! On everyone's part."

Father and son talked the next day and patched up their differences. Listening to Steve, I could almost hear Dana's voice, that voice that Peggy Cummins said was so commanding. Dana once did a recording of passages from the Bible with a voice well suited to play God. If you look and listen to the authoritative Dr. Holden in *Night of the Demon*, you will understand just how compelling Dana could be, why he could be practically worshipped—and also why, to a young son, he could be infuriating. But no one could stay mad at Dana for long. Indeed, Steve wanted to put the blowup with his father in perspective:

In general my childhood relationship to my father was near idolatry but for the alcohol thing. "What is that, why does he do that, he acts like a nut." That was sometimes quite confusing. Of course, as I became older that confusion became a saddening disappointment tinged with anger and a very effective inspiration to seek a different course for myself than the one he had chosen. Today, however, the top of my "longed for, never to be realized" list would be to again be night sailing with him at the helm of the Malabar VII, my head in his lap and to be able to hug him and thank him for all he has shown me and done for me and of course to tell him how much he is loved.

It was easier to be Dana's daughter, Kathy thought. "Dad was goo goo for his daughters. It was harder for him to be equally so for his sons. Imagine the combination of trying to live up to him, this icon, and then the icon being a nut case a portion of the time."

Not that his daughters got a free pass. "He was critical of me when I started puberty because he didn't want me to get fat," Susan said. "When I look at my pictures from that period I am shocked that he spoke to me about dieting. I was a rail!!" Kathy agreed:

> It's true that weight was a concern for Dad. Not about himself, because that didn't seem to be a problem. I, too, received a critical eye when my body began to change in a perfectly normal way. No one has little girl hips forever and, like you, Susan, I can't see any evidence in photos that he needed to worry. He made one remark to me, innocuous enough that I've forgotten what it was. But I did tell Mom and I heard her ask him never to let me think that he was disappointed in who I was, or something to that effect. He denied that he had said anything critical, probably because I was being hypersensitive . . . and I do think I magnified his remark. I must have, because I recall feeling a bit guilty about telling on him.

For his own part, Dana wanted to look good and dress well but did not assign much credit to his physical appearance—"at least not enough credit," Kathy believed. "He told me that he'd have persevered and become successful at whatever career he'd chosen. Mom secretly rolled her eyes at the looks not mattering part of that one."

Dana believed that women, as well as men, earned their place. "Not every father presented his daughter with a copy of *The Feminine Mystique* as soon as it came out," Kathy said. Even though he had not wanted Mary to work, he felt differently about his daughters. "He did not want us to be without careers, to be housewives with too many babies. It didn't seem to matter that those careers weren't highly lucrative. Being respected and comfortable seems to have been enough. (Annis and her undeservedly, inescapably hard life was always with him, I believe)," Kathy concluded.

Dana was elected president of the Screen Actors Guild on December 13, 1963. He had been elected second vice president in 1950 and first vice president in 1960, before heading up the organization, which then had nearly 15,000 members. He had chaired committees, including one that met on August 9, 1963, refusing to endorse Darryl Zanuck's attack on a book about the making of *Cleopatra*, a picture that went millions over budget as Elizabeth Taylor and Richard Burton carried on their off screen romance. Kathy remembered her father reacting to the negative press about how much Taylor was getting for the picture. That was the marketplace, Dana told his daughter as he defended Taylor. She was earning what she was worth to the studio, or she would not be getting paid that much.

Executive secretary Jack Dales summed up Dana's accomplishments as SAG president:

> During his eventful tenure as Guild President, Andrews secured the first affirmative action agreement with producers, the first pay TV contract, and the first residuals for foreign sales of American TV shows. As SAG President, Andrews met with President Lyndon B. Johnson in Washington and encouraged the establishing of the National Endowment for the Arts in 1965. In later years, he was active with SAG's Senior Performers Committee.

This bald summary does not do justice to Dana's prophetic view of the future of his business. Someday, a box would sit atop televisions, he told his family, and actors would be paid appropriately for their work wherever it was shown. And Dana did not just talk about pay TV; SAG minutes show that he went to New York to negotiate with network executives, and opposed motion picture exhibitors who wanted pay TV only in theaters. On May 14, 1964, Dana issued a Guild press release advocating for the public's right to choose where they wanted to watch pay TV. He formed a group to fight a state initiative in California that would have prohibited the spread of subscription television, already a factor in Los Angeles and San Francisco.

Dana also dealt with pressures on Hollywood, such as censorship campaigns waged by various parents' groups. He was sympathetic, often expressing his disgust that actresses had to disrobe in scenes of dubious dramatic value. In "Movie Nudity Hit by Dana Andrews," Murray Schmach in the *New York Times* reported that Dana "blamed the use of naked women in movies on the greed of producers and studios and on the competition of television." If the public did not protest, actresses, especially those just beginning their careers, would be especially vulnerable.

Dana worried about young actresses, whose only alternative to the growing sexual explicitness of motion pictures was heavily censored television, which he considered a medium with "built-in mediocrity because it is not drama. It is just an adjunct of the advertising business." This is why pay TV appealed to him. He clearly foresaw the advantages of what is today taken for granted with Home Box Office, Showtime, and other cable TV productions. At the time, however, Dana's stand had its risks. As Murray Schmach reported, "the guild president said he was aware that two-thirds of the income of guild members came from that medium." Dana reiterated his criticism in another *New York Times* article (October 17, 1964), telling Peter Bart the present trend in television was "demoralizing the acting profession" and "lowering public taste." Only financial necessity would drive him to do more work in the medium, he declared. He had rejected six TV roles that would have paid between $5,000 and $10,000 each, as well as a three-year $300,000 contract to do television commercials for a cigarette brand. "I think pay TV would bring back the halcyon days of the motion picture business," he predicted.

Ken Orsatti, SAG's western regional director during Dana's presidency, remembered a genial and unassuming man who spoke very little at board meetings, even when he was chairing them. Orsatti, who came from a show business background, was nevertheless overwhelmed by the star power in the room when he attended his first board meeting. It was like an old boys club, he recalled, with meetings that lasted less than three hours. Board members ate a catered lunch (usually just a sandwich) and got down to business, expecting SAG's executives to work on the details and carry on the day-to-day union work. Stars generally were not interested in union politics per se. Dana ran a very good meeting, with just the right of firmness and humor. He seemed to enjoy the work and the honor of his position, Orsatti said. Orsatti accompanied Dana on a trip to Colorado on union business and remembered that an old photographer assigned to take Dana's picture did not seem to know who Dana was and kept asking him to smile. Afterwards, as they were walking away, Dana said to Ken, "I'll bet he has not seen any of my pictures." Then Dana paused and added, "Or maybe he has."

Perhaps Dana's proudest moment came when Lyndon Johnson invited him, as president of the Screen Actors Guild, to the White House. Dana flew in from Hawaii, where he was playing a small role in *In Harm's Way*. When he met President Johnson, Dana said that they had done pretty well for two poor boys from Texas.

After 1964, Dana's own television work was fitful and mostly unsatisfying, with guest appearances on *Night Gallery*, *Ironside*, *Ellery Queen*, *The Love Boat*, and *Falcon Crest*. He also starred in made-for-TV movies: *The*

Failing of Raymond, (aired November 27, 1971) and *The Last Hurrah* (aired November 6, 1977), as well as pilots that did not make it as television series: *A Shadow in the Streets* (aired January 28, 1975) and *The First 36 Hours of Dr. Durant* (aired May 13, 1975). None of these roles was especially challenging, not even a performance as General George C. Marshall, in Robert Duvall's 1979 television drama, *Ike*—although Dana retains his ramrod posture and captures his character's mordant sense of humor.

Susan suggests her father liked playing dignitaries, but he also realized, as he told an interviewer, "You begin playing generals and admirals with Bill Holden and Duke Wayne and, well, it's not very rewarding. You don't feel like you're doing anything." Dana was referring not to television productions, but to big budget pictures such as *In Harm's Way* (released in April 6, 1965), the last Preminger picture he appeared in, playing Admiral Broderick in a John Wayne war epic. Screenwriter Wendell Mayes singled out Dana's performance as "very believable . . . not a caricature." In *The Devil's Brigade* (released May 15, 1968) Dana appeared as Brigadier General Walter Naylor, Holden's superior officer, in a routine role.

Two parts broke Dana's string of perfunctory performances. In *Brainstorm* (released May 5, 1965) he is Cort Benson, a cruel husband and powerful industrialist who shows little sympathy for his suicidal wife, Lorrie (Anne Francis). This was a two-week job for Dana that paid him $10,000. Most of his scenes were done in one take, the daily production and progress report noted. Francis, who appeared in four pictures with Dana, never saw him drink, she told me. She admired but never got to know a man who just went about his work calmly and professionally. His calm in this picture is sinister, however—and unnerving. He has some good lines, threatening to ruin Lorrie's lover, who has also had a mental breakdown: "Shall we call it your days of wine and neuroses. A nervous breakdown, they call it. Isn't that just a polite name for insanity."

In *The Loved One* (released October 11, 1965), a satire on the southern California funeral business, he plays General Buck Brinkman, who plans to dispose of dead bodies by shooting them into space and make money by converting the cemetery into a luxury spa. Dana plays another military stiff, as he might have been the first to say—but here the somewhat ponderous, mannered majesty of his latter-day depictions of the top brass gets a send-up reminiscent of George C. Scott's much admired rendition of General "Buck" Turgidson in *Dr. Strangelove* (1964). Dana loved this role and thought it among his best, even though his screen time is brief.

Most of the time, as Dana realized, he was just filling out the Hollywood dance card, so that pictures could be promoted as filled with star-studded casts. An especially pitiful, slow-moving dud of this type is *Battle of the Bulge* (released December 15, 1965), where Dana, as a rather nasty Colonel Pritchard, gives Lieutenant Colonel Dan Kiley (Henry Fonda) a hard time. Was there some kind of unwritten rule in Hollywood that stars on the wane got to outrank the stars still riding high?

CHAPTER 19

Ruin and Recovery
1964–72

ON FEBRUARY 15, 1964, Dana's thirty-year-old son David died during brain surgery. He had been semi-conscious for a month after suffering a cerebral hemorrhage. Susan recalled, "David died when we were teens and our father was devastated. He had been sober for a good while, but that changed after the funeral."

Dana was again drinking so heavily that Ken Annakin, who directed *Battle of the Bulge*, said that Dana's co-stars, Henry Fonda and Robert Ryan, had to prop him up physically. As a result, Dana went for one of his periodic stays at the Compton sanatorium to dry out from an alcohol binge. His family was losing patience with him. At this point, no one really believed he would ever sober up for good. One of the patients called Dana a has-been. "Better a has-been than a never-was-never-will-be," he answered.

Before the Compton stay, Dana had come home one night with blood on his forehead after a car accident. Kathy's friend Paula went to his side, spoke kindly to him, and tried to clean him up. Kathy told her to leave him alone and practically pulled her out of the room. "He wasn't a little boy who fell off his bike," Kathy said. "He was a grown man behaving badly. I didn't think he deserved to have us taking care of him." She did visit him at Compton, though, because she thought he was trying. "The paraldehyde they always gave him smelled disgusting. It was natural to be the loving and caring daughter then. But when he wasn't trying I simply stayed away. I thought he was beyond help, but still hoped that just maybe if he had to live with the consequences and to feel alone, without the people he loved, he might have a reason to work hard enough to change. Also, I didn't want to see him like that."

Why did Mary put up with it? Kathy believed that her mother would have left him if Dana had been abusive to her or the children. But Kathy could not recall her father raising his voice when he was drinking, and he never struck his children. Kathy remembered how her father played loud music at night, a sure sign he was drinking. On a few occasions, Leon, one of the household help, carried Dana, draped over a shoulder, up to his room. Neighborhood and school friends knew of his problem, but they didn't seem to mind. In fact, they'd often strike up conversations with him while Kathy tried to get them to head in another direction. She wasn't particularly embarrassed, just bored by his long stories or conversations. "One friend of either Susan's or Stephen's was forbidden to come to our house because of our alcoholic father," Kathy recalled. "The parents of our other friends, and there were many, must have determined that he was harmless." It was a big house, and Kathy could usually avoid her drunken father.

Ken Orsatti was quite circumspect when I asked him about Dana's drinking. Apparently not wanting to diminish Dana's stature as a SAG president, Orsatti emphasized that "from time to time it was clear there was a problem," but it never affected Dana's work as president. Just after leaving the presidency he also managed a fifteen-week East Coast tour of *A Remedy for Winter*, playing a distinguished historian in love with an actress.

Dana's appearances in pictures from 1965 to 1969—mostly in mediocre westerns, science fiction, and caper pictures—were undistinguished. In *Johnny Reno* (released June 13, 1966), he is competent but without the inspiration that good direction and writing might have stimulated. His pairing with Jane Russell, playing Nona Williams, Reno's former sweetheart in a plot that has Dana trying to save another innocent man from a lynching, seems a rather desperate bid to recapture their glory days of the 1940s. Dana looks too old to be fighting as he did in *Canyon Passage*. He cannot spring back with alacrity. He does better in *Town Tamer* (released October 14, 1965), an awful title but actually a moderately interesting study of an aging gunfighter. As Tom Rosser—at one time a formidable lawman hired to clean up frontier towns—he is humiliated in a barroom fight by a younger and stronger man, but refuses to back down from doing one more dangerous job. In this case, Dana is playing close to his age rather than pretending be a decade younger, as he does in the *Johnny Reno* action scenes.

Then Dana descended into the world of Euro trash film productions, which had the appeal of quick paydays. This foray resulted in his very worst pictures, although he started well with *Crack in the World* (released April 15, 1965), shot in England. As Dr. Stephen Sorenson, Dana has gravitas and hubris reminiscent of Dr. Holden in *Night of the Demon*. Sorenson is trying to tap the molten mass of the earth's core to generate a new energy source. To do so, however, he has to set off a thermonuclear device, with disastrous consequences that you can now assess on a recently issued DVD. Shot at the beginning of his European adventure, *Crack in the World* exhibits Dana looking fit and pleased to be playing his age, appearing quite handsome with silver-grey hair. The *New York Daily News* quoted him as saying, "I had to keep telling those studio bankers to quit tampering with my hair and let me look my age. The romantic phase is now over." Indeed, Sorenson is precisely the "character-lead" that Dana had set out to play all along. Sorenson is testy—and why not? He has a terminal illness. He is also dealing with a problematic marriage and the presence of his young wife's ex-lover. He is hoping to make one more scientific breakthrough that will ensure his fame. In short, he is a complex character rarely seen in the plot-driven melodramas of low budget science fiction pictures. Just how good an actor Dana Andrews was is apparent in a fascinating passage in Alexander Knox's memoir. In *Crack in the World*, Knox plays Sir Charles Eggerston, a government official involved in funding Sorenson's project. Knox disliked the long speeches scientists and dignitaries were given, especially in science fiction pictures. How to lend credibility to claptrap always seemed a strain. Then he watched Dana:

> He would say the words slowly, in order and without inflexion. The absence of all effort to make the jargon credible succeeded in doing so, while the presence of effort on my part succeeded in exposing the flatulences. The conclusion: say the words as if their content is the most obvious thing in the world, so obvious as to make verbal proof redundant and even boring. Or put it another way: if you, the character, give a strong impression that you are uttering truisms so generally accepted as to be boring, the audience is likely to disregard the content of the argument and accept the character's conclusion.

Not quite as good but still respectable is *The Satan Bug* (released March 26, 1965), in which Dana plays General Williams, on a mission to retrieve a lethal virus stolen from a top secret military installation. The script gives Williams less of a backstory than Dr. Sorenson had, and as a result Dana has less to work with, relying on his wrinkled brow and staring eyes to make up for what is left blank in the script. Then Dana descended farther towards mediocrity with *Spy in Your Eye* (released January 1966), in which he is US intelligence chief Colonel Lancaster, who becomes an unwitting Soviet spy after a camera is implanted in his eye. Dana had been too optimistic when he spoke to the *Daily News*, suggesting that he would now get "good, meaty" roles, the "kind I like at this time in my life." He had children in college and needed to work, even when the roles offered were downright silly. *Hot Rods to Hell* (released January 27, 1967), reunites him with Jeanne Crain. Complete with dye jobs and the lacquered look that aging stars too often sport, they confront a gang of juvenile delinquents determined to make the couple's purchase of a motel into—you guessed it: a living hell. Dana's character prevails, bad back and all. In *The Ten Million Dollar Grab* (released August 25, 1967), Dana is George Kimmins, seeking to bilk an insurance company by claiming as a loss a diamond he has actually recovered. As Maurizio, a jewelry shop owner in *No Diamonds for Ursula* (released August 7, 1967), he is involved in yet another insurance company fraud caper. In *The Cobra* (released March 27, 1968), Dana is so obviously drunk that his effort to act like an action hero in his role as Captain Kelly, a CIA officer, is painful to watch.

On April 24, 1967, Dana's mother died. She had been a mainstay, and he had kept her close to him in her final years. He sold his Palos Verdes home. The house seemed too large now that Stephen was in college and soon Susan would be, too. Buying Jacques Tourneur's home, virtually a smaller replica of the Toluca Lake home, seemed perfect. Also, there were too many Republicans in the old neighborhood for an actor with liberal sympathies who wanted to socialize, at least occasionally, with theater and picture people. When Reagan was elected governor of California in 1967, Dana told his son-in-law Tim: "No good will come off this."

During this period (1966–67) Dana and Mary had dinner a few times with Kathy and Tim in their Encino cottage. Dana was on his best behavior. They all drank grape juice in wine glasses. "Soon afterward, we all had good reason to expect bad news at any moment, and finally did," Kathy said. "He was badly beaten and robbed in an alley, probably behind a bar. He needed stitches on his face and was very banged up. At least one Rolex disappeared that way. That undoubtedly wasn't the only time that happened, but it was the only one I ever heard about."

Dana made one more effort to sober up for good. He checked into Hazelden, a treatment facility in Center City, Minnesota, founded in 1949 by Austin Ripley, a recovering alcoholic. Dedicated to curing alcoholics of "the professional class," it more or less followed the Alcoholics

Anonymous twelve-step program. But by the 1960s, Hazelden was experimenting with the holistic and "interdisciplinary team approach," which is perhaps one reason why Dana decided to try it, since the quasi-religious AA way had put him off.

Kathy never forgot Dana's Hazelden letter, written in a voice he had never used before, "apologizing for the terrible effects that his drinking had had on our lives." She knew it was part of the program and was supposed to help make amends, but it made her feel terribly sad for him, and she cried like mad over it:

> I wanted to write back instantly and say, *No, you have not done anything awful to me! It's OK, you haven't ruined my life. You sound so miserable, and I don't want you to feel that way. I love you and want you to be at home!* I was living in Connecticut by then. Of course I didn't write, because I knew he was supposed to do that, but having him dredge up all that misery was very depressing to me.

She destroyed the lengthy letter, which had few specifics and seemed formula driven. "I wasn't too sure what he was apologizing for . . . except being a drunk, I guess." The Hazelden treatment had no lasting effect. And that is what Kathy feared: Her father would humiliate himself without benefit of a cure. She knew she could not help him. In the end, Dana would heal himself the hard way: doing it on his own, which was the only way to preserve his dignity. He had done the same with smoking. When he stopped smoking cigarettes in the early 60s, he didn't tell anyone. "I think he was kind of annoyed when no one noticed, not even Mom, and he finally had to tell us," Kathy said. "Maybe we didn't notice because he had been such a neat smoker. Dad once watched Tim put out a cigarette and leave the butt in the ashtray. Dad pointedly picked up the ashtray, carried it away, and brought it back to the living room clean and dry. Tim never did that again. And that was when Dad was still a smoker."

Dana tried theater once again in a production of *The Odd Couple*, taking the part of Oscar, the sloppy one, but his drinking had become dire. An article in the *Los Angeles Times* (January 11, 1968) reported that Dana had been hospitalized for six days with a skull fracture "apparently suffered in a mysterious fall while on tour with a road company." The accident was attributed to the "flu," but in truth Dana could no longer function unless he took a drink. During the tour, Dana visited with Kathy. She was out of college, married, and living with her husband Tim in Westport,

Connecticut. She remembered that her father was accompanied by Noel Drayton, an English actor who had a small part in *Elephant Walk* and had become Dana's factotum. Kathy dreaded the hanger-on, plying her father with "booze & honey treatments for his ravaged voice." How Dana could drag himself on the stage and remember his lines baffled her:

> I saw him in his little dressing room between two performances. He looked like a character in a movie between torture sessions. He had no color and was dripping wet, something I had never seen before. He didn't have that wonderful Dad smell about him at all. Noel said I should leave so that Dad could take a short rest on his cot before the next performance. I listened to the matinee audience reminisce about his screen performances while I expected someone to say, "Call him an ambulance."

After the tour, Dana was house bound, hallucinating and talking to people who were not there. The days when he could stay up drinking around the clock and still be up while everyone else had passed out were over. He had twenty-four-hour care. He was so ill he could not attend Susan's wedding. Still he drank, until this debilitating regime reduced him to a death-like state after he suffered a grand mal seizure. At one point he bit his tongue so hard it had to be stitched up.

On May 29, 1968, Mary filed papers for a divorce, stating that he had caused her "great mental and physical suffering." She told him she could not remain married to him if he continued to drink. She moved out and took an apartment near UCLA. In truth, Mary was never far away and was watchful. When Dana did not improve, Mary asked Minnie to take charge, discovering that the nursing care had been a sham: The "nurses" had taken Dana's car to Mexico to get drugs. Minnie slowly brought Dana back, spooning grapefruit juice into him and gradually getting him on a nourishing diet.

The separation from Mary lasted several months and ended sometime in early 1969 only when Dana stopped drinking. After Mary's ultimatum and Dana's hospitalization, he began a remarkable recovery. Why he stopped drinking can perhaps never been adequately explained. Certainly, he did not want to lose Mary. The birth of grandchildren Abigail, Matthew, and Ilena, made a difference as well. Dana was enormously pleased with them and wanted to be around to entertain them and enjoy their company. Dana can be heard on a recording describing an incident in which Matthew (Susan's son) began imitating the adult voices around him. He carried on his own conversation, Dana noted, as if he were an adult. Dana got so carried away in describing his delight that he began imitating Matthew.

Dana made abstinence a defining characteristic of his public persona, describing in 1972 the consequences of his addiction to millions of people in the television commercials he did for the Department of Transportation. The original script began, "I am Dana Andrews and I *was* an alcoholic." Dana insisted taking out "was." Dana no longer drank because he had come to accept the fact that "I *am* an alcoholic."

The first stage in Dana's recovery resulted in his commitment to star as college president Thomas Boswell in *Bright Promise* (September 29, 1969–March 31, 1972), a television soap opera. The role was sold to Dana on the basis that it would deal with the pressing controversies on many of the nation's campuses. A soap opera was a real comedown for a movie star, a sure sign that an actor was no longer employable on the big screen. But the show's scripts were good, he insisted at the start of the series, adding: "Some people in my profession have a low opinion of daytime TV because its major audience is women. Well I think women have a great deal more taste and knowledge of the theater than men." Pictures had very little to offer Dana at this point, and the daily grind of television production actually appealed to an actor who had already proven, ten years earlier in New York, that he had remarkable powers of rejuvenation and concentration. Besides, as Dana told Don Page, a *Los Angeles Times* reporter, "I was educated to be a teacher, and this whole idea is very appealing to me. . . . Another aspect I like is that this show is taped live, the nearest thing to a live performance. It gives you the chance to create as if it were happening right now."

Eric James, who played Dana's son, remembered that at the beginning Dana was tremendously proud of the show and even bought a table at the Emmy Awards for the whole cast. He was making a statement, Eric thought, about a series that he hoped would make television history. Eric watched a usually very private and reserved man—never very demonstrative with cast or crew—commandeer the Emmy table, beaming with pride. Eric shared Dana's obsession with real estate, and they talked about how their ventures put them in contact with a real world quite unlike the Hollywood they worked in. Eric remembered how excited Dana was when he bought his first hotel. Real estate became a kind of high, a substitute for drinking. Dana told Eric as much, saying that alcoholism had been his "release" from the tensions and make believe of Hollywood. Dana shared little about his own emotions with the actor who played his son. Only one subject besides real estate animated Dana: Mary. When Dana spoke about her "there was deep love, even reverence in his voice." If he spoke about family, it was about her and his father.

Susan regarded the soap opera as instrumental in his recovery. It seemed a miracle to her that he could do the show. At the time a college student with an infant son, she watched the show and found it mortifying. But after visiting the set and seeing that her father was getting better, she thought the "greater good outweighed the thinness of the project." *Bright Promise* capitalized on Dana's screen persona as the noble hero. A typical episode featured Dana risking his presidency by testifying on behalf of a faculty member and friend, Bill Ferguson, accused of murder. But the dramatic value of this plotline is vitiated by the soap opera's need to swell the story with romantic subplots and other scandals.

By April 16, 1970, Dana had conceded to reporter Bob Williams that the series had not done "too much" with the "raging reality of campus dissent across the country. It's too controversial. Mostly the series is love, jealousy and hate with a college background. We have dealt with the drug problem, however." Eric thought Dana had been deceived by producers who almost immediately began to trivialize the show's subject matter, so that it became just like any other soap opera. Dana made no secret of his scorn for the diminishing quality of the scripts. Indeed, he would stand on the set and complain about the writing to Eric. Eric was certain that the producer in the control room could hear these conversations. There was so much tension on the set. They shot a continuous half hour on videotape, and God help the actor who did anything to stop the taping. One time it happened when Eric blew his lines four times in a row, and then Dana ran into a pillar. He said to Eric, "I thought you would do that." It was the only time Eric saw letter-perfect Dana do anything to delay production. Dana lasted only a year before being fired.

Although Dana continued to perform sporadically on television and in pictures, his principal occupation in the 1970s was the theater. In April 1973, he and Mary did a three-week USO tour to entertain the troops in Europe. During this same period he performed in dinner theater productions of *The Marriage-Go-Round* and *Our Town* (co-starring with Mary), *Come Back, Little Sheba*, and *Any Wednesday*, as well as appearing as Thomas Jefferson in Norman Corwin's play, *Together Tonight! Jefferson, Hamilton and Burr* on the Sam Houston State University campus on March 22 and 23, 1976. "I wish a recording existed of Dad's one-way conversations with his audiences after the curtain call in dinner theatre," Kathy said. "He must have been given a time limit, because he could have gone on with his (literally) captive audience all night. Talking about the forties. They loved it. He loved it. Affirmation."

Dana's niece Angela saw him when his theater group did a stop in New Orleans. She could tell how much Dana love this period with Mary, on the road together. "I'm just her foil," Dana told Angela. It was Mary's turn to star. Dana's grandchild Abigail (Kathy's daughter) loved watching her grandparents on stage. She thought Mary was as good as Dana. She never knew the Dana of the hectic Hollywood years. What she saw was a couple madly in love who always seemed in motion—traveling to a theater date, smartly dressed, learning their lines along the way, and gracious to the dinner crowd audiences who mobbed them. In fact, they had come full circle, enjoying, in a way, what they had when they performed at the Pasadena Playhouse.

Abigail realized that Dana, on a personal level, had made a huge difference in her father Tim's life. When Tim met Dana, he had no family on which he could count, no mentor that could stand by him. Tim got his political education from Dana and much more—as did Charles's son, named after Dana. Dana helped his nephew with college tuition, bought him a car, and in countless ways looked after Charles's son. Out on a sailboat, Dana never reminisced about his past or about Hollywood. He was very much in the present, engaged with them.

Tim, who began sailing at six and had experience on various kinds of vessels, never saw a better boat-handler than Dana, a patient man who never chewed you out if you made a mistake. Dana was always neat and careful about his boats. He loved bright work. Unlike other sailors who would hose off their boats, Dana would have his crew (or in this case, Tim) chamois down everything so that no water spots showed. Dana could sail right into a mooring, a maneuver that made Tim nervous when he first saw his father-in-law do it. "If the wind shifts we're in trouble," Tim said. Dana replied in an even voice, "Don't worry about it. Just do what I tell you." At the dock a guy told Tim, "The first time Dana did it, it scared the hell out of us. But now we know he can do it." Sterling Hayden, quite a sailor himself, told Tim how much he admired Dana's handling of boats. "He wasn't one of these Hollywood guys," Hayden emphasized—an allusion to John Ford and others who had impressive boats, but knew very little about how to sail them.

CHAPTER 20

Curtain Call
1972-92

ON OCTOBER 30, 1972, after a performance of *Marriage-Go-Round* at the Friar's Dinner Theater in Minneapolis, Dana got the *This Is Your Life* treatment. This popular show, hosted by Ralph Edwards, specialized in surprising celebrity subjects with appearances by friends and family who would recount a life story in a hectic half hour. The program opened with the yearning theme from *Laura*. Outside the dinner theater, Edwards introduced the program and spoke of Dana's victory over "one of the most common and disabling diseases, alcoholism." Then Edwards walked on the stage just as Dana was addressing the audience after the performance. Dana, realizing what was about to happen, said, "I don't believe it. That's marvelous." Then the program cut to the Department of Transportation commercial:

> I'm Dana Andrews, and I'm an alcoholic. I don't drink anymore, but I used to—all the time. And when I was drunk I was about as good a driver as my two-year-old grandson. I had accidents. I never killed anybody. If it had gone on, I probably would have. Because the people who were responsible for 19,000 traffic deaths each year were people just like I was—drunk. Get the problem drinker off the road—for his sake and yours.

Dana looked subdued and cast his eyes down as Edwards reprised a life that began as Carver Dana Andrews, a clergyman's son brought up in several Texas towns. A bald Wilton emerged, with Texas accent intact, to tell the story of the hale storm when little Carver, "a mean little devil" frightened by a storm pounding the tin roof like the world was going to end said, "Read the Bible, Mama. Read the Bible, Mama." That became a family refrain, Wilton said. Dana laughed, again looking down, perhaps a little embarrassed but also happy to hear his brother say how much Dana had done to help his own family. "You're prejudiced," Dana told him, slapping Wilton on the back and laughing.

Edwards brought Jeanne, Charles's wife, on stage, to describe Dana's first days in California, when he picked figs for a living. Dana explained how the Andrews brothers tended to pair off: Wilton and Harlan, Dana and Charles. "It was a great loss to me when he [Charles] died," Dana said. Just for a moment he became solemn, his mouth tightening. As Edwards whisked Jeanne off the stage, he told the fabled story of Twomey and Wardlaw in a few sentences and rushed on to introduce Dorothy Adams, the maid in *Laura* and one of Dana's closest friends from his days at the Pasadena Playhouse. "He was a fine actor, but a better singer. He was acting as a sideline," Dorothy said. Dana mentioned he was studying singing with Florence Russell, "I learned five complete operatic roles and never used them." Dorothy then introduced Mary, who briefly told their story of working on *First Lady* and watching Dana

> going around with a very glamorous girl.... Before this I had been very serious about my career but not about my boyfriends. In fact, I used to laugh at them and that always broke everything up. But when Dana used to pick up this girl at the rehearsal, I thought, "Oh, wouldn't it be marvelous to have somebody like that take me home from rehearsal." I thought, "Well, if he ever looks in my direction, I'm going to play it straight [she clenched her fist] I'm going to be serious. But as it turned out, he liked my sense of humor. It worked out fine."

During this sequence Mary and Dana did not look at one another, their avoidance testimony to the difficulty of discussing intimate matters in a sentence or two on television. Edwards described the contract with Goldwyn and Dana's decision to get married. And Dorothy said, "I'll never forget Mary telling her roommate the news. She came in and she said, 'I'm in love. I'm in love. I'm in love.' And with that she threw herself on the bed, the slats broke, and she fell down with it."

Among the program's highlights is Harold Russell, appearing on stage to express his gratitude for Dana's help with Harold's role in *The Best Years of Our Lives*. Russell embraced Dana, who took both of his hands and put them around Russell's neck. Then Edwards breezed through an account of Dana's pictures in the 1940s, as well as his work on television and on Broadway.

Edwards turned to Mary to describe the impact of Dana's drinking:

> Well, I think a man's family is always affected, but I tried to explain to the children that [she looked down, her right hand touching the right side of her brow] that this wasn't something he did purposely. Alcoholism is something like diabetes. A diabetic can't eat certain things, and an alcoholic can't drink certain things.

Dana held his head high during her explanation and when he complied with Edwards's request to describe his doctor's warning:

> He said, "Dana, I'm not giving you any scare tactics at all." But he said, "I think I should tell you I don't know that you will pull through another one of these." I'd just been in the hospital for quite a few days. I knew him quite well. He had been my doctor for fifteen years or so. I knew he meant every word he said. You see, the person with alcoholism, the thing is, the problem is the alcohol. You can start for psychological reasons, but it's the alcohol that's the fly in the ointment, and as long as you have that.... Ask my friends... they all ask the psychiatrist the same question. Well, now we've got all the psychological turmoil over, can I then drink? And the answer is always the same. "I wondered how long it was going to take before you asked that question. And the answer is, 'No, you can't.'"

As Mary looked down, Edwards played a clip showing Secretary of Transportation John A. Volpe talking about Dana's commercial: "You did it without hesitation, and that took guts." Dana bowed his head, smiled, and thanked Volpe for appearing on the program.

Now, the program almost over, Edwards mentioned Dana's new career in real estate, introduced John Gavin, then president of SAG presenting a tribute to Dana, and brought Kathy, Stephen, and Susan on stage as they were welcomed into Dana's embrace. Dana's eyes gleamed as Edwards described him as one of the finest actors of our time and "one of the most courageous men of our time," ending with "This is your life," as Dana, sitting on a sofa, kissed Mary.

No mention was made of David's untimely death or that of Norma Felder on November 28, 1970. She had been suffering from multiple sclerosis for several years. Dana saw her in the hospital shortly before she died. They had kept in touch sporadically, but Dana never spoke of her to his children, who learned about her from Mary.

Very few of Dana's final screen appearances in the 1970s are consequential. In *Innocent Bystanders* (released July 23, 1972), he heads the American Secret Service. In *Airport 1975* (released October 18, 1974), Dana plays businessman Scott Freeman, who dies crashing his small plane into an airliner, piloted by Captain Stacy (Efrem Zimbalist Jr.). In *Take a Hard Ride* (released October 29, 1975), he is Morgan, a rancher who dies in the first scene, extracting a promise from his loyal cowboy (played by Jim Brown) to deliver to Morgan's widow the $86,000 earned from their last cattle drive.

In *The Last Tycoon* (released November 19, 1976), Elia Kazan's last picture, Dana has a short, though effective scene. Kazan gives Dana a wonderful entrance. Just after a take featuring Tony Curtis and Jeanne Moreau playing old movie stars, Dana's character, director Red Ridingwood, enters the movie set, walking into the center of the frame toward the audience. He seems in command, but his air of authority diminishes when he cannot convince his leading lady, (Jeanne Moreau), that she has done the scene as well as can be expected. Reluctantly, he agrees to another take. Later Robert DeNiro, playing Monroe Stahr (based on the legendary MGM production boss Irving Thalberg) has Ridingwood removed from the set, saying that the director does not know how to get the best out of his actress.

A part that did count for something came rather surprisingly in *Good Guys Wear Black* (released June 1978), a Chuck Norris martial arts picture. As a critic in the *Los Angeles Times* put it: "Dana Andrews gives a poignant performance as an alcoholic career diplomat who can no longer control his better impulses." In *Born Again* (released October 1978), Dana plays Tom Phillips, a born-again Christian who helps Charles Colson (one of the Watergate felons) redeem himself. Dana was playing a character whose beliefs were anathema to him. He had turned hostile to organized religion, calling himself a Humanist. But he had his pride as an actor who had done many different kinds of roles, and perhaps the director, Irving Rapper, an old friend, convinced Dana to do the job in this stillborn picture.

By 1980, Dana's career in pictures was virtually over. He made a very brief appearance as an airline executive in *The Pilot* (1980), a riveting picture starring Cliff Robertson as an alcoholic so desperate for a drink that he has to turn over controls to his co-pilot so that he can drink from a flask hidden in the airplane restroom. Robertson's brilliantly understated performance could almost be a tribute to Dana, who would have been magnificent in the role twenty years earlier. In *Prince Jack* (released in December 1985), a docudrama about John F. Kennedy, Dana plays a cunning old cardinal in an extended scene with another old pro, Lloyd Nolan (1902–85), acting as Joseph Kennedy. Dana confessed he could no longer remember his lines. Nolan laughed and pointed to the huge cue cards he said he had been using for years.

The 1980s were discouraging for a lifelong Democrat. Dana hated Richard Nixon and referred to him as a "shit heel." Reagan was no better, a buffoon in Dana's estimation. Dana liked to tell the story of the time he tried to repair Reagan's disintegrating marriage to Jane Wyman. At the Toluca Lake house they sat down to dinner and Reagan immediately began to talk the politics that had so bored Wyman. She left in disgust, telling him he was the same old windbag.

During the Reagan era of the 1980s, Katharine's daughter Abigail, educated in private schools and living in a prosperous Connecticut community, observed little concern for the underprivileged. But she saw her grandfather give away a good deal of his expensive wardrobe and contribute to causes that helped those in need. He was putting in action what he had always taught his children: Any society that does not take care of its least well-off members only demeaned itself. That idea had gotten Dana's father into trouble in Rockdale, Texas, although politically, CF was certainly not a man of the left. Dana was contributing significant sums to groups like the Black Panthers and Cesar Chavez's United Farm Workers.

Dana's niece Angela remembered seeing him for the last time in the early 1980s. She had flown to Los Angeles from Paris, and he insisted on taking her out to dinner at her choice of restaurant. She picked Chasen's, a Hollywood hangout for the stars since the mid-1930s. It was there that Orson Welles punched Dana and later wrote an apologetic note. There, too, Dana would see Bogart, whose sailboat was moored close to Dana's. In his smaller sailboat, named *Katharine,* Dana raced Bogart's boat near Catalina, the only place Dana really fraternized with stars like John Wayne, Maureen O'Hara, and Dick Powell. Angela remembered driving to the restaurant in Dana's gorgeous vintage Mercedes convertible. He was a bit forgetful, so Mary kept telling him which turns to make. Everyone at Chasen's greeted him like royalty and treated his guest with lavish attention. He was the same generous old Dana.

Into the early 1980s, Dana continued to speak on college campuses, including a visit to Mississippi State University, where Clyde Williams hosted "A Film Retrospective Honoring the Career and Work of Dana Andrews," February 19–24, 1984. On the 21st Dana gave a talk, "The

Hollywood Industry, Its People, Its Role in American Life." On Friday the 24th, he met with students, had a luncheon with the university's president, held a press conference at 2 p.m., and at a banquet gave another talk, "Hollywood—Winners and Why?" followed by a showing of *Madison Avenue* and *Daisy Kenyon*. Williams, a native Mississippian, had struck up a friendship with Dana. They even sang old church hymns on the phone to one another, Dana beginning with "Almost Persuaded" and Williams joining in with "Just as I Am." The two men had a good laugh about the old revival meetings, where such songs were kept going so that everyone had a chance to come forward and be saved.

In 1986, Dana visited Huntsville for the last time and made, perhaps, his last public appearance. He could handle audience questions, provided they were delivered to him beforehand in writing so that he could have time to consider his answers. Professor Ralph Pease, who hosted Dana and Mary during their visit, remembered that Dana would sometimes blank out and Mary would finish his stories for him. By the following year, Dana's mind began to go. He still had good days, but the bad ones began to overtake him. He seemed normal picking Abigail up at the airport. But the next day he was in a panic, saying, "I have to be on stage." He looked at Abigail as if he did not know her. It was a frightening experience for a fifteen-year-old who did not know what was happening. "It was as if a channel had been changed in his brain," she said. Another time, he began singing opera in a restaurant.

Dana still enjoyed going to the pictures, but he became confused about what he saw and what it meant. Coming home from one movie, he asked Mary, "Did we have sex?" How did he think they had three children? she replied. She told the story to Dana's niece, Angela, the daughter of his brother David. Mary laughed when she told the story. No one told stories better than Mary, everyone agreed. But behind the laughter was much anguish, as the man she knew was ebbing away. He would sometimes go out and get lost, then eventually find his way home. It got worse, and a neighbor brought him home. Sometimes he spoke in a Texas accent. People would call and he could not remember who they were, but he would answer, "Darling! Good to hear from you!"

By 1989, Mary could no longer continue caring for Dana. He was diagnosed with multi-infarct dementia, although the exact nature of his malady is uncertain. His dementia may well have been the result of seizures; he had about five of them during his last decade of intense drinking. His family found a comfortable place for him at the John Douglas French Center in Los Alamitos, which described itself as the first freestanding facility in the country to deal exclusively with patients afflicted with Alzheimer's-related syndromes. Dana's first days were a tough adjustment. He showed up at the front desk and demanded to know where his script was. He worried about the day's shooting. He could not remember his lines. "Dad," Susan told him, "you are retired. You don't need to worry about your lines." Not long afterward, when his pictures were shown at the French Center, he no longer recognized himself on the screen. And keeping track of what happened in a story had become became impossible for him some years earlier.

On a visit to the French Center, Linda Viertel watched her mother, who had been a cineaste but had lost her memory and become a patient there, hold hands with Dana Andrews. Another time Linda saw him stoop to tie her mother's shoes; it was a sad and sweet and poignant scene. He still looked movie star marvelous to Linda. Susan later recalled a visit she made to her father: "He proudly pointed to the star on his door (every patient had one), and grinned. He had arrived. Finally. And he was at peace with it." For a while Mary took Dana's clothes to the cleaners and brought him clean sports jackets and sweaters. She ran into another wife who said, "Oh no. There'll be none of that. From now on it's things that can be washed here and won't shrink much." Mary bought Dana a wardrobe of washables some time after that. She gave him a cashmere cardigan for Father's Day or his birthday, and Susan and Kathy went along for the visit. "That was the time we heard him sing 'Moon River' with a guitar accompaniment, sitting in a tiny room with a few others and some empty chairs," Kathy recalled. "They had a songbook with large print including the words to each patient's choice. He looked at us (strangers) as though we'd arrived at a theatre late and disturbed the performance." Dana did not like group activities, except when he was called upon to sing. "I saw him refuse to go for 'sports activities,'" Kathy recalled. "He crossed his arms and said, not particularly loudly, 'I am not going.' I'm sure he was not dragged to throw a ball around with a bunch of foggy old men that day. He didn't deteriorate physically the way that my mother did, another reason to believe that he had multi-infarct dementia rather than Alzheimer's . . . not that it matters much in the end, except perhaps for heritability."

Near the end, Mary could not bear to see it. Susan remembered: "My mother said goodbye to him, very simply, with no tears. She did not cry in front of us. She clearly wanted to go. I was there for her as well as myself, but if it had been up to me, we would have stayed the night. But I had to remember that this was HER husband, not mine, and she was going to live, and he was not. I said goodbye to him and kissed his beautiful hand for the last time." Dana was breathing heavily, gasping for air, as Mary would later when Stephen watched her succumb to Alzheimer's. Dana was long past the time when he could remember his lines, when he could remember anything. His son Stephen was holding his hand, telling his dad how much he loved him, and for an instant Dana, struggling hard to keep his eyes open, seemed to recover himself. What happened next is like a Hollywood picture, but it happens to be true: Dana, slowly fading away in a final dissolve, said, as if on cue, "I love you, Son."

Dana died two weeks later on December 17, 1992. Susan remembered all the times she held his big wide hand with its heavy fingers. Kathy held his hand the last time she saw him, remembering the thousands of times he'd held her own while they walked together, remembering when his big hands had rubbed her stockinged feet warm on a freezing morning at the Rose Parade on New Year's Day—and remembering how he'd greet her after an absence, putting one of his hands over and the other under her own, exclaiming, "Kaaaathy! Darling!"

SOURCES

For full citations, see the bibliography. Unless otherwise noted below, my quotations of letters to and from Dana Andrews are in the possession of the Andrews family. Similarly, my references to Clyde Williams, who began a biography of Dana Andrews in the 1970s, are based on transcripts given to me by the Andrews family. In addition, Williams has deposited some material in the special collections department of the Mississippi State University Library.

ABBREVIATIONS

AA	Annis Andrews
AFP	Andrews Family Papers
AMP	Academy of Motion Picture Arts and Sciences
CA	Charles Andrews
CF	Charles Forrest Andrews
CR	Carl Rollyson
CWMSU	Clyde Williams/Dana Andrews Collection, Mississippi State University
CUOH	Columbia University Oral History Office, New York City
DA	Dana Andrews
ELP	El Progresso Archives, Uvalde, Texas
IMDB	Internet Movie Database
MSU	Mississippi State University
NYPL	Billy Rose Theatre Collection, NYPL
SAG	Screen Actors Guild
SHSU	Sam Houston State University Archives, Huntsville, Texas
UCLA	University of California, Los Angeles
USC	University of Southern California, Cinema Arts Library

INTRODUCTION

See Smith for a discussion of the "masculine ideal of steely impassivity." Eddie Muller makes the connection between Dana's tightly wound style and his alcoholism in the special features section of the *Fallen Angel* DVD. For a sample of Dana's statements as SAG president, see Bart.

SOURCES

CHAPTER 1

Shawn Pearson: "Descendants of Thomas Andrews 1795," myfamily.com.
The description of the First Baptist Church: August Lawrence, *A Brief History of the First Baptist Church of Huntsville*, 1941, a pamphlet in SHSU.
The Felder family history: SHSU.
Sam Parish: Crews.

CHAPTER 2

My description of Charles Forrest Andrews derives from the novel his son Charles never completed. The character is clearly based on his father and jibes with Charles's letter to Dana (12/2/35).
CF's own comments about growing up: CF to DA, 2/19/39.
"Dinner on the ground": Rhett Farrior email to CR.
Many of the details of CF's early years, of what it was like to live in his part of Florida are, as he later confirmed to Dana, congruent with the descriptions in Marjorie Kinnan Rawlings's novel, *The Yearling*, on which I have drawn to give an idea of the world that shaped CF's attitudes and affections.
Details of CF's early education come from his obituary, written by Edwin C. Boynton, "Fallen on Zion's Battle Field," *Huntsville Item*, 3/7/40.
A good deal of detail about CF's early years is recorded in the reminiscences of his oldest son, Wilton, who was the closest of all CF's children to his father. Wilton took the trouble to do some of his own research, but he was still relying on hearsay, so I regard the details he provides as at least part legend. In one sense, factuality does not matter, because the point about CF is that he loomed larger than life in his family's imagination. Wilton's cousins heard other stories about CF that contradict some of his account, and Wilton had a tendency to take a rather benign view of his father's failings.
DA's comments on CF: ELP transcript.
CF's love notes: ELP transcript.
Annis's visit to CF's Florida family: CWMSU.
Annis's devotion to CF and her responses to family life: CA's novel.
Details of Dana's birth: CF to DA, 4/29/39.
Description of Collins: taken from *Mississippi: A Guide to the Magnolia State*.
CF's recollections of Dana as an infant: CF to DA, 4/29/39.
CF as father: CWMSU.
The San Antonio hailstorm: CF to DA, 4/29/39.
Margaret Alton: I don't have her precise birthdate, although it had to be in 1915.
Dana's love of candy: CA to DA, 4/29/39.

SOURCES

Description of Rockdale: *Texas: A Guide to the Lone Star State.*
Sleeping sideways: ELP transcript.
Dana's return visit to Rockdale: Jeanne Williams, "Portrait of a Minister's Son," USC clipping files.
Description of Uvalde: *Texas: A Guide to the Lone Star State.*
CF and W. D. Bunting: CF to DA, 8/16/35.
David's recollections of his mother and infant sisters: CWMSU, ELP.
John Nance Garner: Timmons.
CF in the Klan: CWMSU. According to the Dolph Briscoe Center for American History, University of Texas at Austin, CF remained a member of the Klan until 1930.
Dana's amusements in Uvalde: ELP.
Dana's running way: DA to R. L. Standifer, 12/18/45; Mary Todd Andrews, "Dana Andrews: A Distinguished Career," Pasadena Playhouse Hall of Fame (program booklet, May 8, 1982).
CF on the Uvalde years: CF to DA, 4/29/39.

CHAPTER 3

Carver's work in Huntsville: Hedda Hooper, "And Where Is The Wolf of Yesteryear," *Chicago Tribune*, 8/24/45, USC clipping file.
Norma's diary: I am indebted to Mary Sue Coffman for allowing me to read her mother's diary.
David's on Norma's trip abroad: CWMSU.
Mrs. Felder: author interview with her granddaughter, Mary Sue Coffman; AA to DA, 2/16/44.
Richard Arlen: "And Where is The Wolf of Yesteryear," *Chicago Tribune*, 8/12/45, USC clipping file.
CF's preaching: reported in *Huntsville Item*, 9/6/28.
Sam Houston: *Texas: A Guide to the Lone Star State.*
Charles Stewart: "Teacher's Nagging Led to Film Career," *Huntsville Item* in SHSU clipping file.
The Austin party and hitchhiking to California: Channing Chase, "Confidential Report on Dana Andrews," *Screen Guide*, Constance McCormick Collection, USC; John Chapman, "The Man Who Loved Laura," 3/45, USC clipping files.

CHAPTER 4

The correspondence that forms the basis of this chapter is part of the AFP archive.

CHAPTER 5

Dana's strict Baptist upbringing: DA, "This I Believe," *Screenland*, c. 1946–47 in the Constance McCormick Collection, USC.
Janet's Romany costume: *Van Nuys News*, 6/10/27.
Working twenty-one jobs: Jack Hirschberg, "Dana Andrews: Ex-School Bus Driver Would Sooner Have been Born Rich," AMP clipping file.
Janet's charm and appearance: Sheila Simpson to CR, 3/13/11; Lawrence Martin to Janet Murray, 7/13/32.
David on Carver's "respect" for Janet: CWMSU.

CHAPTER 6

Aggie: Sheila Simpson to CR, 3/20/11.
Mrs. Twomey: CWMSU; *Van Nuys News*, 2/15/32.
"I almost did give up": Dana Andrews, "This I Believe," *Screenland* c. 1946–47, Constance McCormick Collection, USC.

CHAPTER 7

Maudie and Oliver Prickett oral history: UCLA
Description of Pasadena Playhouse: This account is based on my visit and on O'Sullivan.
Stan Twomey: Ida Zeitlin transcript of interview with DA in AFP.
"You'll work now and then": CUOH, http://www.fathom.com/feature/121572/index.html.
Florence Russell: CWMSU; Russell.
Aggie: Zeitlin, AFP.
First Lady: Excerpts and commentary on the play are included in Mantle.
Mary Todd's account of meeting Dana appears in her article, "Dana Andrews: A Distinguished Career," Pasadena Playhouse Hall of Fame program booklet, May 8, 1982, AFP.
Twentieth Century-Fox press release: AMP.
"She knew more about acting": *New York Post*, July 23, 1958, in AMP clipping file.
"character leads": AMP.
Stuart Heisler to DA: AFP; Berg.
Lou Golder: Zeitlin, AFP.

CHAPTER 8

Dana's Goldwyn Contract: Fox Legal Files, UCLA.
The Murrays as Republicans: email from Sheila Simpson.

SOURCES

Reeves Espy: CUOH, http://www.fathom.com/feature/121573/index.html.
I UNDERSTAND: Easton.
"I was afraid": McClelland.
"pooling agreement": Fox legal files, UCLA.
"When this comes out": Zeitlin, AFP.
"a terrific new personality": Sharpe.

CHAPTER 9

"I don't know if": "Why I Adore My Wife," *Screen Guide*, c. 1949–50, Constance McCormick Collection, USC.
Louella Parsons: *Los Angeles Examiner*, 12/31/41 USC.
Bugsy Siegel: Anger; Wolfe.
Fox staffer: All internal Fox memos are in the Twentieth Century-Fox production files at USC.
Jean Renoir: Renoir.
"Renoir wrote Zanuck": Thomson and LoBianco.
"Zanuck replied": Behlmer.
"the next big star": Jean Renoir Papers, UCLA.
Shepperd Strudwick: McKay.
"I got good performances": Thomson and LoBianco.
Zanuck concurred: Behlmer.
Annis's responses to *Swamp Water* are described in her letter to Mary, 1/14/42, and Sue Felder's to Dana, 1/12/42, AFP.
Reviews of *Swamp Water*: USC clipping file; Renoir Papers, UCLA.
"two-fisted sort of man": CUOP, http://www.fathom.com/feature/121587/index.html.
"Dana dammit" . . . Clyde Williams: CWMSU.
"I'm just no good": Rollyson.
"benchmark film of his career": Mosely.
Otis Ferguson: unfinished article in AMP file on Milestone.
Dana's collaboration with Milestone: CUOP, http://www.fathom.com/feature/121587/index.html.
"I cast everything": AMP clipping file, 8/13/74.
"Dana had a quality": quoted in McKay.
"Our story is our characters": Fox production file, USC.

CHAPTER 10

Behlmer: *America's Favorite Movies*.
"easy going:" Hirsch.
Mamoulian "had no concept": Fujiwara, *The World and Its Double*.

CHAPTER 11

"unprintable" note . . . got a lot out of me: Elder.
"a man's man": Hirsch.
"Andrews could suggest unease": *The New Biographical Dictionary of Film*.
Darryl Zanuck: Fujiwara, *The World and Its Double*.
"That's the best god-damned war picture": CWMSU.
Howard Barnes: Morella.
a war veteran's memory: See imdb entry on *A Walk in the Sun*, user reviews section.
a poet with a camera: CUOH, http://www.fathom.com/feature/121587/index.html.
Otis Ferguson: AMP.
"Bond came at me": clipping file, AMP.
Walter Wanger: Linet.
"what you pay me for": Bernstein.
Tourneur's direction delighted him: Fujiwara, *The Cinema of Nightfall*.
He liked to drink . . . no one lectured him: *Los Angeles Herald Examiner*, 6/15/77; *Valley News*, May 29, 77, USC.
"Success is a frightening thing": press release for *Innocent Bystanders*, USC.
Dana believed: to Eddie Darling, 12/20/45, AFP.
Vernon Wood estimated: to DA, 4/20/45, AFP.
GET OUTTA MY OFFICE: Easton.

CHAPTER 12

Sam Goldwyn: Berg.
"What happened to you!": McClelland.
"I would surely like you to watch": Michael Highton, liner notes to CD, *Music from the Movies of Dana Andrews 1944–1949*.
Wyler "*loved*" Dana: Herman.
"very quiet and intelligent": CWMSU.
he later told interviewers: Miller.
He will do a scene over and over . . . Mr. Wyler: CUOH, http://www.fathom3.com/feature/121587/index.html.

CHAPTER 13

Gregory Peck: Fox publicity material, AMP.
"a piece of mechanism": Baer.
"a pretty fair director": CWMSU.

CHAPTER 14

"In February 1947": My account of Dana's reluctance to perform in *Daisy Kenyon* is drawn from the Fox legal files, UCLA.
"She overdramatized everything": CWMSU.
"An underestimated actor": Chandler.
"jewel-encrusted jockstrap": Wayne.
"If we do not succeed": Custen.
"I produced": Behlmer, *Memo from Darryl F. Zanuck*.
"critics crucified us": Negulesco; Higham and Greenberg.

CHAPTER 15

"On the flight back" . . . historian Larry Ceplair: http://www.cobbles.com/simpp_archive/linkbackups/huac_blacklist.htm.
SAG: My account is drawn from SAG files.

CHAPTER 16

"I was built up": http://www.fathom.com/feature/121592/index.html.
Reviews of *The Glass Menagerie*: quoted in Parish.
"eaten with ambition": "My Brother Dana," fragment of an article in the Billy Rose Theatre Collection, NYPL.
"Sometimes he was in such bad shape": Kelley.
"Fuck You Club": Walker.
Interview with Hedda Hopper: Constance McCormick Collection, USC.

CHAPTER 17

"Garson was a literal chatterbox": *Huntsville Item*, November 5, 1975, SHSU.
In one harrowing incident: McGilligan.
On another occasion: Hannsberry.
The film's producer: Grant.
Process shot: Fujiwara, *The Cinema of Nightfall*.
"He knows": AMP.

CHAPTER 18

"My coping mechanism":http://www.podtech.net/home/3848/robert-ryan-and-dana-andrews-had-daughters.

Charles D. Davis, Jr.: "Actor Finds Success—as Real Estate Operator," *Los Angeles Times*, May 24, 1964, Constance McCormick Collection, USC.
"very kind": neighborhood newsletter, courtesy Kathy Andrews Smith.
"Their psychology was all wrong": Parish.
Murray Schumach: SAG clipping file.
"You begin playing generals": *Houston Post*, SHSU.
"very believable": McGilligan, *Backstory*.
daily production and progress report: Warner Brothers Archive, UCLA.

CHAPTER 19

Ken Annakin: Earnshaw.
"The romantic phase": Parish.
The separation from Mary: Dora Albert, "Catching Up With Dana Andrews," *Modern Screen*, October 1975, Constance McCormick Collection, USC.
"Some people in my profession": Hannsberry.
"I was educated": "Dana Andrews has promise," 10/4/69, Bob Thomas Collection, UCLA.
A typical episode: I'm indebted to Mattie Abraham at Mississippi State for sending me on DVD an episode of *Bright Promise* that did not seem available from any other source.
"raging reality of campus dissent": Billy Rose Theatre Collection clipping file, NYPL.

FILMOGRAPHY

1985	*Prince Jack*
1980	*The Pilot*
1978	*Good Guys Wear Black*
1978	*Born Again*
1976	*The Last Tycoon*
1974	*Take a Hard Ride*
1974	*Airport 1975*
1973	*Innocent Bystanders*
1968	*The Cobra*
1968	*The Devil's Brigade*
1967	*The Frozen Dead*
1967	*Hot Rods to Hell*
1966	*Johnny Reno*
1966	*Spy in Your Eye*
1965	*In Harm's Way*
1965	*The Loved One*
1965	*Town Tamer*
1965	*Brainstorm*
1965	*Battle of the Bulge*
1965	*Crack in the World*
1965	*The Satan Bug*
1962	*Madison Avenue*
1960	*The Crowded Sky*
1958	*Enchanted Island*
1958	*The Fearmakers*
1957	*Spring Reunion*
1957	*Zero Hour*
1957	*Night of the Demon/Curse of the Demon*
1956	*While the City Sleeps*
1956	*Comanche*
1956	*Beyond a Reasonable Doubt*
1955	*Smoke Signal*
1955	*Strange Lady in Town*

1954	*Elephant Walk*
1954	*Duel in the Jungle*
1954	*Three Hours to Kill*
1952	*Assignment-Paris*
1951	*I Want You*
1951	*Sealed Cargo*
1951	*The Frogmen*
1950	*Edge of Doom*
1950	*Where the Sidewalk Ends*
1949	*The Forbidden Street*
1949	*Sword in the Desert*
1949	*My Foolish Heart*
1948	*Deep Waters*
1948	*No Minor Vices*
1948	*The Iron Curtain*
1947	*Night Song*
1947	*Daisy Kenyon*
1947	*Boomerang!*
1946	*Canyon Passage*
1946	*The Best Years of Our Lives*
1945	*Fallen Angel*
1945	*A Walk in the Sun*
1945	*State Fair*
1944	*Laura*
1944	*The Purple Heart*
1944	*Up in Arms*
1944	*Wing and a Prayer*
1943	*The North Star*
1943	*The Ox-Bow Incident*
1943	*Crash Dive*
1942	*Berlin Correspondent*
1941	*Swamp Water*
1941	*Tobacco Road*
1941	*Belle Starr*
1941	*Ball of Fire*
1940	*Kit Carson*
1940	*Sailor's Lady*
1940	*Lucky Cisco Kid*
1940	*The Westerner*

BIBLIOGRAPHY

Agee, James. *Film Writing and Selected Journalism*. Library of America, 2005.
Anderson, Christopher. *A Star, Is a Star, Is a Star: The Lives and Loves of Susan Hayward*. Doubleday, 1980.
Andrews, Dana. "Why Don't You Take Up Acting?" Dana Andrews Arrives in Hollywood. From Columbia University Oral History Research Office: http://www.fathom.com/feature/121572/index.html.
———. "Let Your Hair and Your Beard Grow": Dana Andrews on His First Meeting with Sam Goldwyn. From Columbia University Oral History Research Office: http://www.fathom.com/feature/121573/index.html.
———. "Strictly for Money": Dana Andrews on the Movie Business. From Columbia University Oral History Research Office: http://www.fathom.com/feature/121592/index.html.
———. "Acting like Children": Dana Andrews on Working with Otto Preminger. From Columbia University Oral History Research Office: http://www.fathom.com/feature/121585/index.html.
———. "The Most Indefatigable Perfectionist": Dana Andrews on Director William Wyler. From Columbia University Oral History Research Office: http://www.fathom.com/feature/121587/index.html.
Anger, Kenneth. *Hollywood Babylon*. Straight Arrow Books, 1975.
Arceri, Gene. *Brooklyn's Scarlett: Susan Hayward, Fire in the Wind*. BearManor Media, 2010.
Baer, William, ed. *Elia Kazan: Interviews*. University Press of Mississippi, 2000.
Barbas, Samantha. *The First Lady of Hollywood: A Biography of Louella Parsons*. University of California Press, 2006.
Bart, Peter. "Actor Deplores TV's Standards." *New York Times*, October 17, 1964.
Barton, Ruth. *Hedi Lamarr: The Most Beautiful Woman in Film*. University Press of Kentucky, 2010.
Basinger, Jeanine. *The Star Machine*. Alfred A. Knopf, 2007.
Behlmer, Rudy. *Memo from Darryl F. Zanuck: The Golden Years at Twentieth Century-Fox*. Grove Press, 1993.
———. *America's Favorite Movies behind the Scenes*. Ungar, 1982.
Bell, Vereen. *Swamp Water*. University of Georgia Press, 2008.
Bellour, Raymond. "Believing in Cinema." *Psychoanalysis and Cinema*, ed. E. Ann Kaplan. Routledge, 1990.

Berg, A. Scott. *Goldwyn: A Biography*. Riverhead, 1998.
Bernstein, Walter. *Walter Wanger: Hollywood Independent*. University of Minnesota Press, 2000.
Borde, Raymond, and Etienne Chaumeton. *A Panorama of American Film Noir*. City Lights Books, 2002.
Capua, Michelangelo. *William Holden: A Biography*. McFarland, 2009.
Chandler, Charlotte. *Not the Girl Next Door: Joan Crawford, A Personal Biography*. Simon & Schuster, 2010.
Coursodon, Jean-Pierre, and Pierre Sauvage. *American Directors*. McGraw-Hill, 1983.
Crews, D'Anne McAdams, ed. *Huntsville & Walker County Texas*. Sam Houston State University Press, 1976.
Custen, George. *Twentieth Century's Fox: Darryl Zanuck and the Culture of Hollywood*. Basic Books, 1997.
Davis, Ronald L. *Zachary Scott: Hollywood's Sophisticated Cad*. University Press of Mississippi, 2006.
———. *The Glamour Factory: Inside Hollywood's Big Studio System*. Southern Methodist University Press, 1993.
Dickstein, Morris. *Dancing in the Dark: A Cultural History of the Great Depression*. W. W. Norton, 2010.
Durgnat, Raymond. *Jean Renoir*. University of California Press, 1974.
Earnshaw, Tony. *Beating the Devil: The Making of "The Night of the Demon."* Tomahawk Press, 2010.
Easton, Carol. *In Search of Sam Goldwyn*. Morrow, 1976.
Eastwood, Clint. "My Hollywood Heroes," *Melbourne Sunday Age*, October 1, 1995.
Elder, Jane Lentz. *Alice Faye: A Life Beyond the Silver Screen*. University Press of Mississippi, 2011.
Eyles, Allen. "Interview with Dana Andrews." *Focus on Film* #26 (1977).
Fujiwara, Chris. *The World and Its Double: The Life and Work of Otto Preminger*. Faber and Faber, 2009.
———. *Jacques Tourneur: The Cinema of Nightfall*. Johns Hopkins University Press, 2001.
Garbicz, Adam, and Jacek Klinowski. *Cinema: The Magic Vehicle: A Guide to Its Achievement*. Schocken Books, 1983.
Granger, Farley. *Include Me Out: My Life from Goldwyn to Broadway*. St. Martin's Press, 2008.
Grant, Barry Keith. *Fritz Lang: Interviews*. University Press of Mississippi, 2003.
Guiles, Fred Lawrence. *Tyrone Power*. Mercury House, 1990.
Hannsberry, Karen Burroughs. *Bad Boys: The Actors of Film Noir*. Volume 1. McFarland, 2003.
Harvey, James. *Movie Love in the Fifties*. Da Capo Press, 2002.

Haskell, Molly. *From Reverence to Rape: The Treatment of Women in the Movies.* University of Chicago Press, 1971.

Herman, Jan. *A Talent for Trouble: The Life of Hollywood's Most Acclaimed Director, William Wyler.* Da Capo Press, 1997.

Higham, Charles, and Joel Greenberg. *The Celluloid Muse: Hollywood Directors Speak.* Henry Regnery, 1969.

Higham, Charles, and Roy Moseley. *Princess Merle: The Romantic Life of Merle Oberon.* Pocket Books, 1985.

Hirsch, Foster. *Otto Preminger: The Man Who Would Be King.* Knopf, 2007.

Issacs, Susan. *After All These Years.* HarperTorch, 1994.

Kazan, Elia. *Elia Kazan: A Life.* Da Capo Press, 1997.

———. *Kazan on Directing.* Vintage, 2010.

Kelley, Kitty. *Elizabeth Taylor: The Last Star.* Simon & Schuster, 2011.

Kemp, Phillip. "Allan Dwan." John Wakeman, ed. *World Film Directors.* Volume 1. H. W. Wilson, 1987.

Knox, Alexander. *On Actors and Acting.* Scarecrow Press, 1998.

Krutnik, Frank. *In a Lonely Street.* Taylor & Francis, 2002.

Laurie, Piper. *Learning to Live Out Loud: A Memoir.* Crown, 2011.

Leider, Emily W. *Myrna Loy: The Only Good Girl in Town.* University of California Press, 2011.

Linet, Beverly. *Susan Hayward: Portrait of a Survivor.* Atheneum, 1980.

Lloyd, Norman. *Stages: Of Life in Theatre, Film and Television.* Limelight Editions, 1993.

McClelland, Doug. *Forties Film Talk: Oral Histories of Hollywood.* McFarland, 1992.

McGilligan, Patrick. *Fritz Lang: The Nature of the Beast.* St. Martin's Press, 1997.

———. *Backstory 3: Interviews with Screenwriters of the 1960s.* University of California Press, 1997.

McKay, James. *Dana Andrews: The Face of Noir.* McFarland, 2010.

Malden, Karl. *When Do I Start: A Memoir.* Limelight Editions, 2004.

Mantle, Burns, ed. *The Best Plays of 1935–1936.* Dodd, Mead & Company, 1936.

Miller, Gabriel, ed. *William Wyler: Interviews.* University Press of Mississippi, 2010.

Mississippi: A Guide to the Magnolia State. Hastings House, 1938.

Morella, Joe, Edward Z. Epstein, and John Griggs, *The Films of World War II.* Citadel Press, 1973.

Mosley, Leonard. *Zanuck: The Rise and Fall of Hollywood's Last Tycoon.* McGraw-Hill, 1985.

Munro, Alice. "The Spanish Lady." In *Something I've Been Meaning to Tell You.* Vintage, 2004.

Negulesco, Jean. *The Things I Did and Things I Think I Did.* Simon & Schuster, 1984.

O'Hara, Maureen. *'Tis Herself: An Autobiography*. Simon & Schuster, 2005.
O'Sullivan, Judy. *The Pasadena Playhouse: A Celebration of One of the Older Theatrical Producing Organizations in America*. (Pasadena Playhouse, n.d.)
Palmer, Lilli. *Change Lobsters and Dance: An Autobiography*. Macmillan, 1999.
Parrish, James. *The Hollywood Reliables*. Arlington House, 1980.
Percy, Walker. *The Moviegoer*. Vintage, 1988.
Pratley, Gerald. *The Cinema of Otto Preminger*. A. S. Barnes & Company, 1971.
Preminger, Otto. *Preminger: An Autobiography*. Bantam Books, 1978.
Price, Victoria. *Vincent Price: A Daughter's Biography*. St. Martin's Press, 2000.
Rawlings, Marjorie Kinnan. *The Yearling*. Scribner's, 1938.
Renoir, Jean. *My Life and My Films*. Atheneum, 1974.
Rollyson, Carl. *Lillian Hellman: Her Life and Legend*. iUniverse, 2009.
Rosenbaum, Jonathan. "Otto Preminger." *Cinema: A Critical Dictionary*, ed. Richard Roud. Viking, 1980.
Ross, Lillian, *The Player: A Profile of an Art*. Simon & Schuster, 1962.
Schatz, Thomas. *The Genius of the System: Hollywood Filmmaking in the Studio Era*. Henry Holt, 1988.
Schickel, Richard. *Elia Kazan: A Biography*. HarperCollins, 2005.
Server, Lee. *Robert Mitchum: "Baby I Don't Care."* St. Martin's Press, 2001.
Sesonske, Alexander. "Jean Renoir in Georgia: *Swamp Water*." *Georgia Review* 26 (Spring 1982).
Sharpe, Howard. "The Remarkable Andrews." *Photoplay*, April 1943.
Smith, David L. *Sitting Pretty: The Life and Times of Clifton Webb*. University Press of Mississippi, 2011.
Smith, Imogen, Sara. "The Forties Hero and His Shadow." http://www.brightlightsfilm.com/62/62dana.php.
Spoto, Donald. *Possessed: The Life of Joan Crawford*. HarperCollins, 2010.
Starr, Kevin. *Endangered Dreams: California in the Depression*. Oxford University Press, 1997.
———. *Embattled Dreams: California in War and Peace 1940–1950*. Oxford University Press, 2003.
Texas: A Guide to the Lone Star State. Hastings House, 1940.
Thomas, Bob. *Golden Boy: The Untold Story of William Holden*. St. Martin's Press, 1983.
Thomson, David. *The New Biographical Dictionary of Film*. Fifth Edition, Completely updated and expanded, Knopf, 2011.
———. *The Whole Equation: A History of Hollywood*. Knopf, 2004.
Thomson, David, and Loraine LoBianco, ed. *Jean Renoir: Letters*. Faber and Faber, 1994.
Thompson, Frank. *William A. Wellman*. Scarecrow Press, 1983.
Tierney, Gene. *Self-Portrait*. Berkeley, 1980.
Timmons, Bascom N. *Garner of Texas*. Garnsey Press, 2007.

Troyan, Michael. *A Rose for Mrs. Miniver: The Life of Greer Garson.* The University Press of Kentucky, 1999.

Vogel, Michelle. *Gene Tierney: A Biography.* McFarland, 2005.

Wakeman, John. *World Film Directors.* H. W. Wilson, 1987.

Walker, Alexander. *Elizabeth: The Life of Elizabeth Taylor.* Grove Press, 2001.

Wayne, Jane Ellen. *Crawford's Men.* Robson Books, 1988.

Webb, Clifton, and David L. Smith. *Sitting Pretty: The Life and Times of Clifton Webb.* University Press of Mississippi, 2011.

Williams, Jeanne. "Dana Andrews' childhood included a stint in Rockdale." *Temple (Texas) Telegram,* October 31, 2010.

Winnington, Richard. *Film Criticism and Caricatures, 1943–1953.* Elek Books, 1975.

Wolfe, Don. *The Black Dahlia Files: The Mob, the Mogul, and the Murder That Transfixed Los Angeles.* Harper, 2006.

Wolfe, Thomas. *You Can't Go Home Again.* Harper Brothers, 1940.

Wood, Robin. "Jacques Tourneur." *Cinema: A Critical Dictionary,* ed. Richard Roud. Viking, 1980.

INDEX

ACLU (American Civil Liberties Union), 225
Actors Studio, 257
Actress, The, 195
Adams, Dorothy, 83, 100, 118, 159–60, 280
After All These Years (Isaacs), 3
Agee, James, 141, 144, 146, 166, 178, 201, 236
Airport, 282
Alcoa Premier Theatre, 262
Algiers, 97
Algonquin Hotel, 6, 259
All Quiet on the Western Front (Milestone), 139
Allen, Red, 69
Ameche, Don, 147, 148, 227
Amendt, Rudolph, 75, 79–80, 83, 84
Ames, Richard Sheridan, 78–79
Anderson, Judith, 151, 157
Andrews, Abigail (grandchild), 275, 278, 283, 284
Andrews, Anne (sister-in-law), 34
Andrews, Annis Speed (mother), 7, 18–24, 29–30, 31, 33, 38, 41, 44, 45, 52, 55–56, 64–65, 79, 101–2, 109, 112, 116, 129, 137, 145, 188, 265
Andrews, Carver Dana: alcoholism of, 4, 84, 103, 107, 137, 140, 156, 160, 177, 180, 187, 193–95, 200–201, 206, 213, 227–29, 233–35, 246, 249, 252–54, 264, 270–71, 274–77, 279, 281–82, 284; death of, 284–86; Horatio Alger figure, 94, 118; little theatre movement, 70–72; marriage to Janet Murray, 63; marriage to Mary Todd, 109; politics of, 183, 216–17, 225; president of the Screen Actors Guild, 265; reactions to the studio system, 186, 212; reactions to success, 187, 199–200; religious views of, 23, 29, 31, 34–35, 55–56, 65, 73, 282; sailing, 44, 210, 231–33, 242, 264, 278, 283; singing career and performances, 66, 71–73, 82, 85; singing lessons, 57–58, 67, 73, 75, 91
Andrews, Charles Forrest (father), 9, 14–15, 17–36, 40, 44, 46–49, 50, 51, 52, 53, 55–56, 64–65, 67–68, 69, 72, 73, 75–76, 79, 80, 83–84, 86, 87, 90, 96, 101–2, 109, 112, 125, 126–27, 129, 137, 138, 145, 172, 283
Andrews, Charles (brother), 7–8, 9, 14, 17, 19, 20, 23, 25, 28–29, 33, 37, 45–46, 47, 49, 50, 53, 56, 64, 65, 66, 67, 69, 70, 75–76, 80, 87, 102, 112, 137, 138, 139, 207–8, 233, 234, 242, 280
Andrews, Dana (nephew), 278
Andrews, David (brother), 9, 19, 21, 22, 29–30, 31, 32, 33, 38, 40–41, 66, 103, 112, 284
Andrews, David (son), 14, 66, 67–68, 70, 72, 74, 79, 80, 83, 84, 86, 90–91, 93, 94, 98, 100, 101, 107, 108, 109, 110, 114, 136, 188,

197, 228, 233, 240–41, 261, 263, 270, 281
Andrews, Evelyn, 24, 28
Andrews, Harlan (brother), 9, 20, 21, 46, 280
Andrews, Hazel, 21
Andrews, Ilena (grandchild), 275
Andrews, Jeanne (sister-in-law), 14, 50, 66, 80, 87, 171, 233, 280
Andrews, John (brother), 9, 33, 34, 35, 81, 145, 177
Andrews, Katharine "Kathy" (daughter), 68, 83, 87, 122, 136, 165, 180, 183, 188, 211, 231, 232–33, 238, 239–43, 247, 257, 260, 261, 264, 265, 270–71, 273–76, 277–78, 281, 285–86
Andrews, Margaret Alton, 23, 28
Andrews, Mary (sister), 9, 30, 65, 74, 81, 82, 101–2, 115, 145
Andrews, Mary Todd (wife), 15, 87–94, 97, 100, 102, 103–5, 107–10, 114–15, 117, 122, 125, 126, 136, 138, 155, 157, 165, 176, 179, 186, 192, 193, 197, 202, 204, 205, 207, 208–9, 210, 211, 212, 227–29, 230–31, 232–34, 235, 236, 237, 239, 242, 243, 247, 255, 259, 270–71, 273, 275, 277–78, 280–81, 283, 284–86
Andrews, Matthew, 275–76
Andrews, Ralph (brother), 9, 21, 23, 34, 41, 55, 137
Andrews, Stephen (son), 177, 179, 211, 232–33, 240, 242, 256, 260, 261, 263–64, 281, 286
Andrews, Susan (daughter), 3–4, 5, 7, 14, 15, 32, 64, 140, 142, 155, 156, 172, 173, 175, 188, 194, 211, 225, 227, 233, 238, 239–40, 253, 255, 256, 259–60, 261, 265, 268, 270, 275, 277, 281, 285–86

Andrews, William "Billy" (brother), 9, 19, 80, 145, 187–89, 231–32
Andrews, Wilton (brother), 9, 18, 20, 21, 22, 23, 24, 26, 27, 28, 31, 32, 33, 37, 40–41, 44, 55, 64, 81, 112, 167, 279–80
Anger, Kenneth, 122
Annakin, Ken, 270
Antony and Cleopatra, 77
Any Wednesday, 277
Arceri, Gene, 184
Arlen, Richard, 11, 39
Arnold, Edward, 221
Asher, Irving, 233
Assignment Paris, 230
Astaire, Fred, 153
Aurelius, Marcus, 94
Austin, Texas, 13, 42, 44, 46, 56, 61, 68
Autry, Gene, 114

Babbitt (Lewis), 53
Back to Methuselah (Shaw), 95–96, 97
Ball of Fire, 120–22, 129
Balzac, Honoré de, 239
Bancroft, Anne, 257
Banky, Vilma, 105–6, 121
Barbara Stanwyck Show, The, 262
Barnes, Howard, 178
Barrymore, John, 87
Bart, Peter, 267
Battle of the Bulge, The, 269–70
Baxter, Anne, 125, 126, 127, 129, 136, 137, 140, 209
Bayne, Beverly, 25
Beating the Devil (Earnshaw), 252
Behlmer, Rudy, 151, 153, 156
Beilenson, Laurence, 222–23
Bell, Vereen, 123, 126
Belle Starr, 119–20, 124
Bellour, Raymond, 252
Benchley, Robert, 6
Berg, Scott, 212

Berlin Correspondent, 129–30, 215
Bernhardt, Sarah, 155
Best Years of Our Lives, The, 5, 182, 186, 190, 191–99, 215, 216, 217, 254, 280
Beyond a Reasonable Doubt (Lang), 247–51
Bickford, Charles, 176
Big Heat, The, 248
Black Panthers, 283
Blackmer, Sidney, 250
Blaine, Vivien, 167
Blue Dahlia, 237
Blue Gardenia, The (Lang), 248
Bodne, Ben and Mary, 259
Bogart, Humphrey, 104, 107, 118, 122, 141, 177, 215, 218, 283
Bolton, Whitney, 258
Bond, Ward, 129, 183
Boomerang, 199, 200–202, 208
Born Again, 282
Bow, Clara, 40
Boyton, Edwin C., 9
Brainstorm, 268
Braxton, Mississippi, 21
Brennan, Walter, 107, 123–24, 129, 140
Brent, George, 104
Bridge on the River Kwai, The, 230
Bright Promise, 276–77
Bringing Up Baby, 121
Brittania Mews. See *Forbidden Street, The*
Broadway, 156
Brooks, Mel, 244
Brown, Gilmor, 71, 80
Brown, Harry, 178
Brown, Jim, 282
Browning, Elizabeth Barrett, 44
Browning, Robert, 44, 48
Brubeck, Dave, 227
Bulwer-Lytton, Edward George, 53
Bunting, W. D., 28

Burr, Raymond, 166
Bus Stop, 151
Bushman, Francis X., 25

Cabell, James Branch, 53
Cady, Jerome, 147, 148
Cagney, James, 122
Caldwell, Erskine, 119
Cantor, Eddie, 146
Canyon Passage, 181–87, 189, 197, 271
Captains and the Kings, The, 260
Carlson, Richard, 221
Carmichael, Hoagy, 193
Carnegie, Dale, 86
Carradine, John, 129, 168
Carter, Minnie, 90, 211, 275
Casablanca, 131
Cashin, Bonnie, 173
Caspary, Vera, 151
Casselberry, Dr. William S., 95–96, 97, 100
"Casual Grace," 238–39
Ceplair, Larry, 218
Cerf, Bennett, 217
Chadwick School, 261
Chan, Charlie, 113, 262
Chaplin, Charlie, 64, 181, 219
Chaplin, Sydney, 256
Chatterton, Ruth, 87
Chavez, Cesar, 283
Chester, Hal, 252–53
Cinema of Otto Preminger, The, 205
City Lights (Chaplin), 64
Civil Rights Congress, 221
Clark, Tom, 221
Cleopatra, 66
Cobb, Irving, 78
Cobra, The, 273
Coe, Fred, 257
Cohn, Harry, 105
Collins, Joan, 262
Collins, Mississippi, 6, 7, 9

Colman, Ronald, 11, 40, 86, 105, 119, 121, 141, 174, 184
Colson, Charles, 282
Columbo, John, 75
Columbo, Russ, 75
Comanche, 246–47
Come Back, Little Sheba, 277
Committee for the First Amendment, 215, 218
Compton sanatorium, 170
Confessions of a Nazi Spy, 215
Conroy, Frank, 131
Conte, Richard, 216, 248
Cooke, Richard, 260
Cooper, Gary, 11, 99, 107, 118, 121, 122, 123, 141, 182, 218
Cory, Wendell, 203
Cotten, Joseph, 203
Crack in the World, 271–72
Craig, James, 249
Crain, Jeanne, 6, 166, 236, 244, 262, 273
Crash Dive, 7, 136–37, 138, 178, 189
Crawford, Joan, 187, 203, 204–5, 210
"Crazy Sunday," 262
Cream of the Jest, The (Cabell), 53
Cregar, Laird, 153
Criminal at Large, 92
Cromwell, John, 210
Crossfire, 216
Crowded Sky, The, 260
Crowther, Bosley, 135, 137, 141, 235
Cumin, Irving, 80
Cummings, Irving, 120
Cummins, Peggy, 252, 254, 264
Curse of the Demon. See *Night of the Demon*
Curtis, Tony, 282
Cvetic, Matt, 225
Cymbeline, 77

Daisy Kenyon, 168, 199, 203–6, 208, 231, 235, 284

Dales, Jack, 221, 224, 266
Dana Andrews: The Face of Noir, 120
Dark Angel, The, 193
Dark Victory, 104
Darnell, Linda, 169, 171, 246
Davenport, Harry, 131
Davis, Bette, 104, 107, 108, 177
Davis, Charles D., Jr., 261
De Mille, Cecil B., 12, 86
De Funiak Springs, Florida, 18, 125
de Havilland, Olivia, 221
Dead End, 107
Dean, James, 156
Dear Octopus, 107
"Death of the Ball Turret Gunner, The," 192
Deep Waters, 206–7, 215
DeNiro, Robert, 282
"Desert Song, The," 14
Devil's Brigade, The, 268
Dick, Bernard, 119
Dick Powell Show, 262
Dickson, Neely, 97
Dietrich, Marlene, 237
Dmytryk, Edward, 216
Dodsworth, 87
Donlevy, Brian, 182
Don't, Mississippi, 6, 7, 9, 18–20
Doolittle, Colonel James, 141
Douglas, Kirk, 140, 208
Dowling, Constance, 146
Dratler, Jay, 151, 158
Drayton, Noel, 276
Duel in the Jungle, 236, 244
Duggan, Shirle, 238
Durgnat, Raymond, 125
Duryea, Dan, 113, 221, 223
Duvall, Robert, 268
Dwan, Allan, 111, 119, 255

Earnshaw, Tony, 252
Easton, Carol, 212–14
Eastwood, Clint, 130, 135

Edge of Doom, 212
Edwards, Ralph, 279–81
Eighteen Actors, 118
Elephant Walk, 233–36, 254, 276
Ellery Queen, 267
Ellington, Duke, 150
Emile Zola, 86
Emma, 87
Enchanted Island, 254–56
Enterprise Pictures, 208
Espy, Reeves, 97, 102, 105, 106, 108
Eyles, Allen, 110, 168, 201
Eythe, William, 148

Fabry, Angela (niece), 9, 278, 283, 284
Failing of Raymond, The, 268
Fairbanks, Douglas, Jr., 217
Fairbanks, Douglas, Sr., 11, 12, 111, 181
Fairless, Benjamin, 212
Falcon Crest, 267
Fallen Angel, 3, 4, 168–77, 189, 204, 205, 246, 263
Farr, Dorothy Parrish, 81
Farrar, David, 236
Fatal Interview (Millay), 93
Faye, Alice, 169–77
Faulkner, William, 18
FBI, 223
Fearmakers, The (Tourneur), 254
Felder, Mary Sue Coffman, 16, 69, 86
Felder, Moselle, 16, 80
Felder, Mrs., 38, 52, 69, 70, 115
Felder, Norma, 14, 36–40, 42, 43–64, 65, 68, 69–70, 72, 80–81, 86, 90, 103, 104–5, 109, 113, 115, 116, 126, 127, 281
Felder, Victor, 16
Feldman, Charles, 189, 203
Feminine Mystique, The, 265
Ferguson, Otis, 143, 181

film noir, 3, 130, 150, 152, 158, 168, 169, 173, 176, 182, 248
Finch, Peter, 233, 234
Firestone, Leonard, 212
First Baptist Church (Huntsville), 14–15
First Baptist Church (Uvalde), 28
First Lady (Kaufman and Dayton), 88–89, 280
First 36 Hours of Dr. Durant, The, 268
Fitzgerald, F. Scott, 262
Fitzgerald, Geraldine, 104
Flaherty, Robert, 12
Fleming, Rhonda, 249
Florida State Normal College, 18
Flynn, Errol, 185
Fonda, Henry, 119, 120, 123, 132, 135, 136, 141, 199, 203, 204–5, 257, 258, 269, 270
Fontaine, Joan, 143, 250–51
Forbidden Street, The, 209–10, 239
Ford, Francis, 132
Ford, John, 3, 119–22, 129, 278
Forde, Eugene, 130
Foreign Correspondent, 130
Formosa, The, 122
Forrest, Sally, 249
Forrest, Steve. *See* Andrews, William
Foulger, Brian, 117
Fowler, Gene, Jr., 249
Francis, Anne, 268
Franco, Francisco, 221
Frankovich, Mike, 252
Friedlob, Bert, 249
Frogmen, The, 227
Frozen Dead, The, 252
Fujiwara, Chris, 186–87, 206, 253

Gable, Clark, 129, 138, 167, 177
Garbo, Greta, 97
Garland, Judy, 216
Garner, John Nance, 10, 30
Garnett, Tay, 144

INDEX

Garson, Greer, 244–45
Gavin, John, 281
Gaynor, Janet, 84
General Electric Theatre, The, 262
Gershwin, George, 12, 150
Gilmore, Virginia, 126, 127, 130
Glass Menagerie, The, 4, 199, 230, 259
Gloria's Romance, 25
Goddess, The, 25
Golder, Lew, 97, 189
Goldwyn, Frances, 212–13
Goldwyn, Samuel, 4, 96–97, 99–116, 118, 120–22, 139–40, 144, 146, 157, 177, 189–91, 195, 200, 203, 211–13, 216, 224, 230, 238, 262
Gone with the Wind, 199
Good Guys Wear Black, 282
Gouzenko, Igor, 208
Grable, Betty, 143
Grand Illusion, 124
Granger, Farley, 139, 140, 142, 144, 190, 212
Grant, Cary, 141, 209
Grapes of Wrath, 119
Griffiths, Andy, 243
Gurie, Sigrid, 97

Hall, Jon, 111, 114, 115, 153
Hamm, John, 262
Harris, Buck, 223
Harrison, Rex, 209
Haskell, Molly, 164
Hathaway, Henry, 144, 147, 202
Hawks, Howard, 120, 121, 122, 189
Haycox, Ernest, 185
Hayden, Sterling, 278
Haymes, Dick, 166, 167
Hayward, Susan, 168, 182, 184–86, 187, 189, 209, 211–12
Hazelden, 273–74
Hecht, Ben, 208
Heflin, Van, 220
Heidi, 111

Heisler, Stuart, 96, 97
Hellman, Lillian, 139, 140
Hemingway, Ernest, 6, 239
Herzberg, Bob, 246
High Noon, 182
Hill, Napoleon, 66, 261
Hill, Virginia, 122
Hinsdale, Oliver, 79
Hiss, Alger, 224
Hitchcock, Alfred, 130
Hitler, Adolf, 102, 106, 221
Hodiak, John, 153, 157
Hoffenstein, Samuel, 151, 158
Hogan's Heroes, 130
Holden, William, 4, 218, 221, 230, 268
Holland, Marty, 170
Hollywood, 13, 45, 137, 138, 164, 184, 212–14, 248, 277
Hollywood Babylon, 122
"Hollywood Fights Back," 215–18, 222, 224
Hollywood Ten, The, 218–19
Hollywood Writers Mobilization for Defense, 221
Hopper, Hedda, 39, 153, 208, 218, 234
Hopper, Jerry, 245
Hot Rods from Hell, 273
House Committee on Un-American Activities (HUAC), 215–24
Houston, Texas, 42
Houston, Sam, 15
Howard, Gordon, 137
How I Turned $1000 into a Million in Real Estate, 261
How To Win Friends and Influence People (Carnegie), 86
Howe, James Wong, 141
Humberstone, H. Bruce, 113, 262
Hunt, Marsha, 216, 218
Huntsville, Texas, 11, 13, 14–16, 36–40, 46, 48, 52, 56, 57, 69, 80–81, 131, 284

Huston, John, 216
Huston, Walter, 125, 127, 141
Hutton, Betty, 247

"I Am No Communist," 218
I Wake Up Screaming, 153, 262
I Want to Live, 184
I Want You, 212
I Was a Communist for the FBI, 225
Ibsen, Henrik, 71
Ike, 268
In Harm's Way, 267, 268
Include Me Out (Granger), 144
Innocent Bystanders, 282
Institute of Living, 227
Iron Curtain, The, 208
Ironside, 267
Isaacs, Susan, 3

Jackie Gleason Show, The, 244
Jagger, Dean, 124
James, Eric, 276–77
Jarrell, Randall, 192
Jefferson, Thomas, 195
Jezebel, 107
John Douglas French Center, 284–86
Johnny Reno, 271
Johnson, Julian, 123
Johnson, Lyndon, 266, 267
Johnson, Van, 177
Johnston, Eric, 219
Joint Anti-Fascist Refugee Committee, 221
Jones, Jennifer, 153
Jory, Victor, 83, 110, 117
Jourdain, Louis, 208, 209
Julius Caesar, 77

Kahn, Ivan, 96
Kantor, MacKinley, 195
Karloff, Boris, 221
Karpeles, Eric, 155
Kaye, Danny, 146, 166, 216

Kazan, Elia, 3, 200–202, 257, 282
Kazan on Directing, 201
Kellogg, Dr. Edward, 73
Kelly, Gene, 215, 216
Kelly, Nancy, 111
Kennedy, John F., 283
Kennedy, Joseph, 28
Kerr, John, 260
Keys of the Kingdom, 200
King, Henry, 207
King of Kings, 12
Kipling, Rudyard, 239
Kit Carson, 114, 119, 129, 183
Kleiner, Harry, 170
Knights of Song, 91
Knox, Alexander, 223, 272
Ku Klux Klan, 30–31, 33, 137, 216

Lady Windermere's Fan, 11, 37–38, 174
Lamarr, Hedi, 150
Lancaster, Burt, 140
Landis, Carole, 153, 209
Lang, Fritz, 3, 130, 247–51
Lardner, Ring, Jr., 219
LaRoque, Rod, 106
LaShelle, Joseph, 163, 174
Last Days of Pompeii (Bulwer-Lytton), 53
Last Hurrah, The, 268
Last Mile, The, 97
"Last of the Big Spenders, The," 262–63
Last Tycoon, The, 282
Laub, Marjorie ("Margo," Janet Murray's sister), 71, 77, 93, 102
Laura, 3, 4, 129, 144, 146, 147, 150–65, 168, 170–71, 172, 176, 186, 189, 279
Laurie, Piper, 245–46
Law of Success, The (Hill), 66
Le Roy, Mervyn, 3
Leaf River Baptist Church, 7

Leaf River School, 18
Learning How to Learn, 94
Learning to Live Out Loud, 246
Leave Her to Heaven, 168
Leech, Richard, 253
Leigh, Vivien, 233
Lewis, Sinclair, 53
Life and Work of Otto Preminger, The, 206
Lifeboat, 153
Lincoln Brigade, 221
Little Foxes, The, 195
Litvak, Anatole, 212
Lloyd, Norman, 8–9, 179–81
Long, R. L., 25
Lost Horizon, 86
Louisville, Kentucky, 20
Love Boat, The, 267
Loved One, The, 268
"Love's Philosophy" (Shelley), 44
Loy, Myrna, 216, 217
Lucky Cisco Kid, 111–13
Ludwig, Emil, 50
Lupino, Ida, 207, 249–50
Lux Radio Theatre, 158, 231

M (Lang), 248
MacGinnis, Niall, 251
MacGowan, Stephen, 123
Madison Avenue, 261–62, 284
Madisonville, Texas, 36, 40, 45, 49, 50, 51, 64
Madmen, 3, 261–62
Major Barbara (Shaw), 94
Malden, Karl, 200–201
Mamoulian, Rouben, 150, 156, 157–58
Man Who Came to Dinner, The, 153
March, Fredric, 84, 192, 193
Marriage Go Round, The, 277, 279
Marshall, George, 237
Marx, Groucho, 86
Massey, Raymond, 108

Matthau, Walter, 230–31
Mature, Victor, 100, 177
Mayer, L. B., 105, 213, 219–20
Mayes, Wendell, 268
Mayo, Archie, 138
Mayo, Virginia, 197, 213
McCarthy, Joseph, 215
McCrea, Joel, 107
McGilligan, Patrick, 251
McKay, James, 120
McKinnon, John, 18
Melville, Herman, 254
Menjou, Adolf, 218
Menzies, William Cameron, 141
Mercer, Johnny, 151
Merrily, We Roll Along (Kaufman and Hart), 91
Michael (Dana's cocker spaniel), 108, 240
Milestone, Lewis, 3, 121, 139–42, 143–44, 149, 153, 177–81, 186, 202, 208, 227
Millay, Edna St. Vincent, 93
Miller, R. W., 48
Mission to Moscow, 215
Mississippi State University, 283–84
Mitchell, Thomas, 249
Mitchum, Robert, 166, 177
Modern Screen, 74, 75, 78, 118, 165, 188
Monroe, Marilyn, 11, 151, 156, 166, 258
Moody, Dwight, 9
Moore, Ruth, 207
Moreau, Jeanne, 282
Morgan, Harry, 147, 166, 210
Motion Picture Association of America (MPAA), 219–20
Motion Picture Production Code, 176, 183, 219
Moviegoer, The, 3
"Movie Nudity Hit by Dana Andrews," 266

310   INDEX

Muni, Paul, 86, 108
Munro, Alice, 3
Murphy, George, 223
Murray, Don, 151
Murray, Janet, 13–14, 15, 58, 60, 62–68, 70, 72–73, 74, 81, 85, 101, 106
Murray, Mrs. Agnes (Aggie), 71, 74–75, 77, 84, 85, 89, 93, 101, 106, 108–9, 110, 114–15, 145, 188, 197–98, 233, 240
Murray, William, 63, 74, 101, 102, 108, 110, 114
Mussolini, Benito, 102, 221
My Foolish Heart, 168, 209, 211–12, 231
My Six Convicts, 231

Nanook of the North, 12
Negulesco, Jean, 210
New York City, 13
Nichols, Dudley, 123, 124, 126
Nickerson, William, 261
Night Gallery, 267
Night of the Demon, 251–54, 264, 272
Night Song, 209, 231
Niven, David, 107
Nixon, Richard, 215, 283
No Diamonds for Ursula, 273
No Minor Vices, 208–9
Nolan, Lloyd, 221, 283
Norris, Chuck, 282
North Star, The, 139–41, 214, 215

O Evening Star, 96, 97
Oberon, Merle, 3, 209–10
O'Brien, Pat, 156
Odd Couple, The, 274–75
O'Donnell, Cathy, 193
O'Hara, Maureen, 3, 209, 210, 283
Olivier, Lawrence, 234
On Being Human (Wilson), 50

One Foot in Heaven, 231
O'Neill, Eugene, 71
Orsatti, Ken, 267, 271
Our Town, 277
Ox-Bow Incident, The, 79, 130–36, 143, 182, 185, 186, 204, 244

Page, Don, 276
Palmer, Lilli, 208–9
Panorama of Film Noir, A, 176
Paramount, 97, 234, 254
Parker, Dorothy, 6
Parker, Eleanor, 262
Parker, Suzy, 262
Parks, Larry, 221
Parrish, Maud, 16
Parrish, Sam, 11, 16, 39, 48
Parsons, Louella, 121, 137, 211
Pasadena Playhouse, 71, 75, 77–79, 83, 87–96, 100–101, 107, 117, 160, 278, 280
Pat the Bunny, 241
Paths of Glory (Cobb), 78, 89
Patten, James, 14
Pearson, Shawn, 9
Pease, Ralph, 245, 284
Peck, Gregory, 140, 200
Penn, Arthur, 257
People's Radio Foundation, 221
Percy, Walker, 3
Perry, Fred, 86
Perry Como Show, The, 247
Peters, Jean, 206, 207
Petrarch, 151
Phil, 82–83
Phillips, Robert, 16
Pichel, Irving, 125
Picnic, 230
Pidgeon, Walter, 203, 221
Pilot, The, 282
Playhouse 90, 257
Poe, Edgar Allan, 151

INDEX

Powell, Dick, 283
Power, Tyrone, 7, 124, 136, 137, 138, 143, 148, 153, 169, 221
Pratley, Gerald, 172, 205
Pratt, John, 66
Preminger, Otto, 3, 5, 144, 150–51, 153, 156–57, 163, 168, 171–76, 186, 202–6, 226, 248, 268
Preston, Robert (Preston Meservy), 83, 100
Price, Vincent, 150, 151, 156, 157, 163, 248, 252
Prickett, Maudie, 77, 78
Prickett, Oliver, 77, 78, 118
Prince Jack, 282–83
Purple Heart, The, 141–44, 146, 147, 153, 178, 216, 227

Quinn, Anthony, 132, 135, 140

Raffles, 107
Raksin, David, 150
Ralston, Jobyna, 39
Rapper, Irving, 200, 282
Reagan, Ronald, 183, 218, 220–24, 283
Redford, Robert, 263
Reed, Donna, 244
Reiner, Carl, 244
Reinhardt, Betty, 151
Remarque, Erich Maria, 178
Remedy for Winter, A, 271
Renoir, Jean, 3, 124–27, 129, 181, 257
Revere, Anne, 169, 221, 224
"Rhapsody in Blue," 12
Rickover, Hyman, 260
"Right-Hand Man, The," 257
RKO, 80
Robertson, Cliff, 282
Robin Hood, 111
Robson, Mark, 211–12

Roc, Patricia, 182
Rockdale, Texas, 23–28, 36, 112, 283
Rockdale Baptist Church, 10
Rogers, Buddy, 39, 40
Romeo and Juliet (movie), 25
Romero, Cesar, 113, 206
Roosevelt, Franklin (FDR), 10, 106, 215, 216
Rosary, The, 25
Rose, Harold, 254
Rosenbaum, Jonathan, 176
Rosenberg, Ethel, 224–25
Rosenberg, Julius, 224–25
Ross, Lillian, 4, 6–7, 9–14, 39, 73, 75, 79, 257, 259–60
Rules of the Game, 124
Russell, Florence, 82, 83, 91
Russell, Harold, 191, 192, 193, 280
Russell, Jane, 271
Ryan, Jim, 106
Ryan, Robert, 216, 270

Sailor's Lady, 110, 113, 255
Salinger, J. D., 211
Sam Houston State Teachers College, 11, 13, 36
Sam Houston State University, 277
San Antonio, Texas, 7, 21, 32
Sanders, George, 249–50
Sandy Creek, Florida, 17
Satan Bug, The, 272
Savages and Saints (Herzberg), 246
Scarface, 121
Schary, Dore, 219–20
Schenck, Joseph, 220
Schickel, Richard, 201
Schmach, Murray, 266–67
Schreiber, Lou, 96, 106, 203
Scott, Randolph, 119, 153
Screen Actors Guild (SAG), 4, 217, 219–24, 265–67, 281
Screen Directors Guild, 219

Screen Director's Playhouse, 209
Screen Writers Guild, 219
Sealed Cargo, 226
Seitz, George, 115
Selznick, David O., 184
Sesonske, Alexander, 124, 126
Shadow in the Streets, A, 268
Shepperd, John. *See* Struckwick, Shepperd
Sherwood, Robert, 195
Shore, Dinah, 146
Siegel, Bugsy, 122
Simpson, Sheila, 65, 74
Skouras, Spyros, 142
Small, Edward, 119
Smith, Gerald L. K., 216
Smith, Imogen Sara, 226
Smith, Tim, 121, 273–74, 275, 278
Smither, Wilbur "Doc," 63, 65
Smoke Signal, 245–46
"Sophisticated Lady," 150
Sorry Wrong Number, 212
Spanish Civil War, The, 221
"Spanish Lady, The" (Munro), 3
Speed family, 7, 8, 9
Speed, James Monroe, 18, 19
Spoonhandle, 207
Spoto, Donald, 195
Spring Reunion, 247
Spurgeon, Charles, 9
Spy in Your Eye, 273
Stage Coach, 119
Stage Struck, 111
Stalin, Josef, 221
Stander, Lionel, 223
Standish, Robert, 235
Stanwyck, Barbara, 121, 122, 212
Star Is Born, A, 84, 193
Starr, Kevin, 13
State Fair, 6, 166, 174, 197
Steinbeck, John, 239
Stella Dallas, 96
Sten, Anna, 121

Stevens, George, 220
Stewart, Charles O., 11, 42
Stewart, Jimmy, 138, 177
Stingaree, 25
Stockwell, Dean, 207
Storm, Leslie, 235
Strange Lady in Town, 244–45
Strangelove, Dr., 268
Strudwick, Shepperd, 119, 124
Sullivan, Barry, 262
"Summertime," 150
Sunday, Billy, 9
Swamp Water, 120, 123–29, 140, 183, 207, 256
Swanson, Gloria, 111
Sword in the Desert, 226

Take a Hard Ride, 282
Taylor, Elizabeth, 233, 266
Taylor, Robert, 79, 218
Ten Million Dollar Grab, 273
Tennyson, Alfred, 76
Thief of Baghdad, The, 12
Thirteen Chair, The, 58, 60
30 Seconds Over Tokyo, 142
This Is Your Life, 279–81
Thomas, Parnell, 217
Thompson, Frank, 130
Thomson, David, 150, 174
Three Hours to Kill, 237–38, 244
Tibbet, Lawrence, 14
Tierney, Gene, 3, 119–20, 150–53, 157–58, 163, 168, 208, 226
Tobacco Road, 119, 124, 129, 183
Tobin, Jack, 42
Todd, J. W., 239
Todds, The, 108–9,
Together Tonight, 277
Toland, Gregg, 97, 192
Torn, Rip, 262
Tourneur, Jacques, 144, 181, 184–85, 202, 209, 251, 252, 254
Town Tamer, 271

Tracy, Spencer, 97, 195
Trojan Women, The, 87
Tucker, Forrest, 109
Twelfth Night, 87
Twelve O'Clock High, 200
Twentieth Century-Fox, 96, 124, 170, 219
Twilight Zone, 262
Two for the Seesaw, 4, 87, 257–60
Twomey, Mrs., 74
Twomey, Stanley, 74–75, 79, 93, 97, 100, 102, 104, 118, 146, 280
Typee (Melville), 254

"Uncle Wiggily in Connecticut," 211
United Artists, 100, 213
Up in Arms, 146, 166, 167
Uvalde, Texas, 10, 28–35, 36, 137

Valley Forge, 100–101, 104, 108
Van Nuys, California, 13, 42, 44, 58, 70, 98
Van Nuys, Woman's Club, 58, 63, 66, 71, 72, 93
Vidal, Gore, 262
Viertel, Linda, 285
Volpe, John A., 281
von Stroheim, Erich, 141

Waelder, Texas, 21, 22
Wakeman, John, 186
Walk in the Sun, A, 144, 177–80, 197, 216
Walker, June, 230
Walton County, Florida, 18
Wanger, Walter, 184–86, 216, 219–20
War of the Worlds, 232
Wardlaw, John, 74–75, 93, 102, 118, 146, 280
Wardlaw's Motor Inn, 64
Warner, Jack, 218
Warner's, 80

Wasson, George, 203
Watts, Richard, Jr., 258
Wayne, John, 119, 140, 183, 189, 268, 283
Weather Is a Weapon, 231
Webb, Clifton, 151, 153–57, 167–68, 206
Welles, Orson, 179, 283
Wellman, William, 3, 39, 130–32, 134–36, 202
Wells, H. G., 232
Westerner, The, 107, 108, 110
When Do I Start?, 201
Where the Sidewalk Ends, 3, 4, 205, 226, 231
While the City Sleeps, 232, 247, 248
Whole Equation, The, 150
Widmark, Richard, 227
Wilde, Cornell, 168
Wilde, Oscar, 11
Williams, Bob, 277
Williams, Clyde, 34–35, 74, 94, 129, 136, 191, 193, 194, 202, 205, 208–9, 210, 236, 247–48, 257, 260, 283
Williams, Tennessee, 199–200
Wills, Chill, 109
Wilson, 143, 223
Wilson, Woodrow, 50
Wing and a Prayer, 144, 146–49, 178, 227
Wings, 39, 131
Winnington, Richard, 210
Winston, Archer, 197
Winters, Jonathan, 244
Winter's Tale, The, 160
Withers, Jane, 139
Wolfe, Thomas, 5, 48
Woman in the Window, The, 248
Wood, Helen, 49, 50
Wood, Robin, 185–86, 248
Wood, Vernon, 146, 189
Wooley, Monty, 153

Woollcott, Alexander, 153
World Film Directors, 186
Wright, Teresa, 192, 193–94, 195, 216
Wuthering Heights, 107, 195
Wyler, Talli, 107
Wyler, William, 3, 107–10, 191–96, 202, 216
Wylie, Philip, 232
Wyman, Jane, 283

Young, Portia, 93

Zanuck, Darryl, 4, 105, 111, 120, 122–24, 126, 131, 136, 141, 143, 147–49, 153, 156–57, 171, 203, 208, 210, 223, 259, 266
Zanuck, Virginia, 135, 149, 185
Zeitlin, Ida, 74, 75, 78, 80, 88, 89, 118, 120, 188
Zero Hour, 254
Zimbalist, Efrem, Jr., 260
Zukor, Adolph, 105

Printed in the USA
CPSIA information can be obtained
at www.ICGtesting.com
CBHW030736261223
2915CB00004B/10